Demographic Scenario of the North East India

Other Books of the Author

English

1. *Human Capital and Manpower Planning in North East*, Published by Himalayan Publishers, Itanagar–Delhi in 2007.
2. *Socio-Economic Scenario of the North East India*, Published by Concept Publishing Company Pvt. Ltd, New Delhi-110 059 in 2013.
3. *A Tale of Two Jails*—Under Publication

Bengali

1. *Nabadiganta* (Novel), Published by Chiro Sobuj Prakashani, Kolkata in April, 2010.
2. *Chadmabeshi* (Novel), Published by Annapurna Prakashani, Kolkata in February, 2014.
3. *Maner Kotha*, Published by Annapurna Prakashani, Kolkata in August, 2012.
4. *Maner Kotha* (2nd part), Published by Annapurna Prakashani, Kolkata in January, 2016.
5. *Jiban-Darpan*, Published by Annapurna Prakashani, Kolkata in January, 2017.
6. *Maner Kotha* (3rd part), Published by Annapurna Prakashani, Kolkata in January, 2018.
7. *Maner Kotha* (4th part), Published by Annapurna Prakashani, Kolkata in January, 2020.
8. *Pratiksha*, Published by Annapurna Prakashani, Kolkata in January, 2019.
9. *Maner Kotha* (5th Part) writing in progress.

About the Author

R.K. Das Choudhury did his graduation in Science from Gauhati University in 1969 and M. Sc. in Statistics from Dibrugarh University in 1971. He started his service career in 1972 with the Directorate of Economics and Statistics, Government of Assam and thereafter, he joined the Directorate of Economics and Statistics, Government of Arunachal Pradesh in 1978. Finally, he retired from there as Joint Director, on 31st December, 2007. While in service, he did his Ph.D. from the North Eastern Hill University (NEHU), Shillong. Apart from administrative and financial experience, Dr. Das Choudhury has vast knowledge in National Sample Survey (NSS), both in Field Operations as well as in Tabulations and Publication of NSS Reports. He had special contribution in the field of improvement of Sample Design for selection of sample households/ sample enterprises for detailed survey in the Hilly Areas. Moreover, he has enough knowledge on Population Census and other Socio-Economic Subjects *viz.* IRDP, BPL, NFHS etc. Dr. Das Choudhury also worked in the North Eastern Council (NEC), Shillong for more than 10 (ten) years (on deputation) in various capacities and gathered enough experience in Planning, processing of projects for financial sanction, Evaluation and Monitoring of completed projects, preparation of Data Bank etc. There are another 2 (two) English and 8 (eight) Bengali published Books in his credit. Presently, he is writing 1 (one) more Bengali Book. He writes Bengali Books in Pseudonym–'BINAYAK'.

Demographic Scenario of the North East India

R.K. Das Choudhury

CONCEPT PUBLISHING COMPANY PVT. LTD.
NEW DELHI-110059

ISBN: 978-93-5439-054-8

First Published 2021

Published and Printed by

Concept Since 1974

Concept Publishing Company Pvt. Ltd.
A/15-16, Commercial Block, Mohan Garden,
New Delhi-110059 (INDIA)
T: 91 11 41101460, 91 11 25351460, 91 11 25351794
E : publishing@conceptpub.com; *W* : www.conceptpub.com

Cataloging in Publication Data--Courtesy: D.K. Agencies (P) Ltd. <docinfo@dkagencies.com>

Das Choudhury, R. K., 1949- **author.**
Demographic scenario of the North East India / R.K. Das Choudhury.
pages cm
Includes bibliographical references and index.
ISBN 9789354390548

1. India, Northeastern—Population—Statistics. 2. India, Northeastern—Census. 3. India—Census. I. Title.

LCC HB3640.I53D37 2021 | DDC 304.609541021 23

Preface

I spent my College and University life and also the entire service life, which was a long period of little more than 35 (thirty five) years, in the North Eastern Region. Initially, I joined the Directorate of Economics and Statistics, Government of Assam on 31st October, 1972 and thereafter, I joined the Directorate of Economics and Statistics, Government of Arunachal Pradesh on 22nd February, 1978. Finally, I retired from there as Joint Director on the last day of December, 2007. During my service period, I got the opportunity of serving in the North Eastern Council (NEC), Shillong (on deputation) on 3 (three) occasions with a total duration of more than 10 (ten) years.

This gave me enough scope of knowing this region, particularly its land and people, socio-economic conditions, education and employment scenario, nature and implementation of development schemes and projects etc. In addition to that, being an officer of the Directorate of Economics and Statistics, I had a close contact with the Directorate of Census Operations, which is like a sister-concern. On many occasions, I was actively associated with conducting the Census Operations in the State and imparting training to the Census Enumerators and Supervisors.

This gave me the scope of knowing the objective and coverage of the Census Operations in details and the utility of this. Actually, Census is the only source of getting the Population and Socio-Cultural Data or the Demographic Information, with greater details. Demography is the scientific study of human population, particularly their size, composition and distribution, which changes over time or space, primarily due to Birth, Death and Migration.

But, the Census information has its own style and limitations, and that primarily serves the general purposes, not the specific one. However, using this information, it is possible to do any kind of Demographic Study. And the present work, entitled "Demographic Scenario of the North East India" is mainly based on the Census Information. This is actually, my 3rd book on North Eastern Region. In this book, an attempt has been made to show the Demographic changes, that had been taken place within a period of last 50 (fifty) years, i.e. from 1961 to 2011, in each of the North Eastern States, *vis-à-vis* the North Eastern Region, together with the position of the Country as a whole. However, there are some lapses, due to non-availability of information on different aspects and occasions.

I am very much grateful to the Registrar General of India, New Delhi. I have used the Census Data from their Publications and also from the Digital Library, which is available in their website. I am also grateful to the Director of Census Operations, West Bengal, particularly to Shri Tarun Sarkar, who is in-charge of the Library. I could use their Library fully and up to my satisfaction. I am also thankful to the Library staff, who helped me in finding out the relevant Publications, whenever I wanted. I cannot, but to thank Shri Kaushik Bhattacharjee and Shri Partha Biswas of the Directorate, who helped me in many ways. I am also thankful to Mrs. Gita Choudhury, Librarian of Bipin Chandra Pal Memorial Trust Library, New Delhi, who provided me many important books.

I am thankful to my friend, Shri Abhijit Roy Choudhury, Rtd. Deputy Director of Census Operations, Meghalaya, Shillong, who helped me in many ways for improvement of my book. I am also thankful to my brother-in-law, Shri Bikash Purkayastha, who inspired me for writing this book and also suggested the name of some books on this subject, which helped me a lot. I cannot, but to thank my son, Shri Abhimanyu Das Choudhury, who helped me in using Excel for addition and calculation of ratio and proportion etc. using huge data from different tables simultaneously. I am also thankful to my daughter and to my wife, who gave me constant moral support for completing this book.

My special thanks are due to Prof. B.S. Butola of Jawaharlal Nehru University, New Delhi, who has been a continuous source of inspiration and encouragement for me. For his able guidance and suggestions, I could improve my book in many ways and for that, I am very much grateful to him. I am also thankful to all of them, whose name I could not mention separately, for helping me in different ways.

I hope, my book will present a new dimension in the field of North East Demography. This will perhaps, be useful for the Social Scientists, Research Scholars and for the General Readers. I will be extremely happy, if I find that, this book is useful and people are reading it with interest. That will be my satisfaction and I will feel that, my endeavour is successful. There might be some unintentional omission and commission and for that, I hope, the readers will excuse me and will suggest for improvement.

Kolkata, **R.K. Das Choudhury**
January, 2018

Contents

Appendices

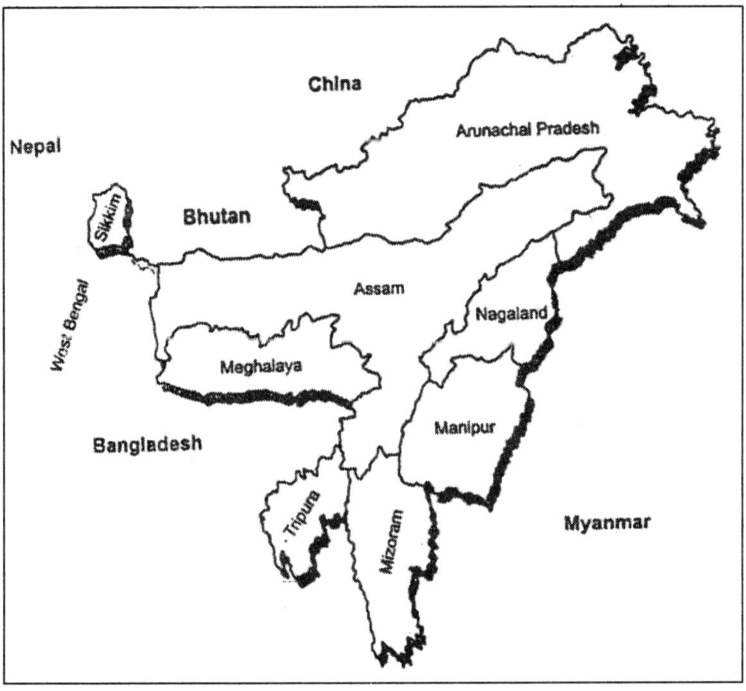

Map of the North East India

1
Physiography of the Region

The North Eastern Region is situated in the North East extremity of our country. It is bounded by China in the North, Myanmar and Bangladesh in the South, Myanmar in the East and Nepal and West Bengal in the West. The total Geographical Area (notional area) of the North Eastern Region including Sikkim is 2,62,191 sq. kms. Historically, successive legal and administrative decisions taken between 1874 and 1935 gave distinct identity to the areas of this Region. The British administration initially treated the hill areas of the North East as a "Non-Regulated Areas", and then declared them as "Backward Tracts" and finally "Excluded Areas" and "Partially Excluded Areas". A brief history of each of the North Eastern States is given below:

Arunachal Pradesh

Arunachal Pradesh is a thinly populated mountainous state lies roughly between 26° 28′ N and 29° 30′ N latitudes and 91° 30′ E and 97° 30′ E longitudes on the North East extremity of India. The State is having a total area of 83,743 sq. kms forming India's international boundaries with Bhutan in the West, Tibet in the North-West, China in the North and Myanmar in the South-East. From the south it is bordered by the state of Assam. The overall hilly feature of the state shows that it gradually rises from about 350 metres height in the foothills in north bank of river Brahmaputra to mighty convolutions of mountain ranges and spurs over 6,000 metres in the Greater and Trans-Himalayas. It is a tangle of deep gorge like valleys, densely wooded mountain slopes, dissected by numerous torrents and rivers, deep river valleys and a belt of tropical rain forest.[1]

Arunachal Pradesh is one of the very few states of India which has a very large area under forest. According to the published land-use statistics provided by the State as well as the Central Government, the total forest cover is legally notified as 52,000 sq. km. (i.e. about 62.1 per cent of the total Geographical area of the State) while the satellite imagery data generated by NRSA, Hyderabad recorded it as 71,405 sq. km. (i.e. about 85.3%).[2] The rich forest cover of the state is also vivid in terms of variety of plant species and vegetation. It ranges from swampy rain forest at the foothills and low-lying areas in the eastern part of the state to the tropical and subtropical vegetation cover up to the height of approximately 2,134 metres. This vegetation zone is distinguished by valuable trees of great size, plentiful climbers and abundant undergrowth. Among the climbers, cane is most noticeable. Orchids of numerous varieties are also in abundance. Beyond 2,134 and up to 2,734 metres, there are deciduous and mixed deciduous forests comprising mainly of walnut, oak, chestnut, pine, spruce and rhododendron. Beyond it and up to an altitude of 3,658 metres, the wide stretch of area is generally claimed by conifers. Going still further up, the flora yields to plentiful rhododendrons of dwarfish stature and wild strawberry bushes. Above 4,877 metres and right up to the snow line, is the region of alpine meadow.

Like the flora, the deeply wooded terrains of Arunachal Pradesh are also rich in fauna. Among the great variety of wild-life in the state, the most commonly noticed are tiger, black panther, black deer, leopard, wild elephant, barking deer, musk deer, monkey and langur, wild buffalo, wild goat, flying fox and many other kinds of birds.[3] Apart from these, the state is very rich in natural resources like water and hydroelectric potentials. Moreover, the unexplored and adventurous terrain of this strategically sensitive state has vast potentials for the development of tourism industry.

The state of Arunachal Pradesh is the homeland of about 20 major tribes and more than 100 sub-tribes. The major tribes are Sherdukpen, Monpa, Aka, Miji, Khoa, Bagni, Nishi, Hill Miri, Apatani, Tagin, Memba and Khamba, Adi, Mishmi, Khamti, Singpoh, Nocte, Wancho, Tangsa, Lisu etc. According to historians and other scholars, the tribal people of the state with Mongoloid characters had a South East Asian origin and their migration to Arunachal Pradesh took place in pre-historic times.[4] The racial affiliation of the people of this state has been described by scholars as Mongoloid, Palio-Mongoloid and so on. But Anthropologists also noticed deviation in racial type among different sections of the same group, particularly among the ethnic groups spreading along the central parts of the state and these are considered to be the earliest migrants to this area.

The tribal people of Arunachal Pradesh are predominantly agriculturists. The rural people mostly depend on agriculture, free collection from surrounding forests, hunting, fishing etc. for their livelihood. Since the area is not much exposed to agricultural development as compared to other areas of the country, the age-old traditional method of shifting (jhum) cultivation is still prevalent in the agricultural pursuits. Limited availability of flat land, lack of protective measures for land development, paucity of irrigation facilities has offered limited choice before the rural people, which made them compelled to pursue the traditional method of jhum cultivation. However, the Apatanis of lower Subansiri district, gifted with some amount of flat land, have been pursuing settled rice cultivation in an improved manner for a long time. Though, improvements have also been noticed among the Adis of Pasighat, Mebo, Roing, Dambuk, Khamtis of Chaukham and Namsai, Monpas of Tawang and Dirang in this regard, but the situation is far from satisfaction.

The historical accounts of Arunachal Pradesh and its people dates back to the late Ahom period in the eighteen century. It appears from the historical evidences that **"Sukapa"** the founder of the Ahom Kingdom came across the Patkoi hills in early thirteenth century. After the conquest of Assam by the Ahoms, it was found that the Akas, Daflas, Miris, Mishmis, Nagas etc. living in the mountains of the North and East of Brahmaputra valley were in the habit of coming down in the plains contiguous to their respective hills and taking by force whatever they found before them. To prevent the tribesmen from such rapacious attacks, the Ahom rulers initially applied force but failed. Ultimately, they introduced the policy of payment of **Posa** (allowance) to the tribesmen in order to maintain a good relation and to keep them in good humour.

The decline of Ahom monarchy dates back to the middle of the eighteenth century. The British annexed the whole of Assam in 1838 and constituted it into a Non-Regulated Province of the British Empire in India.[5] Moreover, to regulate relations with the tribal people of North East India, the British laid down a restrictive line what came to be known as **'Inner Line'** in 1874. Later on, the then Government of India, extended the Assam Frontier Tracts Regulation of 1880 to the hills inhabited by Abors, Miris, Mishmis, Singpohs, Nagas, Khamtis, Bhutias, Akas, Daflas and other tribes in the year 1914 through a notification issued by its Foreign and Political Department. As a result, the hills inhabited by the tribes mentioned above were separated from Darrang and Lakhimpur Districts of Assam and constituted into the **North Eastern Frontier Tract.**[6]

With rapid expansion of administration in the interior of the Frontier Tracts, spatial interaction at the intra and inter-regional levels increased manifolds. Moreover, it was realized that an efficient administrative machinery is a must for executing various developmental programmes. Accordingly, momentous reorganization took place in the year 1954.

The State of Arunachal Pradesh was initially a part of Assam. But on promulgation of the North East Frontier (Administration) Regulation, 1954, inaugurated a full-scale and integrated administrative structure for the entire area under the name of **North East frontier Agency (NEFA)** for the first time.[7] However, the political and constitutional development of late sixties, lead towards a separate direction and on 21st January, 1972, NEFA attained the status of **Union Territory (UT)** with the new name of **Arunachal Pradesh.** On 15th August, 1975, the Union Territory was endowed with the Legislative Assembly and the first general election was held in 1978. The Union Territory of Arunachal Pradesh, finally attained the status of a full-fledged state on 20th February, 1987. As per 2011 Census, the state is having 16 Districts, 27 Urban Towns and 5,589 Villages.[8] The total population of the State, as per 2011 Census, was 13,83,727 with a Density of 17 persons per sq. km. and Sex Ratio of 938.

Assam

The erstwhile state of Assam which was called North-East India, situated between 89° 46′ E and 97° 4′ E longitude and 28° 15′ N and 24° N latitude.[9] The history of the pre-historic and proto-historic periods of Assam is shrouded in mystery and very little is known about this period. The *Mahabharata*, *Vishnupurana*, *Kalika Purana* and *Yoginitantra* indicate that in the early period, it was known as Pragjyotisha and later as Kamarupa and was ruled by Kings who had appellation of *Danaba-Asura* which suggest their non-Aryan origin.[10]

The earliest historic record is found in the account of the Chinese pilgrim Hiuen-Tsang, who visited Kamarupa in 640 A.D. It was a strong and prosperous kingdom ruled by a Hindu King named Bhaskar Varman. Hiuen-Tsang placed the circumference of the kingdom at 10,000 lee from which Winningham infers that it must have included, at that time, the whole of Brahmaputra valley, Coch-Behar and Bhutan.[11]

After the visit of Hiuen-Tsang, the history of Kamarupa again became obscure and the veil was lifted by a dynasty founded by Pralambha about the year 800 A.D. The new dynasty ruled for about 200 years when it gave way to the Palas at about 1000 A.D. After a century and a half, Pala dynasty was brought under the Pala dynasty of Bengal by Ram Pala.[12]

In the 13th century, a new kingdom known as Kamatapura comprising a small portion of the kingdom of Kamarupa came into existence. The establishment of Muslim power in Bengal affected the course of the history of Assam considerably. While Assam became a constant prey of the Muhammadan invasions from Bengal, the Ahoms made their way into Assam early in the 13th century across the Patkai range. At the end of the 15th Century, a new dynasty of Kochas was established by one Biswa Singh. The Kochas then launched a systematic warfare against the Ahoms for territorial expansion. During the latter part of the reign of king Nara-Narayana, the most powerful and glorious king of the dynasty, a division was made in the kingdom with the river Sankosh as the boundary between them. The new branch of the Koch dynasty with their headquarters at Baruagarh ruled over the kingdom which came to be known as Kamarupa. The territory of this kingdom was gradually absorbed by the Ahoms when the last powerful king of the dynasty, Parikshit, was carried off to Delhi by the Muhammadans.[13]

The Ahoms, a Shan tribe, came to the Brahmaputra valley from Burma about the year 1226. After establishing firmly in the upper Brahmaputra valley, they followed a policy of expansion and by 1700 A.D., conquered the territories once included in the kingdom of Kamarupa. In 1695, Rudra Singh, the greatest of Ahom princes, ascended the throne and completed the conquest of the whole Brahmaputra valley. In 1780, Gourinath succeeded to the throne and his reign was marked chiefly by the rising of the Moamarias which shook the foundations of the Ahom kingdom. Gourinath in utter distress applied for help to the British, who succeeded in suppressing the Moamaria rebellion and defeated Kisen Narayan, the king of old Darrang, and in 1809, Chandra Kanta Singh succeeded to the throne.[14]

It was found that Badan Bar Phukan who became jealous of the power of the Bor Gohain, the Ahom Prime Minister, sought the help of the British to oust the Bor Gohain from his position. But, having failed to persuade the British, he went to the Court of the king of Ava in Burma and succeeded eventually in getting his support. As a result, a huge Burmese army came to Assam towards the end of 1816. At this critical juncture, the Ahom Prime Minister died and all responsibility fell on his eldest son who was quite inexperienced in conducting the affairs of the state. The Burmese then continued with their triumphant march, and the new Bor Gohain fled away to Guwahati. The Bor Gohain who suspected the Ahom king Chandra Kanta, having conspired to through him over to the enemy, invited an Ahom prince Purandar Singh and put him up as a pretender to the Ahom throne. In the meantime, the Bor Phukan who enjoyed momentary glory, was assassinated in another court intrigue. But, at one stage, both Chandra Kanta and the pretender Purandar Singh sought British help for driving the Burmese occupation army. But in the meanwhile, Burmese army created great havoc and finally succeeded in enticing Chandra Kanta to leave British protection. He was then immediately seized and confined. The Burmese also continued to give offense to the British across the border and demanded surrender of fugitives who had sought shelter in the British territory. The British finally declared war against Burmese on the 5th March, 1824. The war lasted for about two years and ultimately the Burmese army retreated before the superior might of the British which put an end to the Burmese occupation of Assam.

The British finally annexed the whole of Assam in 1838 and constituted it into a Non-Regulated Province of the British empire in India and the region was brought under direct British rule.[15] The British rule in Assam ended with the independence of India on 15th August, 1947. The present State of Assam is having a geographical area of 78,438 sq. kms. and is surrounded by seven North Eastern States *viz.* Arunachal Pradesh, Nagaland, Manipur, Mizoram, Tripura, Meghalaya, West Bengal and two other countries *viz.* Bhutan and Bangladesh. The total population of Assam was 3,12,05,576 as per 2011 census. The population of the state can be divided into two broad groups *viz.* non-tribal and tribal. The non-tribal people generally lives in the two major river systems in the twenty two districts of the Brahmaputra valley and the three districts of Barak valley. Whereas, the tribal people generally lives in the two hill districts. There are about 23 different tribes, like Bodo Kacharis, Karbis, Lalings, Khasis, Jaintias, Garos, Dimasas, Hmars, Rengma Nagas etc. The overall density of population of the State was 398 persons per sq. km. as per 2011 census. However, the density of population was less in the two hill districts of Karbi-Anglong and the North Cachar Hills. For administrative and revenue purposes, the State has 27 (twenty seven) districts including the newly created Kamrup (Metro) district and 4 (four) districts under the newly created Bodoland Territorial Council (BTC) areas *viz.* Kokrajhar, Baska, Chirang and Udalguri.[16]

Agriculture is the main source of livelihood of majority of the people of this state. The state is also very rich in timber products, tea and oil besides many other industrial and economic activities.

Manipur

Manipur is one of the seven sisters of the North Eastern Region, situated between 93.03° E and 94.78° E longitudes and 23.80° N and 25.68° N latitudes. The State is a charming place encircled by nine hill ranges on all sides with a small and beautiful oval valley at the centre. The state has 352 kms. long international border with Myanmar to the South-East and 502 kms. long border with the adjacent state of Nagaland on the North, while Cachar District of Assam on the West and Mizoram on the South and South-West. The total Geographical area (notional) of the State is 22,327 sq. kms. The altitude of the state, above the mean sea level, varies from 790 metres to 2020 metres. It has sub-tropical temperate climate.

The early history of the State of Manipur can be seen from the State Royal Chronicle, called the Cheitharol Kumbaba which covers the period from 33 AD to 1890 AD. During this period, altogether 74 (seventy four) kings ruled the state, of which Nongda Lairen Pakhangba (33 AD to 121 AD) was the first and Kulachandra was the last. At that time, Manipur was a small independent kingdom.

Manipur lost her independence to the British India in the year, 1891. From 1892 onwards, it became a princely native state under the political control of Government of British India. Accordingly, the administration of the state came to be handed over to a political agent by vesting all executive powers in him. This British Paramountcy continued till 1947 when India got independence.

According to a merger agreement between Maharaja Budhachandra, the then king of Manipur and the Government of India, signed on 21st September, 1949, the state was merged into India as a part C-category on the 15th October, 1949. As a result, Manipur came under the administrative control of a Chief Commissioner assisted by an Advisory Council of 14 (fourteen) members. But from the year

1957, a Territorial Council with 70 (seventy) members headed by a Chairman replaced the Advisory Council and this was continued till 1963 when Manipur became a single district Union Territory. Later on, the Territorial Council was replaced by a Legislative Assembly of 30 (thirty) members and a Council of Ministers. In the year 1972, Manipur became a full-fledged state within the Indian Union with a Governor as the Head of the state and the members of the Legislative Assembly was also doubled to 60 (sixty) .[17]

The state of Manipur is divided naturally into two tracts *viz.* the hills and the dales. The hill comprises of five districts *viz.* Senapati, Tamenglong, Churachandpur, Chandel and Ukhrul. While, the valley comprises of four districts *viz.* Imphal East, Imphal West, Bishnupur and Thoubal. The valley area of Manipur consists of two main parts, one is the Imphal valley, right at the heart of the state and the other is Jiri valley, in the west beyond the hill ranges bordering the Cachar district of Assam.[18] The total population of the state as per 2011 census was 28,55,794. There are 51 Urban Towns and 2,582 Villages with a Density of 128 persons per sq. km. and Sex Ratio of 985.[19] The people include Meiteis, Nagas, Meite Pangals and other communities. Agriculture is the main source of livelihood of majority of the people of Manipur. In the hills, the people follow the traditional method of shifting cultivation. Permanent cultivation is generally practiced in the valley districts. Terrace cultivation is also practiced in some of the pockets of the hills where jhuming or shifting cultivation is widely adopted.[20]

Meghalaya

The State of Meghalaya is situated between 98° 47′ E and 97° 47′ E longitudes and 25° 5′ N and 26° 10′ N latitudes bounded by the Goalpara, Kamrup and Nowgong districts of Assam on the North, Karbi Anglong and North Cachar Hills on the East and Bangladesh on the South West. The State is broadly divided into three natural sectors *viz.* (i) The Central Plateau, (ii) The Southern Border Area, and (iii) The Northern Border Area.

The Central Plateau forms the highest region of the State. It comprises mainly with the high land of the Khasi and Jaintia Hills and situated more or less in the centre of the state having an altitude approximately between 1230 metres and 1850 metres above mean sea level. From the Shillong Peak, it stretches out to a distance of about 50 kms. directly towards the south, 65 kms. towards the south-west and 28 kms. towards the south-east and merges with the Southern Border Areas. Similarly, it stretches out to a distance of about 20 kms. towards the north and merges with Norhern Border Areas. The Central Plateau is the source of most of the streams *viz.* Umngot, Kopili, Umiam Mawphlang, Umiam Khwan, Myntdu, Umkhen, Myntang and others.[21]

The southern Border Area is highly irregular. It is more or less a continuation of the Central Plateau and up to a few kms with interruptions here and there caused by sudden drops and depressions. As it recedes further and moves closer to the border of Bangladesh, the sudden drops and depressions become more prominent till they abruptly end in sheer precipices. This is specially true in the case of Khasi and Jaintia Hills. From the foot of the precipices, the area continues for some more distance in the form of a vast stretch of flat land till it merges with the border of Bangladesh at an elevation of mostly 200 to 300 metres. However, along the border of the Garo Hills, there are no sudden drops, depression or precipices. This region receives the heaviest and most copious rainfall in the state.[22]

The Northern Border Area lies in the north of the state and merges with the districts of Goalpara, Kamrup and Nowgong of Assam. The feature of the Northern Border Area is more or less similar to the Central Plateau with the gradual downward move till it merges with the border of Assam. This region gets less rainfall and has a sub tropical climate.[23]

The State of Meghalaya with its headquarters at Shillong was originally a part of Assam. At its initial stage, it had two districts *viz.* the Garo Hills district and the united Khasi-Jaintia district. It became an Autonomous State on 1st April, 1970, but it did not retain that status for long. Under the North Eastern Areas (Regulation) Act, 1971, Meghalaya became a full-fledged State and it was formally inaugurated on 21st January, 1972. On 22nd February, 1972, the Jaintia Hills district was created. In October, 1976, two new districts *viz.* East Garo Hills district with its headquarters at Williamnagar, and West Khasi Hills district with its headquarters at Nongstoin were created.[24] Later on, in the month of June, 1992, two more districts *viz.* Ri-Bhoi and South Garo Hills were created and thus, the total number of districts in Meghalaya reached to 7 (seven).

The total Geographical area of the state is 22,429 sq. kms. and the total population as per 2011 Census was 29,66,889, having a density of

132 persons per sq. km. and Sex Ratio of 989. The inhabitants of this state are mainly Khasis, Jaintias, Garos, Bhois, Wars etc. The Khasis, Jaintias, Bhois and Wars are collectively known as the Hynniewtrep people predominantly inhabit the districts of East Meghalaya. They are also known to be one of the earliest ethnic group of settlers in the Indian sub-continent, belonging to the Proto-Austroloid Monkhmer race. The Garo Hills are predominantly inhabited by the Garos, belonging to the Bodo family of the Tibeto-Burman race, said to have migrated from Tibet. The Garos prefer to call themselves as Achiks and the land they inhabit as the Achik-land. The Khasi-Pnars inhabit the eastern part of Meghalaya, in the Khasi and Jaintia Hills. Khasis residing in Jaintia Hills are now better known as Jaintias. They are also called Pnars. The Khasis, occupying the northern lowlands and foothills, are generally called Bhois and those who live in the southern tracts are called Wars.[25]

The people of Meghalaya, mainly the rural masses, depend on agriculture. Agriculture is the main source of their livelihood and they primarily follow the age-old method of Jhum cultivation. Terrace cultivation is done in the gentle slopes of the Khasi Hills. Besides this, wet cultivation is also practiced in the inter-mountain plains in the Khasi and Jaintia Hills and in the low-lying border areas of the Garo Hills.[26] The State of Meghalaya is very rich in production of potato, cabbage, cauliflower, ginger, turmeric, orange, banana, pineapple etc.

Mizoram

The state of Mizoram is situated between 22° 19′ N and 24° 19′ N latitude and 92° 16′ E and 93° 26′ E longitude covering an area of 21,087 sq. kms. The state is bounded by Assam and Manipur on the North and North-East, Myanmar on the East and South, Tripura on the North-West and Bangaldesh on the South-West.

Mizoram is a mountainous state. It consists of seven long north-south traversing parallel ranges with intervening valleys which form a panoramic physiographic feature of 'Tongueshaped' area or hogsback, the middle portion is high and tappers downwards in north-south direction.[27] Further, the whole area is divided into three natural regions *viz.* (i) Mountainous region, (ii) Ridges and high land regions, and (iii) Plain land or Flat land (low land areas).

The Mountainous terrain region can be further sub-divided into (a) Mountainous region of north-east, (b) Mountainous region of central Mizoram, and (c) Mountainous region of south-east region.

The Mountainous terrain of north-east is above 1500 metres, having very less population and agricultural facilities. The central region falls under Chalfilh range in which Zopuitlang (1992 metres) and Bualpuitlang are prominent. The highest peak of Blue Mountain (2165 metres, Phawngpui) falls in the southern region and the river Kolodyne passes through it.

Low-lying areas in Mizoram are very rare except a few small patches between mountain ranges. In the north-west Mizoram, between the rivers Longkhaih and Tlawng, there is a small area below 600 metres near Lokichera and Bhairabi. Near Demagiri, the river Karnphuli and its tributaries form another small low-lying area. Down south, the low land lies west of Tuichawng and its tributaries. In the east, near Champhai covering an area of 11 sq. km, is a flat land and in the Mat river basin near Thenzol and north-Vanlaiphai, there is another small low-lying area, which are suitable for wet rice cultivation.[28]

The early history of the Mizos is virtually based on legends, traditions, customs and beliefs. There is common belief among the Mizos that, their ancestors emigrated from a place called 'Chhingluing'. Historians and Anthropologists are of the opinion that this place is in the southern China. In some recent studies too, it was found that the Mizos came from the east and their original home was in Mekong Valley. K. Zawla, a historian asserts that the Mizo people came to the Chindwin belt about 996 A.D. and lived there for about 200 years. Later on, they left that place and during their movement around 1466 A.D., the first place of halt was at Lengtlang and each family grouped together and each sub-tribe settled in separate villages. The sub-tribes were the Lusei, Ralte, Chawangthu, Khiangte, Hauhnar, Chuange, Chuanthang, Ngente, Punte and Parte. Westward movement of the Mizos from Lentlang to the present Mizo state took place between 1700 and 1730 A.D.[29]

The state of Mizoram was initially a part of Assam and was known as Lushai Hills District. In 1954, the nomenclature of the Lushai Hills District was changed to Mizo Hills District by an Act of Parliament. Later on, the District was elevated to the status of Union Territory with the name 'Mizoram' in 1972 and subsequently it became a full-fledged state on 20th February, 1987.[30] At present the state is having 8 (eight) districts *viz.* Mamit, Kolasib, Aizawl, Champhai, Serchhip, Lunglei, Lawngtlai and Saiha.

The total population of Mizoram as per 2011 census was 10,97,206 and most of them are depending on agriculture and allied activities for their livelihood. They are generally practicing the age-old method of Jhum cultivation on hilly slopes. The scope of settled cultivation in Mizoram is very much limited as the availability of flat land is very less. However, wet rice cultivation is being practiced in the low-lying areas available in between the mountain ranges and river basins. The main food crops in Mizoram are paddy, maize, pulse, vegetables, ginger, chilly, sugarcane etc. The state of Mizoram, on the other hand, is very much suitable for pisciculture and sufficient quantity of fish of different kinds is being produced every year.

Nagaland

The state of Nagaland is situated between 25° 60′ N and 27° 40′ N latitude and 93° 20′ E and 95° 15′ E longitude spreading over an area of 16,579 sq. kms. The state is bounded by Assam and Arunachal Pradesh on the North, Manipur on the South, Myanmar on the East and Assam on the West. Nagaland is predominantly a tribal state. The entire tribal population is divided into twenty major tribal groups. The dominant tribes which have their well-defined territorial jurisdiction are—Aos, Angamis, Changs, Chakhesang, Kabuis, Kacharis, Khein Mangas, Konyaks, Kukis, Lothas, Maos, Mikirs, Phoms, Rengmas, Sangtams, Semas, Thankuls, Yimchungars and Zelliang.[31]

The early history of Nagas is not much known as there is hardly any record available on this. However, it is seen that, at about 2000 years B.C., Mongolians came to India through Burma and Tibet. Some of these people settled in Garo Hills, while Kukis and Bodos settled in Cachar Hills. The Cacharis started ruling over northern Assam and Dimapur was said to be the capital of Cacharis. More details about Nagas could be found from the references of emissaries and evidence of cultural relations that grown up with the Cacharis in the later part of 14th century.

It is believed that, Sukhpa, the founder of Ahom Kingdom came to Assam from Burma through Tirap region of Arunachal Pradesh around 1228 A.D. and had their first contacts with the tribal communities of Nocte, Konyak and Wanchas. Later on, with the gradual expansion of the Ahom Kingdom, the Aos and Lothas also came in contact with the Ahoms. However, though there were frequent clashes among these tribes and Lothas, Ahoms could somehow manage to keep their control over this region and also could maintain more or less a good relation with the Nagas. It was found that Nagas used to present gifts and tributes to Ahoms and they in turn allowed Nagas to carry out revenue-free cultivation of paddy in the fields and fishing in the bills. Moreover, so long Nagas were refrained from raids on the plain people, Ahoms did not interfere in the daily activities of the Nagas.

But in the year 1536, Ahom made an expedition against the Nagas to subside the Konyak uprising, but failed. Subsequently, a large Ahom force was sent who brutally murdered hundreds of people at Dimapur and finally defeated the Konyak. But that was not the end, the Konyak and the Lothas carried out their raids on the plain people on different occasions but the Ahom rulers could succeed in defeating the tribal people and finally could establish their authority on the Naga Hills and as such, there was no major untoward incident occurred in these hills in the eighteenth century.[32]

The British came in contact with the Nagas in the early period of the nineteenth century and found that it is very difficult to control the Nagas. Initially, the British made a series of raids and adopted changing policies to contain the Naga hostilities but could not succeed. Later on, they thought of developing friendly relation with the Nagas and accordingly, Lieutenant Bigge made two friendly missions to Naga Hills in 1840-42 and succeeded in that. On demand of the Naga Chief, he opened a salt depot at Dimapur and because of that good gesture, he became very popular among the tribals. Further, with the help of Captain Gordon, Bigge also succeeded in demarcating a boundary, separating the Naga country from Manipur.[33]

The British established its authority and control over the Naga territory in 1866 in pursuance of the decision taken by the Government of India on the recommendations of the Lieutenant Governor of Assam. In 1881, a separate Naga Hills District was formed and the British followed the policy of consolidating their authority in the region and also pursued steady penetration into the interior. In 1890, Mokokchung Sub-division was formed and in 1922, Primi (Akhegwo) and Meloni (Meluri) were annexed to the Naga Hills District. Later on, the Naga Hills District Council was formed in order to bring all the Nagas under one banner. In April, 1946, the Council became Naga National Council (NNC) and had its first Conference at Wokha.[34]

The Naga territory remained split between Assam and North East Frontier Agency even after India's independence in 1947, despite a vocal movement advocating the political union of all Nagas. In 1957, the Indian Government established a single Naga administrative unit under Indian rule. Later on, in 1960, the Indian Government agreed to make Nagaland a self-governing State within India. Finally, the State was officially inaugurated on 1st December, 1963.[35] The State is now having 8 (eight) districts *viz*. Kohima, Dimapur, Phek, Mokokchung, Wokha, Zunheboto, Tuensang and Mon.

Nagaland is a hilly tribal State. The general elevation ranges from 914 metres to 3840 metres above the sea level. The Barail Range locally known as Radliura, enters the state from north Cachar and after passing through Kohima goes in the direction of Wokha. Owing to a sudden rise of the Barail Range on its northern face, about 12 kms. wide miniature type of Dun (valley) is formed in between the Barail Range and Samaguling Hills. The Patkai range forms a watershed which constitutes the International boundary between India and Myanmar. Saraniati situated in Tuensang district is the highest peak of the State which is 3877 metres above sea level.[36]

The State was having a total population of 19,78,502 as per 2011 Census, spreading over a Geographical area of 16,579 sq. km. with a density of 119 persons per sq. km. Agriculture is the mainstay of the people of Nagaland. In the hill slopes, the people generally practice Jhum cultivation. However, in recent times, people have started terrace cultivation and the Government is also encouraging them by giving loans and subsidies for this purpose. The main crops of the State are Paddy, Wheat, Maize, Bajra, Jowar, Millets, Cereals, Pulse, Oil seeds etc. The State is also rich in flora and fauna.

Tripura

The state of Tripura is situated between 22° 56′ N and 24° 32′ N latitude and 91° 09′ E and 92° 20′ E longitude spreading over an area of 10,492 sq. kms.[37] The state is almost surrounded by Bangladesh on three sides with an international border of 856 kms. leaving a small strip of about 30 kms. on the North, by which, it is having the link with the rest of the country through the Karimganj District of Assam. The state is also having a boundary of about 160 kms. with Mizoram on the North Eastern side.[38]

Topographically, the state can broadly be divided into hill ranges, plain lands including valleys, and river basins. The hill ranges gradually gain height from west to east and generally run from north to south losing altitude till they merge with the plains of Bangladesh. The six main hill ranges in Tripura are the Jampui, Sakhan, the Longtharai-Atharamura, the Sardang, the Baramura-Devtamura and Atharamura ranges. The Jampui range is situated in Dharmanagar sub-division and is 74 kms. in lengh. One of its peaks, the Betling Sib (1000 metres) is the highest altitude found in Tripura and is mainly inhabited by the Lushais and the Reangs. The Sakhan range forms the boundary of Dharmanagar and Kailashahar sub-division and its northern part, is known as the Unakuti. The length of this range is 58 kms. and that of Unokuti is 20 kms. Its highest peak is the Sakhan (840 metres) and this range is mainly inhabited by the Lushais and the Darlongs. The Longtharai range forms the boundary of Kailashahar and Kamalpur sub-division and is about 48 kms. long. Its highest peak is Longtharai (515 metres). The Atharamura range starts from the Amarpur sub-division and then runs into the southern part of Khowai sub-division and thereafter along the boundary of Khowai and Kamalpur sub-divisions, it merges into the plains of Bangladesh. It rises at Niungmarueta to a height of 514 metres and derives its name from the fact that, it has eighteen peaks. Two offshoots of this range run towards south-east and west meeting Longtharai and Baramura ranges respectively. The Baramura range is about 47 kms. and that of its lower portion known as the Devata range is about 85 kms.[39]

The early history of Tripura is clouded in mystery and romance. This can be seen from the Bengali poem *Rajmala* or *Chronicles of Tripura*, the early part of which was composed in 1458 A.D. by Tripuri priest Durlabhendra and two of his Brahmin associates, Sukheshwar and Baneshwar. The early King of Tripura, King Chengthum-fa was very weak, but his wife, Queen Tripura Sundari was very brave and strong and once fought a war with her troops against the army of the Emperor of Gaur and won the war. The victorious Queen belonged to a Raj which traces its descent to Drujho, the son of Yajati, the supreme ruler. Drujho ultimately became a *sanyasi* and abdicated his throne in favour of his son Tripur. But Tripur unleashed a reign of terror and oppression. Under his rule, his subjects reached to a stage of great poverty and starvation and ultimately emigrated to Hiramba (Cachar), but had to return soon as they did not get any help from the Raja there. They then worshipped Shiva, who promised to help them if they worship Chaturdash Deveta. Their prayers were answered when Tripur's widow gave birth to Trilochan, who was immediately made the King by his grateful people. The tales of his wisdom then spread far and wide and ultimately Hiramba King offered him his daughter in marriage which was solemnized with great joy.[40]

After a reign of conquest and glory, Trilochan was succeeded by the youngest of his twelve sons, Dakshin, who was the choice of both his father and their subjects. Rajeshwar, the sixty-first king of Tripura had no son; so he in his anger fired an arrow at a Shivalingam. Shiva cursed him that he would have no son, but to propitiate the great God, Rajeshwar offered a human sacrifice which pleased Shiva and Rajeshwar was blessed with a son by the name of Micholee. At the time of Pratit, the seventy-first Raja, Tripura and Cachar were bound in a strong alliance. This treaty survived the storm and stress of subsequent history.

The fame of Tripura nationalism was however, tarnished by Ratan-pha, an exile in Gaur, who invited the Turkish Sultan, Togral to conquer the Kingdom. He successfully invaded the state with the help of the Mohammedan troops and ascended the throne after beheading his brother. The Gaur Sultan conferred upon him the title of **Manik,** probably in 1279 A. D, which the Tripura Rajas retained to these days. Dharma Manikya ascended the throne in 1407 A.D. and ruled till 1458 A.D. Up to his time, human sacrifice was very much in vogue, but he ruled that such sacrifice should only be offered three times a year. Dharma Manikya was a great King and was a patron of learning. Under his patronage, the work on the first part of *Rajmala* was started. He died after a long and peaceful reign. But an inter-regnum followed after his death till Dhanya Manikya became the Raja in 1490 A. D.[41]

Dhanya Manikya was the greatest of the Tripura Kings. With the help of his Queen, Kamala Devi, he tried to remove a number of baneful caste restrictions among his troops. He was a great patron of literature and wanted to popularize Bengali. Dhanya Manikya was also a worshipper of the *lingam* and built many temples and got artists to carve beautiful images. He died in 1520 A.D. and was succeeded by his son Dev Manikya. Dev Manikya was a *tantrik* and a great devotee of Shakti. He was assassinated by a priest, but the priest was in turn killed by the army chief who put first Indra and then Vijoy, the late Raja's two sons, on the throne. Vijoy Manikya (1535-1583 A.D.) was a very powerful ruler, but unfortunately died of small-pox after ruling for 47 years. His son, Anantha Manikya (1583-1585 A.D.) succeeded him. However, Gopi Prasad strangled his son-in-law and sat on the throne as Udai Manikya. Udai Manikya (1585-1596 A.D.) decorated his capital Rangamati with beautiful tanks, buildings, temples and renamed it as Udaipur. He was later on poisoned and his son Jai Manikya (1596-1597 A.D.) succeeded him, but for a very short period. His son, Amar Manikya (1597-1611 A.D.) beheaded his father as well as his uncle

Runag Narayan who was trying to kill him, and ascended the throne.

Up to this time, the Tripura Kings had successfully repelled all external invasions and had carried the glory of their state beyond the bank of the Brahmaputra and the Padma. But when Mughals defeated the Tripura troops and marched on Udaipur, Amar Manikya fled away to the forests and subsequently committed suicide. He was succeeded by his son Rajdhar Manikya (1611-1613 A.D.) who made a temple of Vishnu and distributed land to the Brahmins. He was accidentally drowned in the river Gumti as he bent to drink water in which the image of Vishnu had been washed. After his death, his son Jasadhar Manikya (1613-1623 A.D.) became the King. During his time, he was repeatedly at war with Mughals. In 1620, Nawab Fateh Jung invaded Tripura and after a fierce fighting managed to subdue Jasadhar Manikya and took him to Delhi as prisoner along with a large number of elephants and horses. However, having refused restoration of his throne on condition of paying a tribute, Jasadhar Manikya was exiled to Benaras where he died at the age of 72.[42]

In the meantime, Tripura was systematically plundered by the Mughal Governors of Udaipur, but ultimately a dreadful plague forced them to leave Udaipur. However, in 1625 A.D., Kalyan Manikya, a kinsman was sworn in to the throne of Jasadhar by the people of Tripura. Kalyan Manikya (1625-1659 A.D.) was a kind and religious man, but was a strong ruler. He defied the Mughals and refused to pay any tribute. Kalyan Manikya had to fight several times with the powerful Mughal troops, but finally the valiant Tripura troops were overcome by Shah Shuja in 1658 and for the first time in the history, Tripura came to be included in the rent roll of a foreign power. However, it appears from the available history that, the rent assessed by Shah Shuja was never paid and there was a feeling amongst the people that, Tripura had been independent and ultimately their defeat of 1658 was almost forgotten.

Kalyan Manikya was succeeded by Govind Manikya, whose reign was interrupted by his half-brother, Nakshatra Rai, who ruled between 1660-1666 A.D. as Chattra Manikya. After his death due to small pox, Govind Manikya regained his throne and ruled till 1669. Within this short period, he became very popular and resisted successfully all attempts by the Mughals to oust him from the throne. He was succeeded by his son Ram Manikya (1669-1682 A.D.) whose reign was quite uneventful. But after his death, his younger brother Narendra Manikya usurped the throne, but later on, he was deposed and Ratna

Manikya (1684-1712 A.D.) regained the throne. The throne was then seized by Ghanshyam Thakur, the second son of Ram Manikya and assumed the title of Mahendra Manikya (1712-1714 A.D.) and then, he was succeeded by his younger brother, Dharma Manikya (1714-1744 A.D.).[43]

Tripura then faced many ups and downs and it was also marked by sordid court intrigues, when all the contenders were trying to ingratiate themselves with the Mughal Nawab. But finally Krishna Manikya ascended the throne, when the Muslim glory was on the wane in India. However, at that time, the Mughals occupied the lowlands of Tripura leaving the hill areas under the control of Raja. The East India Company in the meantime, attacked the plains of Tripura and Krishna Manikya (1760-1783 A.D.) was made the Raja of Hill Tripura. He was succeeded by his nephew, Jajdhar Manikya (1785-1804 A.D.). After his death, a five year inter-regnum followed, during which anarchy prevailed in the state. Ultimately in 1808 A.D, the English recognized Durga Manikya (1809-1813 A.D.) and invested him as Raja. Since then, every Raja received investiture from the English and was called upon to pay *nazar*. The rulers of Tripura continued to describe the state as Swadhina Tripura, but the state soon fell in line with the other feudatory states of India.

The relations of the subsequent Rajas of Tripura with the English were based solely on the concern to regain as much of their territory as possible. During the time of Isan Chandra Manikya (1850-1862 A.D.), he tried to receive the sympathetic consideration from the British authorities in the matter of fixation of the boundaries, but could not do that. He was succeeded by Bir Chandra Manikya (1862-1896 A.D.), Radha Kishore Manikya (1896-1909 A.D.), Birendra Kishore Manikya (1909-1923 A.D.) and Bir Bikram Manikya (1923-1946 A.D.). All of them tried to impress the British for fixing their boundaries in accordance with the correct historical position, but could not succeed. The last of these Rajas, Kirit Manikya, retained the title, some privileges, and a sizeable privy purse when his state acceded to the Indian Union in 1949 till these were withdrawn by the President of India in 1970 and he became a commoner, thus ending a dynasty over two millennium old.[44]

Tripura was a Princely State till it acceded to the Indian Union in 1949. Then it became a Union Territory on 1st July, 1963 and finally attained the status of a full-fledged state on 21st January, 1972. Presently, the state is having 4 (four) Districts *viz*. West Tripura, South

Tripura, North Tripura and Dhalai District. The total geographical area of the state is 10,492 sq. kms. having a total population of 36,73,917 as per 2011 Census with a population density of 350 persons per sq. km. The state is mostly hilly and about 60 per cent of the area has been classified as forest and about 27 per cent is available for cultivation. The state has many rain-fed, non-perennial rivers and streams flowing to the neighbouring Bangladesh. The major rivers are Gomati, Howrah, Dhalai, Muhuri, Feni, Juri which swell in monsoons, but they become shallow during the rest of the year. The hill areas of the state is mainly inhabited by the tribal people. There are 19 (nineteen) sub tribes amongst the Scheduled Tribe (ST) people with their own cultural identity. They are Tripuri, Reang, Jamatia, Chakma, Lusai, Mog, Garo, Kuki, Chaimal, Uchai, Halam, Khasia, Bhutia, Kunda, Orang, Lepcha, Santal, Bhil and Noatia.

The hill people mainly pursue the age-old method of Jhum cultivation. However, the high rainfall and good quality soil made the plain areas suitable for settled cultivation. A significant area of the state is under fruits and plantation crops. The major crops grown in plantations are tea, rubber, cashew, orange and pineapple. Jackfruit, banana, lemon, coconut and arecanut are also grown mainly on the homestead. The state is also rich in power potentials.[45]

Sikkim

Sikkim is basically a mountain state belonging to the Eastern Himalayas. It is situated between 27°4′ and 28°7′ north latitude and 88°11′ and 88°56′ east longitude. The State is completely a mountain-locked one, bordering on the north by Tibet (China), on the east by Tibet (China) and Bhutan, on the west by Nepal and on the south, the hill division of Darjeeling District of West Bengal. The state covers an area of 7,096 sq. km. stretching for about 113 km. from south to north and only 64 km. from west to east. The mountain ranges vary from about 3,040 metres to over 8,500 metres on all the three sides of north, west and east.[46]

The early history of Sikkim is not much known. However, the Lepchas are believed to be the original inhabitants of 'Sikkim Proper' and the name 'Sikkim' is said to be derived from two Limbu words 'Su Him', means 'new house' (meant for the Limbu girl, from east Nepal, married to Lepcha boy at that time). The words later changed to 'Sukhim' which ultimately came to be 'Sikkim' in anglicized form. The original Lepchas, however, called their homeland as Nyema-el which means 'the holy land'.

Sikkim has been invaded many times by the Bhutias from the north bringing with them the Tibetan culture, the Tibetan language, the Lamaistic Buddhism along with a mixture of Pastoral and semi-settled agricultural life, while the Nepalese coming from the west, brought in Indo-Aryan languages, Hinduism and a settled agricultural practice. It is seen that, the infiltration of the Tibetans started long before 15th century when traders, farmers and the Lamas came here in search of new opportunities. The Tibetans, at that time, were at a higher cultural level than the Lepchas and as such could provide facilities for various branches of learning including medicine, mathematics and astronomy.[47]

However, it is seen that, the credit of organizing the Lepchas into a society for the first time went to a person known as Tur Ve Pa No who was eventually elected as the leader or king called 'Punu' in around 1400 A.D. By this time, the Limbus from Nepal took occupation of the south-western part of Sikkim and they used to come in conflict with the Lepchas and in one such conflict, Punu was killed. And, the kingship ended after three more Punus following the death of the first one. Thereafter, the Lepchas resorted to electing leaders to advise on religious and social matters of the community which gradually shifted itself to the region around Kanchenjunga under continuous pressure of the Limbus.

In the second quarter of the 17th century A.D., three highly placed Lamas came from Tibet to convert the Sikkimese people into Buddhism and in their search for the descendent of Guru Tashe, a Tibetan noble, they came in contact of a person known as Phuntsog (Panchoo) Namgyal at Gangtok who happened to be his great-grandson and proclaimed him as the Gyalpo or king of Sikkim in 1641 at Yoksam, giving him the title of Chogyal or the Dharmaraj. The kingdom was divided into 12 (twelve) Dzongs or Districts and each of them was placed under a Lepcha Governor. And at that time, the kingdom was spread up to Chumbi valley in the north in Tibet and the present Darjeeling District of West Bengal.

The reign of Chogyal continued for about hundred and fifty years. However, in 1706, the Bhutanese army invaded Sikkim but was finally defeated by Tibet which came to its rescue and in gratitude of that, the great monastery of Pemayangtse was built by the king of Sikkim. But the peace was for a temporary period, and with the emergence of Gurkha power in Nepal, a number of invasions were conducted into

Sikkim in the middle of 18th century causing great hardship besides bringing significant changes to the social structure of Sikkim with a lasting effect. The Gurkhas gradually came to represent an important section of the Nepalese population in Sikkim and ultimately, the Nepalese in general, started encroaching upon the forests of Sikkim and cutting down valuable timber. There was neither much resistance to immigration from Tibet, nor any restrictions to the entry of Nepalese in Sikkim, rather some people welcomed them for various type of construction works and for the development of resources of a less populated area like Sikkim.[48]

The relation between Sikkim and the British represented by the East India Company began some time in 1814-15 and in terms of a treaty signed by Sikkim in 1817, the East India Company agreed to hand over the territory captured by Nepal to Sikkim and the political boundary between Nepal and Sikkim was fixed along the rivers Mahananda and Mechi and the Singalia range. But Sikkim forfeited her independence for good by this treaty, since according to Article 3 of the treaty (Treaty of Titalia), Sikkim lost the right to take any independent decision in any of its disputes with Nepal or other neighbouring states. This was followed by the loss of Darjeeling which Sikkim was forced to cede to the East India Company as a gift in 1835. The East India Company further acquired an additional territory of Sikkim covering 640 sq. miles as a sequel to its military expedition to Sikkim in 1849 on a flimsy pretext. Though the whole of Sikkim was not physically annexed to British India in view of political consideration, affecting its relationship with other Himalayan states like Nepal, Tibet and Bhutan, the Government of India sent a military expedition in 1860 and reduced the power of the king almost to subservience by the Treaty of 1861 which brought Sikkim under the control of British India, making it a *de facto* protectorate of the Government of India.[49]

In 1889, a political officer was appointed with his headquarters at Gangtok, the capital of Sikkim for the first time. During his time, he encouraged Nepalese immigrants who eventually subsided the interests of the original people of Lepcha and the Tibetan origin in Sikkim. But on the other hand, he took up many developmental measures like laying tracks into densely forested hills, introduction of apple cultivation, cloth weaving, carpet making, copper mining, opening schools and hospitals etc. All these, along with the measures taken on improving the land tenure system, land rent etc. contributed very much towards the all-round development of Sikkim.

But the cultural differences between groups of people together with superiority of the Nepalese made the situation acrimonious in terms of political authority, which was vested with the king and his advisers, favouring Bhutia-Lepcha interests. However, at the time of attaining India's independence in 1947, the growing discontent found an opportunity to replace monarchy with an elected Government reflecting majority interest. And the formation of the Sikkim State Congress in December, 1947 was the first step in this direction, demanding among other things a popular interim Government to function till merger with India. This prompted the then Maharaja to organize Sikkim National Party which stood for an independent Sikkim. But later on, the two parties came to an agreement on Sikkim continuing to be an Indian Protectorate in respect of external affairs, defence, communication and enjoy internal autonomy. A treaty to this effect was signed with the India Government in December, 1950. The first general election for local self Government was held in 1953 for which both the Nepalese and the Lepcha-Bhutia groups were allotted six seats each, keeping out another six to be nominated by the king. But in course of time, the relation between the king and the members of the Sikkim Congress gradually became very bitter and finally in 1974 election, the Sikkim Congress won a thumping victory with a tally of 31 out of 32 seats in the Assembly, which advocated Sikkim's participation in the political and economic institutions of India. Accordingly, a special opinion poll was held on 14th April, 1974 and the result went overwhelmingly in favour of merger, which ultimately took place on 26th April, 1975 making Sikkim a full-fledged State of India.[50]

Sikkim is a mountainous State spreading over an area of 7,096 sq. km. having a total population of 6,10,577 with a density of 86 persons per sq. km. as per 2011 Census. The State is divided into four Districts *viz.* North Sikkim, East Sikkim, South Sikkim and West Sikkim. The inhabitants of this State are mainly Lepchas, Bhutias and Nepalese. The majority of population of North Sikkim comprises of Lepchas and Bhutias. The Lepchas are predominantly concentrated in the Dzongu Areas and the Bhutias are seen from Kabi-Tingda to Lachen-Lachung. Nepalese are found mixed up around Phodong, Mangshila and Mangan. Lepchas and Bhutias are usually Buddhists and Nepalese are Hindus.[51]

Another important aspect of the State is that, most of its area comes under forest and under the category of barren land and other non-agricultural area, leaving a small part of it for agriculture. The forest of the state is very rich in stunning varieties of orchids, rhododendron, bamboo groves, medicinal plants, large cardamom, tea etc. However, in the land available for cultivation, the people of Sikkim practices both terrace and jhum cultivation in association with animal husbandry. The agricultural practice in Sikkim is much more advanced and the most remarkable feature of agriculture is that, the practice of mono-cropping has largely been replaced by double or triple cropping system irrespective of altitudinal or agro-climatic handicaps. This has changed the character and nature of production and made it possible to get higher returns with the introduction of short duration, photo-intensive high yielding varieties of paddy, maize and dwarf wheat. Simultaneously, the animal husbandry sector also went up to a significant change with the introduction of improved technology.[52]

Notes

1. J.N. Chowdhury, *Arunachal through the ages*, published by Smt. Jaya Chowdhury, Shillong, 1982, p. 1.
2. Surendra Singh, North Eastern Hill University, Shillong, *A Resource Atlas of Arunachal Pradesh, 1999*, p. 59.
3. J.N. Chowdhury, *Arunachal Panorama*, published by Smt. Jaya Chowdhury, Shillong, 1973, p. 15.
4. J.N. Chowdhury, *Arunachal through the ages, op. cit.*, p. 63.
5. *Ibid.*, pp. 83-86.
6. *Ibid.*, pp. 218-223.
7. *Ibid.*, pp. 242-243.
8. Registrar General of India, National Health Profile, 2011.
9. M.L. Bose, *Social History of Assam,* Concept Publishing Company, New Delhi, p. 15.
10. *Ibid.*, p. 37.
11. *Ibid.*, p. 37.
12. *Ibid.*, p. 37.
13. *Ibid.*, p. 38.
14. *Ibid.*, pp. 38-39.
15. J.N. Chowdhury, *Arunachal through the ages*, *op. cit.*, pp. 83-86.
16. Directorate of Economics and Statistics, Assam, *Economic Survey,* Assam 2005-06, p. 5.
17. Directorate of Economics and Statistics, Government of Manipur, *Economic Survey,* Manipur, 2002-03, p. i.
18. *Ibid.*, p. ii.
19. Registrar General of India, National Health Profile, 2011.
20. Directorate of Economics and Statistics, Govt. of Manipur, *Economic Survey, op. cit.*, pp. 67, 72.

21. D.D. Mali, *An Introduction to the Economy of Meghalaya,* Ratna's Mascot, G.S. Road, Shillong, p. 2.
22. *Ibid.*, p. 2.
23. *Ibid.*, pp. 2-3.
24. *Ibid.*, p. 1.
25. P.L. Sanjeev Reddy and P.C. Shekar Reddy, *Peace and Development in Northeast,* Mittal Publications, New Delhi, p. 22.
26. D.D. Mali, *An Introduction to the Economy of Meghalaya, op. cit.*, p. 39.
27. S.N. Singh, *Mizoram* (*Historical, Geographical, Social, Economic, Political and Administrative*), Mittal Publications, p. 13.
28. *Ibid.*, p. 17.
29. *Ibid.*, pp. 28, 29.
30. *Ibid.*, pp. 4, 5.
31. S.A. Rahman (Chief Editor), *The Beautiful India—Nagaland,* Published by Reference Press, New Delhi, pp. 39, 40.
32. *Ibid.*, pp. 12, 13.
33. *Ibid.*, pp. 14, 15.
34. *Ibid.*, pp. 21, 22.
35. P.L. Sanjeev Reddy and P.C. Shekar Reddy, *Peace and Development in Northeast, op. cit.,* p. 23.
36. S.A. Rahman (Chief Editor), *The Beautiful India—Nagaland,* op. cit, p. 41.
37. Directorate of Economics and Statistics, Planning (Statistics) Department, Govt. of Tripura, *Economic Review of Tripura, 2003-04*, p. 1.
38. Omesh Saigal, *Tripura— Its History and Culture*, Published by Concept Publishing Company, Delhi, 1978, p. 17.
39. *Ibid.*, pp. 18, 19.
40. *Ibid.*, pp. 29-31.
41. *Ibid.*, pp. 32-33.
42. *Ibid.*, pp. 33-36.
43. *Ibid.*, pp. 37-38.
44. *Ibid.*, pp. 38-40.
45. *Economic Review of Tripura, 2003-2004, op. cit.,* pp. 1-5.
46. B. Bhattacharya, *Sikkim—Land and People*, Omsons Publications, New Delhi-110 027, pp. 5, 6.
47. *Ibid.*, pp. 1, 2.
48. *Ibid.*, pp. 2, 3.
49. *Ibid.*, p. 3.
50. *Ibid.*, pp. 4, 5.
51. *Peace and Development in Northeast, op. cit.,* p. 17.
52. B. Bhattacharya, *Sikkim—Land and People*, *op. cit.*, Omsons Publications, New Delhi-110027.

2
Demography—The Subject

The term 'Demography' is derived from two Greek words, 'Demas', the people and 'Grapho', to draw or write. Thus, its meaning stands as, to draw or write about people. There is no specific definition of Demography. However, the economists, geographers, social scientists and others have defined it in their own ways according to their suitability and convenience. In doing so, it has been observed that, some definitions have adopted a narrow outlook on the subject, while, some others made its scope very wide.

The limited view of Demography has been taken by Wrong, who defines it as the statistical description and analysis of human population. The Multilingual Demographic Dictionary defines Demography as the "Scientific study of human populations, primarily with respect to their size, their structure and their development." Further, it differentiates between various aspects of Demography by defining separately Demographic Statistics, Economic Demography and Social Demography; the latter two imply the "study of relations between demographic phenomena on the one hand and economic and social phenomena on the other."[1] According to Peter R. Cox: "Demography is the study of statistical methods of human population involving primarily the measurements of the size, growth and diminution of the numbers of the people, the proportions of living being born or dying within the same area or region and the related functions of fertility, mortality and marriage."[2] According to Von Mayor: "Demography is the numerical analysis of the state and movement of human population inclusive of census enumerations and registration of vital processes and of whatever qualitative analysis can be made of the state and movement of population on the basis of fundamental census and registration data."[3] Hauser and Duncan took a more comprehensive view in defining the discipline of Demography and stated that, "Demography is the study of size, territorial distribution, and composition of population, changes therein, and the components of such changes, which may be identified as natality, mortality, territorial movement (migration), and social mobility (change of status)."[4]

Some more definitions are also there. Frank Lorimer stated that, "In broad sense Demography includes both Demographic analysis and population studies. A broad study of Demography studies both qualitative and quantitative aspects of population." Donald and J. Bogue stated that, "Demography is the mathematical and statistical study of size, composition, and spatial distribution of human population and of changes over time in these aspects through the operations of the five processes of fertility, mortality, marriage, migration and social mobility. Although it maintains a continuous descriptive and comparative analysis of trends, in each of these processes and in their net result, its long run goal is to develop theories to explain the events that it charts and compares."[5] According to W.G. Barckley, "Demography does not deal with the behaviour of individuals but only with the aggregates of people or even part thereof. The numerical portrayal of human population is known as Demography." G.A. Harrison and A.J. Boyee are of the opinion that, "Populations are not merely conglomerations of individual but rather, although to different degrees, ordered coherent systems, which have an entity greater than that of the sum of the individuals of which they are composed." H. Stenford stated that, "In its most formal sense Demography is a very technical and highly mathematical study of the vital statistics of human population (especially birth, death and migration) as well as the characteristics of population structure (including age, sex and marital status) as they contribute to an understanding of population change."[6]

From above definitions, it is very much clear that, Demography is a dynamic and developing discipline and it can be studied either from its technical aspects which involve statistical analysis of the population size and its composition and factors responsible for its growth and its distribution (which is a narrow view of the subject), or from the societal aspects which are concerned with the relationship between Demographic processes on the one hand, social, economic, political, biological and ecological factors on the other.

Further, from the definitions of Demography, it can be seen that, there were no unanimity of views among the different writers. However, depending on their works, the writers can be classified into two groups. Those who want to enlarge the scope can be called the Macro Demographic group and those who maintain narrow views can be put in the Micro Demographic group.

The Macro Demography covers the subjects like causes of slow or rapid growth of birth rate, death rate, population growth, sex ratio and health condition etc. It also covers the subjects, e.g. economic issues like unemployment, income condition of the masses, standard of living, labour conditions and living standard, production, consumption, saving-habits, correlation between population and economic development etc. Social problems, like marital status, composition of the family, growing trend about caste, religion, education, problems of migration, urbanisation etc. also form part of Macro Demography.

In Micro Demography, i.e. according to narrow view, Demography can be studied as small units like individual, family, group etc. In fact, these small units constitute the primary elements of macro analysis. For example, if the fertility rate of women of a particular district of any state is studied, it will form the part of Micro Demography. On the other hand, if the fertility of women for the whole of India or of that state including that particular district, which is a part of that state, which is again a part of the country, is studied, then it will fall within the macro analysis. According to Prof. Bogue, "Micro Demography is the study of the growth, distribution and redistribution of the population within community, state, economic area or other local area. This included both numerical and composition aspects and is performed by using meaningful subdivision of community of local areas."[7]

Now-a-days, it is accepted that, Demography is the study of human society and has very little to do with individualistic human problems. In the World Population Conferences held by the United Nations Organisation in 1954 and 1968, the following topics were discussed: (i) Fertility, (ii) Mortality, (iii) Migration, (iv) Genetic composition, (v) Future prospects, (vi) Population and resources, (vii) Technique of measurement, (viii) Training of Demographers, (ix) Distribution of population, (x) Family planning, (xi) Population projection, (xii) Demographic aspects of housing, education, saving and investment.

According to Whipple, the subject matter of Demography comprises of:

(a) Geneology, Ancestry and their records.
(b) Human Eugenics.
(c) Registration of vital events.

(d) Census of population.
(e) Biometrics dealing with the study of structure, growth and strength of human body.
(f) Pathometrics dealing with the knowledge of disease and anatomy.

In short, in Demography, Population size, Composition of Population, Distribution of Population, Labour Force, Population Policy etc. are studied.[8]

Origin of Demography and its Development

From time immemorial, population, particularly, its growth and size have been in the centre of all discussions related to the socio-economic development of any group, state or country. In olden days, increase of population was considered necessary for protection, showing might, won wars, production of food for leading a happy life. But, gradually that concept started changing when it was found that, land and other resources for production of food are limited, and on the other hand, overpopulation creates scarcity of food, lowers down standard of living and generates social tension etc. On seeing this, some people became curious and wanted to understand the phenomena of population and the problems surrounding it. Actually, the history of Demography is very old and can be traced back to a few thousand years. And the views expressed by them can be divided into three categories:

A. Ancient Demographic thought,
B. Western Demographic thought of mediaeval age, and
C. Modern Demographic thought.

A. Ancient Demographic Thought

The views of the scholars on Demography can be seen from the history of ancient civilisations of China, Babylon, Greece, Rome etc.

1. Ancient Chinese Demographic thought: Chinese Demographer, Confucious believed that, excess of population in any country will have a direct bearing on the productive capacity per head, and it will reduce the standard of living which will create social discontentment and tension. Further, he said that, it is the primary duty of the state to maintain population at the optimum level, avoid social dissatisfaction and strife. He also advocated that, measures like territorial migration, restrictions on marriage and imposition of punitive tax to keep the population within socially desirable bounds.

2. *Greek Demographic thought:* Aristotle and Plato, in their discussions considered the question of optimum population with a view to create favourable conditions for developing the potentialities of man and realisation of his highest good. They believed that good life could be attained only if the population was large enough to be economically self-sufficient and capable of defending itself, but not so large, on the other hand, so as to make Government difficult. Aristotle was in favour of establishing a balance between population and resources. According to him, if these two are not in harmony, poverty would be on the increase, crime would go up and turmoil and upheaval would overtake the country. Regarding controlling the size of population, Aristotle and Plato advocated the measures like (i) ban on the marriage of physically handicapped, (ii) child exposure and abortion, (iii) unnatural sex, (iv) colonization, and (v) migration, to restrict population.

On the other hand, to boost population, (if necessary) they suggested the following measures:

(a) Immigration.
(b) Offering reward.
(c) Social rebuke of those who do not marry, etc.

3. *Demographic thought of the Romans:* In Rome, counting of population for the first time was done in 435 B.C. and thereafter population was counted as many as 69 times in 470 years. Romans were more concerned with the practical problem of encouraging population growth. They viewed celibacy with disfavour, defended marriage and procreation and enacted legislation for promoting marriage and birth. Cicero decried polygamy and community ownership of wives and recommended monogamy to give a fillip to birth rate. He did not approve of out-migration to regulate population increase. However, Pliny supported immigration to overcome stagnation in population.

B. Western Demographic Thought of Mediaeval Age

The Christian writers of mediaeval Europe considered the question of population entirely from moral and ethical angles. Materialistic philosophy of life was relegated to the background, and spiritualism and thought of the other world ruled supreme. Divorce, child killing, abortion etc. were opposed tooth and nail. Biblical tenets were the guidelines for daily life. The people believed that, natural and social calamities could reduce the population and consequently, to keep the population at a particular level, birth rate should be high. In this connection, the views of two prominent thinkers Ibna Khaldun and Givanni Botero, on middle ages Demography, are worth mentioning:

(i) Ibna Khaldun was the leading Muslim social scientist, who in his book "Universal History" tried to explain population transition.

(ii) Givanni Botero held the view that, whatever be the size of population, birth rate will remain high. Countries with deficient resources to support its population will have to face terrible consequences unless the population is controlled.

Mercantilist's Thought

During 17th and 18th centuries, the mercantilist school of political economy flourished in Europe. Their slogan was more gold, more power and more wealth. Their aim was not to increase per capita income, but to raise the natural income over the wage cost of production. They believed that, growth in population will create increased demand for finished goods and consequently consumption will go up and at the same time manpower will also be available to produce more and more. Samuel Forrey stated that, "People and plenty are commonly the begetters, the one of the other, if rightly ordered." Prof. Child maintained that, "increasing population alone could make the people happy and prosperous." Cantillon suggested that, "If agriculture of a country would not be expanded in proportion to the population or if such an expansion would involve diminishing returns, additional agricultural products could be obtained from abroad in exchange for manufactured goods." In France, the Physiocrats believed that, any attempt to check population was only a hindrance on the way of God's will and such population growth was in the interest of society as a whole. They also believed that, "As it is in the physical order that men thus united in society multiply promptly, by natural and necessary parallel to the multiplication they are reduced due to lack of means of subsistence if they do not, at the same time, multiply those means of cultivation."[9]

C. Modern Demographic Thought

It has been found that, Demography as a science of population analysis was developed during 17th century and John Graunt was regarded as the father of Demography. He set forth his findings in a pamphlet published in London in 1662 named 'Natural and Political observation made upon the Bills of Mortality'. According to Willcox, Graunt discovered "the uniformity and predictability of many important biological phenomena taken in the mass." Graunt stressed the importance of measuring the logistics of population by simple indices which were easily calculable, and thus became the founder of modern vital statistics.

Sir William Patty: Since Graunt became the founding father of the new science, Patty became its godfather, by giving it the name 'political arithmetic' and enhancing its social position. His main publications were:

(a) Political Arithmetic.
(b) Observations upon the Dublin Bills of Mortality, 1683.
(c) Political Anatomy of Ireland.

Patty emphasised the need for establishment of a central statistical office and helped in the development of Graunts Life Table with the help of 'arbitrary proportions'. He also stressed the analysis of the following factors:

(a) Structure, composition and projection of population.
(b) Expansion of population.
(c) Urbanisation.
(d) Problems of less developed nations.
(e) Unemployment and national income.
(f) Manpower.

Edmund Halley: Halley achieved immortality by charting a comet, constructed the first empirical life table with the Church records of Breslan, Silesia. He used his data with great ingenuity and obtained estimates of expected numbers of persons in a stationary population by single years of age through eighty four years.

Richard Price: He prepared estimates of the population of England and Wales in 1695. It was the most substantial finding on this subject between the Norman conquest and first Census of England and Wales 1801. He defended his results with considerable sophistication by evidence and inferences.

Johan Peter Susmilch: Johan Susmilch, a Lutheran clergymen, became the leading exponent of Demography in the middle decades of the eighteenth century. His publication "The Principles of Divine Order" appeared in 1741, which he later revised in 1761-62 and in 1765. He rejected the physio-theology by Derham, and emphasised the law of numbers. He noted the—

(i) Men are more prone to accept a new spouse if a first marriage is dissolved by death than are women. There is a tendency among men towards successive polygamy. He concluded that God, in his infinite wisdom, had provided for this propensity.

(ii) In most nations there is normally a moderate excess of births over deaths, giving a gradual increase in population.

(iii) Death is more frequent in the first week of life and declines to a low level in the vicinity of fifteen years.

(iv) It is the duty of Government to preserve this tendency.

(v) In rural districts, decline in the rates of marriage was generally due to compete occupancy on the land and in cities, it is chiefly due to luxury and high prices.[10]

Phases of History of Demography

History of Demography falls under four phases—

(a) **First phase**: The work of Thomas Robert Malthus was considered as the first phase of population study. In 1798, he published his famous brochure. According to him, the principle of population is that, the increase of population, which constantly tends to exceed increase of the means of subsistence. In other words, he concluded that, "if unchecked, populations would be subject to exponential growth." He had a fear that, population growth would tend to outstrip growth in food production, leading to ever-increasing famine and poverty. It could be seen that, when Malthus was expounding his population thesis, a Chinese Philosopher, Hungliang Chi was also engaged in studying the population problem and he too reached identical conclusions to which Malthus reached.

(b) **Second Phase:** Second phase of Demographic studies started with the beginning of 19th century and the following scholars were involved in it:

Joshia Milne: Joshia Milne started improving the studies related to figures.

William Far: He was the leading English vital statistician during the middle decades of the 19th century. He prepared report about population of Victorian era, so that it was possible to undertake social legislation.

Johan Finlaison: He came to the conclusion that for realistic estimation, proper registration of birth, death and marriage was necessary.

Achille Guilliard: He coined the term Demography to designate the science of population studies.

(c) **Third Phase:** The third phase of population studies started in the beginning of 20th century. During this time:

Carr Saunders: Brought out his work entitled "The Population Problem—A Study in Human Evolution." It was an important empirical attempt to present Demography as a new branch of knowledge. He also developed the optimum theory of population.

Thompson and Lewis: They however opined that, "Carr Saunders may be said to sponsor the theory that man's growth in numbers has been largely determined by his denotions of economically desirable numbers under his conditions of life. But since Carr Saunders regards man's growth as wholly within his control and as conditioned by the attitudes of mind that he has developed under his institutions and particular physical conditions of his life, his theory stands in sharp contrast to those who were based on natural law."

During this period, Enxer Ludwig Moser, Alfred Lotka, Bockh etc. also developed quantitative theories of population.

(d) **Fourth Phase**: This is called the modern phase of Demographic studies. During this period, Demography as a discipline has been developed with a rigorous but limited core of analytical theory and well defined statistical techniques.

During this time, use of mathematical approach was taking place. Verhulest developed Logistic curve theory for population studies, Organisations like U.N.O. and individuals like Cannan, Bowley, Whelpton, Pearl, Simon Kuznets,

Dorothy Thomas, Coale, etc. have done commendable work in enlarging the frontiers of Demographic studies. Emphasis was also given to interdisciplinary nature of population studies in place of pure Demography. In the words of Dr. B.N. Ganguli: "It is a field where biologists and sociologists have joined hand to correct the follies of a civilisation caught up in the bold advances of modern science towards specialisation of nature and the eventual exhaustion of natural resources. Economists, Demographers and Sociologists can no longer afford to ignore the ecological dimensions of both population and development."[11]

Development of Demography in India

The development of Demography in India can be seen from the two broad periods: (i) Development of Demography in pre-independent India, and (ii) Development of Demography in post-independent India.

(i) **Development of Demography in pre-independent India:** The necessity of population studies in our country was felt since ancient time. It has been found that, the *Arthashastra* of Kautilya gives a detailed description of how to conduct a population, economic and agricultural census. During the reign of Akbar; The Great, Abul Fazal also compiled the *Ain-e-Akbari* containing comprehensive data on population, industry, wealth and traits of population. During British period, the system of decennial census started with the first census in 1872. Later on, the Imperial Gazetteers made a significant contribution towards the growth of Demography in India. The first Imperial Gazetteer was published in 1881 in 9 volumes at the instance of W.W. Hunter and in 1882, a companion volume entitled 'The Indian Empire: Its History, People and Products', was published. The revised versions of the Imperial Gazetteers were published in 26 volumes during the period from 1907 and 1909.

Further, it is seen that, the First Indian Population Conference was held in 1936 under the auspices of the University of Lucknow and a paper entitled "Future Growth of India's Population" was presented. The Second All India Conference on population and the First Family Hygiene Conference were jointly held in Bombay in 1938 and a paper on differential fertility based on field experience was presented.

The earliest study on India's population based on the analysis of Census data was in the form of a book entitled "The Census of India:

An Analysis and Criticism" by M. Subraya Kamath, was published by the Theosophical Publishing House, Madras in 1914, with an introduction by Annie Besant. Kamat based his study on the Census of India from 1881 to 1911 and draws special attention to infanticide, infant marriages and child widows in India. After that, many other scholars made significant contribution to population studies in various ways at different points of time. The Government of India also took interest on population studies and in 1944, the then Department of Education, Health and Lands set up the Population Data Committee under the Chairmanship of W.M. Yeats "to advise the Government of India on the available data relating to growth of population." In 1946, the Government of India appointed the Health Survey and Development Committee (popularly known as the Bhore Committee) to study health conditions in India and to make recommendations for their improvement.

In 1945, the All India Institute of Hygiene and Public Health, Calcutta conducted several field studies under the guidance of Dr. C. Chandrasekharan. In 1942, Prof. N.V. Sovani of the Gokhale Institute of Politics and Economics, Pune, published a study entitled "The Population Problem in India: A Regional Approach."

(ii) **Development of Demography in post-independent India:** In 1949, the Family Planning Association of India was established in Bombay, which started propagating population control. The importance of teaching formal and technical Demography in Colleges and Universities was first emphasised by a Committee set up by the U.N. Secretary General in December, 1953 and the matter came up for consideration in the Population Commission in March 1955 and the Government of India established its Demographic Advisory Committee in 1958. The founding of the Demographic Advisory Committee in 1958, preceded by the establishment of the Demographic Training and Research Centre (DTRC) at Chembur, Bombay in 1957, led to the official support of six other Centres of Demographic Research at Delhi, Calcutta, Poona, Trivandrum, Dharwar and Madras. The other important landmarks in the growth of Demography are as follows:

(a) **The Indian Census, the Vital Registration System and the National Sample Survey:** The Population Census and the Vital Registration System are the two sources, not only of historical Demography, but also of the study of specific regions and spaces over time. These two are the best sources of information. The Indian Census was primarily designed to provide the administration a working knowledge of the people of the country. Similarly, the vital statistics system was also designed to have a rough idea on mortality, morbidity and natality. The country though had its preliminary Census in 1872, but the first regular Census was taken in 1881 and thereafter, regular Census is being held in every 10 years. However, due to its fixed decadal duration of enumeration and of general nature of information, its scope of application has been limited. The scope has further been reduced due to non-availability of intra-decadal information. Therefore, to overcome such situations, the National Sample Survey (NSS) was introduced in the year 1950 and Prof. P.C. Mahalanobis was the pioneer of this work. The NSS is being conducted every year with different subject(s) depending on the requirements of different users. The aim of NSS is to generate information on specific themes through successive rounds of sample survey, so that, these information could be used for formulating plans, conducting research and for the structural analysis.

(b) **Indian Association for the Study of Population**: Establishment of the Indian Association for the Study of Population (IASP) in 1972 was a significant step forward towards the development of Demography in our country. The IASP, in the same year, started publishing a Journal, entitled 'Demography India' with the financial support from the Family Planning Foundation of India.

(c) **Teaching in Demography**: In the First Asian Population Conference in 1963, the subject of teaching of Demography in the Universities was taken up earnestly and subsequently, the Universities like Aligarh, Allahabad, Banaras, Baroda, Gorakhpur, Lucknow, Jaipur and Saugar instituted post-graduate teaching in Demography as an optional paper in M.A. Economics, but Poona introduced Demography as a compulsory paper in M. Sc. Statistics.

In India, Demography was taught at the post-graduate level leading to M. Sc. degree in the University of Kerala, for the first time. In 1973, a Population Studies Centre was established at Shri Venkateshwara University, Tirupati. From 1974, Demography is being taught in J.N.U. Besides, it formed a part of the syllabi as an optional paper in Economics at Agra, Aligarh, Allahabad, Banaras, Baroda, Bombay, Calcutta, Gorakhpur, Gujarat, Lucknow, Meerut, Rajasthan, Rewa, Saugar. Demography has also become a part of the post-graduate courses in Economics, Statistics and Sociology in many other Universities.

The University of Madras established a Centre for Population Studies. Initially, the Centre started offering two diploma courses in population studies: (i) a Post-Graduate Diploma in Population Studies, and (ii) a Post-M.A., M. Sc. Diploma in Population Studies. However, the Post-Graduate Degree Course in Population Studies has been started from the academic year 1984.

(d) **Demographic Training and Research**: Development of infrastructure in the form of establishment of the Demographic Training and Research Centre at Bombay and setting up of a chain of Demographic Research Centres at several Universities, Research Institutes and Government Departments, was the major achievement for Demographic Training and Research in India. The Demographic Training and Research Centre at Bombay was established with the assistance from the United Nations to serve as a "Regional Training Centre" for the countries in Asia. A co-ordinating Central Family Planning Institute has also been established in New Delhi in order to lay down a strong foundation for continuous Training and long-term Research in Demography in our country.

The International Institute for Population Studies (IIPS), Bombay is also doing a commendable job in the field of Demographic Research and Family Welfare Activities. Besides IIPS, CSO, NSSO, RGI, IMR and many other Government Departments, Institutions, Universities are also engaged in Demographic Research and Family Welfare Activities.[12]

Notes

1. V.C. Sinha and E. Zacharia, *Elements of Demography*, published by Allied Publishers Private Limited, New Delhi, 2012, p. 1.

2. *Ibid.*, pp. 1–2.
3. *Ibid.*, p. 2.
4. *Ibid.*, p. 2.
5. *Ibid.*, pp. 2–3.
6. *Ibid.*, p. 3.
7. *Ibid.*, p. 4.
8. *Ibid.*, pp. 5-6.
9. *Ibid.*, pp. 22-23.
10. *Ibid.*, pp. 24-25.
11. *Ibid.*, pp. 25-26.
12. *Ibid.*, pp. 26-33.

3

Demographic Aspect and Population Growth in NER

In the North Eastern Region, there is no separate Institute, as such, for the study of Demography. The subject is being taught at the post-graduate level in some of the Universities of this Region, as a paper in Statistics. Demography is the Statistical study of human population, particularly their size, composition and distribution, which changes over time or space, primarily due to birth, death and migration. The size normally refers to the number of people living in a given place at a given time, composition refers mainly to age, sex, education, religion, social group, marital and residential (i.e. rural-urban) status, while distribution refers to occupation and activity status of population. The change in the population size due to birth relates to the fertility, i.e. the actual birth performances of the group of women or to the relative frequency with which the births occur in that population. Fertility is again a matter of fecundity, i.e. the physiological capacity of the women to reproduce during their child bearing span. The death has also a vital role in the change of population size. The physiological change in population depends on the absolute increase, i.e. the total number births–(minus) the total number of deaths, over a period of time.

Migration has a very big role in change of population. Migration generally refers to the movement of persons from a locality of origin to a destination place and staying there more or less on a permanent basis. The migration might be of the nature of rural-urban, intra-state, inter-state or inter-country and the reason of migration might be education, employment, business, marriage, family moved, natural calamities, political upheavals etc. The change in the size of population due to migration depends on the absolute increase or decrease of population due to in-migration and out-migration of a place over a period of time.

Measurement of migration is somewhat complex as it is associated with many socio-economic and political factors and to get information of such nature over a short period of time is quite difficult. Moreover, movement of people is also taking place secretly, for which, there is no scope of keeping any record at all. However, during population Census, such information are being collected in every ten years, but it is really difficult to get the information on such events, that are taking place, during inter-censual period.

Population Growth

Initially, North Eastern Region was consisted of Assam and two other Kingsley States *viz.* Manipur and Tripura. Arunachal Pradesh, Meghalaya, Mizoram and Nagaland, all were parts of Assam. Later on, due to political and administrative reasons, these were separated from Assam at different points of time. However, except Brahmaputra and Barak valleys of Assam, entire North Eastern Region is hilly and these hilly areas were inhabited mainly by the people who had migrated from Mongolia, Burma, China, Tibet etc. The early history of Assam is not much known. However, the *Mahabharata*, *Vishnupurana*, *Kalika Purana* and *Yoginitantra* indicate that, Assam was known as Pragjyotisha and later on as Kamarupa and was ruled by Kings who had appellation of *Danaba-Asura*, which suggest their non-Aryan origin. It is seen that, King Pralambha founded a dynasty at around 800 A.D. which lasted for about 200 years, and thereafter came the Pala dynasty. In the 13th century, Ahoms, a Shan tribe came to the Brahmaputra valley from Burma and again in the 15th century, a new dynasty of Kochas was established by Biswa Singh.

The tribal people of Arunachal Pradesh had Mongoloid character and their migration took place in pre-historic times. The ethnic group of Eastern Meghalaya, who are known to be one of the earliest ethnic groups of settlers in Indian Sub-Continent, belongs to the Proto-Austroloid Monkhmer race. While the Garos of Western Meghalaya, belongs to the Bodo family of Tibeto-Burman race, said to have migrated from Tibet. The ancestors of Mizos emigrated from South-East China at the end of 10th century. But the Nagas are far more primitive. They had a Mongoloid origin and had migrated at about 2000 years B.C.

The Kingsley State of Manipur was inhabited mainly by Manipuris, while the Kingsley State of Tripura was inhabited by

Tripuris. The ancestral origin of Tripuris, traces back to Drujho, the son of Yajati, the supreme ruler. Initially, Sikkim was also a Kingsley State inhabited by Lepchas and later on, Nepalese from Nepal came to Sikkim and settled there. All these Kingsley States of Manipur, Tripura and Sikkim became full-fledged States of India at different points of time.

From above, though it is possible to get some idea about the origin of the people of this region, but no such information is available, which can give little idea about their size at that time. Human beings are the most wonderful creation among all the living beings. The early humans had to pass through various stages of development. While undergoing these changes, they could realize the need of increasing their size and strength for securing food, shelter, security, technological and other development. But, they could realize the need of knowing their size at a much later stage. And in case of India, there was no information about the size of population even in ancient or mediaeval era. However, in 1605, Moreland estimated the population of India as 10 crores. And according to Dr. Pradha Kumar Mukherjee, the population of India was 10.50 crores at the beginning of 19th century.

It is seen that, to get a proper idea about the size of population of our country, a comprehensive Census for the first time was conducted in 1872. But the second Census was conducted in 1881 and thereafter Census is being conducted in every ten years, i.e. in 1891, 1901, 1911 and so on ......Initially, in addition to their number the population was also classified under broad activity and occupational groups. For this purpose, the income concept was taken into consideration for determining the economic status of an individual. From 1901 Census, population was divided into categories like actual workers, dependents, engaged in principal or subsidiary occupations etc. However, additions and alterations were made in the methodology of collecting information, depending on the necessity, in the subsequent Census.

The first population Census in our country was though conducted in 1872, but the population record for the North Eastern States except Arunachal Pradesh is available from 1901 Census onwards. In Arunachal Pradesh, the population Census was conducted for the first time in 1961, and thereafter, it is being conducted in every ten years along with other states of the country. The state-wise population of the North Eastern Region as well as the population of the country as a whole from 1901 Census to 2011 Census, i.e. over a period of 110 years can be seen from the Appendix–3.1.

From Appendix–3.1, it can be seen that, the growth of population in the North Eastern States does not follow any particular trend. In case of Arunachal Pradesh, the population was 3.37 lakhs as per 1st census conducted in 1961, but within 30 years, it became more than two and a half times and in next 20 years, the population became more than four times. The population in Assam in the year, 1901 was 32.90 lakhs and it became more than one and a half time within a period of 30 years and in another 30 years, it increased to more than three times. In next 30 years, the population reached to little less than seven times and finally it went up to nine and a half time within a period of next 20 years. The growth of population in Manipur at the initial stages was almost similar to Assam. In 1901, the population of Manipur was 2.84 lakhs and it became more than one and a half time within a period of 30 years, then it went to little less than two and a half time in another 30 years. In the next 30 years, it reached to almost six and a half time and finally it became more than ten times within a period of another 20 years. The population growth in Meghalaya was much slow at the initial stages. In 1901, the population of Meghalaya was 3.41 lakhs and it added little more than a quarter of its original size in next 30 years and became more than two times within a period of another 30 years. Then it picked up the momentum and became more than five times within next 30 years and finally it reached to almost nine times in another 20 years.

The growth of population in the states of Mizoran, Nagaland and Tripura was very fast. In Mizoram, though the population growth at the initial stages was a bit slow, but it increased very rapidly in the later years. In 1901, the population of Mizorzm was though 0.82 lakhs, but it became more than one and a half time within a period of 30 years and within next 30 years, it went up to more than three times. In another 30 years, population increased to more than eight times and finally it reached to more than thirteen times in next 20 years. In Nagaland also, though the growth of population at the initial stages was slow, but at the later years, population increased very rapidly. It is seen that, the population of Nagaland in 1901 was 1.02 lakhs, but it increased to more than one and a half time within a period of 30 years and after that it picked up the momentum and reached to more than three and a half time within next 30 years and to little less than twelve times in another 30 years. The population finally went up to more than nineteen times in the next 20 years. The growth of population of Tripura was also more or less similar to Nagaland. The population of Tripura in the year 1901 was though 1.73 lakhs, but within a period of 30 years, it went up to more than two times and then to more than six and a half time within next 30 years. In another 30 years, it went up to almost sixteen times and finally the population reached to more than twenty one times in next 20 years. The growth of population in Sikkim was not that fast. The population of Sikkim in 1901 was 0.59 lakh and after a period of 30 years, it became little less than double and then within next 30 years, it reached to little less than three times and then in another 30 years, it reached to little less than seven times and finally the population reached to almost ten and a half time within next 20 years.

The population growth in the North Eastern Region as a whole, including Sikkim was not that fast. It is seen that the population of North Eastern Region in 1901 was 43.31 lakhs and it became little less than double within a period of 30 years and then it became little more than three times within a period of another 30 years. The population of this region reached to more than seven times in the next 30 years and finally reached to more than ten and a half time in another 20 years. However, the growth of population of our country as a whole was much slow as compared to the North Eastern States. In 1901, the population of the country was 23.84 crores and within a period of next 30 years, it increased to 27.90 crores i.e. there was an addition of only 4.06 crores. The population could not even become double in next 30 years. It took another 30 years to cross three and a half time mark and finally it could cross five times mark in another 20 years. The details can be seen from the Appendix–3.1.

It is interesting to note that the rate of increase of population in all the North Eastern States was quite slow at the beginning and that trend was more or less maintained till first 50 years starting from 1901. The rate of growth gained momentum from 1961 and thereafter the population started increasing in all the States very rapidly. But from Appendix–3.2, it can be seen that the Natural Growth Rate was not very high in any of the North Eastern States and it was ranging from 17.0 in Arunachal Pradesh to 26.4 in Manipur in 1971 and thereafter it was more or less maintaining a declining trend. Therefore, the phenomenal growth of population in this Region perhaps cannot be attributed to the natural growth process. This high rate of growth of population might be due to the time to time in-migration of people from other states of our country as well as due to the influx of people from other countries because of political and other reasons.

The North Eastern States except Assam are mostly tribal dominated States and there was a dearth of educated and skilled manpower in the early era of Planned Development. Moreover, the States *viz.* Arunachal Pradesh, Meghalaya, Mizoram and Nagaland were initially parts of Assam and in sixties and early seventies they became separate States and everything had to start afresh, for which huge number of educated and skilled manpower from other states were needed.

To study the population growth in the North Eastern States for last 50 years, i.e. from 1961 to 2011, Appendix–3.3.1 to Appendix–3.3.6, have been prepared on the basis of Census Reports of each of these Census years. These are multidimensional tables wherein population has been classified under three categories *viz.* total population, total Scheduled Tribe (ST) population and total Scheduled Caste (SC) population and they have also been distributed according to sex and their residential status. Further, the percentage of ST and SC population has also been calculated for each of the Census years and presented separately in these Appendices.

From Appendix–3.3.1 to Appendix–3.3.6, it can be seen that, the States of Mizoram, Nagaland, Meghalaya and Arunachal Pradesh are tribal dominated States and the percentage of tribal people were very high in all these States. In the State of Mizoram, more than 94 per cent of people were tribal and they maintained almost the same percentage in all the years starting from 1961 to 2011. The other unique characteristic of the tribal people of Mizoram was that, they maintained more or less this high percentage both in rural and urban areas, in the last 50 years. Nagaland also recorded a very high percentage of ST people and it ranges from 93.09 per cent in 1961 to 86.48 per cent in 2011. However, the percentage of tribal people in rural and urban areas was not similar to Mizoram. In rural areas of Nagaland, the percentage of ST people was 95.37 in 1961, but it came down to 92.85 in 2011. Whereas in urban areas it was 51.49 per cent in 1961 and then gradually increased and reached to 70.78 per cent in 2011. The overall position of tribal people of Meghalaya was not the same as of Nagaland. The percentage of ST people of Meghalaya was 83.07 in 1961, but it increased to 86.15 per cent in 2011. In rural areas, the percentage of ST people was 90.59 in 1961 and they maintained this high percentage in all these years till 2011. However, in urban areas, the ST people showed a remarkable change in their percentage and starting from 41.38 per cent in 1961, their percentage reached to 70.36 in 2011. This not only indicates urban migration of ST, but that also caused a sharp change in the composition of urban people.

The position of Arunachal Pradesh was completely different. Initially, Arunachal was a part of Assam, but due to the political and constitutional development in fifties, sixties and seventies, the portions of the Himalayas, inhabited by the tribal people, were separated from Assam and a full-scale administrative structure with the name, North East Frontier Agency (NEFA) was formed in 1954. Later on, NEFA attained the status of Union Territory (UT) in 1972 with a new name, Arunachal Pradesh and shifted its Headquarters to Itanagar from Shillong in 1974. Moreover, for running the administration together with construction of roads and buildings, and for implementing the developmental schemes, a huge number of manpower from other States were required at that time. This actually changed the population composition of the State to a great extent. Therefore, the overall percentage of ST people of Arunachal Pradesh, which was 88.59 in 1961, started declining gradually and reached to 64.22 per cent in 2001, and then again there was an increasing trend and ultimately the percentage reached to 68.79 in 2011. Same trend was maintained in rural areas. Starting from 88.59 per cent in 1961, it came down to 69.60 per cent in 2001 and again reached to 74.07 per cent in 2011. But in urban areas, the percentage of ST people showed a phenomenal increase. Starting from 20.07 per cent in 1971, the percentage of ST people maintained a steady increase and reached to 51.04 in 2011. This shows, there was high rate of urban migration of the ST people in the last 50 years.

In Manipur and Tripura, ST people were comparatively less and they maintained a low proportion in all these years in both the States. In Manipur, the overall percentage of ST people was 31.93 in 1961 and their percentage increased very slowly and finally reached to 40.88 in 2011. In rural areas also, there was no significant increase. Starting from 34.38 per cent in 1961, it reached to 52.23 per cent in 2011, i.e. within a period of 50 years. The increase in the proportion of ST people was also not that much even in urban areas. Their percentage was only 6.12 in 1961 and finally it reached to 13.38 in 2011. In case of Tripura, the overall position of ST people was 31.53 per cent in 1961 and they maintained almost the same percentage throughout this period and reached to 31.76 in 2011. In rural areas, the percentage was slightly higher. It was 34.30 per cent in 1961 and then steadily increased to 41.20 per cent in 2011. The proportion of ST people in urban areas was very less. It was only 3.59 per cent in 1961 and somehow reached to 5.12 per cent over a period of 50 years.

The State of Sikkim was having much less ST population. In Sikkim, the overall percentage of ST people was only 23.27 in 1981 and it reached to 33.80 in 2011. In rural areas, the situation was almost the same. The percentage of ST people in rural areas was 23.60 in 1981 and finally it reached to 36.57 in 2011. In urban areas, the proportion of ST people was comparatively less in all these years. Starting with 21.54 per cent in 1981, it could reach to 25.53 per cent in 2011. The proportion of ST people in Assam was the lowest. The overall percentage was only 10.75 in 1961 and it maintained a very low growth over the years and somehow reached to 12.45 per cent in 2011. In rural areas, the position was almost the same. Starting with 11.51 per cent in 1961, the percentage of ST people reached to 13.67 in 2011. In urban areas, the percentage of ST people was only 0.86 in 1961 and the growth was also very slow in all these years. Within a period of 50 years, it could reach to the maximum of 4.98 per cent only.

The percentage of ST people in Assam was though comparatively less, but the overall percentage of the ST people in the North Eastern Region (NER) as a whole was quite high and it was much higher than the overall percentage of the ST people of our country. The overall percentage of the ST people of NER was 22.61 as compared to 6.86 per cent of the country in 1961, but in 2011, the percentage was 27.70 as compared to 8.63 of the country as a whole. In rural areas, the percentage of ST people of NER was 23.83 as compared to 8.15 of the country in 1961, but in 2011, it was 28.76 and 11.28 respectively. In urban areas, the rate of growth of ST people of NER was much higher. Starting with 7.73 per cent in 1961, it reached to 23.00 per cent in 2011. Whereas, in case of the country as a whole, the percentage of ST people was only 0.98 in 1961 and the growth rate was also less in all these years and the percentage finally reached to 2.77 in 2011.

In the North Eastern States, Scheduled Caste (SC) people are not much. In the tribal dominated States viz. Arunachal Pradesh, Meghalaya, Mizoram and Nagaland, SC population was very very less. In Manipur and Sikkim, though some SC people were there, but their percentage was very less both in rural as well as in urban areas, at the initial stages. But from eighties, the percentage of SC people started increasing moderately, particularly in urban areas. However, in case of urban areas of Manipur, the percentage of SC people was 3.84 in 1991 and it reached to 5.93 in 2011. Whereas, in case of urban areas of Sikkim, situation was reverse. The percentage was 7.67 in 1981, but it came down to 5.17 in 2011. In Assam and Tripura, SC people were comparatively more and their proportion was higher in the urban areas, in both the States. In urban areas of Assam, the percentage of SC people was 7.74 in 1961, but it increased slowly and reached to 9.22 per cent in 2011. Whereas, in urban areas of Tripura, the percentage of SC people was 6.55 in 1961, but their rate of growth was quite high and finally it reached to 22.56 per cent in 2011.

However, it is interesting to note that, in case of NER, the percentage of SC people in urban areas was slightly higher than the percentage of SC people in rural areas and that trend was more or less maintained in last 50 years. In NER, the percentage of SC people of urban areas was 6.10 in 1961 and it gradually increased to 8.17 in 2011. But the situation of the country as a whole was completely different. The percentage of SC people was much higher in the rural areas than the percentage of SC people of urban areas, in all these years. In rural areas, the percentage of SC people was 15.98 in 1961 and it reached to 18.45 in 2011. Whereas in urban areas, it was 8.72 in 1961 and finally it could reach to 12.60 in 2011. Further details can be seen from the Appendix–3.3.1 to Appendix–3.3.6.

Decadal Growth

The population of our country or of any State are primarily classified under 3 (three) categories *viz.* General population, Scheduled Tribe (ST) population and Scheduled Caste (SC) population. In Appendix-3.3.1 to Appendix–3.3.6, the population of each of the North Eastern States were classified as Total population, ST population and SC population with their sex and residential status. Further, taking the total of ST and SC population under a particular category and subtracting this number from the Total Population of that category, General population or Others, under that category was found out and Decadal Growth was calculated in absolute number and in percentage and presented in Appendix–3.3.7. The General population or Others, in any of the tribal dominated States of NE Region, are not the indigenous people of that State. Basically, they are the migrants, who had come there for service, business or for other economic activities.

In the North Eastern Region, the States *viz.* Mizoram, Nagaland, Meghalaya and Arunachal Pradesh are tribal dominated States and there was a dearth of educated and skilled Manpower at the beginning of planning era. Therefore, for running Administration and for executing the Developmental Schemes, huge number of educated and skilled persons, were required from outside, at the initial stages in these States. But later on, the tribal people gradually came forward and started taking active part in administration and in other activities and that paved the way for reducing dependency on outside people. Appendix–3.3.7 will give an idea about the nature and extent of growth of people at different points of time in different States of NE Region.

From Appendix–3.3.7, it can be seen that, in case of Mizoram, the overall Decadal Growth (DG) of ST population was much less to the extent of 20.03 per cent as against 276.86 per cent for Others during 1961–71, and it was also less to the tune of 47.43 per cent as against 66.84 per cent during 1971–81. But after that, the situation started changing. The overall DG became 41.49 per cent for ST and 11.93 per cent for Others, during 1981–91. During 1991–2001, it was 28.42 per cent and 38.00 per cent respectively and during 2001-11, it was 23.45 per cent for ST and 22.21 per cent for Others. Further, it can be seen that, the DG for Others was the highest to the extent of 367.36 per cent in rural areas during 1961-71. This indicates that, the requirement of non-tribal people was more in rural areas at the initial stage. However, from 1971-81 onwards, the growth rate was much more in urban particularly for ST. It can be seen that, in urban areas, within a period of 50 years, the ST people grown by 4066.52 per cent and non-ST by 2598.40 per cent.

In case of Nagaland, the overall DG for Others was more to the extent of 130.75 per cent against 33.14 per cent of ST during 1961–71. During this period, the DG for Others was also more in rural as well as in urban. This was 65.57 per cent against 31.27 per cent for rural and 244.42 per cent against 96.53 per cent for urban respectively. During 1971–81, the overall DG for Others was though more to the tune of 110.79 per cent against 42.24 per cent for ST, but in urban areas, the DG for ST increased considerably to the extent of 228.18 per cent against 76.88 per cent for Others. From 1981–91 onwards, the DG for ST started increasing both in rural as well as in urban, but the DG for Others started declining and lastly registered a negative growth of (-) 2.45 per cent in rural areas during 2001–11. This indicates the gradual reduction of dependency on non-tribal people.

The situation in Meghalaya was slightly different. Initially, Meghalaya was within Assam and the State of Assam was having its capital in Shillong. Later on, Meghalaya was separated and the capital of Assam was also shifted from Shillong to Dispur, Guwahati. On the other hand, after attaining separate statehood, Shillong again became the capital of Meghalaya. Further, during that transitional period, many of the employees of Assam Government, opted for Meghalaya Government service and stayed there. Moreover, from British period, Shillong was the educational hub and as such, the local tribal people, along with the non-tribal, got all opportunities of education. Therefore, there was no much need of non-ST people in sixties and seventies.

In Meghalaya, though the overall DG for Others was more to the tune of 50.11 per cent against 27.39 per cent for ST during 1961–71, but in case of urban, DG for ST was much more to the extent of 38.07 per cent against 13.28 per cent for Others, during that period. From 1971–81 onwards, the DG for ST started increasing, particularly in urban areas. It was 26.18 per cent against 28.56 per cent for Others in rural, whereas in urban, it was much more to the tune of 99.07 per cent for ST against 35.13 per cent for Others, during 1971–81. But in 1981–91, there was a negative growth for Others to the tune of (–) 14.20 per cent against 39.18 per cent for ST in rural, and in urban, it was also much less to the extent of 14.20 per cent against 54.05 per cent for ST. In next two decades, though there was no much difference in DG in case of rural, but in urban, the DG for ST was higher to the extent of 50.70 per cent against 16.43 per cent in 1991-2001 and 35.07 per cent against 22.06 per cent in 2001-11. On the whole, the ST population increased by 299.88 per cent and non-ST people increased by 205.27 per cent within a period of 50 years, starting from 1961.

Arunachal Pradesh though a tribal dominated State, but in sixties and seventies there was a shortage of educated and skilled manpower and as such quite a big number non-tribal people were required for administration and for other activities. It can be seen that, the overall DG for Others was very high to the extent of 154.65 per cent against 23.89 per cent of ST in 1961–71 and it was also high to the tune of 92.05 per cent against 58.07 per cent in 1971–81. However, from 1971–81, the DG for ST in urban areas, started increasing and reached to 121.04 per cent against 119.99 per cent of Others, during that period and in 1981–91, it reached to 219.47 per cent against 154.36 per cent. From 1991-2001 onwards the DG for Others started declining considerably both in rural as well as in urban areas. In 1991-2001, it was 11.98 per cent against 16.99 per cent of ST in rural and in urban, it was 62.83 per cent against 207.76 per cent of ST. But in 2001–11, it further came down to 4.87 per cent against 30.28 per cent in rural and 20.97 per cent against 63.81 per cent of ST in urban. This not only indicates the growth of tribal people, but it also indicates the reduction of dependency on non-tribal people.

Manipur was a princely State and educational facilities were there even in nineteenth century. The State was having its own educated and skilled manpower from that time. In Manipur, ST people are comparatively less. Out of total population, about one third is ST and most of them are living in rural areas. However, the growth of ST people is comparatively more in urban than in rural. During 1961–71, the DG of ST was 30.47 per cent against 31.21 per cent of Others in rural, whereas in urban, it was 260.59 per cent against 98.65 per cent. In 1971–81, the DG for ST was 7.29 per cent against 15.43 per cent in rural, but in urban, it was 202.11 per cent against 159.86 per cent of Others. In Manipur, the growth of ST was not uniform, rather it showed some ups and downs both in rural as well as in urban. In 1981–91, the DG for ST was 68.88 per cent against 6.83 per cent of Others in rural and in urban, it was 17.88 per cent against 32.28 per cent. In 1991-2001, though the DG for ST was 21.93 per cent against 25.62 per cent in rural, but it showed a negative growth in urban. In 2001–11, the DG for ST reached to 49.57 per cent against 6.23 per cent in rural, but in urban, it increased considerably and reached to the extent of 216.82 per cent against 34.21 per cent of Others. The growth rate for ST and Others may not show the actual position, as the final population figures of some of the Census contained estimated population of a few sub-divisions of Manipur.

Tripura was also a princely State and educational facilities were there even much before starting of the planning era. Tripura has mixed population and Scheduled Tribe people are comparatively less. Out of total population, about thirty per cent are ST and most of them are living in rural hilly areas. In Tripura, a considerable number of Scheduled Caste (SC) people, i.e. around seventeen per cent of the total population, are also there. The growth rate of SC was rather more than ST and Others at the initial stages. During 1961–71, the DG of SC was 61.68 per cent against 24.89 per cent of ST and 34.51 per cent of Others in rural and 51.12 per cent against 48.32 per cent of ST and 58.48 per cent of Others in urban. During 1971–81, the DG for SC was also high both in rural as well as in urban. In rural, it was 59.21 per cent against 29.48 per cent of ST and 25.34 per cent of Others and in urban, it was 91.82 per cent against 39.80 per cent of ST and 35.22 per cent of Others. From 1981–91 onwards, the DG for SC started declining in rural areas, but in urban, it maintained the high rate. During 1981–91, though the DG for SC in rural was 30.54 per cent against 45.64 per cent of ST and 16.26 per cent of Others, but in urban, it was quite high to the extent of 265.45 per cent against 83.63 per cent of ST and 69.49 per cent of Others. In 1991-2001, the DG for SC further went down. During this period, it was 20.01 per cent against 15.34 per cent of ST and 10.15 per cent of Others in rural, but in urban, it was 40.10 per cent against 80.59 per cent of ST and 25.00 per cent of Others. During 2001–11, both SC and Others, registered a negative growth in rural, but in urban, the DG for SC was quite high to the extent of 116.71 per cent against 93.66 per cent of ST and 65.46 per cent of Others. The overall growth rate for SC was 447.02 per cent against 224.05 per cent of ST and 179.70 per cent of Others within a period of 50 years starting from 1961.

In the North Eastern Region (NER), Assam is the most populous State. About sixty eight per cent of the total population of NER, are there in Assam alone. The State also having, both ST, about twelve per cent and SC, about seven per cent, of the total population of the State. The ST people are living primarily in the two hill Districts *viz.* Karbi Anglong and North Cachar Hills. In case of Assam, it is seen that, the growth rate for all, i.e. ST, SC and Others was less in rural, but more in urban. It is also seen that, the growth rate of ST was comparatively more than others. That means the ST people were increasing faster. During 1961–71, the DG for ST was 37.52 per cent against 23.23 per cent of SC and 32.69 per cent of Others in rural, but in urban, it was 111.72 per cent against 41.68 per cent of SC and 66.55 per cent of Others. In 1981–91, the DG for ST was 74.41 per cent against 72.96 per cent of SC and 43.99 per cent of Others in rural, but it was very high to the extent of 581.40 per cent against 167.47 per cent of SC and 81.74 per cent of Others, in urban. From 1991-2001 onwards, the growth rate started declining for all. During 1991-2001, the DG for ST was 13.58 per cent against 8.64 per cent of SC and 17.74 per cent of Others in rural and in urban, it was 58.57 per cent against 18.74 per cent of SC and 39.40 per cent of Others. In 2001–11, the DG for ST was 16.19 per cent against 17.51 per cent of SC and 15.17 per cent of Others in rural and in urban, it was 42.16 per cent against 48.96 per cent of SC and 25.26 per cent of Others. On the whole, the ST people increased at a rate of 233.53 per cent against 205.04 per cent of SC and 180.61 per cent of Others within a period of 50 years starting from 1961.

In Sikkim, both ST and SC people are there. About one third of the total population are ST, but SC population are not much, it is about five per cent of the total population of the State. However, proper records on ST and SC were not available at the initial stages. Moreover, the growth rate was also not uniform. It showed some ups and downs, both in rural as well as in urban. During 1981–91, the DG for ST was 33.32 per cent against 48.51 per cent of SC and 40.53 per cent of Others in rural, whereas in urban, all three, registered a negative growth. In 1991-2001, the DG for ST was 22.07 per cent against 11.90 per cent of SC and 34.22 per cent of Others in rural, but in urban, it was 28.06 per cent against 19.70 per cent of SC and 75.41 per cent of Others. In 2001–11, growth rate showed again a different picture. During this period, though the DG for ST in rural was 64.01 per cent, but other two, registered a negative growth. Whereas, in urban, the DG for ST was quite high to the extent of 312.95 per cent against 141.12 per cent of SC and 126.04 per cent of Others.

The growth rate in North Eastern Region and in India showed some similarity. It has been found that, the DG in rural areas was comparatively less than in urban, both in NER and in the country in last 50 years starting from 1961. Further, the overall DG in NER was higher in the initial three decades, but in later two decades, there was no much difference in the DG of NER and in the country. During 1961-71, the overall DG in NER for ST was 31.08 per cent against 31.13 per cent of SC and 36.54 per cent of Others. But in the country, it was 26.17 per cent against 24.14 per cent of SC and 24.74 per cent of Others. The difference between the overall DG was quite high during 1981–91. During this period, the overall DG for ST in NER was 89.44 per cent against 92.46 per cent of SC and 50.48 per cent of Others, but in India, it was 31.24 per cent against 31.95 per cent of SC and 25.82 per cent of Others. During 1991-2001 and in 2001–11, the difference between the overall DG of the respective categories of NER and India, was not much. In 1991-2001, the overall DG in NER for ST was 27.11 per cent against 13.77 per cent of SC and 20.30 per cent of Others and in India, it was 24.45 per cent against 20.56 per cent of SC and 21.45 per cent of Others. In 2001–11, the overall DG in NER for ST was 21.15 per cent against 21.88 per cent of SC and 16.05 per cent of Others, whereas in India, it was 23.98 per cent against 20.85 per cent of SC and 16.37 per cent of Others.

Further, it can be seen that, though the rural growth rate for ST, SC and Others, within a period of last 50 years starting from 1961, was not that high, but in urban areas it was quite high, both in NER and in India. The rural growth rate for ST was 232.72 per cent against 193.59

per cent of SC and 154.90 per cent of Others in NER, but in India, the rural growth rate for ST was 220.47 per cent against 167.26 per cent of SC and 114.29 per cent of Others. But, the growth rate in urban areas, particularly for ST was very high. In NER, the urban growth rate for ST was very high to the extent of 2154.22 per cent against 914.67 per cent of SC and 504.80 per cent of Others and in India, it was also high to the tune of 1254.47 per cent against 590.58 per cent of SC and 347.68 per cent of Others, during the period of last 50 years.

This high growth rate in urban, cannot be attributed to the natural growth alone. This is a clear indication of urban development *vis-à-vis* urban migration. Further, it indicates that, the urban migration in respect of ST people was comparatively more than SC and Others. That means, the ST people are becoming more and more interested for education and employment and for raising their standard of living, day by day.

Growth within a Period of 50 Years

The growth of population in NER and in India during a period of last 50 years, starting from 1961, can be looked at in another way. It is seen that, in 1961 census, in NER, out of total rural population, 23.83 per cent was ST, 5.89 per cent was SC and 70.28 per cent was Others. And in urban, it was 7.73 per cent, 6.10 per cent and 86.17 per cent respectively. After a gap of 50 years, i.e. in 2011, the rural percentage for ST became 28.76, SC became 6.27 and Others became 64.97 and in urban, it became 23.00 for ST, 8.17 for SC and 68.83 for Others. That indicates, in NER, after a gap of 50 years, the proportion increased by an additional percentage of (+) 4.93 for ST and (+) 0.38 for SC and in case of Others, it decreased by a percentage of (–) 5.31, in rural. But in urban, the proportion increased by an additional percentage of (+) 15.27 for ST, (+) 2.07 for SC and in case of Others, the proportion decreased by a very higher percentage of (–) 17.34.

In India, the position was more or less similar except the case of ST people. In rural areas, the proportion increased by an additional percentage of (+) 3.14 for ST and (+) 2.47 for SC. But for Others, the proportion decreased by (–) 5.61 per cent. In case of urban, the proportion increased by an additional percentage of (+) 1.80 for ST and (+) 3.88 for SC. Whereas for Others, the proportion decreased by (-) 5.68 per cent.

From this, again it appears that, compared to the position of India, the growth rate for ST people was more in NER. Particularly, the growth rate in urban areas of NER was very high. But in case of SC, the growth rate was more, both in rural as well as in urban areas of the country as a whole, than in NER. However, in case of Others (i.e. population other than ST and SC), there was a decline in the growth rate, both in rural as well as in urban for NER and India, in the last 50 years. In the urban areas of NER, the rate of decline was very high and that cannot be attributed to the death rate alone. That was perhaps due to outmigration of the General category of people.

Appendix-3.1

Population Trend in the North Eastern Region from 1901-2011

(In thousand population)

Census Year	Name of the North Eastern States / NER										India @**#
	Arunachal Pradesh*	Assam@	Manipur	Meghalaya	Mizoram	Nagaland	Tripura	Sub-Total, NER	Sikkim	Total, NER	
1	2	3	4	5	6	7	8	9	10	11	12
1901	0	3290	284	341	82	102	173	4272	59	4331	238396
1911	0	3849	346	394	91	149	230	5059	88	5147	252093
1921	0	4637	384	422	98	159	304	6004	82	6086	251321
1931	0	5560	446	481	124	179	382	7172	110	7282	278977
1941	0	6695	512	556	153	190	513	8619	122	8741	318661
1951	0	8029	578	606	196	213	639	10261	138	10399	361088
1961	337	10837	780	769	266	339	1142	14500	162	14662	439235
1971	468	14625	1073	1012	332	516	1556	19582	210	19792	548160
1981	632	18041	1421	1336	494	775	2053	24752	316	25068	683329
1991	865	22414	1837	1775	690	1210	2757	31548	406	31954	846421
2001	1098	26656	2294	2319	889	1990	3199	38445	541	38986	1028737
2011	1384	31206	2856	2967	1097	1979	3674	45163	611	45774	1210855

Note: Census in Arunachal Pradesh for the first time in 1961.

@ The 1981 Census could not be held in Assam. The population figure for 1981 has been worked out by interpolation.

** The 1991 Census was not held in Jammu & Kashmir. The population for 1991 has been worked out by interpolation.

India and Manipur figures include estimated figures for three sub-divisions viz. Mao Maran, Paomata and Purul of Senapati District of Manipur as census results of 2001 were cancelled in these sub-divisions due to technical reasons.

Source: (i) Registrar General of India, New Delhi.
(ii) 2011 census figures are from Primary Census Abstract of R.G.I.

Annexure-3.2

Estimates of Birth rate, Death rate, Natural Growth rate, Infant Mortality rate and Total Fertility rate by residence in different years

Sl. No.	Name of State/ India	Year	Birth rate			Death rate			Natural Growth rate			Infant Mortality rate			Total Fertility rate		
			Total	Rural	Urban	Total	Rural	Urban	Total	Rural	Urban	Total	Rural	Urban	Total	Rural	Urban
1	2	3	4	5	6	7	8	9	10	11	12	13	14	15	16	17	18
1	Arunachal Pradesh	1971	NA	36.8	NA	NA	19.8	NA	NA	17.0	NA	NA	NA	NA	NA	NA	NA
		1975	NA	28.7	NA	NA	16.6	NA	NA	12.1	NA	NA	NA	NA	NA	NA	NA
		1980	NA	25.9	NA	NA	14.8	NA	NA	11.1	NA	NA	NA	NA	NA	NA	NA
		1985	35.5	35.9	30.5	14.3	15.2	2.2	21.2	20.7	28.3	NA	NA	NA	NA	NA	NA
		1990	30.1	31.0	20.9	13.2	14.1	4.4	16.9	16.9	16.5	NA	NA	NA	NA	NA	NA
		1995	23.8	24.5	15.8	6.0	6.3	1.9	17.8	18.2	13.9	NA	NA	NA	NA	NA	NA
		2000	22.3	23.1	13.9	6.0	6.3	2.5	16.3	16.8	11.4	44	45	11	NA	NA	NA
		2009	21.1	22.6	14.9	6.1	7.0	2.5	15.0	15.6	12.4	32	35	14	NA	NA	NA
		2010	20.5	22.1	14.6	5.9	6.9	2.3	14.6	15.2	12.3	31	34	12	NA	NA	NA
		2011	19.8	21.4	14.2	5.8	6.8	2.5	14.0	14.7	11.6	32	36	10	NA	NA	NA
		2012	19.4	21.0	13.9	5.8	6.7	2.7	13.6	14.3	11.3	33	37	13	NA	NA	NA
		2013	19.3	20.8	13.8	5.8	6.7	2.7	13.4	14.1	11.1	32	36	14	NA	NA	NA
		2015	18.8	19.5	15.3	6.0	6.5	3.7	12.7	13.0	11.6	30	32	19	NA	NA	NA
		2016	18.9	19.5	16.1	6.2	6.5	4.5	12.7	13.0	11.6	36	38	23	NA	NA	NA
2	Assam	1971	38.5	39.3	31.0	17.8	18.7	9.5	20.7	20.6	21.5	139	144	73	5.7	5.8	4.3
		1975	30.1	30.7	23.7	16.9	17.6	9.6	13.2	13.1	14.1	144	147	96	4.1	4.2	3.1

1	2	3	4	5	6	7	8	9	10	11	12	13	14	15	16	17	18
		1980	31.9	32.7	22.5	10.7	11.0	6.9	21.2	21.7	15.6	103	105	64	4.0	4.1	2.6
		1985	34.3	35.0	25.0	13.2	13.5	8.4	21.1	21.5	16.6	111	112	96	4.1	4.2	2.6
		1990	29.7	30.3	22.1	10.5	10.8	7.6	19.2	19.5	14.5	76	78	39	3.4	3.5	2.2
		1995	29.3	30.2	21.8	9.6	10.0	6.7	19.7	20.2	15.1	77	78	59	3.5	3.7	2.2
		2000	26.9	27.9	18.6	9.6	10.0	6.1	17.4	17.9	12.6	75	78	35	3.1	3.3	1.8
		2009	23.6	24.9	15.9	8.4	8.8	5.9	15.2	16.1	10.1	61	64	37	2.6	2.8	1.6
		2010	23.2	24.4	15.8	8.2	8.6	5.8	14.9	15.8	10.1	58	60	36	2.5	2.7	1.6
		2011	22.8	24.0	15.5	8.0	8.4	5.6	14.8	15.6	9.9	55	58	34	2.4	2.6	1.5
		2012	22.5	23.7	15.6	7.9	8.3	5.6	14.6	15.4	10.0	55	58	33	2.4	2.5	1.5
		2013	22.4	23.5	15.4	7.8	8.2	5.6	14.5	15.3	9.9	54	56	32	2.3	2.4	1.5
		2015	22.0	23.2	15.3	7.1	7.4	5.1	15.0	15.8	10.2	47	50	25	NA	NA	NA
		2016	21.7	22.8	15.0	6.7	7.1	4.9	14.9	15.8	10.1	44	46	22	NA	NA	NA
3	Manipur	1971	33.3	34.0	26.4	6.9	7.1	5.5	26.4	26.9	20.9	NA	NA	NA	NA	NA	NA
		1975	24.5	25.3	18.7	5.6	5.6	5.5	18.9	19.7	13.2	NA	NA	NA	NA	NA	NA
		1980	30.9	31.6	24.1	6.3	6.4	4.6	24.6	25.2	19.5	NA	NA	NA	NA	NA	NA
		1985	28.5	29.8	24.4	7.7	7.9	7.1	20.8	21.9	17.3	NA	NA	NA	NA	NA	NA
		1990	21.1	22.2	17.4	5.9	5.8	6.3	15.2	16.4	11.1	NA	NA	NA	NA	NA	NA
		1995	20.6	21.4	18.4	6.7	7.0	6.0	13.9	14.4	12.4	NA	NA	NA	NA	NA	NA
		2000	18.3	19.1	16.2	5.6	5.4	6.0	12.7	13.6	10.2	23	23	25	NA	NA	NA
		2009	15.4	15.4	15.5	4.7	4.6	5.0	10.7	10.8	10.5	16	18	11	NA	NA	NA
		2010	14.9	14.8	15.3	4.2	4.3	4.0	10.7	10.5	11.3	14	15	9	NA	NA	NA
		2011	14.4	14.2	15.0	4.1	4.1	4.2	10.3	10.2	10.8	11	11	12	NA	NA	NA
		2012	14.6	14.4	15.2	4.0	4.0	4.2	10.6	10.4	11.0	10	10	11	NA	NA	NA

1	2	3	4	5	6	7	8	9	10	11	12	13	14	15	16	17	18
		2013	14.7	14.5	15.1	4.0	4.0	4.2	10.6	10.5	10.9	10	10	10	NA	NA	NA
		2015	14.4	14.4	14.5	4.0	3.9	4.2	10.4	10.5	10.3	9	10	8	NA	NA	NA
		2016	12.9	13.2	12.4	4.5	4.4	4.8	8.4	8.8	7.6	11	12	10	NA	NA	NA
4	Meghalaya	1971	NA	NA	NA	NA	NA	NA	NA	NA	NA	NA	NA	NA	NA	NA	NA
		1976	33.5	36.1	20.6	15.5	17.6	5.1	18.0	18.5	15.5	NA	NA	NA	NA	NA	NA
		1980	31.2	33.6	18.8	11.1	12.3	4.7	20.1	21.3	14.1	NA	NA	NA	NA	NA	NA
		1985	39.1	42.4	24.1	12.7	14.3	5.6	26.4	28.1	18.5	NA	NA	NA	NA	NA	NA
		1990	31.8	35.4	15.5	7.8	8.7	3.4	24.0	26.7	12.1	NA	NA	NA	NA	NA	NA
		1995	29.0	31.8	14.8	8.9	9.7	5.1	20.1	22.1	9.7	NA	NA	NA	NA	NA	NA
		2000	28.5	31.0	15.3	9.2	10.1	4.6	19.3	20.9	10.7	58	61	32	NA	NA	NA
		2009	24.4	26.4	15.0	8.1	8.6	5.7	16.3	17.9	9.4	59	61	40	NA	NA	NA
		2010	24.5	26.6	14.8	7.9	8.4	5.6	16.6	18.2	9.2	55	58	37	NA	NA	NA
		2011	24.1	26.2	14.6	7.8	8.3	5.5	16.3	17.9	9.1	52	54	38	NA	NA	NA
		2012	24.1	26.2	14.4	7.6	8.1	5.4	16.5	18.1	9.0	49	50	40	NA	NA	NA
		2013	23.9	26.1	14.2	7.6	8.0	5.4	16.4	18.0	8.8	47	48	40	NA	NA	NA
		2015	23.7	25.7	15.0	7.4	7.8	5.5	16.3	17.9	9.5	42	44	34	NA	NA	NA
		2016	23.7	25.9	14.0	6.6	7.0	5.0	17.1	18.9	9.0	39	40	26	NA	NA	NA
5	Mizoram	1971	NA	NA	NA	NA	NA	NA	NA	NA	NA	NA	NA	NA	NA	NA	NA
		1975	NA	NA	NA	NA	NA	NA	NA	NA	NA	NA	NA	NA	NA	NA	NA
		1980	NA	NA	NA	NA	NA	NA	NA	NA	NA	NA	NA	NA	NA	NA	NA
		1985	NA	NA	NA	NA	NA	NA	NA	NA	NA	NA	NA	NA	NA	NA	NA
		1990	NA	NA	NA	NA	NA	NA	NA	NA	NA	NA	NA	NA	NA	NA	NA
		1995	NA	NA	NA	NA	NA	NA	NA	NA	NA	NA	NA	NA	NA	NA	NA

1	2	3	4	5	6	7	8	9	10	11	12	13	14	15	16	17	18
		2000	16.9	18.8	14.5	5.2	6.3	3.7	11.7	12.6	10.7	21	24	15	NA	NA	NA
		2009	17.6	21.7	13.2	4.5	5.0	4.1	13.0	16.7	9.2	36	45	19	NA	NA	NA
		2010	17.1	21.1	13.0	4.5	5.4	3.7	12.5	15.7	9.3	37	47	21	NA	NA	NA
		2011	16.6	20.6	12.6	4.4	5.4	3.4	12.2	15.2	9.2	34	43	19	NA	NA	NA
		2012	16.3	20.2	12.2	4.4	5.5	3.1	11.9	14.7	9.1	35	44	19	NA	NA	NA
		2013	16.1	20.0	12.0	4.3	5.5	3.1	11.8	14.5	9.0	35	44	19	NA	NA	NA
		2015	16.2	19.3	13.0	4.2	5.2	3.3	12.0	14.1	9.8	32	39	22	NA	NA	NA
		2016	15.5	18.2	12.6	4.2	4.4	4.1	11.3	13.8	8.5	27	35	14	NA	NA	NA
6	Nagaland	1971	NA	NA	NA	NA	NA	NA	NA	NA	NA	NA	NA	NA	NA	NA	NA
		1975	NA	NA	NA	NA	NA	NA	NA	NA	NA	NA	NA	NA	NA	NA	NA
		1983	23.1	24.0	18.6	6.3	7.3	1.4	16.8	16.7	17.2	NA	NA	NA	NA	NA	NA
		1985	25.3	28.4	11.2	6.3	7.0	3.0	19.0	21.4	8.2	NA	NA	NA	NA	NA	NA
		1990	16.2	16.7	14.0	4.1	5.0	0.0	12.1	11.7	14.0	NA	NA	NA	NA	NA	NA
		1995	NA	NA	13.3	NA	NA	1.5	NA	NA	11.8	NA	NA	NA	NA	NA	NA
		2000	NA	NA	12.2	NA	NA	3.0	NA	NA	9.2	NA	NA	23	NA	NA	NA
		2009	17.2	17.4	16.3	3.6	3.7	3.1	13.6	13.7	13.2	26	27	23	NA	NA	NA
		2010	16.8	17.0	16.0	3.6	3.7	3.3	13.2	13.3	12.7	23	24	20	NA	NA	NA
		2011	16.1	16.3	15.5	3.3	3.4	2.9	12.8	12.9	12.5	21	21	20	NA	NA	NA
		2012	15.6	15.7	15.1	3.2	3.3	2.8	12.4	12.5	12.3	18	18	18	NA	NA	NA
		2013	15.4	15.5	15.0	3.1	3.2	2.7	12.3	12.3	12.3	18	18	19	NA	NA	NA
		2015	14.8	15.0	14.6	3.0	3.2	2.7	11.8	11.8	11.8	12	11	15	NA	NA	NA
		2016	14.0	14.4	13.3	4.5	5.6	2.8	9.5	8.8	10.5	12	11	14	NA	NA	NA

1	2	3	4	5	6	7	8	9	10	11	12	13	14	15	16	17	18
7	Tripura	1971	35.8	37.2	23.1	15.3	16.1	7.6	20.5	21.1	15.5	NA	NA	NA	NA	NA	NA
		1975	29.2	30.3	17.8	9.4	9.7	6.9	19.8	20.6	10.9	NA	NA	NA	NA	NA	NA
		1980	25.9	26.3	21.2	7.8	8.1	4.9	18.1	18.2	16.3	NA	NA	NA	NA	NA	NA
		1985	27.3	27.6	24.5	9.9	10.1	8.0	17.4	17.5	16.5	NA	NA	NA	NA	NA	NA
		1990	24.9	25.7	17.4	7.1	7.3	5.1	17.8	18.4	12.3	NA	NA	NA	NA	NA	NA
		1995	18.9	19.0	18.0	7.7	7.9	6.6	11.2	11.1	11.4	NA	NA	NA	NA	NA	NA
		2000	16.5	17.0	14.0	5.4	5.3	5.6	11.1	11.6	8.4	41	42	32	NA	NA	NA
		2009	14.8	15.5	11.6	5.1	5.0	5.5	9.7	10.5	6.1	31	33	20	NA	NA	NA
		2010	14.9	15.6	11.5	5.0	4.8	5.7	9.9	10.8	5.8	27	29	19	NA	NA	NA
		2011	14.3	15.1	11.0	5.0	4.9	5.4	9.4	10.2	5.6	29	31	19	NA	NA	NA
		2012	13.9	14.6	10.7	4.8	4.7	5.1	9.2	10.0	5.6	28	29	19	NA	NA	NA
		2013	13.7	14.3	10.6	4.7	4.6	5.1	9.0	9.8	5.5	26	27	19	NA	NA	NA
		2015	14.7	15.7	12.3	5.2	4.9	6.0	9.5	10.8	6.3	20	19	25	NA	NA	NA
		2016	13.7	14.6	11.3	5.5	5.2	6.1	8.2	9.4	5.2	24	21	32	NA	NA	NA
8	Sikkim	1971	NA	NA	NA	NA	NA	NA	NA	NA	NA	NA	NA	NA	NA	NA	NA
		1975	NA	NA	NA	NA	NA	NA	NA	NA	NA	NA	NA	NA	NA	NA	NA
		1981	31.0	32.2	26.6	8.9	9.9	5.4	22.1	22.3	21.2	NA	NA	NA	NA	NA	NA
		1985	33.1	35.1	24.2	10.7	11.7	6.2	22.4	23.4	18.0	NA	NA	NA	NA	NA	NA
		1990	26.3	28.0	18.4	7.3	7.7	5.2	19.0	20.3	13.2	NA	NA	NA	NA	NA	NA
		1995	22.5	22.8	16.4	6.9	7.0	3.0	15.6	15.8	13.4	NA	NA	NA	NA	NA	NA
		2000	21.8	22.1	14.8	5.7	5.7	4.0	16.2	16.4	10.7	49	49	36	NA	NA	NA
		2009	18.1	18.4	16.0	5.7	6.0	3.9	12.3	12.4	12.1	34	36	21	NA	NA	NA
		2010	17.8	18.1	16.1	5.6	5.9	3.8	12.3	12.3	12.3	30	31	19	NA	NA	NA

1	2	3	4	5	6	7	8	9	10	11	12	13	14	15	16	17	18
		2011	17.6	17.7	16.6	5.6	5.9	3.5	12.0	11.8	13.1	26	28	17	NA	NA	NA
		2012	17.2	17.3	16.7	5.4	5.7	3.3	11.9	11.7	13.4	24	25	16	NA	NA	NA
		2013	17.1	17.1	16.7	5.2	5.6	3.2	11.8	11.6	13.5	22	23	15	NA	NA	NA
		2015	17.0	15.9	18.7	5.0	5.9	3.5	12.0	10.0	15.2	18	20	14	NA	NA	NA
		2016	16.6	15.5	18.5	4.7	5.5	3.4	11.9	10.0	15.1	16	18	13	NA	NA	NA
9	India	1971	36.9	38.9	30.1	14.9	16.4	9.7	22.0	22.5	20.4	129	138	82	5.2	5.4	4.1
		1975	35.2	36.7	28.5	15.9	17.3	10.2	19.3	19.4	18.3	140	151	84	4.9	5.2	3.7
		1980	33.3	34.6	28.1	12.4	13.5	8.0	20.9	21.1	20.1	114	124	65	4.4	4.7	3.4
		1985	32.9	34.3	28.1	11.8	13.0	7.8	21.1	21.3	20.3	97	107	59	4.3	4.6	3.3
		1990	30.2	31.7	24.7	9.7	10.5	6.8	20.5	21.2	17.9	80	86	50	3.8	4.1	2.8
		1995	28.3	30.0	22.7	9.0	9.8	6.6	19.3	20.2	16.1	74	80	48	3.5	3.9	2.6
		2000	25.8	27.5	20.7	8.5	9.3	6.3	17.3	18.3	14.4	68	74	43	NA	NA	NA
		2009	22.5	24.1	18.3	7.3	7.8	5.8	15.2	16.3	12.5	50	55	34	2.6	NA	NA
		2010	22.1	23.7	18.0	7.2	7.7	5.8	14.9	15.9	12.2	47	51	31	2.5	NA	NA
		2011	21.8	23.3	17.6	7.1	7.6	5.7	14.7	15.7	11.9	44	48	29	2.4	2.7	1.9
		2012	21.6	23.1	17.4	7.0	7.6	5.6	14.5	15.5	11.8	42	46	28	NA	NA	NA
		2013	21.4	22.9	17.3	7.0	7.5	5.6	14.4	15.4	11.7	40	44	27	2.3	NA	NA
		2015	20.8	22.4	17.3	6.5	7.1	5.4	14.3	15.4	11.9	37	41	25	NA	NA	NA
		2016	20.4	22.1	17.0	6.4	6.9	5.4	14.0	15.2	11.7	34	38	23	NA	NA	NA

Source: Compendium of India's Fertility and Mortality Indicators - 1971 - 1997 and other related SRS Bulletins of the Registrar General, India, New Delhi.

Appendix-3.3.1

State-wise Distribution of Total Population, Scheduled Tribe (ST) and Scheduled Caste (SC) Population and their Sex ratio and Percentage with Rural-Urban Break-up in different Census Years

Sl. No.	Name of the State/ NER/India	Total/ Rural/ Urban	Census Year, 1961							
			Total population				ST population			
			Person	Male	Female	Sex ratio	Person	Male	Female	Sex ratio
1	2	3	4	5	6	7	8	9	10	11
1	Arunachal Pradesh*	T	336558	177680	158878	894	298167	148116	150051	1013
		R	336558	177680	158878	894	298167	148116	150051	1013
		U	0	0	0	0	0	0	0	0
2	Assam	T	10837329	5798376	5038953	869	1164641	607247	557394	918
		R	10056041	5328139	4727902	887	1157908	603066	554842	920
		U	781288	470237	311051	661	6733	4181	2552	610
3	Manipur	T	780037	387058	392979	1015	249049	123162	125887	1022
		R	712320	352937	359383	1018	244903	120753	124150	1028
		U	67717	34121	33596	985	4146	2409	1737	721
4	Meghalaya**	T	769380	397288	372092	937	639161	319354	319807	1001
		R	651897	330701	321196	971	590549	295395	295154	999
		U	117483	66587	50896	764	48612	23959	24653	1029
5	Mizoram***	T	266063	132465	133598	1009	261014	128830	132184	1026
		R	251806	124835	126971	1017	248326	122450	125876	1028
		U	14257	7630	6627	869	12688	6380	6308	989

1	2	3	4	5	6	7	8	9	10	11
6	Nagaland	T	369200	191027	178173	933	343697	171233	172464	1007
		R	350043	179261	170782	953	333834	165991	167843	1011
		U	19157	11766	7391	628	9863	5242	4621	882
7	Tripura	T	1142005	591237	550768	932	360070	184174	175896	955
		R	1039008	536580	502428	936	356372	182168	174204	956
		U	102997	54657	48340	884	3698	2006	1692	843
8	Sub-Total, NER	T	14500572	7675131	6825441	889	3315799	1682116	1633683	971
		R	13397673	7030133	6367540	906	3230059	1637939	1592120	972
		U	1102899	644998	457901	710	85740	44177	41563	941
9	Sikkim	T	162189	85193	76996	904	-	-	-	-
		R	155341	81285	74056	911	-	-	-	-
		U	6848	3908	2940	752	-	-	-	-
10	Total, NER	T	14662761	7760324	6902437	889	3315799	1682116	1633683	971
		R	13553014	7111418	6441596	906	3230059	1637939	1592120	972
		U	1109747	648906	460841	710	85740	44177	41563	941
11	India	T	439234771	226293201	212941570	941	30130184	15161672	14968512	987
		R	360298168	183504095	176794073	963	29357790	14754124	14603666	990
		U	78936603	42789106	36147497	845	772394	407548	364846	895

Source: Census of India, 1961, Volume I, Part II-A(ii), Registrar General and ex-officio Census Commissioner, New Delhi.

* the then NEFA which was declared as Rural at that time.

** total information of Garo Hills and United Khasi & Jaintia Hills.

*** information of the then Mizo Hills District of Assam.

– information on ST population is not available.

Appendix-3.3.1 (*cont.*)

State-wise Distribution of Total Population, Scheduled Tribe (ST) and Scheduled Caste (SC) Population and their Sex ratio and Percentage with Rural-Urban Break-up in different Census Years

Sl. No.	Name of the State/NER/India	Total/ Rural/ Urban	Census Year, 1961									
			SC population				Percentage of ST population			Percentage of SC population		
			Person	Male	Female	Sex ratio	Person	Male	Female	Person	Male	Female
1	2	3	12	13	14	15	16	17	18	19	20	21
1	Arunachal Pradesh*	T	-	-	-	-	88.59	83.36	94.44	-	-	-
		R	-	-	-	-	88.59	83.36	94.44	-	-	-
		U	-	-	-	-	-	-	-	-	-	-
2	Assam	T	731490	388564	342926	883	10.75	10.47	11.06	6.75	6.70	6.81
		R	670984	354423	316561	893	11.51	11.32	11.74	6.67	6.65	6.70
		U	60506	34141	26365	772	0.86	0.89	0.82	7.74	7.26	8.48
3	Manipur	T	13376	6886	6490	942	31.93	31.82	32.03	1.71	1.78	1.65
		R	13218	6785	6433	948	34.38	34.21	34.55	1.86	1.92	1.79
		U	158	101	57	564	6.12	7.06	5.17	0.23	0.30	0.17
4	Meghalaya**	T	1261	702	559	796	83.07	80.38	85.95	0.16	0.18	0.15
		R	1102	610	492	807	90.59	89.32	91.89	0.17	0.18	0.15
		U	159	92	67	728	41.38	35.98	48.44	0.14	0.14	0.13
5	Mizoram***	T	5	5	0	0	98.10	97.26	98.94	0.002	0.004	-
		R	0	0	0	0	98.62	98.09	99.14	-	-	-
		U	5	5	0	0	88.99	83.62	95.19	0.04	0.07	-

1	2	3	12	13	14	15	16	17	18	19	20	21
6	Nagaland	T	126	80	46	575	93.09	89.64	96.80	0.03	0.04	0.03
		R	31	26	5	192	95.37	92.60	98.28	0.01	0.01	0.003
		U	95	54	41	759	51.49	44.55	62.52	0.50	0.46	0.55
7	Tripura	T	119725	62069	57656	929	31.53	31.15	31.94	10.48	10.50	10.47
		R	112980	58500	54480	931	34.30	33.95	34.67	10.87	10.90	10.84
		U	6745	3569	3176	890	3.59	3.67	3.50	6.55	6.53	6.57
8	Sub-Total, NER	T	865983	458306	407677	890	22.87	21.92	23.94	5.97	5.97	5.97
		R	798315	420344	377971	899	24.11	23.30	25.00	5.96	5.98	5.94
		U	67668	37962	29706	783	7.77	6.85	9.08	6.14	5.89	6.49
9	Sikkim	T	-	-	-	-	-	-	-	-	-	-
		R	-	-	-	-	-	-	-	-	-	-
		U	-	-	-	-	-	-	-	-	-	-
10	Total, NER	T	865983	458306	407677	890	22.61	21.68	23.67	5.91	5.91	5.91
		R	798315	420344	377971	899	23.83	23.03	24.72	5.89	5.91	5.87
		U	67668	37962	29706	783	7.73	6.81	9.02	6.10	5.85	6.45
11	India	T	64449275	32937280	31511995	957	6.86	6.70	7.03	14.67	14.56	14.80
		R	57566964	29282272	28284692	966	8.15	8.04	8.26	15.98	15.96	16.00
		U	6882311	3655008	3227303	883	0.98	0.95	1.01	8.72	8.54	8.93

Source: Census of India, 1961, Volume I, Part II-A(ii), Registrar General and ex-officio Census Commissioner, New Delhi.

* information of the then NEFA is not available.

** total information of Garo Hills and United Khasi & Jaintia Hills

*** information of the then Mizo Hills District of Assam.

— information on ST & SC is not available.

Appendix-3.3.2

State-wise Distribution of Total Population, Scheduled Tribe (ST) and Scheduled Caste (SC) Population and their Sex ratio and Percentage with Rural-Urban Break-up in different Census Years

Sl. No.	Name of the State/NER/ India	Total/ Rural/ Urban	Census Year, 1971							
			Total population				ST population			
			Person	Male	Female	Sex ratio	Person	Male	Female	Sex ratio
1	2	3	4	5	6	7	8	9	10	11
1	Arunachal Pradesh	T	467511	251231	216280	861	369408	184076	185332	1007
		R	450223	239369	210854	881	365939	182111	183828	1009
		U	17288	11862	5426	457	3469	1965	1504	765
2	Assam	T	14625152	7714240	6910912	896	1606648	819653	786995	960
		R	13335930	6975131	6360799	912	1592393	811252	781141	963
		U	1289222	739109	550113	744	14255	8401	5854	697
3	Manipur	T	1072753	541675	531078	980	334466	166490	167976	1008
		R	931261	470231	461030	980	319516	158746	160770	1013
		U	141492	71444	70048	980	14950	7744	7206	930
4	Meghalaya	T	1011699	520967	490732	942	814230	407859	406371	996
		R	864529	441533	422996	958	747113	375627	371486	989
		U	147170	79434	67736	853	67117	32232	34885	1082
5	Mizoram	T	332390	170824	161566	946	313299	155015	158284	1021
		R	294631	151322	143309	947	278290	137497	140793	1024
		U	37759	19502	18257	936	35009	17518	17491	998

1	2	3	4	5	6	7	8	9	10	11
6	Nagaland	T	516449	276084	240365	871	457602	231921	225681	973
		R	465055	241171	223884	928	438218	221671	216547	977
		U	51394	34913	16481	472	19384	10250	9134	891
7	Tripura	T	1556342	801126	755216	943	450544	230544	220000	954
		R	1393982	717227	676755	944	445059	227590	217469	956
		U	162360	83899	78461	935	5485	2954	2531	857
8	Sub-Total, NER	T	19582296	10276147	9306149	906	4346197	2195558	2150639	980
		R	17735611	9235984	8499627	920	4186528	2114494	2072034	980
		U	1846685	1040163	806522	775	159669	81064	78605	970
9	Sikkim	T	209843	112662	97181	863	-	-	-	-
		R	190175	100959	89216	884	-	-	-	-
		U	19668	11703	7965	681	-	-	-	-
10	Total, NER	T	19792139	10388809	9403330	905	4346197	2195558	2150639	980
		R	17925786	9336943	8588843	920	4186528	2114494	2072034	980
		U	1866353	1051866	814487	774	159669	81064	78605	970
11	India	T	547949809	283936614	264013195	930	38015162	19181450	18833712	982
		R	438855500	225218984	213636516	949	36720681	18498874	18221807	985
		U	109094309	58717630	50376679	858	1294481	682576	611905	896

Source: Census of India, 1971, Series I, Final Population & Paper 1 of 1975, Registrar General & Census Commissioner, New Delhi.

information on ST population is not available.

Appendix-3.3.2 (*cont.*)

State-wise Distribution of Total Population, Scheduled Tribe (ST) and Scheduled Caste (SC) Population and their Sex ratio and Percentage with Rural-Urban Break-up in different Census Years

Sl. No.	Name of the State/NER/ India	Total/ Rural/ Urban	Census Year, 1971									
			SC population				Percentage of ST population			Percentage of SC population		
			Person	Male	Female	Sex ratio	Person	Male	Female	Person	Male	Female
1	2	3	12	13	14	15	16	17	18	19	20	21
1	Arunachal Pradesh	T	339	178	161	904	79.02	73.27	85.69	0.07	0.07	0.07
		R	335	175	160	914	81.28	76.08	87.18	0.07	0.07	0.08
		U	4	3	1	333	20.07	16.57	27.72	0.02	0.03	0.02
2	Assam	T	912557	476150	436407	917	10.99	10.63	11.39	6.24	6.17	6.31
		R	826834	430287	396547	922	11.94	11.63	12.28	6.20	6.17	6.23
		U	85723	45863	39860	869	1.11	1.14	1.06	6.65	6.21	7.25
3	Manipur	T	16376	8556	7820	914	31.18	30.74	31.63	1.53	1.58	1.47
		R	15802	8183	7619	931	34.31	33.76	34.87	1.70	1.74	1.65
		U	574	373	201	539	10.57	10.84	10.29	0.41	0.52	0.29
4	Meghalaya	T	3887	2048	1839	898	80.48	78.29	82.81	0.38	0.39	0.37
		R	1673	823	850	1033	86.42	85.07	87.82	0.19	0.19	0.20
		U	2214	1225	989	807	45.61	40.58	51.50	1.50	1.54	1.46
5	Mizoram	T	82	79	3	38	94.26	90.75	97.97	0.02	0.05	0.002
		R	77	74	3	41	94.45	90.86	98.24	0.03	0.05	0.002
		U	5	5	0	0	92.72	89.83	95.80	0.01	0.03	0.00

1	2	3	12	13	14	15	16	17	18	19	20	21
6	Nagaland	T	-	-	-	-	88.61	84.00	93.89	-	-	-
		R	-	-	-	-	94.23	91.91	96.72	-	-	-
		U	-	-	-	-	37.72	29.36	55.42	-	-	-
7	Tripura	T	192860	99423	93437	940	28.95	28.78	29.13	12.39	12.41	12.37
		R	182667	94103	88564	941	31.93	31.73	32.13	13.10	13.12	13.09
		U	10193	5320	4873	916	3.38	3.52	3.23	6.28	6.34	6.21
8	Sub-Total, NER	T	1126101	586434	539667	920	22.19	21.37	23.11	5.75	5.71	5.80
		R	1027388	533645	493743	925	23.61	22.89	24.38	5.79	5.78	5.81
		U	98713	52789	45924	870	8.65	7.79	9.75	5.35	5.08	5.69
9	Sikkim	T	9502	5159	4343	842	-	-	-	-	-	-
		R	7766	4167	3599	864	-	-	-	-	-	-
		U	1736	992	744	750	-	-	-	-	-	-
10	Total, NER	T	1135603	591593	544010	920	21.96	21.13	22.87	5.74	5.69	5.79
		R	1035154	537812	497342	925	23.35	22.65	24.12	5.77	5.76	5.79
		U	100449	53781	46668	868	8.56	7.71	9.65	5.38	5.11	5.73
11	India	T	80005398	41343194	38662204	935	6.94	6.76	7.13	14.60	14.56	14.64
		R	70449154	36265715	34183439	943	8.37	8.21	8.53	16.05	16.10	16.00
		U	9556244	5077479	4478765	882	1.19	1.16	1.21	8.76	8.65	8.89

Source: Census of India, 1971, Paper 1 of 1975, Registrar General & Census Commissioner, New Delhi.

- information is not available.

Appendix-3.3.3

State-wise Distribution of Total Population, Scheduled Tribe (ST) and Scheduled Caste (SC) Population and their Sex ratio and Percentage with Rural-Urban Break-up in different Census Years

Sl. No.	Name of the State/NER/ India	Total/ Rural/ Urban	Census Year, 1981							
			Total population				ST population			
			Person	Male	Female	Sex ratio	Person	Male	Female	Sex ratio
1	2	3	4	5	6	7	8	9	10	11
1	Arunachal Pradesh	T	631839	339322	292517	862	441167	220046	221121	1005
		R	590411	313886	276525	881	431110	214471	216639	1010
		U	41428	25436	15992	629	10057	5575	4482	804
2	Assam*	T	19896843	10467461	9429382	901	-	-	-	-
		R	17849657	9309726	8539931	917	-	-	-	-
		U	2047186	1157735	889451	768	-	-	-	-
3	Manipur	T	1420953	721006	699947	971	387977	196455	191522	975
		R	1045493	530331	515162	971	342811	173481	169330	976
		U	375460	190675	184785	969	45166	22974	22192	966
4	Meghalaya	T	1335819	683710	652109	954	1076345	537635	538710	1002
		R	1094486	556958	537528	965	942734	472954	469780	993
		U	241333	126752	114581	904	133611	64681	68930	1066
5	Mizoram	T	493757	257239	236518	919	461907	231261	230646	997
		R	371943	192874	179069	928	353436	177296	176140	993
		U	121814	64365	57449	893	108471	53965	54506	1010

1	2	3	4	5	6	7	8	9	10	11
6	Nagaland	T	774930	415910	359020	863	650885	332943	317942	955
		R	654696	344699	309997	899	587270	299058	288212	964
		U	120234	71211	49023	688	63615	33885	29730	877
7	Tripura	T	2053058	1054846	998212	946	583920	297612	286308	962
		R	1827490	939558	887932	945	576252	293471	282781	964
		U	225568	115288	110280	957	7668	4141	3527	852
8	Sub-Total, NER	T	26607199	13939494	12667705	909	3602201	1815952	1786249	984
		R	23434176	12188032	11246144	923	3233613	1630731	1602882	983
		U	3173023	1751462	1421561	812	368588	185221	183367	990
9	Sikkim	T	316385	172440	143945	835	73623	38211	35412	927
		R	265301	142341	122960	864	62621	32387	30234	934
		U	51084	30099	20985	697	11002	5824	5178	889
10	Total, NER	T	26923584	14111934	12811650	908	3675824	1854163	1821661	982
		R	23699477	12330373	11369104	922	3296234	1663118	1633116	982
		U	3224107	1781561	1442546	810	379590	191045	188545	987
11	India**	T	665287849	343930423	321357426	934	51628638	26038535	25590103	983
		R	507607678	260054020	247553658	952	48427604	24364350	24063254	988
		U	157680171	83876403	73803768	880	3201034	1674185	1526849	912

Source: Census of India, 1981, Series 1, Paper 2 of 1984, Registrar General & Census Commissioner, New Delhi.

* Projected Population (Census was not conducted).

** Excluding Projected Population of Assam.

– information not available.

Appendix-3.3.3.(cont.)

State-wise Distribution of Total Population, Scheduled Tribe (ST) and Scheduled Caste (SC) Population and their Sex ratio and Percentage with Rural-Urban Break-up in different Census Years

Sl. No.	Name of the State/ NER/ India	Total/ Rural/ Urban	Census Year, 1981									
			SC population				Percentage of ST population			Percentage of SC population		
			Person	Male	Female	Sex ratio	Person	Male	Female	Person	Male	Female
1	2	3	12	13	14	15	16	17	18	19	20	21
1	Arunachal Pradesh	T	2919	1833	1086	592	69.82	64.85	75.59	0.46	0.54	0:37
		R	1940	1198	742	619	73.02	68.33	78.34	0.33	0.38	0.27
		U	979	635	344	542	24.28	21.92	28.03	2.36	2.50	2.15
2	Assam	T	-	-	-	-	-	-	-	-	-	-
		R	-	-	-	-	-	-	-	-	-	-
		U	-	-	-	-	-	-	-	-	-	-
3	Manipur	T	17753	9075	8678	956	27.30	27.25	27.36	1.25	1.26	1.24
		R	14795	7534	7261	964	32.79	32.71	32.87	1.42	1.42	1.41
		U	2958	1541	1417	920	12.03	12.05	12.01	0.79	0.81	0.77
4	Meghalaya	T	5492	3068	2424	790	80.58	78.63	82.61	0.41	0.45	0.37
		R	2950	1593	1357	852	86.13	84.92	87.40	0.27	0.29	0.25
		U	2542	1475	1067	723	55.36	51.03	60.16	1.05	1.16	0.93

1	2	3	12	13	14	15	16	17	18	19	20	21
5	Mizoram	T	135	120	15	125	93.55	89.90	97.52	0.03	0.05	0.006
		R	97	90	7	78	95.02	91.92	98.36	0.03	0.05	0.004
		U	38	30	8	267	89.05	83.84	94.88	0.03	0.05	0.01
6	Nagaland	T	-	-	-	-	83.99	80.05	88.56	-	-	-
		R	-	-	-	-	89.70	86.76	92.97	-	-	-
		U	-	-	-	-	52.91	47.58	60.65	-	-	-
7	Tripura	T	310384	159796	150588	942	28.44	28.21	28.68	15.12	15.15	15.09
		R	290832	149702	141130	943	31.53	31.24	31.85	15.91	15.93	15.89
		U	19552	10094	9458	937	3.40	3.59	3.20	8.67	8.76	8.58
8	Sub-Total, NER	T	336683	173892	162791	936	13.54	13.03	14.10	1.27	1.25	1.29
		R	310614	160117	150497	940	13.80	13.38	14.25	1.33	1.31	1.34
		U	26069	13775	12294	892	11.62	10.58	12.90	0.82	0.79	0.86
9	Sikkim	T	18281	9558	8723	913	23.27	22.16	24.60	5.78	5.54	6.06
		R	14365	7522	6843	910	23.60	22.75	24.59	5.41	5.28	5.57
		U	3916	2036	1880	923	21.54	19.35	24.67	7.67	6.76	8.96
10	Total, NER	T	354964	183450	171514	935	13.65	13.14	14.22	1.32	1.30	1.34
		R	324979	167639	157340	939	13.91	13.49	14.36	1.37	1.36	1.38
		U	29985	15811	14174	896	11.77	10.72	13.07	0.93	0.89	0.98
11	India	T	104754623	54210594	50544029	932	7.76	7.57	7.96	15.75	15.76	15.73
		R	87996992	45354781	42642211	940	9.54	9.37	9.72	17.34	17.44	17.23
		U	16757631	8855813	7901818	892	2.03	2.00	2.07	10.63	10.56	10.71

Source: Census of India, 1981, Series 1, Paper 2 of 1984, Registrar General & Census Commissioner, New Delhi.

– information not available.

Appendix-3.3.4

State-wise Distribution of Total Population, Scheduled Tribe (ST) and Scheduled Caste (SC) Population and their Sex ratio and Percentage with Rural-Urban Break-up in different Census Years

Sl. No.	Name of the State/ NER/ India	Total/ Rural/ Urban	Census Year, 1991							
			Total population				ST population			
			Person	Male	Female	Sex ratio	Person	Male	Female	Sex ratio
1	2	3	4	5	6	7	8	9	10	11
1	Arunachal Pradesh	T	864558	465004	399554	859	550351	275397	274954	998
		R	753930	400966	352964	880	518222	258595	259627	1004
		U	110628	64038	46590	728	32129	16802	15327	912
2	Assam	T	22414322	11657989	10756333	923	2874441	1461560	1412881	967
		R	19926527	10304161	9622366	934	2777308	1409364	1367944	971
		U	2487795	1353828	1133967	838	97133	52196	44937	861
3	Manipur	T	1837149	938359	898790	958	632173	322720	309453	959
		R	1331504	682395	649109	951	578930	295691	283239	958
		U	505645	255964	249681	975	53243	27029	26214	970
4	Meghalaya	T	1774778	907687	867091	955	1517927	760234	757693	997
		R	1444731	734865	709866	966	1312093	659859	652234	988
		U	330047	172822	157225	910	205834	100375	105459	1051

1	2	3	4	5	6	7	8	9	10	11
5	Mizoram	T	689756	358978	330778	921	653565	329819	323746	982
		R	371810	194414	177396	912	358113	182212	175901	965
		U	317946	164564	153382	932	295452	147607	147845	1002
6	Nagaland	T	1209546	641282	568264	886	1060822	545156	515666	946
		R	1001323	522235	479088	917	933145	478579	454566	950
		U	208223	119047	89176	749	127677	66577	61100	918
7	Tripura	T	2757205	1417930	1339275	945	853345	434225	419120	965
		R	2335484	1202529	1132955	942	839264	426741	412523	967
		U	421721	215401	206320	958	14081	7484	6597	881
8	Sub-Total, NER	T	31547314	16387229	15160085	925	8142624	4129111	4013513	972
		R	27165309	14041565	13123744	935	7317075	3711041	3606034	972
		U	4382005	2345664	2036341	868	825549	418070	407479	975
9	Sikkim	T	406457	216427	190030	878	90901	47504	43397	914
		R	369451	195277	174174	892	83486	43477	40009	920
		U	37006	21150	15856	750	7415	4027	3388	841
10	Total, NER	T	31953771	16603656	15350115	924	8233525	4176615	4056910	971
		R	27534760	14236842	13297918	934	7400561	3754518	3646043	971
		U	4419011	2366814	2052197	867	832964	422097	410867	973
11	India*	T	846302688	439230458	407072230	927	67758380	34363271	33395109	972
		R	628691676	324321614	304370062	938	62751026	31755930	30995096	976
		U	217611012	114908844	102702168	894	5007354	2607341	2400013	920

Source: Census of India, 1991, State Profile & Paper 1 of 1993, Union Primary Census Abstract, Registrar General & Census Commissioner, New Delhi.

Included estimated total population of Jammu & Kashmir, but excluded information on ST of Jammu & Kashmir.

Appendix-3.3.4 (*cont.*)

State-wise Distribution of Total Population, Scheduled Tribe (ST) and Scheduled Caste (SC) Population and their Sex ratio and Percentage with Rural-Urban Break-up in different Census Years

Sl. No.	Name of the State/NER/ India	Total/Rural/ Urban	Census Year, 1991									
			SC population				Percentage of ST population			Percentage of SC population		
			Person	Male	Female	Sex ratio	Person	Male	Female	Person	Male	Female
1	2	3	12	13	14	15	16	17	18	19	20	21
1	Arunachal Pradesh	T	4052	2491	1561	627	63.66	59.22	68.82	0.47	0.54	0.39
		R	2858	1782	1076	604	68.74	64.49	73.56	0.38	0.44	0.30
		U	1194	709	485	684	29.04	26.24	32.90	1.08	1.11	1.04
2	Assam	T	1659412	864617	794795	919	12.82	12.54	13.14	7.40	7.42	7.39
		R	1430131	743834	686297	923	13.94	13.68	14.22	7.18	7.22	7.13
		U	229281	120783	108498	898	3.90	3.86	3.96	9.22	8.92	9.57
3	Manipur	T	37105	18806	18299	973	34.41	34.39	34.43	2.02	2.00	2.04
		R	17705	9075	8630	951	43.48	43.33	43.64	1.33	1.33	1.33
		U	19400	9731	9669	994	10.53	10.56	10.50	3.84	3.80	3.87
4	Meghalaya	T	9072	4981	4091	821	85.53	83.76	87.38	0.51	0.55	0.47
		R	4972	2697	2275	844	90.82	89.79	91.88	0.34	0.37	0.32
		U	4100	2284	1816	795	62.37	58.08	67.08	1.24	1.32	1.16
5	Mizoram	T	691	597	94	157	94.75	91.88	97.87	0.10	0.17	0.03
		R	456	399	57	143	96.32	93.72	99.16	0.12	0.21	0.03
		U	235	198	37	187	92.93	89.70	96.39	0.07	0.12	0.02

1	2	3	12	13	14	15	16	17	18	19	20	21
6	Nagaland	T	-	-	-	-	87.70	85.01	90.74	-	-	-
		R	-	-	-	-	93.19	91.64	94.88	-	-	-
		U	-	-	-	-	61.32	55.92	68.52	-	-	-
7	Tripura	T	451116	231516	219600	948	30.95	30.62	31.29	16.36	16.33	16.40
		R	379664	195079	184585	946	35.94	35.49	36.41	16.26	16.22	16.29
		U	71452	36437	35015	961	3.34	3.47	3.20	16.94	16.92	16.97
8	Sub-Total, NER	T	2161448	1123008	1038440	925	25.81	25.20	26.47	6.85	6.85	6.85
		R	1835786	952866	882920	927	26.94	26.43	27.48	6.76	6.79	6.73
		U	325662	170142	155520	914	18.84	17.82	20.01	7.43	7.25	7.64
9	Sikkim	T	24084	12424	11660	938	22.36	21.95	22.84	5.93	5.74	6.14
		R	21333	11013	10320	937	22.60	22.26	22.97	5.77	5.64	5.93
		U	2751	1411	1340	950	20.04	19.04	21.37	7.43	6.67	8.45
10	Total, NER	T	2185532	1135432	1050100	925	25.77	25.15	26.43	6.84	6.84	6.84
		R	1857119	963879	893240	927	26.88	26.37	27.42	6.74	6.77	6.72
		U	328413	171553	156860	914	18.85	17.83	20.02	7.43	7.25	7.64
11	India*	T	138223277	71928960	66294317	922	8.01	7.82	8.20	16.33	16.38	16.29
		R	112343797	58342419	54001378	926	9.98	9.79	10.18	17.87	17.99	17.74
		U	25879480	13586541	12292939	905	2.30	2.27	2.34	11.89	11.82	11.97

Source: Census of India, 1991, Paper 1 of 1993, Union Primary Census Abstract, Registrar General & Census Commissioner, New Delhi.

* excluding information on SC of Jammu & Kashmir.

— information on SC not available.

Appendix-3.3.5.

State-wise Distribution of Total Population, Scheduled Tribe (ST) and Scheduled Caste (SC) Population and their Sex ratio and Percentage with Rural-Urban Break-up in different Census Years

Sl. No.	Name of the State/NER/ India	Total/ Rural/Urban	Census Year, 2001							
			Total population				ST population			
			Person	Male	Female	Sex ratio	Person	Male	Female	Sex ratio
1	2	3	4	5	6	7	8	9	10	11
1	Arunachal Pradesh	T	1097968	579941	518027	893	705158	352017	353141	1003
		R	870087	454680	415407	914	606278	303072	303206	1000
		U	227881	125261	102620	819	98880	48945	49935	1020
2	Assam	T	26655528	13777037	12878491	935	3308570	1678117	1630453	972
		R	23216288	11939945	11276343	944	3154546	1598267	1556279	974
		U	3439240	1837092	1602148	872	154024	79850	74174	929
3	Manipur	T	2166788	1095634	1071154	978	741141	374319	366822	980
		R	1590820	808953	781867	967	705912	357052	348860	977
		U	575968	286681	289287	1009	35229	17267	17962	1040
4	Meghalaya	T	2318822	1176087	1142735	972	1992862	996567	996295	1000
		R	1864711	946999	917712	969	1682670	846830	835840	987
		U	454111	229088	225023	982	310192	149737	160455	1071
5	Mizoram	T	888573	459109	429464	935	839310	422963	416347	984
		R	447567	232726	214841	923	430883	219919	210964	959
		U	441006	226383	214623	948	408427	203044	205383	1012

1	2	3	4	5	6	7	8	9	10	11
6	Nagaland	T	1990036	1047141	942895	900	1774026	913203	860823	943
		R	1647249	859716	787533	916	1544022	795008	749014	942
		U	342787	187425	155362	829	230004	118195	111809	946
7	Tripura	T	3199203	1642225	1556978	948	993426	504320	489106	970
		R	2653453	1363638	1289815	946	967997	491080	476917	971
		U	545750	278587	267163	959	25429	13240	12189	921
8	Sub-Total, NER	T	38316918	19777174	18539744	937	10354493	5241506	5112987	975
		R	32290175	16606657	15683518	944	9092308	4611228	4481080	972
		U	6026743	3170517	2856226	901	1262185	630278	631907	1003
9	Sikkim	T	540851	288484	252367	875	111405	56940	54465	956
		R	480981	255774	225207	880	101909	52249	49660	950
		U	59870	32710	27160	830	9496	4691	4805	1024
10	Total, NER	T	38857769	20065658	18792111	937	10465898	5298446	5167452	975
		R	32771156	16862431	15908725	943	9194217	4663477	4530740	972
		U	6086613	3203227	2883386	900	1271681	634969	636712	1003
11	India	T	1028610328	532156772	496453556	933	84326240	42640829	41685411	978
		R	742490639	381602674	360887965	946	77338597	39045650	38292947	981
		U	286119689	150554098	135565591	900	6987643	3595179	3392464	944

Sources: Census of India, 2001, Primary Census Abstract, Registrar General & Census Commissioner, New Delhi.

Appendix-3.3.5. (*cont.*)

State-wise Distribution of Total Population, Scheduled Tribe (ST) and Scheduled Caste (SC) Population and their Sex ratio and Percentage with Rural-Urban Break-up in different Census Years

Sl. No.	Name of the State/NER/ India	Total/ Rural/ Urban	Census Year, 2001									
			SC population				Percentage of ST population			Percentage of SC population		
			Person	Male	Female	Sex ratio	Person	Male	Female	Person	Male	Female
1	2	3	12	13	14	15	16	17	18	19	20	21
1	Arunachal Pradesh	T	6188	3590	2598	724	64.22	60.70	51.80	0.56	0.62	0.50
		R	3062	1769	1293	731	69.60	66.65	72.99	0.35	0.39	0.31
		U	3126	1821	1305	717	43.39	39.07	48.66	1.37	1.45	1.27
2	Assam	T	1825949	943674	882275	935	12.41	12.18	12.66	6.85	6.85	6.85
		R	1553691	802548	751143	936	13.59	13.39	13.89	6.69	6.72	6.66
		U	272258	141126	131132	929	4.48	4.35	4.63	7.92	7.68	8.18
3	Manipur	T	60037	29934	30103	1006	34.20	34.16	34.25	2.77	2.73	2.81
		R	20802	10595	10207	963	44.37	44.14	44.62	1.31	1.31	1.31
		U	39235	19339	19896	1029	6.12	6.02	6.21	6.81	6.75	6.88
4	Meghalaya	T	11139	5920	5219	882	85.94	84.74	87.19	0.48	0.50	0.46
		R	7065	3750	3315	884	90.24	89.42	91.08	0.38	0.40	0.36
		U	4074	2170	1904	877	68.31	65.36	71.31	0.90	0.95	0.85

1	2	3	12	13	14	15	16	17	18	19	20	21
5	Mizoram	T	272	212	60	283	94.46	92.13	96.95	0.03	0.05	0.01
		R	65	62	3	48	96.27	94.50	98.20	0.01	0.03	0.001
		U	207	150	57	380	92.61	89.69	95.69	0.05	0.07	0.03
6	Nagaland	T	-	-	-	-	89.15	87.21	91.30	-	-	-
		R	-	-	-	-	93.73	92.47	95.11	-	-	-
		U	-	-	-	-	67.10	63.06	71.97	-	-	-
7	Tripura	T	555724	283186	272538	962	31.05	30.71	31.41	17.37	17.24	17.50
		R	455623	232667	222956	958	36.48	36.01	36.98	17.17	17.06	17.29
		U	100101	50519	49582	981	4.66	4.75	4.56	18.34	18.13	18.56
8	Sub-Total, NER	T	2459309	1266516	1192793	942	27.02	26.50	27.58	6.42	6.40	6.43
		R	2040308	1051391	988917	941	28.16	27.77	28.57	6.32	6.33	6.31
		U	419001	215125	203876	948	20.94	19.88	22.12	6.95	6.79	7.12
9	Sikkim	T	27165	13807	13358	967	20.60	19.74	21.58	5.02	4.79	5.29
		R	23872	12146	11726	965	21.19	20.43	22.05	4.96	4.75	5.21
		U	3293	1661	1632	983	15.86	14.43	17.69	5.50	5.08	6.01
10	Total, NER	T	2486474	1280323	1206151	942	26.93	26.41	27.50	6.40	6.38	6.42
		R	2064180	1063537	1000643	941	28.06	27.66	28.48	6.30	6.31	6.29
		U	422294	216786	205508	948	20.89	19.82	22.08	6.94	6.77	7.13
11	India	T	166635700	86088760	80546940	936	8.20	8.01	8.40	16.20	16.18	16.22
		R	133010878	68603342	64407536	939	10.42	10.23	10.61	17.91	17.98	17.85
		U	33624822	17485418	16139404	923	2.44	2.39	2.50	11.75	11.61	11.91

Sources: Census of India, 2001, Primary Census Abstract, Registrar General & Census Commissioner, New Delhi.

\- Information on SC is not available.

Appendix-3.3.6

State-wise Distribution of Total Population, Scheduled Tribe (ST) and Scheduled Caste (SC) Population and their Sex ratio and Percentage with Rural-Urban Break-up in different Census Years

Sl. No.	Name of the State/NER/India	Total/Rural/ Urban	Census Year, 2011							
			Total population				ST population			
			Person	Male	Female	Sex ratio	Person	Male	Female	Sex ratio
1	2	3	4	5	6	7	8	9	10	11
1	Arunachal Pradesh	T	1383727	713912	669815	938	951821	468390	483431	1032
		R	1066358	546011	520347	953	789846	390625	399221	1022
		U	317369	167901	149468	890	161975	77765	84210	1083
2	Assam	T	31205576	15939443	15266133	958	3884371	1957005	1927366	985
		R	26807034	13678989	13128045	960	3665405	1847326	1818079	984
		U	4398542	2260454	2138088	946	218966	109679	109287	996
3	Manipur	T	2855794	1438586	1417208	985	1167422	588279	579143	984
		R	2021640	1026884	994756	969	1055808	533856	521952	978
		U	834154	411702	422452	1026	111614	54423	57191	1051
4	Meghalaya	T	2966889	1491832	1475057	989	2555861	1269728	1286133	1013
		R	2371439	1194260	1177179	986	2136891	1070557	1066334	996
		U	595450	297572	297878	1001	418970	199171	219799	1104
5	Mizoram	T	1097206	555339	541867	976	1036115	516294	519821	1007
		R	525435	269135	256300	952	507467	257987	249480	967
		U	571771	286204	285567	998	528648	258307	270341	1047

1	2	3	4	5	6	7	8	9	10	11
6	Nagaland	T	1978502	1024649	953853	931	1710973	866027	844946	976
		R	1407536	725472	682064	940	1306838	665351	641487	964
		U	570966	299177	271789	908	404135	200676	203459	1014
7	Tripura	T	3673917	1874376	1799541	960	1166813	588327	578486	983
		R	2712464	1387173	1325291	955	1117566	563908	553658	982
		U	961453	487203	474250	973	49247	24419	24828	1017
8	Sub-Total, NER	T	45161611	23038137	22123474	960	12473376	6254050	6219326	994
		R	36911906	18827924	18083982	960	10579821	5329610	5250211	985
		U	8249705	4210213	4039492	959	1893555	924440	969115	1048
9	Sikkim	T	610577	323070	287507	890	206360	105261	101099	960
		R	456999	242797	214202	882	167146	86059	81087	942
		U	153578	80273	73305	913	39214	19202	20012	1042
10	Total, NER	T	45772188	23361207	22410981	959	12679736	6359311	6320425	994
		R	37368905	19070721	18298184	959	10746967	5415669	5331298	984
		U	8403283	4290486	4112797	959	1932769	943642	989127	1048
11	India	T	1210854977	623270258	587584719	943	104545716	52547215	51998501	990
		R	833748852	427781058	405967794	949	94083844	47263733	46820111	991
		U	377106125	195489200	181616925	929	10461872	5283482	5178390	980

Source: Web-site of the Registrar General and Census Commissioner, New Delhi.

Appendix-3.3.6. (*cont.*)

State-wise Distribution of Total Population, Scheduled Tribe (ST) and Scheduled Caste (SC) Population and their Sex ratio and Percentage with Rural-Urban Break-up in different Census Years

Sl. No.	Name of the State/ NER/India	Total/ Rural/ Urban	Census Year, 2011									
			SC population				Percentage of ST population			Percentage of SC population		
			Person	Male	Female	Sex ratio	Person	Male	Female	Person	Male	Female
1	2	3	12	13	14	15	16	17	18	19	20	21
1	Arunachal Pradesh	T	-	-	-	-	68.79	65.61	72.17	-	-	-
		R	-	-	-	-	74.07	71.54	76.72	-	-	-
		U	-	-	-	-	51.04	46.32	56.34	-	-	-
2	Assam	T	2231321	1145314	1086007	948	12.45	12.28	12.63	7.15	7.19	7.11
		R	1825761	938664	887097	945	13.67	13.50	13.85	6.81	6.86	6.76
		U	405560	206650	198910	963	4.98	4.85	5.11	9.22	9.14	9.30
3	Manipur	T	97328	48863	48465	992	40.88	40.89	40.87	3.41	3.40	3.42
		R	47849	24275	23574	971	52.23	51.99	52.47	2.37	2.36	2.37
		U	49479	24588	24891	1012	13.38	13.22	13.54	5.93	5.97	5.89
4	Meghalaya	T	17355	9157	8198	895	86.15	85.11	87.19	0.58	0.61	0.56
		R	11573	6086	5487	902	90.11	89.64	90.58	0.49	0.51	0.47
		U	5782	3071	2711	883	70.36	66.93	73.79	0.97	1.03	0.91
5	Mizoram	T	1218	807	411	509	94.43	92.97	95.93	0.11	0.15	0.08
		R	298	209	89	426	96.58	95.86	97.34	0.06	0.08	0.03
		U	920	598	322	538	92.46	90.25	94.67	0.16	0.21	0.11

1	2	3	12	13	14	15	16	17	18	19	20	21
6	Nagaland	T	-	-	-	-	86.48	84.52	88.58	-	-	-
		R	-	-	-	-	92.85	91.71	94.05	-	-	-
		U	-	-	-	-	70.78	67.08	74.86	-	-	-
7	Tripura	T	654918	334370	320548	959	31.76	31.39	32.15	17.83	17.84	17.81
		R	437993	224498	213495	951	41.20	40.65	41.78	16.15	16.18	16.11
		U	216925	109872	107053	974	5.12	5.01	5.24	22.56	22.55	22.57
8	Sub-Total, NER	T	3002140	1538511	1463629	951	27.62	27.15	28.11	6.65	6.68	6.62
		R	2323474	1193732	1129742	946	28.66	28.31	29.03	6.29	6.34	6.25
		U	678666	344779	333837	968	22.95	21.96	23.99	8.23	8.19	8.27
9	Sikkim	T	28275	14454	13821	956	33.80	32.58	35.16	4.63	4.47	4.81
		R	20335	10496	9839	937	36.57	35.44	37.86	4.45	4.32	4.59
		U	7940	3958	3982	1006	25.53	23.92	27.30	5.17	4.93	5.43
10	Total, NER	T	3030415	1552965	1477450	951	27.70	27.22	28.20	6.62	6.65	6.59
		R	2343809	1204228	1139581	946	28.76	28.40	29.14	6.27	6.31	6.23
		U	686606	348737	337869	969	23.00	21.99	24.05	8.17	8.13	8.22
11	India	T	201378372	103535314	97843058	945	8.63	8.43	8.85	16.63	16.61	16.65
		R	153850848	79118287	74732561	945	11.28	11.05	11.53	18.45	18.50	18.41
		U	47527524	24417027	23110497	946	2.77	2.70	2.85	12.60	12.49	12.72

Source: Web-site of the Registrar General and Census Commissioner, New Delhi.

\- information not available.

Appendix-3.3.7

State-wise Decadal Growth of Scheduled Tribe (ST) Population, Scheduled Caste (SC) Population and Others with Rural-Urban Break-up

Sl. No.	Name of the State/NER/ India	Total/ Rural/ Urban	Decadal Growth (absolute / per cent)								
			During 1961 - 71			During 1971 - 81			During 1981 - 91 (for Assam & NER, it is 1971 - 91)		
			ST Population	SC Population	Others	ST Population	SC Population	Others	ST Population	SC Population	Others
1	2	3	4	5	6	7	8	9	10	11	12
1	Arunachal Pradesh	T	71241 (23.89)	339 *	59373 (154.65)	214512 (58.07)	2580 (761.06)	89989 (92.05)	109184 (24.75)	1133 (38.81)	122402 (65.19)
		R	67772 (22.73)	335 *	45558 (118.67)	210313 (57.47)	1605 (479.10)	73412 (87.45)	87112 (20.21)	918 (47.32)	75489 (47.97)
		U	3469 *	4 *	13815 *	4199 (121.04)	975 (24375.00)	16577 (119.99)	22072 (219.47)	215 (21.96)	46913 (154.36)
2	Assam	T	442007 (37.95)	181067 (24.75)	3164749 (35.40)	^	^	^	1267793 (78.91)	746855 (81.84)	5774522 (47.70)
		R	434485 (37.52)	155850 (23.23)	2689554 (32.69)	^	^	^	1184915 (74.41)	603297 (72.96)	4802385 (43.99)
		U	7522 (111.72)	25217 (41.68)	475195 (66.55)	^	^	^	82878 (581.40)	143558 (167.47)	972137 (81.74)
3	Manipur	T	85417 (34.30)	3000 (22.43)	204299 (39.47)	53511 (16.00)	1377 (8.41)	293312 (40.63)	244196 (62.94)	19352 (109.01)	152648 (15.04)
		R	74613 (30.47)	2584 (19.55)	141744 (31.21)	23295 (7.29)	(-) 1007 (-) (6.37)	91944 (15.43)	236119 (68.88)	2910 (19.67)	46982 (6.83)
		U	10804 (260.59)	416 (263.29)	62555 (98.65)	30216 (202.11)	2384 (415.33)	201368 (159.86)	8077 (17.88)	16442 (555.85)	105666 (32.28)

1	2	3	4	5	6	7	8	9	10	11	12
4	Meghalaya	T	175069 (27.39)	2626 (208.25)	64624 (50.11)	262115 (32.19)	1605 (41.29)	60400 (31.20)	441582 (41.03)	3580 (65.19)	(-) 6203 (-) (2.44)
		R	156564 (26.51)	571 (51.81)	55497 (92.12)	195621 (26.18)	1277 (76.33)	33059 (28.56)	369359 (39.18)	2022 (68.54)	(-) 21136 (-) (14.20)
		U	18505 (38.07)	2055 (1292.45)	9127 (13.28)	66494 (99.07)	328 (14.81)	27341 (35.13)	72223 (54.05)	1558 (61.29)	14933 (14.20)
5	Mizoram	T	52285 (20.03)	77 (1540.00)	13965 (276.86)	143608 (47.43)	53 (64.63)	12706 (66.84)	191658 (41.49)	556 (411.85)	3785 (11.93)
		R	29964 (12.07)	77	12784 (367.36)	75146 (27.00)	20 (25.97)	2146 (13.19)	4677 (1.32)	359 (370.10)	(-) 5169 (-) (28.08)
		U	22321 (175.92)	0	1181 (75.51)	73462 (209.84)	33 (660.00)	10560 (384.70)	186981 (172.38)	197 (518.42)	8954 (67.30)
6	Nagaland	T	113905 (33.14)	^	33344 (130.75)	193283 (42.24)	^	65198 (110.79)	409937 (62.98)	^	24679 (19.90)
		R	104384 (31.27)	^	10628 (65.57)	149052 (34.01)	^	40589 (151.24)	345875 (58.90)	^	752 (1.12)
		U	9521 (96.53)	^	22716 (244.42)	44231 (223.18)	^	24609 (76.88)	64062 (100.70)	^	23927 (42.26)
7	Tripura	T	90474 (25.13)	73135 (61.09)	250728 (37.86)	133376 (29.60)	117524 (60.94)	245816 (26.93)	269425 (46.14)	140732 (45.34)	293990 (25.39)
		R	88687 (24.89)	69687 (61.68)	196600 (34.51)	131193 (29.48)	108165 (59.21)	194150 (25.34)	263012 (45.64)	88832 (30.54)	156150 (16.26)
		U	1787 (48.32)	3448 (51.12)	54128 (58.48)	2183 (39.80)	9359 (91.82)	51666 (35.22)	6413 (83.63)	51900 (265.45)	137840 (69.49)

1	2	3	4	5	6	7	8	9	10	11	12
8	Sub-Total, NER	T	1030398 (31.08)	260118 (30.04)	3791208 (36.74)	(-) 743996# (-) (17.12)	(-) 789418# (-) (70.10)	8558317 (60.65)	3796427 (87.35)	1035347 (91.94)	7133244 (50.55)
		R	956469 (29.61)	229073 (28.69)	3152396 (33.65)	(-) 952915# (-) (22.76)	(-) 716774# (-) (69.77)	7368254 (58.84)	3130547 (74.78)	808398 (78.68)	5490753 (43.85)
		U	73929 (86.22)	31045 (45.88)	638812 (67.28)	208919# (130.85)	(-) 72644# (-) (73.59)	1190063 (74.93)	665880 (417.04)	226949 (229.91)	1642491 (103.41)
9	Sikkim	T	^	^	47654 (29.38)	^	8779 (92.39)	97763 (48.80)	17278 (23.47)	5803 (31.74)	66991 (29.84)
		R	^	^	34834 (22.42)	^	6599 (84.97)	68527 (37.57)	20865 (33.32)	6968 (48.51)	76317 (40.53)
		U	^	^	12820 (187.21)	^	2180 (125.58)	29236 (163.04)	(-) 3587 (-) (32.60)	(-) 1165 (-) (29.75)	(-) 9326 (-) (25.79)
10	Total, NER	T	1030398 (31.08)	269620 (31.13)	3829360 (36.54)	(-) 670373# (-) (15.42)	(-) 780639# (-) (68.74)	8582457 (59.97)	3887328 (89.44)	1049929 (92.46)	7224375 (50.48)
		R	956469 (29.61)	236839 (29.67)	3179464 (33.38)	(-) 890294# (-) (21.27)	(-) 710175# (-) (68.61)	7374160 (58.05)	3214033 (76.77)	821965 (79.41)	5572976 (43.87)
		U	73929 (86.22)	32781 (48.44)	649896 (67.96)	219921# (137.74)	(-)70464# (-) (70.15)	1208297 (75.23)	673295 (421.68)	227964 (226.95)	1651399 (102.81)
11	India	T	7884978 (26.17)	15556123 (24.14)	85273937 (24.74)	13613476 (35.81)	24749225 (30.93)	78975339 (18.37)	16129742 (31.24)	33468654 (31.95)	131416443 (25.82)
		R	7362891 (25.08)	12882190 (22.38)	58312251 (21.33)	11706923 (31.88)	17547838 (24.91)	39497417 (11.91)	14323422 (29.58)	24346805 (27.67)	82413771 (22.20)
		U	522087 (67.59)	2673933 (38.85)	26961686 (37.82)	1906553 (147.28)	7201387 (75.36)	39477922 (40.18)	1806320 (56.43)	9121849 (54.43)	49002672 (35.58)

Source: This Table has been generated on the basis of the information available in other Tables.

* figures are of 1971 Census, # Assam figures of 1981 Census not included, ^ information not available. Figure within bracket indicates growth in per cent.

Appendix-3.3.7 (*cont.*)

State-wise Decadal Growth of Scheduled Tribe (ST) Population, Scheduled Caste (SC) Population and Others with Rural-Urban Break-up

Sl. No.	Name of the State/NER/ India	Total/ Rural/ Urban	Growth (absolute / percent)								
			During 1991 -2001			During 2001 - 11			During 1961 - 2011* (i.e. within a period of 50 years)		
			ST Population	SC Population	Others	ST Population	SC Population	Others	ST Population	SC Population	Others
1	2	3	13	14	15	16	17	18	19	20	21
1	Arunachal Pradesh	T	154807 (28.13)	2136 (52.71)	76467 (24.65)	246663 (34.98)	^	39096 (10.11)	582413 (157.66)	^	333803 (340.26)
		R	88056 (16.99)	204 (7.14)	27897 (11.98)	133568 (30.28)	^	12703 (4.87)	423907 (115.84)	^	192228 (228.07)
		U	66751 (207.76)	1932 (161.81)	48570 (62.83)	63095 (63.81)	^	26393 (20.97)	158506 (4569.21)	^	141575 (1024.50)
2	Assam	T	434129 (15.10)	166537 (10.04)	3640540 (20.36)	575801 (·7.40)	405372 (22.20)	3568875 (16.58)	2719730 (233.53)	1499831 (205.04)	16148686 (180.61)
		R	377238 (13.58)	123560 (8.64)	2788963 (17.74)	510859 (·6.19)	272070 (17.51)	2807817 (15.17)	2507497 (216.55)	1154777 (172.10)	13088719 (159.09)
		U	56891 (58.57)	42977 (18.74)	851577 (39.40)	64942 (42.16)	133302 (48.96)	761058 (25.26)	212233 (3152.13)	345054 (570.28)	3059967 (428.54)
3	Manipur	T	108968 (17.24)	22932 (61.80)	197739 (16.93)	426281 (57.52)	37291 (62.11)	225434 (16.51)	918373 (368.75)	83952 (627.63)	1073432 (207.38)
		R	126982 (21.93)	3097 (17.49)	17629 (25.62)	349896 (49.57)	27047 (130.02)	53877 (6.23)	810905 (331.11)	34631 (262.00)	463784 (102.11)
		U	(-) 18014 (-) (33.83)	19835 (102.24)	68502 (15.82)	76385 (216.82)	10244 (26.11)	171557 (34.21)	107468 (2592.09)	49321 (31215.82)	609648 (961.39)

1	2	3	13	14	15	16	17	18	19	20	21
4	Meghalaya	T	474935 (31.29)	2067 (22.78)	67042 (27.06)	562999 (28.25)	6216 (55.80)	78852 (25.05)	1916700 (299.88)	16094 (1276.29)	264716 (205.27)
		R	370577 (28.24)	2093 (42.10)	47310 (37.06)	454221 (26.99)	4508 (63.81)	47999 (27.43)	1546342 (261.85)	10471 (950.18)	162729 (270.11)
		U	104358 (50.70)	(-) 26 (-) 0.63	19732 (16.43)	108778 (35.07)	1708 (41.92)	30853 (22.06)	370358 (761.87)	5623 (3536.48)	101986 (148.42)
5	Mizoram	T	185745 (28.42)	(-) 419 (-) (60.64)	13491 (38.00)	196805 (23.45)	946 (347.79)	10882 (22.21)	775101 (296.96)	1213 (24260.00)	54829 (1087.01)
		R	72770 (20.32)	(-) 391 (-) (85.75)	3378 (25.51)	76584 (17.77)	233 (358.46)	1051 (6.32)	259141 (104.36)	298 (absolute)	14190 (407.76)
		U	112975 (38.24)	(-) 28 (-) (20.74)	10113 (45.43)	120221 (29.44)	713 (344.44)	9831 (30.37)	515960 (4066.52)	915 (18300.00)	40639 (2598.40)
6	Nagaland	T	713204 (67.23)	^	67286 (45.24)	(-) 63053 (-) (3.55)	^	51519 (23.85)	1367276 (397.81)	^	242026 (949.01)
		R	610877 (65.46)	^	35049 (51.41)	(-) 237184 (-) (15.36)	^	(-) 2529 (-) (2.45)	973004 (291.46)	^	84489 (521.25)
		U	102327 (80.15)	^	32237 (40.02)	174131 (75.71)	^	54048 (47.92)	394272 (3997.49)	^	157537 (1695.04)
7	Tripura	T	140081 (16.42)	104608 (23.19)	197309 (13.58)	173387 (17.45)	99194 (17.85)	202133 (12.25)	806743 (224.05)	535193 (447.02)	1189976 (179.70)
		R	128733 (15.34)	75959 (20.01)	113277 (10.15)	149569 (15.45)	(-) 17630 (-) (3.87)	(-) 72928 (-) (5.93)	761194 (213.60)	325013 (287.67)	587249 (103.09)
		U	11348 (80.59)	28649 (40.10)	84032 (25.00)	23818 (93.66)	116824 (116.71)	275061 (65.46)	45549 (1231.72)	210180 (3116.09)	602727 (651.22)
8	Sub-Total, NER	T	2211869 (27.16)	297861 (13.78)	4259874 (20.05)	2118883 (20.46)	542831 (22.07)	4182979 (16.40)	9157577 (276.18)	2136157 (246.67)	19367305 (187.69)
		R	1775233 (24.26)	204522 (11.14)	3145111 (17.46)	1487513 (16.36)	283166 (13.88)	2851052 (13.48)	7349762 (227.54)	1525159 (191.05)	14639312 (156.25)
		U	436636 (52.89)	93339 (28.66)	1114763 (34.50)	631370 (50.02)	259665 (61.97)	1331927 (30.65)	1807815 (2108.48)	610998 (902.93)	4727993 (497.95)

1	2	3	13	14	15	16	17	18	19	20	21
9	Sikkim	T	20504 (22.56)	3081 (12.79)	110809 (38.02)	94955 (85.23)	1110 (4.09)	(-) 26339 (-) (6.55)	^	18773 (197.57)	175601 (87.65)
		R	18423 (22.07)	2539 (11.90)	90568 (34.22)	65237 (64.01)	(-) 3537 (-) (14.82)	(-) 85682 (-) (2.41)	^	12569 (161.85)	87109 (47.75)
		U	2081 (28.06)	542 (19.70)	20241 (75.41)	29718 (312.95)	4647 (141.12)	59343 (126.04)	^	6204 (357.37)	88492 (493.49)
10	Total, NER	T	2232373 (27.11)	300942 (13.77)	4370683 (20.30)	2213838 (21.15)	543941 (21.88)	4156640 (16.05)	9363937 (282.40)	2164432 (249.94)	19581058 (186.82)
		R	1793656 (24.24)	207061 (11.15)	3235679 (17.70)	1552750 (16.89)	279629 (13.55)	2765370 (12.85)	7516908 (232.72)	1545494 (193.59)	14753489 (154.90)
		U	438717 (52.67)	93881 (28.59)	1135004 (34.84)	661088 (51.98)	264312 (62.59)	1391270 (31.67)	1847029 (2154.22)	618938 (914.67)	4827569 (504.80)
11	India	T	16567860 (24.45)	28412423 (20.56)	137327357 (21.45)	21219476 (23.98)	34742672 (20.85)	127282501 (16.37)	74415532 (246.98)	136929097 (212.46)	560275577 (162.56)
		R	14587571 (23.25)	20667081 (18.40)	78544311 (17.32)	15745247 (21.65)	20839970 (15.67)	53672996 (10.09)	64726054 (220.47)	96283884 (167.26)	312440746 (114.29)
		U	1980289 (39.55)	7745342 (29.93)	58783046 (31.48)	5474229 (49.72)	13902702 (41.35)	73609505 (29.98)	9689478 (1254.47)	40645213 (590.58)	247834831 (347.68)

Source: This Table has been generated on the basis of the information available in other Appendices.

^ information not available, Figure within bracket indicates growth in per cent.

* For Arunachal Pradesh, it is 1971-2011.

4

Growth of Religious Groups

The term 'Religion', is very wide and perhaps there is no single definition to explain it properly and to the satisfaction of all human beings. It is seen that, Religion deals with ideas that cannot be proved. It depends on intuition and takes its stand on spiritual ideas. The goal of Religion is realization and the truth of it will have to be taken on trust. Therefore, it can be said that, it is a belief with which people live their life and do their work for the fulfilment of their wishes, getting peace of mind, purification of soul, leading a disciplined life, worshipping and getting the blessings of the God.

Religion played a very vital role in the evolution of human civilization and culture. Very often, it spreads out from the land of its origin. Human civilization of the world is divided into so many religious groups and every group is worshipping the God (as they believe) in their own ways. In India, people of so many religious groups, are living. However, for the purpose of population Census, information of 6 (six) major religious groups is being collected separately. These groups are (i) Hindus, (ii) Muslims, (iii) Christians, (iv) Sikhs, (v) Buddhists, and (vi) Jains. The people of other religious groups, are being put together and is being categorized as 'Others'. But the people, who cannot state their religion, are being categorized as 'Religion not stated', for the purpose of the Census.

In the North Eastern States, mainly, people of 4 (four) major religious groups *viz.* (i) Hindus, (ii) Muslims, (iii) Christians, and (iv) Buddhists, are living. The people of other 2 (two) religious groups, i.e. Sikhs and Jains are also there in all the States of this region, but their numbers are very less. Appendix–4.1 to Appendix–4.6, will give a clear idea about the number of people of each of these religious groups, who are living in different States, showing their position in each of the Census years, from 1961 to 2011, i.e. of the last 50 (fifty) years. Apart from the total number of population in each religious group, the details of the total number of males and the total number of females, with their residential status, are also available in these Appendices, for each of these Census Years.

The Appendix–4.7 will however give an idea about the proportion of people of each religious group of each North Eastern States as well as of India, in each census year with their residential status, and also the changes that took place in their proportion, in the subsequent census years from 1961 to 2011. Further, it can also be seen that, in some of the states, quite a big number of people were there, who were of other religious groups [i.e. other than the 6 (six) religious groups mentioned above] and also a big number of people, who could not state their religion at the time of population Census, conducted in different years.

In case of Arunachal Pradesh, it is seen that, at the initial stages, the people were divided into 3 (three) broad groups on the basis of their socio-cultural affinities. The first group, i.e. the people of the western part and of the mountainous regions along the northern border, were following Buddhism. The second group, i.e. the people of the central region, were worshipping the Sun and the Moon God, namely Donyi-Polo and Abo-Tani, the mythical first man who is believed to have been the original ancestor for many of the tribal people. The people of the eastern region were in the third group. They were maintaining a very close contact with the plain people of Assam for trade and were also exchanging cultural traits and social customs. This ultimately paved the way for spreading 'Vaishnavism', which they imbibed from the many Vaishnava Satras of Assam.

From the Appendix–4.7, it can be seen that, in 1961, out of the total population of Arunachal Pradesh, 7.61 per cent were Hindus, 0.30 per cent Muslims, 0.51 per cent Christians and 1.73 per cent Buddhists. Whereas, 89.10 per cent of the people, did not or could not, tell their religion. However, the situation changed in 1971. The percentage of Hindus increased to 21.99, Christians increased to 0.79, Buddhists to 13.13 and 63.46 per cent of the people were categorized as Others. In 1981, the percentage of Hindus further increased to 29.24, Muslims to 0.80, Christians to 4.32, Buddhists to 13.69, but the percentage of Others came down to 51.60. In 1991 also, the Hindus, the Muslims and the Christians maintained their respective growth and reached to 37.04 per cent, 1.38 per cent and 10.30 per cent respectively. After that there was a sharp change in the proportion of different constituent groups. The percentage of Hindus started declining and it came down to 34.60

in 2001 and it further went down to 29.04 in 2011. Whereas, the Muslims and the Christians, started increasing very rapidly. The percentage of Muslims though reached to 1.88 in 2001 and 1.95 in 2011, but the percentage of Christians reached to 18.72 in 2001 and it went further to the extent of 30.26 per cent in 2011.

Further, it is observed that, the proportion of people categorized as 'Others' started declining rapidly. Their percentage, which was 63.46 in 1971, came down to 26.20 in 2011. This automatically raises a question as to where these people are going? On the other hand, it is also observed that, the Christian people are increasing very fast. Therefore, there might be a possibility that, the people who were categorized as 'Others', opted for Christianity. A large number of Buddhist people are also there in Arunachal Pradesh. In 1971, their percentage was 13.13 and they maintained more or less that proportion till 1981. After that, it started declining slightly and reached to 11.77 per cent in 2011.

In Assam, mainly 2 (two) religious groups *viz.* Hindus and Muslims are living. The people of other religious groups are comparatively very less. Among the 2 (two) main groups, Hindus were the majority. In 1961, the percentage of Hindus was 66.41 and it increased to 72.51 in 1971 but, thereafter, it started declining. It came down to 67.13 per cent in 1991, 64.89 per cent in 2001 and finally went down to 61.46 per cent in 2011. On the other hand, Muslims started increasing rapidly. In 1961, though the percentage of Muslims was 23.29, but it reached to 24.56 per cent in 1971, 28.43 per cent in 1991, 30.92 per cent in 2001 and finally it reached to 34.22 per cent in 2011.

In Manipur, main religious groups are Hindus, Muslims and Christians. Among these 3 (three), Hindus are the majority, followed by Christians and Muslims. But, it is very much surprising to see that, the proportion of Hindus was declining very fast. In 1961, the percentage of Hindus was 61.68, but it came down to 60.04 per cent in 1981, 57.67 per cent in 1991, 46.01 per cent in 2001 and finally, it came down to 41.38 per cent in 2011. On the other hand, the proportion of Christians started increasing very rapidly. In 1961, the percentage of Christians was 19.49, but it became 26.03 per cent in 1971, 29.68 per cent in 1981, 34.11 per cent in 1991, 34.04 per cent in 2001 and finally it reached to 41.29 per cent in 2011, i.e. it attained almost the same percentage of Hindus. This high rate of growth of Christian cannot be attributed to the birth alone. Therefore, there might be a possibility that, some Hindus opted for Christianity, which is also evident from the declining trend in the growth of Hindus. However in case of Muslims, though there was an increasing trend, but the rate was not that high. In 1961, the percentage of Muslims was 6.23 and with a very low pace, it reached to 8.40 per cent in 2011.

The state of Meghalaya is a Tribal dominated state and majority of its people are Christians. Hindus and Muslims are also there, but their proportion is comparatively less. However, a large number of people were also there in the state, who could not be put under any of the 6 (six) religious groups considered in Census, were categorized as Others. In Meghalaya, though the Christian people are the majority, but in sixties and seventies, their proportion was not that high. In 1971, the percentage of Christians was only 46.98. After that, it started increasing very rapidly. It reached to 52.62 per cent in 1981, 64.58 per cent in 1991, 70.25 per cent in 2001 and finally reached to 74.59 per cent in 2011. On the other hand, Hindus showed a declining trend. The percentage of Hindus, which was 18.50 in 1971, came down to 18.03 per cent in 1981, 14.67 per cent in 1991, 13.27 per cent in 2001 and finally to only 11.53 per cent in 2011.

In case of Muslims, though their proportion at the initial stages was less, but gradually it started increasing. In 1971, the percentage of Muslims was 2.60, but it reached to 3.10 per cent in 1981, 3.46 per cent in 1991, 4.28 per cent in 2001 and then to 4.40 per cent in 2011. However, the people who were classified as Others, registered a declining trend. In 1971, their percentage was 31.45, but it came down to 25.77 per cent in 1981, 16.82 per cent in 1991, 11.53 per cent in 2001 and then to 8.71 per cent in 2011. In this case, a question comes, as to where these people had gone. Is there any relation between the high growth rate of Christians and the rapid decline in the proportion of Others? It might be a fact that, some of the people, who were categorized as Others, opted for Christianity, as this high rate of growth of Christians cannot be justified by birth alone.

In the North Eastern Region, Mizoram is one state, where the proportion of Christian people is very high. And their unique feature is that, they maintained that high proportion all along with slight ups and downs. In 1971, the percentage of Christians was 86.08 and in 1981 and 1991 though their percentage was slightly lower, but again it reached to 86.97 per cent in 2001 and 87.16 per cent in 2011. Another feature of Mizoram is that, a sizeable number of Buddhists are there and they also maintained more or less a uniform proportion with slight variations. In 1971, the percentage of Buddhists was 6.81 and gradually it reached to 8.51 per cent in 2011.

In Mizoram, Hindus are comparatively very less and their proportion also gradually came down with the passes of time. The percentage of Hindus was only 6.39 in 1971 and it came down to 5.05 per cent in 1991, 3.55 per cent in 2001 and finally to the lowest of 2.75 per cent in 2011. The Muslim people are also there, though their number was very less in the initial stages. But they showed an increasing trend gradually. In 1971, the percentage of Muslims was only 0.57 and it increased to 0.66 per cent in 1991, 1.14 per cent in 2001 and to 1.35 per cent in 2011.

Nagaland is another Christian dominated state in the North Eastern Region. In sixties and seventies, though their proportion was not that high, but from eighties, they started increasing vary fast. In 1961, the percentage of Christians was 52.98 and it increased to 66.76 per cent in 1971, 80.21 per cent in 1981, 87.47 per cent in 1991, 89.97 per cent in 2001 and then it came down a bit to 87.93 per cent in 2011. It is seen that, in the initial stages, a large number of people were classified under Others, but their proportion started decreasing very rapidly subsequently. The percentage of people classified as Others was 37.23 in 1961, which came to 20.94 per cent in 1971, 3.59 per cent in 1981, 0.48 per cent in 1991, 0.31 per cent in 2001 and finally it came down to only 0.16 per cent in 2011. Here also, this rapid decline in their proportion, raises the question as to where this people had gone? On the other hand, it is seen that, the Christians had grown very rapidly and keeping that in view, it can perhaps be considered that, many of these people, who were categorized as Others—had opted for Christianity, as this high growth rate of Christians cannot be justified by birth alone.

In Nagaland, Hindus and Muslims are also there, though their numbers are comparatively less. The percentage of Hindus was 9.39 in 1961 and though it showed an increasing trend and reached to 11.43 per cent in 1971 and 14.36 per cent in 1981, but after that, it started declining. In 1991, the percentage of Hindus came down to 10.13 and finally it went down to only 8.75 per cent in 2011. The Muslims, on the other hand, increased steadily. In 1961, though their percentage was only 0.24, but it increased to 0.58 per cent in 1971, 1.52 per cent in 1981, 1.71 per cent in 1991, 1.76 per cent in 2001 and finally reached to 2.47 per cent in 2011.

The state of Tripura is a Hindu majority state, but a considerable number of Muslims, Christians and Buddhists are also there. The Hindus were though the majority, but their proportion showed some ups and downs with the passes of times. It is seen that, in 1961, the percentage of Hindus was 76.01 and it reached to 89.55 per cent in 1971 and thereafter, it started declining and reached to 89.34 per cent in 1981, 86.50 per cent in 1991, 85.62 per cent in 2001 and finally it came down to 83.40 per cent in 2011.

The Muslims and the Christians however showed an increasing trend. The Muslims, starting with 6.68 per cent in 1971, reached to 7.13 per cent in 1991, 7.95 per cent in 2001 and then reached to 8.60 per cent in 2011. However, the Christians starting with a lower percentage of only 0.88 in 1961, started increasing rapidly and reached to 1.01 per cent in 1971, 1.68 per cent in 1991, 3.20 per cent in 2001 and then to the level of 4.35 per cent in 2011. The Buddhists, on the other hand, showed some ups and downs in their growth rate in different times. In 1961, the percentage of Buddhists was 2.95, but it came down to 2.72 per cent in 1971 and then to 2.67 per cent in 1981. Then it increased to 4.65 per cent in 1991 and again it declined to 3.09 per cent in 2001 and finally it again showed an upward trend and reached to 3.41 per cent in 2011. It is difficult to find out the reason(s) of such ups and downs. However, there might have been some problem(s) in identifying the religion of some groups of people at the time of filling up the census schedule in different years.

In Sikkim, Hindus and Buddhists are the 2 (two) main groups, though Muslims and Christians are also living there. In 1961, the percentage of Hindus was 66.69 per cent and though it increased slightly and reached to 68.88 per cent in 1971, but thereafter, it started declining. It reached to 67.25 per cent in 1981, 60.93 per cent in 2001 and finally came down to 57.76 per cent in 2011. The Buddhists however, showed some ups and downs in their proportion in different times. In 1961, the percentage of Buddhists was 30.76, but it came down to 29.84 per cent in 1971, 28.71 per cent in 1981 and then to 27.16 per cent in 1991. After that, there was an increase in their proportion and the percentage reached to 28.11 and again, it decreased to 27.39 per cent in 2011.

Muslims also showed some ups and downs in their proportion in different times. In 1961, the percentage of Muslims was 0.75 and in 1981, it reached to 1.03 per cent, then it came down to 0.95 per cent in 1991. After that, it showed an increasing trend and reached to 1.42 per cent in 2001 and finally reached to 1.62 per cent in 2011. The Christians, on the other hand, registered a steady increase in their proportion. In 1961, the percentage of Christians was 1.74 and it increased to 2.22 per cent in 1981, 3.30 per cent in 1991, 6.68 per cent in 2001 and then, it reached to 9.91 per cent in 2011.

The position of North Eastern Region, as a whole, is slightly different from the position of the country as a whole. In this region, mainly the people of 3 (three) religious groups *viz.* Hindu, Muslim and Christian, are living. However, though some Buddhists are also there, but their proportion is very low. And the people of other religious groups are quite insignificant.

In NE Region, Hindus are though the majority, but their proportion was much low in comparison to the position of the country as a whole. Further, their growth rate was also declining very fast. In 1961, the percentage of Hindus in this region was 64.12 and in 1971, though it increased to 66.42 per cent, but again it started declining and came down to 61.05 per cent in 1991, 57.22 per cent in 2001 and finally came down to 54.02 per cent in 2011. On the other hand, though it appears that, the growth rate of Hindus in the country as a whole also started declining, but that was not as fast as it happened in the North Eastern Region. In India, the percentage of Hindus was 83.45 in 1961 and thereafter, it started declining slowly and reached to 82.73 per cent in 1971, 82.63 per cent in 1981, 82.00 per cent in 1991, 80.46 per cent in 2001 and finally came down to 79.80 per cent in 2011.

The Muslims however, registered a steady increase in their growth rate over the years, both in NE Region as well as in the Country as a whole. In this region, the percentage of Muslims was 20.78 in 1961 and then it reached to 21.30 per cent in 1991, 22.80 per cent in 2001 and finally to 25.05 per cent in 2011. However, in case of the country as a whole, starting with a percentage of 10.69, the percentage of Muslims reached to 11.21 in 1971, 12.12 per cent in 1991, 13.43 per cent in 2001 and then to 14.23 per cent in 2011.

In the North Eastern Region as a whole, the Christians also registered an increasing trend over the years. In 1961, the percentage of Christians was 7.69 and in 1971, it became 9.03 per cent, in 1991, it reached to 13.50 per cent, then to 16.11 per cent in 2001 and finally reached to 17.25 per cent in 2011. But in case of the country as a whole, the position was different. In 1961, the percentage of Christians in the country was 2.44, but in 1971, there was a slight increase and it became 2.60 per cent. After that, there was a declining trend and the percentage reached to 2.34 in 2001 and to 2.30 per cent in 2011.

Decadal Growth of Religious Groups

The details of Decadal Growth (DG) of different religious groups can be seen from the Appendix–4.8. It has been observed that, amongst the major religious groups, *viz.* Hindus, Muslims and Christians, the growth of Hindus was comparatively less and over the years it showed a declining trend in all the North Eastern States. Whereas, the Muslims were growing rapidly in all the NE States and the growth of Christians was also very fast, particularly in Arunachal Pradesh, Manipur, Meghalaya, Mizoram and Nagaland, though the growth rate showed some ups and down at different points of time.

In Arunachal Pradesh, the Decadal Growth (DG) of Hindus was more to the extent of 301.70 per cent in 1961–71 and after that, it started declining. The DG of Hindus reached to 79.64 per cent in 1971–81, 18.65 per cent in 1991–2001 and finally came down to 5.77 per cent in 2001–11. Further, it has been found that, within a period of 50 (fifty) years, i.e. from 1961 to 2011, the growth of Hindus was 14.70 times. The Muslims were though comparatively less in number at the initial period, but their DG was the highest to the extent of 502.49 per cent in 1971–81. After that, the Decadal Growth rate was not that intense and it came down to 135.01 per cent in 1981–91 and to 30.81 per cent in 2001–11. However, within a period of 50 (fifty) years, the Muslims increased by 25.83 times. But the Christians registered a phenomenal increase over the years. As per 1961 census, the Christian population in Arunachal Pradesh was only 0.51 per cent of the total population of the state, but their DG reached to 115.06 per cent in 1961–71 and it increased to the highest of 641.21 per cent in 1971–81. After that, the growth rate slightly came down and reached to 225.98 per cent in 1981–91 and finally to 103.71 per cent in 2001–11. That means, within a period of 50 (fifty) years, i.e. from 1961 to 2011, the Christian people of Arunachal Pradesh increased by 243.44 times. In other words, the Christians became the second largest religious group and occupied 30.26 per cent of the total population of the State by 2011. Perhaps, this again indicates that, many of the people who were the worshipper of the Sun and the Moon God, i.e. Donyi-Polo and Abo-Tani, and were classified under 'Others' in the initial years of Census, opted for Christianity subsequently.

The State of Assam, though a Hindu majority state, but the Decadal Growth of Hindus was not very high and gradually, it showed a declining trend. The DG of Hindus was 34.49 per cent in 1961–71 and though it increased to 41.89 per cent in 1981–91, but after that, there was a sharp decline and it came down to 14.95 per cent in 1991-2001 and then to 10.89 per cent in 2001–11, and it appears that, within a period of 50 (fifty) years, i.e. from 1961 to 2011, the Hindus of Assam increased by 1.43 times. The Muslims, on the other hand, increased much faster. The DG of Muslims was though 29.89 per cent in 1961–71, but it increased to 77.42 per cent in 1981–91. After that, the growth rate was a bit slow and the DG came down to 29.59 per cent in 2001–11. However, within this period of 50 (fifty) years, the Muslims of Assam increased by 2.86 times, i.e. almost 3 (three) times. The Christian people in Assam, was comparatively much less in sixties. But during 1971–91, they had the Growth of 95.37 per cent. Thereafter, the DG came down to 32.54 per cent in 1991-2001 and to 18.17 per cent in 2001–11.

The State of Manipur was though a Hindu majority State, but over the years, it changed its characteristics. The Decadal Growth of Hindus was 31.49 per cent in 1961–71 and though it increased to 34.87 per cent in 1971–81, but thereafter, it came down very sharply and registered a negative DG of (–) 5.91 per cent in 1991-2001. However, during 2001–11, it again showed an increasing trend and reached to 18.56 per cent. But, it appears that, within a period of 50 (fifty) years, the Hindus of Manipur increased by only 1.45 times. The Christians, on the other hand, increased very rapidly. The DG of Christians was 83.66 per cent in 1961–71, but after that, there was some ups and downs in their growth rate. In 1971–81, the DG was 51.02 per cent and in 1981–91, it was 48.60 per cent and again it reached to 59.85 per cent in 2001–11. However, from 1961 to 2011, i.e. within a period of 50 (fifty) years, the Christians increased by 6.75 times, and touched the proportion of Hindus.

The Decadal Growth rate of Muslims was also not uniform always. The DG of Muslims was 46.06 per cent in 1961–71 and thereafter, there was a declining trend. The DG reached to 39.96 per cent in 1971–81, 34.44 per cent in 1981–91 and then there was an increasing trend. In 1991-2001, it reached to 42.99 per cent and again, it came down to 25.61 per cent in 2001-11. However, in that period of 50 (fifty) years, the Muslims of Manipur increased by 3.94 times, i.e. almost four times.

Meghalaya is a Christian majority State and Hindus are comparatively much less there and their growth rate also came down over the years. The Decadal Growth of Hindus was though 28.69 per cent in 1971–81, but it came down to 18.25 per cent in 1991-2001 and to 11.13 per cent in 2001–11. However, within a period of 40 (forty) years, i.e. from 1971 to 2011, the Hindus of Meghalaya increased only by 0.83 time, that means, they could not even double their number of 1971. On the other hand, the DG of Christians was 47.89 per cent in 1971–81, which increased to 63.06 per cent in 1981–91. After that, the rate declined a bit and the DG reached to 42.13 per cent in 1991-2001 and to 35.85 per cent in 2001–11. But in that period of 40 (forty) years, the Christians of Meghalaya increased by 3.66 times. The DG of Muslims was though not uniform but it was quite high. In 1971–81, the DG of Muslims was 57.26 per cent and then, it came down a bit and reached to 48.34 per cent in 1981-91. In 1991-2001, the DG again increased and reached to 61.35 per cent and thereafter, it again came down to 31.49 per cent in 2001–11, and within a period of 40 (forty) years, the Muslims of Meghalaya increased by 3.95, i.e. almost four times.

Amongst all the North Eastern States, Mizoram was unique at least in two counts. It is seen that, the proportion of Christians in Mizoram, was very high from the beginning and they maintained that high proportion all along. On the other hand, the proportion of Hindus was very low and from 1981 onwards, they always registered a negative growth. In 1971, the proportion of Christians was as high as 86.08 per cent and the Decadal Growth in 1971–81 was 44.63 per cent. The Decadal Growth however, showed a declining trend and reached to 42.89 per cent in 1981–91, 30.69 per cent in 1991-2001 and then to 23.75 per cent in 2001–11. But, within a period of 40 (forty) years, the Christians of Mizoram increased by 2.34 times.

On the other hand, the proportion of Hindus in 1971, was as low as 6.39 per cent and though the DG was 66.02 per cent in 1971–81, but after that, the growth rate was always negative. The DG was (–) 1.20 per cent in 1981–91, (–) 9.27 per cent in 1991-2001 and (–) 4.52 per cent in 2001–11, and in that 40 (forty) years, the Hindus increased by only 0.42 times, i.e. they could not even added nine thousand people. The growth rate of Muslims was however, increasing steadily. The DG of Muslims was though 17.16 per cent in 1971–81, but it increased to 105.80 per cent in 1981–91, 122.54 per cent in 1991-2001 and then it came down to 46.87 per cent in 2001–11. However, in 40 (forty) years, the Muslims of Mizoram increased by 6.88 times.

The State of Nagaland is also a Christion majority State and they were increasing very rapidly. The Decadal Growth of Christian was 76.29 per cent in 1961–71 and it increased to 80.28 per cent in 1971–81. After that, the growth rate started declining. In 1981–91, the DG was 70.20 per cent, in 1991-2001, it was 69.23 and thereafter, there was a negative DG of (–) 2.83 per cent in 2001-11. However, during a period of 50 (fifty) years, i.e. from 1961 to 2011, the Christian people of Nagaland, increased by 7.89 times.

The Hindus were comparatively much less in Nagaland and initially, though the DG was a bit high, but it started declining rapidly. In 1961–71, the DG of Hindus in Nagaland was 70.23 per cent and in 1971–81, it reached to 88.49 per cent and thereafter, it came down to 10.07 per cent in 1981-91. Then it increased a bit and reached to 25.06 per cent in 1991-01 and again it came down to 12.99 per cent in 2001-11 and in that 50 (fifty) years, the Hindus increased by 3.99 times, i.e. almost four times.

The Muslims were though very less in number in the initial stages, but they were increasing very fast. In 1961–71, the DG of Muslims in Nagaland was 232.88 per cent and it reached to 298.04 in 1971–81. After that, the DG was not that high and there was a declining trend. In 1981–91, it was 74.84 per cent, in 1991-2001, it was 69.58 per cent and then it came down to 39.87 per cent in 2001–11. But in that time period of 50 (fifty) years, the Muslims of Nagaland, increased by 53.95 times, i.e. almost fifty four times.

The State of Tripura is a Hindu majority State and though their Decadal Growth was a bit high in sixties, but it started declining in the subsequent years. In 1961–71, the DG of Hindus in Tripura was 60.56 per cent and then it came down to 31.61 per cent in 1971–81, 30.02 per cent in 1981–91, 14.86 per cent in 1991-2001 and finally it came down to 11.85 per cent in 2001–11. And in 50 (fifty) years, the Hindus of Tripura could increase only by 2.53 times.

Muslims were second highest in number in Tripura, but their Decadal Growth was higher than the Hindus. It is seen that, the DG was 33.25 per cent in 1971–81, 41.84 per cent in 1981–91, 29.49 per cent in 1991-2001 and 24.21 per cent in 2001–11 and from 1971 to 2011, i.e. in 40 (forty) years, the Muslims of Tripura increased by 2.04 times.

The Christians were comparatively much less in number, but their Decadal Growth was quite high. In 1961-71, the DG of Christians was though 56.52 per cent, but thereafter, it started increasing and reached to 58.29 per cent in 1971–81, 86.84 per cent in 1981–91, 120.54 per cent in 1991-2001 and after that, it came down to 56.00 per cent in 2001–11. And within a period of 50 (fifty) years, the Christians of Tripura increased by 14.93, i.e. almost fifteen times.

Sikkim is also a Hindu Majority State and their Decadal Growth was though not much, but it showed some ups and down in subsequent years.

The DG of Hindus was 33.63 per cent in 1961–71 and then it reached to 47.21 per cent in 1971–81 and again it came down to 30.60 per cent in 1981–91, 18.59 per cent in 1991-2001 and to the lowest of 7.01 per cent in 2001–11 and in 50 (fifty) years, the Hindus increased by 2.26 times.

In Sikkim, Muslims and Christians were very less in sixties, but they started growing very fast from seventies though some ups and downs were there, in their Decadal Growth. The DG of Muslims was 867.46 per cent in 1971–81, but it came down to 18.76 per cent in 1981–91 and again it went up to 99.87 in 1991-2001 and finally came down to 28.26 per cent in 2001–11. But in 40 (forty) years, i.e. from 1971 to 2011, the Muslims of Sikkim, increased by 28.45 times. The Christians also showed a similar trend. The DG of Christian was 321.83 per cent in 1971–81, then it came down to 91.20 per cent in 1981–91 and again increased to 169.25 per cent in 1991-2001 and thereafter came down to 67.58 per cent in 2001–11 and in that time period of 40 (forty) years, the Christians increased by 35.39 times.

The situation of the North Eastern Region as a whole was not much different from the States. Over the years, the proportion of Hindus was declining and on the other hand, the proportion of Muslims and the Christians was going up. The Decadal Growth (DG) of Hindus of NE Region was 39.81 per cent in 1961–71 and it increased a bit and reached to 48.39 per cent in 1981–91. But after that, there was a sharp decline and the DG reached to 13.98 per cent in 1991-2001 and then to 11.21 per cent in 2001–11 and within a period of 50 (fifty) years, i.e. from 1961 to 2011, the Hindus of NE Region increased by only 1.63 times.

The Decadal Growth of Muslims and the Christians was comparatively high and also showed some ups and downs. In 1961-71, the DG of Muslims was 24.69 per cent and then it went up to 79.12 per cent in 1981–91. Thereafter, it came down to 30.17 per cent in 1991-2001 and to 29.44 per cent in 2001–11, and in that period of 50 (fifty) years, the Muslims increased by 2.76 times. The Decadal Growth of Christians was however, higher than the Muslims. In 1961-71, the DG of Christians was 58.64 per cent, and then it went up to the extent of 141.41 per cent in 1981–91. After that, there was a declining trend, and in 1991-2001, it reached to 45.08 per cent and finally to 26.08 per cent in 2001–11. But in 50 (fifty) years, the Christians of North Eastern Region increased by 6.01 times.

The position of the country as a whole was slightly different from the position of the North Eastern Region. The Decadal Growth of Hindus in the country was 23.67 per cent in 1961–71 and then it came down to 21.27 per cent in 1971–81. After that, it increased slightly and the DG reached to 25.09 per cent in 1981–91 and then again came down to 20.35 per cent in 1991-2001 and finally reached to 16.76 per cent in 2001–11, and within a period of 50 (fifty) years, the Hindus of the country increased only by 1.64 times.

The Decadal Growth of Muslims and Christians also showed some ups and downs, but the Muslims were increasing at a faster pace. The DG of Muslims was 30.84 per cent in 1961–71 and then came down to 23.04 per cent in 1971–81. After that, it increased to 34.44 per cent in 1981–91, 36.02 per cent in 1991-2001 and finally came down to 24.65 per cent in 2001–11. But, in that 50 (fifty) years, the Muslims of the country, increased by 2.67 times. The DG of Christians was comparatively less and in 1961–71, it was 32.58 per cent and then it came down to 13.72 per cent in 1971–81. Thereafter, it again increased and reached to 21.43 per cent in 1981–91, 22.61 per cent in 1991-2001 and again came down to 15.53 per cent in 2001–11 and in 50 (fifty) years, the Christians increased by 1.59 times.

Further it appears that, the proportion of Hindus of the country was much higher than the proportion of Hindus of NE Region, in all the census years. But on the other hand, the proportion of Muslims as well as of the Christians of NER was higher than their respective proportion in the country as a whole. It also appears that, the growth of both Muslims and Christians was faster in the NE Region than their growth in the country as a whole. However, in respect of Hindus, there was one similarity, both in NER and in the country. It is seen that, the proportion of Hindus was going down over the years in the North Eastern Region and also in the country, though it was much faster in NE Region. It is seen that, in last 50 (fifty) years, i.e. from 1961 to 2011, the proportion of Hindus of NE Region decreased by 10.10 per cent as against 3.65 per cent of the country in that period.

Most of the North Eastern States are hilly and tribal dominated. In the initial stages of planning era, there was acute shortage of educated and skilled manpower for administration and implementation of different developmental schemes and for other activities in these states. Therefore, in sixties and seventies a large number of people from neighbouring Assam and other parts of the country went there for employment and for other economic activities. These people were mostly Hindus. But gradually, the local people became educated and started taking over the jobs and other activities, and therefore, the dependency on outside people started decreasing.

Appendix-4.1

State-wise Distribution of Population by Religion in different Census Years

Sl. No.	Name of the States/Region/India	Religious Communities	Number of persons in different Census years					
			1961	1971	1981	1991	2001	2011
1	2	3	4	5	6	7	8	9
1	Arunachal Pradesh	Hindus	25599	102832	184732	320212	379935	401876
		Muslims	1008	842	5073	11922	20675	27045
		Christians	1713	3684	27306	89013	205548	418732
		Sikhs	745	1255	1231	1205	1865	3287
		Buddhists	5809	61400	86483	111372	143028	162815
		Jains	14	39	42	64	216	771
		Others	1784	296674	326000	313118	337399	362553
		Religion not stated	299886	785	972	17652	9302	6648
		All Religions	336558	467511	631839	864558	1097968	1383727
2	Assam	Hindus	7884921	10604618	*	15047293	17296455	19180759
		Muslims	2765509	3592124	*	6373204	8240611	10679345
		Christians	764553	381010	*	744367	986589	1165867
		Sikhs	9686	11920	*	16492	22519	20672
		Buddhists	36513	22565	*	64008	51029	54993
		Jains	9468	12917	*	20645	23957	25949
		Others	394089	-	*	138230	22999	27118
		Religion not stated	8033	-	*	10083	11369	50873
		All Religions	11872772	14625154	*	22414322	26655528	31205576
3	Manipur	Hindus	481112	632597	853180	1059470	996894	1181876
		Muslims	48588	70969	99327	133535	190939	239836

1	2	3	4	5	6	7	8	9
		Christians	152043	279243	421702	626669	737578	1179043
		Sikhs	523	1028	992	1301	1653	1527
		Buddhists	325	495	473	711	1926	7084
		Jains	778	1408	975	1337	1461	1692
		Others	-	83167	35490	14066	235280	233767
		Religion not stated	96668	3846	8814	60	1057	10969
		All Religions	780037	1072753	1420953	1837149	2166788	2855794
4	Meghalaya	Hindus	***	187140	240831	260306	307822	342078
		Muslims	***	26347	41434	61462	99169	130399
		Christians	***	475267	702854	1146092	1628986	2213027
		Sikhs	***	1262	1674	2612	3110	3045
		Buddhists	***	1878	2739	2934	4703	9864
		Jains	***	268	542	445	772	627
		Others	***	318168	344215	298466	267245	258271
		Religion not stated	***	1369	1530	2461	7015	9578
		All Religions	***	1011699	1335819	1774778	2318822	2966889
5	Mizoram	Hindus	**	21229	35245	34788	31562	30136
		Muslims	**	1882	2205	4538	10099	14832
		Christians	**	286141	413840	591342	772809	956331
		Sikhs	**	427	421	299	326	286
		Buddhists	**	22647	40429	54024	70494	93411
		Jains	**	-	11	4	179	376
		Others	**	62	1606	1859	2443	808
		Religion not stated	**	2	0	2902	661	1026
		All Religions	**	332390	493757	689756	888573	1097206
6	Nagaland	Hindus	34677	59031	111266	122473	153162	173054
		Muslims	891	2966	11806	20642	35002	48963
		Christians	195588	344798	621590	1057940	1790349	1739651

1	2	3	4	5	6	7	8	9
		Sikhs	255	687	743	732	1152	1890
		Buddhists	42	179	517	581	1356	6759
		Jains	263	627	1153	1202	2093	2655
		Others	137444	108159	27852	5870	6108	3214
		Religion not stated	40	2	3	106	814	2316
		All Religions	369200	516449	774930	1209546	1990036	1978502
7	Tripura	Hindus	867998	1393689	1834218	2384934	2739310	3063903
		Muslims	230002	103962	138529	196495	254442	316042
		Christians	10039	15713	24872	46472	102489	159882
		Sikhs	49	318	285	740	1182	1070
		Buddhists	33716	42285	54806	128260	98922	125385
		Jains	195	375	297	301	477	860
		Others	4	-	27	2	1277	1514
		Religion not stated	2	-	24	1	1104	5261
		All Religions	1142005	1556342	2053058	2757205	3199203	3673917
8	Sub-Total, NER	Hindus	9294307	13001136	3259472	19229476	21905140	24373682
		Muslims	3045998	3799092	298374	6801798	8850937	11456462
		Christians	1123936	1785856	2212164	4301895	6224348	7832533
		Sikhs	11258	16897	5346	23381	31807	31777
		Buddhists	76405	151449	185447	361890	371458	460311
		Jains	10718	15634	3020	23998	29155	32930
		Others	533321	806230	735190	771611	872751	887245
		Religion not stated	404629	6004	11343	33265	31322	86671
		All Religions	14500572	19582298	6710356	31547314	38316918	45161611
9	Sikkim	Hindus	108165	144544	212780	277881	329548	352662
		Muslims	1207	335	3241	3849	7693	9867
		Christians	2813	1663	7015	13413	36115	60522
		Sikhs	72	94	322	375	1176	1868

1	2	3	4	5	6	7	8	9
		Buddhists	49894	62617	90848	110371	152042	167216
		Jains	19	191	108	40	183	314
		Others	-	399	1987	374	12926	16300
		Religion not stated	19	0	84	154	1168	1828
		All Religions	162189	209843	316385	406457	540851	610577
10	Grand-Total, NER	Hindus	9402472	13145680	3472252	19507357	22234688	24726344
		Muslims	3047205	3799427	301615	6805647	8858630	11466329
		Christians	1126749	1787519	2219179	4315308	6260463	7893055
		Sikhs	11330	16991	5668	23756	32983	33645
		Buddhists	126299	214066	276295	472261	523500	627527
		Jains	10737	15825	3128	24038	29338	33244
		Others	533321	806629	737177	771985	885677	903545
		Religion not stated	404648	6004	11427	33419	32490	88499
		All Religions	14662761	19792141	7026741	31953771	38857769	45772188
11	India	Hindus	366526866	453292086	549779481	687646721	827578868	966257353
		Muslims	46940799	61417934	75512439	101596057	138188240	172245158
		Christians	10728086	14223382	16165447	19640284	24080016	27819588
		Sikhs	7845915	10378797	13078146	16259744	19215730	20833116
		Buddhists	3256036	3812325	4719796	6387500	7955207	8442972
		Jains	2027281	2604646	3206038	3352706	4225053	4451753
		Others	1498895	2184556	2766285	3269355	6639626	7937734
		Religion not stated	410893	36083	60217	431621	727588	2867303
		All Religions	439234771	547949809	665287849	838583988	1028610328	1210854977

Source: Census of India, 2001 (First Report on Religion Data, Abstract), Registrar General and Census Commissioner, India, New Delhi.

Note: * means No Census conducted. ** means information included under Assam. ***information not available.

Appendix-4.2

State-wise Distribution of Population by Religion with Rural-Urban break-up in different Census Years

Sl. No.	Name of the States/Region/India	Religious Communities	Census year, 1971								
			Total			Rural			Urban		
			Person	Male	Female	Person	Male	Female	Person	Male	Female
1	2	3	4	5	6	7	8	9	10	11	12
1	Arunachal Pradesh	Hindus	102832	68080	34752	90597	59335	31262	12235	8745	3490
		Muslims	842	641	201	523	401	122	319	240	79
		Christians	3684	2276	1408	3301	2009	1292	383	267	116
		Sikhs	1255	987	268	997	795	202	258	192	66
		Buddhists	61400	31612	29788	60136	30825	29311	1264	787	477
		Jains	39	28	11	9	9	0	30	19	11
		Others	296674	147227	149447	293875	145615	148260	2799	1612	1187
		Religion not stated	785	380	405	785	380	405	0	0	0
		All Religions	467511	251231	216280	450223	239369	210854	17288	11862	5426
2	Assam	Hindus	10604618	5617020	4987598	9489620	4976477	4513143	1114998	640543	474455
		Muslims	3592124	1872507	1719617	3447593	1790644	1656949	144531	81863	62668
		Christians	381010	198226	182784	368447	191574	176873	12563	6652	5911
		Sikhs	11920	6643	5277	5110	2842	2268	6810	3801	3009

1	2	3	4	5	6	7	8	9	10	11	12
		Buddhists	22565	12033	10532	20467	10895	9572	2098	1138	960
		Jains	12914	7810	5104	4692	2698	1994	8222	5112	3110
		Others	2	2	0	1	1	0	1	1	0
		Religion not stated	0	0	0	0	0	0	0	0	0
		All Religions	14625153	7714241	6910912	13335930	6975131	6360799	1289223	739110	550113
3	Manipur	Hindus	632597	321209	311388	512939	261148	251791	119658	60061	59597
		Muslims	70969	35937	35032	69265	35056	34209	1704	881	823
		Christians	279243	139668	139575	267202	133312	133890	12041	6356	5685
		Sikhs	1028	713	315	410	341	69	618	372	246
		Buddhists	495	264	231	449	264	185	46	0	46
		Jains	1408	769	639	418	198	220	990	571	419
		Others	83167	41226	41941	76732	38023	38709	6435	3203	3232
		Religion not stated	3846	1889	1957	3846	1889	1957	0	0	0
		All Religions	1072753	541675	531078	931261	470231	461030	141492	71444	70048
4	Meghalaya	Hindus	187140	105177	81963	115839	63576	52263	71301	41601	29700
		Muslims	26347	14238	12109	22042	11510	10532	4305	2728	1577
		Christians	475267	238895	236372	415131	209528	205603	60136	29367	30769
		Sikhs	1262	736	526	125	76	49	1137	660	477
		Buddhists	1878	1054	824	1311	726	585	567	328	239
		Jains	268	162	106	147	88	59	121	74	47
		Others	318168	160008	158160	308577	155341	153236	9591	4667	4924
		Religion not stated	1369	697	672	1357	688	669	12	9	3
		All Religions	1011699	520967	490732	864529	441533	422996	147170	79434	67736

1	2	3	4	5	6	7	8	9	10	11	12
5	Mizoram	Hindus	21229	16409	4820	18864	14731	4133	2365	1678	687
		Muslims	1882	1256	626	1477	871	606	405	385	20
		Christians	286141	140822	145319	251182	123400	127782	34959	17422	17537
		Sikhs	427	421	6	420	415	5	7	6	1
		Buddhists	22647	11878	10769	22624	11867	10757	23	11	12
		Jains	3	3	0	3	3	0	0	0	0
		Others	61	35	26	61	35	26	0	0	0
		Religion not stated	0	0	0	0	0	0	0	0	0
		All Religions	332390	170824	161566	294631	151322	143309	37759	19502	18257
6	Nagaland	Hindus	59031	42414	16617	30731	20844	9887	28300	21570	6730
		Muslims	2966	2300	666	1228	883	345	1738	1417	321
		Christians	344798	175266	169532	325452	164618	160834	19346	10648	8698
		Sikhs	687	518	169	87	65	22	600	453	147
		Buddhists	179	126	53	91	70	21	88	56	32
		Jains	627	403	224	5	3	2	622	400	222
		Others	108159	55055	53104	107459	54686	52773	700	369	331
		Religion not stated	2	2	0	2	2	0	0	0	0
		All Religions	516449	276084	240365	465055	241171	223884	51394	34913	16481
7	Tripura	Hindus	1393689	717124	676565	1237146	636351	600795	156543	80773	75770
		Muslims	103962	53374	50588	98736	50597	48139	5226	2777	2449
		Christians	15713	8202	7511	15457	8058	7399	256	144	112
		Sikhs	318	147	171	288	124	164	30	23	7

1	2	3	4	5	6	7	8	9	10	11	12
		Buddhists	42285	22001	20284	42140	21924	20216	145	77	68
		Jains	375	278	97	215	173	42	160	105	55
		Others	0	0	0	0	0	0	0	0	0
		Religion not stated	0	0	0	0	0	0	0	0	0
		All Religions	1556342	801126	755216	1393982	717227	676755	162360	83899	78461
8	Sub-Total, NER	Hindus	13001136	6887433	6113703	11495736	6032462	5463274	1505400	854971	650429
		Muslims	3799092	1980253	1818839	3640864	1889962	1750902	158228	90291	67937
		Christians	1785856	903355	882501	1646172	832499	813673	139684	70856	68828
		Sikhs	16897	10165	6732	7437	4658	2779	9460	5507	3953
		Buddhists	151449	78968	72481	147218	76571	70647	4231	2397	1834
		Jains	15634	9453	6181	5489	3172	2317	10145	6281	3864
		Others	806231	403553	402678	786705	393701	393004	19526	9852	9674
		Religion not stated	6002	2968	3034	5990	2959	3031	12	9	3
		All Religions	19582297	10276148	9306149	17735611	9235984	8499627	1846686	1040164	806522
9	Sikkim	Hindus	144544	78461	66083	131271	70231	61040	13273	8230	5043
		Muslims	335	261	74	131	106	25	204	155	49
		Christians	1663	935	728	1231	721	510	432	214	218
		Sikhs	94	80	14	68	62	6	26	18	8
		Buddhists	62617	32581	30036	56900	29506	27394	5717	3075	2642
		Jains	191	112	79	175	101	74	16	11	5
		Others	399	232	167	399	232	167	0	0	0
		Religion not stated	0	0	0	0	0	0	0	0	0
		All Religions	209843	112662	97181	190175	100959	89216	19668	11703	7965

1	2	3	4	5	6	7	8	9	10	11	12
10	Grand-Total, NER	Hindus	13145680	6965894	6179786	11627007	6102693	5524314	1518673	863201	655472
		Muslims	3799427	1980514	1818913	3640995	1890068	1750927	158432	90446	67986
		Christians	1787519	904290	883229	1647403	833220	814183	140116	71070	69046
		Sikhs	16991	10245	6746	7505	4720	2785	9486	5525	3961
		Buddhists	214066	111549	102517	204118	106077	98041	9948	5472	4476
		Jains	15825	9565	6260	5664	3273	2391	10161	6292	3869
		Others	806630	403785	402845	787104	393933	393171	19526	9852	9674
		Religion not stated	6002	2968	3034	5990	2959	3031	12	9	3
		All Religions	19792140	10388810	9403330	17925786	9336943	8588843	1866354	1051867	814487
11	India	Hindus	453292086	234837669	218454417	370110765	189861236	180249529	83181321	44976433	38204888
		Muslims	61417934	31961789	29456145	43732953	22519401	21213552	17684981	9442388	8242593
		Christians	14223382	7161792	7061590	10666676	5356761	5309915	3556706	1805031	1751675
		Sikhs	10378797	5583846	4794951	8402738	4510483	3892255	1976059	1073363	902696
		Buddhists	3812325	1942757	1869568	2849277	1430717	1418560	963048	512040	451008
		Jains	2604646	1342870	1261776	1046406	523992	522414	1558240	818878	739362
		Others	2184556	1086525	1098031	2021667	1003791	1017876	162889	82734	80155
		Religion not stated	36083	19366	16717	25018	12603	12415	11065	6763	4302
		All Religions	547949809	283936614	264013195	438855500	225218934	213636516	109094309	58717630	50376679

Source: Census of India, 1971 (Series-1), Registrar General & Census Commissioner, New Delhi.

Appendix-4.3
State-wise Distribution of Population by Religion with Rural-Urban Break-up in different Census Years

Sl. No.	Name of the States/Region/ India	Religious Communities	Census year, 1981								
			Total			Rural			Urban		
			Person	Male	Female	Person	Male	Female	Person	Male	Female
1	2	3	4	5	6	7	8	9	10	11	12
1	Arunachal Pradesh	Hindus	184732	112349	72383	157082	95071	62011	27650	17278	10372
		Muslims	5073	3608	1465	3260	2342	918	1813	1266	547
		Christians	27306	14752	12554	25887	13812	12075	1419	940	479
		Sikhs	1231	711	520	948	530	418	283	181	102
		Buddhists	86483	44638	41845	84180	43386	40794	2303	1252	1051
		Jains	42	27	15	12	8	4	30	19	11
		Others	326000	162685	163315	318237	158312	159925	7763	4373	3390
		Religion not stated	972	552	420	805	425	380	167	127	40
		All Religions	631839	339322	292517	590411	313886	276525	41428	25436	15992
2	Assam*	Hindus	*	*	*	*	*	*	*	*	*
		Muslims	*	*	*	*	*	*	*	*	*
		Christians	*	*	*	*	*	*	*	*	*
		Sikhs	*	*	*	*	*	*	*	*	*

1	2	3	4	5	6	7	8	9	10	11	12
		Buddhists	*	*	*	*	*	*	*	*	*
		Jains	*	*	*	*	*	*	*	*	*
		Others	*	*	*	*	*	*	*	*	*
		Religion not stated	*	*	*	*	*	*	*	*	*
		All Religions	*	*	*	*	*	*	*	*	*
3	Manipur	Hindus	853180	432564	420616	557388	283143	274245	295792	149421	146371
		Muslims	99327	50507	48820	76492	38704	37788	22835	11803	11032
		Christians	421702	214146	207556	374507	189711	184796	47195	24435	22760
		Sikhs	992	634	358	148	134	14	844	500	344
		Buddhists	473	278	195	289	171	118	184	107	77
		Jains	975	572	403	8	8	0	967	564	403
		Others	35490	17815	17675	30033	15066	14967	5457	2749	2708
		Religion not stated	8814	4490	4324	6628	3394	3234	2186	1096	1090
		All Religions	1420953	721006	699947	1045493	530331	515162	375460	190675	184785
4	Meghalaya	Hindus	240831	132062	108769	141819	76578	65241	99012	55484	43528
		Muslims	41434	22087	19347	34219	17696	16523	7215	4391	2824
		Christians	702854	354203	348651	593102	299907	293195	109752	54296	55456
		Sikhs	1674	855	819	403	22[illegible]	182	1271	634	637
		Buddhists	2739	1453	1286	1023	520	503	1716	933	783
		Jains	542	374	168	200	130	70	342	244	98
		Others	344215	171867	172348	322298	161160	161138	21917	10707	11210
		Religion not stated	1530	809	72[illegible]	1422	746	676	108	63	45
		All Religions	1335819	683710	652109	1094486	556958	537528	241333	126752	114581

1	2	3	4	5	6	7	8	9	10	11	12
5	Mizoram	Hindus	35245	25660	9585	24423	17621	6802	10822	8039	2783
		Muslims	2205	1812	393	1064	826	238	1141	986	155
		Christians	413840	207485	206355	304409	152423	151986	109431	55062	54369
		Sikhs	421	376	45	238	238	0	183	138	45
		Buddhists	40429	21073	19356	40336	21009	19327	93	64	29
		Jains	11	7	4	0	0	0	11	7	4
		Others	1606	826	780	1473	757	716	133	69	64
		Religion not stated	-	-	-	-	-	-	-	-	-
		All Religions	493757	257239	236518	371943	192874	179069	121814	64365	57449
6	Nagaland	Hindus	111266	72081	39185	66959	43193	23766	44307	28888	15419
		Muslims	11806	7881	3925	7223	4498	2725	4583	3383	1200
		Christians	621590	320241	301349	552370	282564	269806	69220	37677	31543
		Sikhs	743	531	212	281	241	40	462	290	172
		Buddhists	517	300	217	183	108	75	334	192	142
		Jains	1153	691	462	15	12	3	1138	679	459
		Others	27852	14182	13670	27662	14080	13582	190	102	88
		Religion not stated	3	3	0	3	3	0	0	0	0
		All Religions	774930	415910	359020	654696	344699	309997	120234	71211	49023
7	Tripura	Hindus	1834218	941722	892496	1616165	830488	785677	218053	111234	106819
		Muslims	138529	71428	67101	132169	68079	64090	6360	3349	3011
		Christians	24872	12950	11922	24358	12627	11731	514	323	191

1	2	3	4	5	6	7	8	9	10	11	12
		Sikhs	285	223	62	188	148	40	97	75	22
		Buddhists	54806	28307	26499	54476	28122	26354	330	185	145
		Jains	297	186	111	101	76	25	196	110	86
		Others	27	16	11	14	8	6	13	8	5
		Religion not stated	24	14	10	19	10	9	5	4	1
		All Religions	2053058	1054846	998212	1827490	939558	887932	225568	115288	110280
8	Sub-Total, NER	Hindus	3259472	1716438	1543034	2563836	1346094	1217742	695636	370344	325292
		Muslims	298374	157323	141051	254427	132145	122282	43947	25178	18769
		Christians	2212164	1123777	1088387	1874633	951044	923589	337531	172733	164798
		Sikhs	5346	3330	2016	2206	1512	694	3140	1818	1322
		Buddhists	185447	96049	89398	180487	93316	87171	4960	2733	2227
		Jains	3020	1857	1153	336	234	102	2684	1623	1061
		Others	735190	367391	367799	699717	349383	350334	35473	18008	17465
		Religion not stated	11343	5868	5475	8877	4578	4299	2466	1290	1176
		All Religions	6710356	3472033	3238323	5584519	2878306	2706213	1125837	593727	532110
9	Sikkim	Hindus	212780	116207	96573	179506	96242	83264	33274	19965	13309
		Muslims	3241	2708	533	1513	1335	178	1728	1373	355
		Christians	7015	3753	3262	5112	2732	2380	1903	1021	882
		Sikhs	322	209	113	171	112	59	151	97	54
		Buddhists	90848	48408	42440	77006	40879	36127	13842	7529	6313
		Jains	108	79	29	16	16	0	92	63	29
		Others	1987	1023	964	1902	978	924	85	45	40

1	2	3	4	5	6	7	8	9	10	11	12
		Religion not stated	84	53	31	75	47	28	9	6	3
		All Religions	316385	172440	143945	265301	142341	122960	51084	30099	20985
10	Grand-Total, NER	Hindus	3472252	1832645	1639607	2743342	1442336	1301006	728910	390309	338601
		Muslims	301615	160031	141584	255940	133480	122460	45675	26551	19124
		Christians	2219179	1127530	1091649	1879745	953776	925969	339434	173754	165680
		Sikhs	5668	3539	2129	2377	1624	753	3291	1915	1376
		Buddhists	276295	144457	131838	257493	134195	123298	18802	10262	8540
		Jains	3128	1936	1192	352	250	102	2776	1686	1090
		Others	737177	368414	368763	701619	350361	351258	35558	18053	17505
		Religion not stated	11427	5921	5506	8952	4625	4327	2475	1296	1179
		All Religions	7026741	3644473	3382268	5849820	3020647	2829173	1176921	623826	553095
11	India	Hindus	549724717	284365289	265359428	429086621	219882993	209203628	120638096	64482296	56155800
		Muslims	75571514	39019643	36551871	49855797	25503283	24352514	25715717	13516360	12199357
		Christians	16174498	8118081	8056417	11458726	5739231	5719495	4715772	2378850	2336922
		Sikhs	13078146	6957891	6120255	10245347	5445357	4799990	2832799	1512534	1320265
		Buddhists	4719900	2416824	2303076	3209856	1616225	1593631	1510044	800599	709445
		Jains	3192572	1644578	1547994	1155174	577987	577187	2037398	1066591	970807
		Others	2766285	1376106	1390179	2551606	1265464	1286142	214679	110642	104037
		Religion not stated	60217	32011	28206	44551	23480	21071	15666	8531	7135
		All Religions	665287849	343930423	321357426	507607678	260054020	247553658	157680171	83876403	73803768

Source: Census of India, 1981, Series-1, Paper 3 of 1984, Registrar General & Census Commissioner, New Delhi.

* Census was not conducted in Assam.

\- means information not available.

Appendix-4.4

State-wise Distribution of Population by Religion with Rural-Urban Break-up in different Census Years

Sl. No.	Name of the States/Region/India	Religious Communities	Census year, 1991								
			Total			Rural			Urban		
			Person	Male	Female	Person	Male	Female	Person	Male	Female
1	2	3	4	5	6	7	8	9	10	11	12
1	Arunachal Pradesh	Hindus	320212	187501	132711	248520	144619	103901	71692	42882	28810
		Muslims	11922	7788	4134	6395	4230	2165	5527	3558	1969
		Christians	89013	46234	42779	84419	43677	40742	4594	2557	2037
		Sikhs	1205	808	397	729	508	221	476	300	176
		Buddhists	111372	57064	54308	106378	54336	51992	4994	2678	2316
		Jains	64	42	22	17	13	4	47	29	18
		Others	313118	156809	156309	290124	144908	145216	22994	11901	11093
		Religion not stated	17652	8758	8894	17348	8625	8723	304	133	171
		All Religions	864558	465004	399554	753930	400966	352964	110628	64038	46590
2	Assam	Hindus	15047293	7858071	7189222	12967859	6723515	6244344	2079434	1134556	944878
		Muslims	6373204	3289295	3083909	6036072	3108598	2927474	337132	180697	156435
		Christians	744367	381564	362803	714736	366011	348725	29631	15553	14078

1	2	3	4	5	6	7	8	9	10	11	12
		Sikhs	16492	9272	7220	5153	2922	2231	11339	6350	4989
		Buddhists	64008	33267	30741	59528	30821	28707	4480	2446	2034
		Jains	20645	11512	9133	4512	2577	1935	16133	8935	7198
		Others	138230	69501	68729	136846	68785	68061	1384	716	668
		Religion not stated	10083	5507	4576	1821	932	889	8262	4575	3687
		All Religions	22414322	11657989	10756333	19926527	10304161	9622366	2487795	1353828	1133967
3	Manipur	Hindus	1059470	540204	519266	650102	333606	316496	409368	206598	202770
		Muslims	133535	68201	65334	94236	48083	46153	39299	20118	19181
		Christians	626669	320840	305829	577221	295516	281705	49448	25324	24124
		Sikhs	1301	912	389	418	363	55	883	549	334
		Buddhists	711	383	328	561	289	272	150	94	56
		Jains	1337	706	631	27	11	16	1310	695	615
		Others	14066	7080	6986	8914	4512	4402	5152	2568	2584
		Religion not stated	60	33	27	25	15	10	35	18	17
		All Religions	1837149	938359	898790	1331504	682395	649109	505645	255964	249681
4	Meghalaya	Hindus	260306	144641	115665	146151	78958	67193	114155	65683	48472
		Muslims	61462	32887	28575	53470	27813	25657	7992	5074	2918
		Christians	1146092	575628	570464	965185	486953	478232	180907	88675	92232
		Sikhs	2612	1494	1118	206	158	48	2406	1336	1070
		Buddhists	2934	1554	1380	1103	564	539	1831	990	841
		Jains	445	254	191	49	26	23	396	228	168
		Others	298466	149961	148505	276863	139497	137366	21603	10464	11139

1	2	3	4	5	6	7	8	9	10	11	12
		Religion not stated	2461	1268	1193	1704	896	808	757	372	385
		All Religions	1774778	907687	867091	1444731	734865	709866	330047	172822	157225
5	Mizoram	Hindus	34788	25327	9461	17825	13211	4614	16963	12116	4847
		Muslims	4538	4126	412	732	690	42	3806	3436	370
		Christians	591342	298630	292712	298337	151824	146513	293005	146806	146199
		Sikhs	299	268	31	179	165	14	120	103	17
		Buddhists	54024	28193	25831	53234	27739	25495	790	454	336
		Jains	4	4	0	0	0	0	4	4	0
		Others	1859	970	889	845	451	394	1014	519	495
		Religion not stated	2902	1460	1442	658	334	324	2244	1126	1118
		All Religions	689756	358978	330778	371810	194414	177396	317946	164564	153382
6	Nagaland	Hindus	122473	78928	43545	61207	38874	22333	61266	40654	21212
		Muslims	20642	12864	7778	12438	7293	5145	8204	5571	2633
		Christians	1057940	544892	513048	921225	472679	448546	136715	72213	64502
		Sikhs	732	520	212	220	185	35	512	335	177
		Buddhists	581	319	262	248	129	119	333	190	143
		Jains	1202	690	512	12	9	3	1190	681	509
		Others	5870	3011	2859	5868	3009	2859	2	2	0
		Religion not stated	106	58	48	105	57	48	1	1	0
		All Religions	1209546	641282	568264	1001323	522235	479088	208223	119047	89176
7	Tripura	Hindus	2384934	1226645	1158289	1977471	1018725	958746	407463	207920	199543
		Muslims	196495	100799	95696	184647	94665	89982	11848	6134	5714

1	2	3	4	5	6	7	8	9	10	11	12
		Christians	46472	24202	22270	45265	23522	21743	1207	680	527
		Sikhs	740	636	104	692	610	82	48	26	22
		Buddhists	128260	65465	62795	127323	64949	62374	937	516	421
		Jains	301	181	120	85	57	28	216	124	92
		Others	2	1	1	0	0	0	2	1	1
		Religion not stated	1	1	0	1	1	0	0	0	0
		All Religions	2757205	1417930	1339275	2335484	1202529	1132955	421721	215401	206320
8	Sub-Total, NER	Hindus	19229476	10061317	9168159	16069135	8351508	7717627	3160341	1709809	1450532
		Muslims	6801798	3515960	3285838	6387990	3291372	3096618	413808	224588	189220
		Christians	4301895	2191990	2109905	3606388	1840182	1766206	695507	351808	343699
		Sikhs	23381	13910	9471	7597	4911	2686	15784	8999	6785
		Buddhists	361890	186245	175645	348375	178877	169498	13515	7368	6147
		Jains	23998	13389	10609	4702	2693	2009	19296	10696	8600
		Others	771611	387333	384278	719460	361162	358298	52151	26171	25980
		Religion not stated	33265	17085	16180	21662	10860	10802	11603	6225	5378
		All Religions	31547314	16387229	15160085	27165309	14041565	13123744	4382005	2345664	2036341
9	Sikkim	Hindus	277881	148305	129576	252888	133956	118932	24993	14349	10644
		Muslims	3849	2735	1114	2252	1553	699	1597	1182	415
		Christians	13413	6927	6486	11790	6089	5701	1623	838	785
		Sikhs	375	202	173	290	154	136	85	48	37
		Buddhists	110371	57945	52426	101812	53294	48518	8559	4651	3908
		Jains	40	26	14	0	0	0	40	26	14

1	2	3	4	5	6	7	8	9	10	11	12
		Others	374	210	164	301	171	130	73	39	34
		Religion not stated	154	77	77	118	60	58	36	17	19
		All Religions	406457	216427	190030	369451	195277	174174	37006	21150	15856
10	Grand-Total, NER	Hindus	19507357	10209622	9297735	16322023	8485464	7836559	3185334	1724158	1461176
		Muslims	6805647	3518695	3286952	6390242	3292925	3097317	415405	225770	189635
		Christians	4315308	2198917	2116391	3618178	1846271	1771907	697130	352646	344484
		Sikhs	23756	14112	9644	7887	5065	2822	15869	9047	6822
		Buddhists	472261	244190	228071	450187	232171	218016	22074	12019	10055
		Jains	24038	13415	10623	4702	2693	2009	19336	10722	8614
		Others	771985	387543	384442	719761	361333	358428	52224	26210	26014
		Religion not stated	33419	17162	16257	21780	10920	10860	11639	6242	5397
		All Religions	31953771	16603656	15350115	27534760	14236842	13297918	4419011	2366814	2052197
11	India	Hindus	687646721	357252833	330393883	522896625	269935107	252961518	164750096	87317726	77432370
		Muslims	101596057	52631365	48964692	65563695	33714204	31849491	36032362	18917161	17115201
		Christians	19640284	9848930	9791354	13485261	6772296	6712965	6155023	3076634	3078389
		Sikhs	16259744	8610508	7649236	12473430	6604366	5869064	3786314	2006142	1780172
		Buddhists	6387500	3272200	3115300	4127484	2095172	2032312	2260016	1177028	1082988
		Jains	3352706	1722715	1629991	997718	505578	492140	2354988	1217137	1137851
		Others	3269355	1649354	1620001	2981632	1501547	1480085	287723	147807	139916
		Religion not stated	415569	220253	195316	270479	142935	127544	145090	77318	67772
		All Religions	838567936	435208158	403359778	622796324	321271205	301525119	215771612	113936953	101834659

Source: Census of India, 1991, Paper 1 of 1995, Registrar General & Census Commissioner, India, New Delhi.

Appendix-4.5

State-wise Distribution of Population by Religion with Rural-Urban Break-up in Different Census Years

Sl. No.	Name of the States/Region/ India	Religious Communities	Census year, 2001								
			Total			Rural			Urban		
			Person	Male	Female	Person	Male	Female	Person	Male	Female
1	2	3	4	5	6	7	8	9	10	11	12
1	Arunachal Pradesh	Hindus	379935	217195	162740	258225	146466	111759	121710	70729	50981
		Muslims	20675	12726	7949	10369	6411	3958	10306	6315	3991
		Christians	205548	102606	102942	183338	91695	91643	22210	10911	11299
		Sikhs	1865	1475	390	864	706	158	1001	769	232
		Buddhists	143028	72618	70410	132323	67107	65216	10705	5511	5194
		Jains	216	130	86	86	52	34	130	78	52
		Others	337399	168613	168786	275798	137749	138049	61601	30864	30737
		Religion not stated	9302	4578	4724	9084	4494	4590	218	84	134
		All Religions	1097968	579941	518027	870087	454680	415407	227881	125261	102620
2	Assam	Hindus	17296455	8951108	8345347	14477966	7444777	7033189	2818489	1506331	1312158
		Muslims	8240611	4252691	3987920	7714619	3973086	3741533	525992	279605	246387
		Christians	986589	502756	483833	936008	476178	459830	50581	26578	24003
		Sikhs	22519	13508	9011	7634	4633	3001	14885	8875	6010

1	2	3	4	5	6	7	8	9	10	11	12
		Buddhists	51029	26322	24707	44546	22834	21712	6483	3488	2995
		Jains	23957	12840	11117	3603	1994	1609	20354	10846	9508
		Others	22999	11795	11204	21608	11028	10580	1391	767	624
		Religion not stated	11369	6017	5352	10304	5415	4889	1065	602	463
		All Religions	26655528	13777037	12878491	23216288	11939945	11276343	3439240	1837092	1602148
3	Manipur	Hindus	996894	505108	491783	586114	301175	284939	410780	203933	206847
		Muslims	190939	96787	94152	135494	68759	66735	55445	28028	27417
		Christians	737578	373173	364405	704673	356769	347904	32905	16404	16501
		Sikhs	1653	1091	562	843	634	209	810	457	353
		Buddhists	1926	1025	901	1768	924	844	158	101	57
		Jains	1461	793	668	92	51	41	1369	742	627
		Others	235280	117106	118174	161101	80256	80845	74179	36850	37329
		Religion not stated	1057	551	506	735	385	350	322	166	156
		All Religions	2166788	1095634	1071154	1590820	808953	781867	575968	286681	289287
4	Meghalaya	Hindus	307822	168517	139305	181473	99028	82445	126349	69489	56860
		Muslims	99169	52455	46714	87021	45182	41839	12148	7273	4875
		Christians	1628986	812961	816025	1344515	675876	668639	284471	137085	147386
		Sikhs	3110	1810	1300	876	592	284	2234	1218	1016
		Buddhists	4703	2513	2190	2431	1335	1096	2272	1178	1094
		Jains	772	405	367	340	179	161	432	226	206
		Others	267245	133899	133346	241619	121561	120058	25626	12338	13288
		Religion not stated	7015	3527	3488	6436	3246	3190	579	281	298
		All Religions	2318822	1176087	1142735	1864711	946999	917712	454111	229088	225023

1	2	3	4	5	6	7	8	9	10	11	12
5	Mizoram	Hindus	31562	23528	8034	10290	8588	1702	21272	14940	6332
		Muslims	10099	7946	2153	3318	2101	1217	6781	5845	936
		Christians	772809	389155	383654	362553	185013	177540	410256	204142	206114
		Sikhs	326	251	75	192	135	57	134	116	18
		Buddhists	70494	36540	33954	69385	35962	33423	1109	578	531
		Jains	179	103	76	134	72	62	45	31	14
		Others	2443	1231	1212	1442	722	720	1001	509	492
		Religion not stated	661	355	306	253	133	120	408	222	186
		All Religions	888573	459109	429464	447567	232726	214841	441006	226383	214623
6	Nagaland	Hindus	153162	96808	56354	73299	47274	26025	79863	49534	30329
		Muslims	35005	21690	13315	16632	9691	6941	18373	11999	6374
		Christians	1790349	922406	867943	1549221	798398	750823	241128	124008	117120
		Sikhs	1152	774	378	615	428	187	537	346	191
		Buddhists	1356	761	595	656	395	261	700	366	334
		Jains	2093	1130	963	109	63	46	1984	1067	917
		Others	6108	3150	2958	6025	3104	2921	83	46	37
		Religion not stated	811	422	389	692	363	329	119	59	60
		All Religions	1990036	1047141	942895	1647249	859716	787533	342787	187425	155362
7	Tripura	Hindus	2739310	1405428	1333882	2217025	1139427	1077598	522285	266001	256284
		Muslims	254442	130788	123654	236748	121586	115162	17694	9202	8492
		Christians	102489	52815	49674	99820	51326	48494	2669	1489	1180
		Sikhs	1182	1074	108	613	558	55	569	516	53

1	2	3	4	5	6	7	8	9	10	11	12
		Buddhists	98922	50575	48347	97148	49639	47539	1774	966	808
		Jains	477	249	228	190	106	84	287	143	144
		Others	1277	726	551	1107	611	496	170	115	55
		Religion not stated	1104	570	534	802	415	387	302	155	147
		All Religions	3199203	1642225	1556978	2653453	1363638	1289815	545750	278587	267163
8	Sub-Total, NER	Hindus	21905140	11367692	10537448	17804392	9186735	8617657	4100748	2180957	1919791
		Muslims	8850940	4575083	4275857	8204201	4226816	3977385	646739	348267	298472
		Christians	6224348	3155872	3068476	5180128	2635255	2544873	1044220	520617	523603
		Sikhs	31807	19983	11824	11637	7686	3951	20170	12297	7873
		Buddhists	371458	190354	181104	348257	178166	170091	23201	12188	11013
		Jains	29155	15650	13505	4554	2517	2037	24601	13133	11468
		Others	872751	436520	436231	708700	355031	353669	164051	81489	82562
		Religion not stated	31319	16020	15299	28306	14451	13855	3013	1569	1444
		All Religions	38316918	19777174	18539744	32290175	16606657	15683518	6026743	3170517	2856226
9	Sikkim	Hindus	329548	177900	151643	290384	156202	134182	39164	21698	17466
		Muslims	7693	5346	2347	4913	3393	1520	2780	1953	827
		Christians	36115	18428	17687	32192	16485	15707	3923	1943	1980
		Sikhs	1176	1061	115	1084	1009	75	92	52	40
		Buddhists	152042	78191	73851	138597	71364	67233	13445	6827	6618
		Jains	183	110	73	57	37	20	126	73	53
		Others	12926	6519	6407	12668	6397	6271	258	122	136
		Religion not stated	1168	929	239	1086	887	199	82	42	40
		All Religions	540851	288484	252367	480981	255774	225207	59870	32710	27160

1	2	3	4	5	6	7	8	9	10	11	12
10	Grand-Total, NER	Hindus	22234688	11545592	10689096	18094776	9342937	8751839	4139912	2202655	1937257
		Muslims	8858633	4580429	4278204	8209114	4230209	3978905	649519	350220	299299
		Christians	6260463	3174300	3086163	5212320	2651740	2560580	1048143	522560	525583
		Sikhs	32983	21044	11939	12721	8695	4026	20262	12349	7913
		Buddhists	523500	268545	254955	486854	249530	237324	36646	19015	17631
		Jains	29338	15760	13578	4611	2554	2057	24727	13206	11521
		Others	885677	443039	442638	721368	361428	359940	164309	81611	82698
		Religion not stated	32487	16949	15538	29392	15338	14054	3095	1611	1484
		All Religions	38857769	20065658	18792111	32771156	16862431	15908725	6086613	3203227	2883386
11	India	Hindus	827578868	428678554	398900314	611263295	314437535	296825760	216315573	114241019	102074554
		Muslims	138188240	71374134	66814106	88794744	45473491	43321253	49393496	25900643	23492853
		Christians	24080016	11984663	12095353	15893958	7943541	7950417	8186058	4041122	4144936
		Sikhs	19215730	10152298	9063432	14106481	7443893	6662588	5109249	2708405	2400844
		Buddhists	7955207	4074155	3881052	4893610	2499409	2394201	3061597	1574746	1486851
		Jains	4225053	2177398	2047655	1009347	521033	488314	3215706	1656365	1559341
		Others	6639626	3332551	3307075	6002468	3008524	2993944	637158	324027	313131
		Religion not stated	727588	383019	344569	526736	275248	251488	200852	107771	93081
		All Religions	1028610328	532156772	496453556	742490639	381602674	360887965	286119689	150554098	135565591

Source: Census of India, 2001, First Report on Religion Data, Registrar General & Census Commissioner, India, New Delhi.

Appendix-4.6

State-wise Distribution of Population by Religion with Rural-Urban Break-up in different Census Years

Sl. No.	Name of the States/Region/India	Religious Communities	Census year, 2011								
			Total			Rural			Urban		
			Person	Male	Female	Person	Male	Female	Person	Male	Female
1	2	3	4	5	6	7	8	9	10	11	12
1	Arunachal Pradesh	Hindus	401876	225172	176704	256727	142358	114369	145149	82814	62335
		Muslims	27045	15553	11492	12488	7215	5273	14557	8338	6219
		Christians	418732	205796	212936	349180	172208	176972	69552	33588	35964
		Sikhs	3287	2800	487	1587	1318	269	1700	1482	218
		Buddhists	162815	80988	81827	143726	71613	72113	19089	9375	9714
		Jains	771	371	400	561	268	293	210	103	107
		Others	362553	180044	182509	297021	148506	148515	65532	31538	33994
		Religion not stated	6648	3188	3460	5068	2525	2543	1580	663	917
		All Religions	1383727	713912	669815	1066358	546011	520347	317369	167901	149468
2	Assam	Hindus	19180759	9796805	9383954	15699871	8006062	7693809	3480888	1790743	1690145
		Muslims	10679345	5463393	5215952	9877218	5052341	4824877	802127	411052	391075
		Christians	1165867	587196	578671	1102715	555891	546824	63152	31305	31847
		Sikhs	20672	11815	8857	8242	5021	3221	12430	6794	5636
		Buddhists	54993	28089	26904	47732	24332	23400	7261	3757	3504

1	2	3	4	5	6	7	8	9	10	11	12
		Jains	25949	13543	12406	2858	1520	1338	23091	12023	11068
		Others	27118	13699	13419	25543	12897	12646	1575	802	773
		Religion not stated	50873	24903	25970	42855	20925	21930	8018	3978	4040
		All Religions	31205576	15939443	15266133	26807034	13678989	13128045	4398542	2260454	2138088
3	Manipur	Hindus	1181876	596220	585656	644751	331011	313740	537125	265209	271916
		Muslims	239836	120404	119432	156420	78777	77643	83416	41627	41789
		Christians	1179043	595478	583565	1067403	540712	526691	111640	54766	56874
		Sikhs	1527	964	563	735	513	222	792	451	341
		Buddhists	7084	3654	3430	4587	2407	2180	2497	1247	1250
		Jains	1692	862	830	368	197	171	1324	665	659
		Others	233767	115715	118052	139866	69540	70326	93901	46175	47726
		Religion not stated	10969	5289	5680	7510	3727	3783	3459	1562	1897
		All Religions	2855794	1438586	1417208	2021640	1026884	994756	834154	411702	422452
4	Meghalaya	Hindus	342078	183622	158456	190258	100081	90177	151820	83541	68279
		Muslims	130399	67827	62572	115041	58804	56237	15358	9023	6335
		Christians	2213027	1100492	1112535	1817419	911129	906290	395608	189363	206245
		Sikhs	3045	1640	1405	613	376	237	2432	1264	1168
		Buddhists	9864	5144	4720	6547	3397	3150	3317	1747	1570
		Jains	627	342	285	273	157	116	354	185	169
		Others	258271	127983	130288	232659	116026	116633	25612	11957	13655
		Religion not stated	9578	4782	4796	8629	4290	4339	949	492	457
		All Religions	2966889	1491832	1475057	2371439	1194260	1177179	595450	297572	297878

1	2	3	4	5	6	7	8	9	10	11	12
5	Mizoram	Hindus	30136	20013	10123	7194	4799	2395	22942	15214	7728
		Muslims	14832	9550	5282	6549	3615	2934	8283	5935	2348
		Christians	956331	476464	479867	419398	213209	206189	536933	263255	273678
		Sikhs	286	216	70	88	62	26	198	154	44
		Buddhists	93411	47970	45441	91112	46881	44231	2299	1089	1210
		Jains	376	208	168	260	140	120	116	68	48
		Others	808	402	406	434	222	212	374	180	194
		Religion not stated	1026	516	510	400	207	193	626	309	317
		All Religions	1097206	555339	541867	525435	269135	256300	571771	286204	285567
6	Nagaland	Hindus	173054	104851	68203	62934	38453	24481	110120	66398	43722
		Muslims	48963	28527	20436	23007	12723	10284	25956	15804	10152
		Christians	1739651	881927	857724	1310838	668171	642667	428813	213756	215057
		Sikhs	1890	1531	359	1116	999	117	774	532	242
		Buddhists	6759	3513	3246	4478	2385	2093	2281	1128	1153
		Jains	2655	1373	1282	421	230	191	2234	1143	1091
		Others	3214	1620	1594	2997	1514	1483	217	106	111
		Religion not stated	2316	1307	1009	1745	997	748	571	310	261
		All Religions	1978502	1024649	953853	1407536	725472	682064	570966	299177	271789
7	Tripura	Hindus	3063903	1563730	1500173	2168395	1110363	1058032	895508	453367	442141
		Muslims	316042	160930	155112	269621	137112	132509	46421	23818	22603
		Christians	159882	81480	78402	152170	77511	74659	7712	3969	3743
		Sikhs	1070	782	288	733	543	190	337	239	98

1	2	3	4	5	6	7	8	9	10	11	12
		Buddhists	125385	63545	61840	116608	59126	57482	8777	4419	4358
		Jains	860	453	407	421	209	212	439	244	195
		Others	1514	791	723	1224	630	594	290	161	129
		Religion not stated	5261	2665	2596	3292	1679	1613	1969	986	983
		All Religions	3673917	1874376	1799541	2712464	1387173	1325291	961453	487203	474250
8	Sub-Total, NER	Hindus	24373682	12490413	11883269	19030130	9733127	9297003	5343552	2757286	2586266
		Muslims	11456462	5866184	5590278	10460344	5350587	5109757	996118	515597	480521
		Christians	7832533	3928833	3903700	6219123	3138831	3080292	1613410	790002	823408
		Sikhs	31777	19748	12029	13114	8832	4282	18663	10916	7747
		Buddhists	460311	232903	227408	414790	210141	204649	45521	22762	22759
		Jains	32930	17152	15778	5162	2721	2441	27768	14431	13337
		Others	887245	440254	446991	699744	349335	350409	187501	90919	96582
		Religion not stated	86671	42650	44021	69499	34350	35149	17172	8300	8872
		All Religions	45161611	23038137	22123474	36911906	18827924	18083982	8249705	4210213	4039492
9	Sikkim	Hindus	352662	189972	162690	258280	139660	118620	94382	50312	44070
		Muslims	9867	6536	3331	3658	2683	975	6209	3853	2356
		Christians	60522	30290	30232	45678	23103	22575	14844	7187	7657
		Sikhs	1868	1592	276	1672	1477	195	196	115	81
		Buddhists	167216	85302	81914	130174	66943	63231	37042	18359	18683
		Jains	314	181	133	139	86	53	175	95	80
		Others	16300	8323	7977	15765	8070	7695	535	253	282
		Religion not stated	1828	874	954	1633	775	858	195	99	96
		All Religions	610577	323070	287507	456999	242797	214202	153578	80273	73305

1	2	3	4	5	6	7	8	9	10	11	12
10	Grand-Total, NER	Hindus	24726344	12680385	12045959	19288410	9872737	9415623	5437934	2807598	2630336
		Muslims	11466329	5872720	5593609	10464002	5353270	5110732	1002327	519450	482877
		Christians	7893055	3959123	3933932	6264801	3161934	3102867	1628254	797189	831065
		Sikhs	33645	21340	12305	14786	10309	4477	18859	11031	7828
		Buddhists	627527	318205	309322	544964	277034	267880	82563	41121	41442
		Jains	33244	17333	15911	5301	2807	2494	27943	14526	13417
		Others	903545	448577	454968	715509	357405	358104	188036	91172	96864
		Religion not stated	88499	43524	44975	71132	35125	36007	17367	8399	8968
		All Religions	45772188	23361207	22410981	37368905	19070721	18298184	8403283	4290486	4112797
11	India	Hindus	966257353	498306968	467950385	684093951	351423647	332670304	282163402	146883321	135280081
		Muslims	172245158	88273945	83971213	103504739	52870001	50634738	68740419	35403944	33336475
		Christians	27819588	13751031	14068557	16657065	8295745	8361320	11162523	5455286	5707237
		Sikhs	20833116	10948431	9884685	14930792	7839048	7091744	5902324	3109383	2792941
		Buddhists	8442972	4296010	4146962	4814849	2457022	2357827	3628123	1838988	1789135
		Jains	4451753	2278097	2173656	904809	467577	437232	3546944	1810520	1736424
		Others	7937734	3952064	3985670	7199007	3583894	3615113	738727	368170	370557
		Religion not stated	2867303	1463712	1403591	1643640	844124	799516	1223663	619588	604075
		All Religions	1210854977	623270258	587584719	833748852	427781058	405967794	377106125	195489200	181616925

Source: website of the Registrar General and Census Commissioner, India, New Delhi.

Appendix-4.7

State-wise Percentage Distribution of Different Religious Groups to Total of All Religious Groups with Rural-Urban Break-up in different Census Years

Sl. No.	Name of the States/ Region/India	Religious Communities	Percentage distribution in Census year								
			1961			1971			1981		
			Total	Rural	Urban	Total	Rural	Urban	Total	Rural	Urban
1	2	3	4	5	6	7	8	9	10	11	12
1	Arunachal Pradesh	Hindus	7.61	-	-	21.99	20.12	70.77	29.24	26.61	66.74
		Muslims	0.30	-	-	0.18	0.12	1.85	0.80	0.55	4.38
		Christians	0.51	-	-	0.79	0.73	2.22	4.32	4.38	3.43
		Sikhs	0.22	-	-	0.27	0.22	1.49	0.19	0.16	0.68
		Buddhists	1.73	-	-	13.13	13.36	7.31	13.69	14.26	5.56
		Jains	0.001	-	-	0.008	0.002	0.17	0.006	0.002	0.07
		Others	0.53	-	-	63.46	65.27	16.19	51.60	53.90	18.74
		Religion not stated	89.10	-	-	0.17	0.18	0	0.15	0.14	0.40
		All Religions	100.00	-	-	100.00	100.00	100.00	100.00	100.00	100.00
2	Assam	Hindus	66.41	-	-	72.51	71.16	86.49	-	-	-
		Muslims	23.29	-	-	24.56	25.85	11.21	-	-	-
		Christians	6.44	-	-	2.61	2.76	0.97	-	-	-
		Sikhs	0.08	-	-	0.08	0.04	0.53	-	-	-

1	2	3	4	5	6	7	8	9	10	11	12
		Buddhists	0.31	-	-	0.15	0.15	0.16	-	-	-
		Jains	0.08	-	-	0.09	0.04	0.64	-	-	-
		Others	3.32	-	-	0	0	0	-	-	-
		Religion not stated	0.07	-	-	0	0	0	-	-	-
		All Religions	100.00	-	-	100.00	100.00	100.00	-	-	-
3	Manipur	Hindus	61.68	-	-	58.97	55.08	84.57	60.04	53.31	78.78
		Muslims	6.23	-	-	6.62	7.44	1.20	6.99	7.32	6.08
		Christians	19.49	-	-	26.03	28.69	8.51	29.68	35.82	12.57
		Sikhs	0.07	-	-	0.09	0.04	0.44	0.07	0.02	0.23
		Buddhists	0.04	-	-	0.05	0.05	0.03	0.03	0.03	0.05
		Jains	0.10	-	-	0.13	0.05	0.70	0.07	0.001	0.26
		Others	0.00	-	-	7.75	8.24	4.55	2.50	2.87	1.45
		Religion not stated	12.39	-	-	0.36	0.41	0	0.62	0.63	0.58
		All Religions	100.00	-	-	100.00	100.00	100.00	100.00	100.00	100.00
4	Meghalaya	Hindus	-	-	-	18.50	13.40	48.45	18.03	12.96	41.03
		Muslims	-	-	-	2.60	2.55	2.93	3.10	3.13	2.99
		Christians	-	-	-	46.98	48.02	40.86	52.62	54.19	45.48
		Sikhs	-	-	-	0.12	0.01	0.77	0.13	0.03	0.53
		Buddhists	-	-	-	0.19	0.15	0.39	0.20	0.09	0.71
		Jains	-	-	-	0.03	0.02	0.08	0.04	0.02	0.14
		Others	-	-	-	31.45	35.69	6.52	25.77	29.45	9.08
		Religion not stated	-	-	-	0.13	0.16	0.008	0.11	0.13	0.04
		All Religions	-	-	-	100.00	100.00	100.00	100.00	100.00	100.00

1	2	3	4	5	6	7	8	9	10	11	12
5	Mizoram	Hindus	-	-	-	6.39	6.40	6.23	7.14	6.57	8.88
		Muslims	-	-	-	0.57	0.50	1.07	0.45	0.29	0.94
		Christians	-	-	-	86.08	85.26	92.58	83.81	81.84	89.83
		Sikhs	-	-	-	0.13	0.14	0.02	0.09	0.06	0.15
		Buddhists	-	-	-	6.81	7.68	0.06	8.19	10.84	0.08
		Jains	-	-	-	0.00	0.00	0.00	0.002	0.00	0.01
		Others	-	-	-	0.02	0.02	0.00	0.32	0.40	0.11
		Religion not stated	-	-	-	0.00	0.00	0.00	0.00	0.00	0.00
		All Religions	-	-	-	100.00	100.00	99.96	100.00	100.00	100.00
6	Nagaland	Hindus	9.39	-	-	11.43	6.61	55.07	14.36	10.23	36.85
		Muslims	0.24	-	-	0.58	0.26	3.38	1.52	1.10	3.81
		Christians	52.98	-	-	66.76	69.98	37.64	80.21	84.37	57.57
		Sikhs	0.07	-	-	0.13	0.02	1.17	0.10	0.04	0.38
		Buddhists	0.01	-	-	0.04	0.02	0.17	0.07	0.03	0.28
		Jains	0.07	-	-	0.12	0.001	1.21	0.15	0.002	0.95
		Others	37.23	-	-	20.94	23.11	1.36	3.59	4.23	0.16
		Religion not stated	0.01	-	-	0.00	0.00	0.00	0.00	0.00	0.00
		All Religions	100.00	-	-	100.00	100.00	100.00	100.00	100.00	100.00
7	Tripura	Hindus	76.01	-	-	89.55	88.75	96.42	89.34	88.44	96.67
		Muslims	20.14	-	-	6.68	7.08	3.22	6.75	7.23	2.82
		Christians	0.88	-	-	1.01	1.11	0.15	1.21	1.33	0.23
		Sikhs	0.001	-	-	0.02	0.02	0.02	0.01	0.01	0.04

1	2	3	4	5	6	7	8	9	10	11	12
		Buddhists	2.95	-	-	2.72	3.02	0.09	2.67	2.98	0.15
		Jains	0.02	-	-	0.02	0.02	0.10	0.02	0.01	0.09
		Others	0.00	-	-	0.00	0.00	0.00	0.001	0.001	0.001
		Religion not stated	0.00	-	-	0.00	0.00	0.00	0.001	0.001	0.001
		All Religions	100.00	-	-	100.00	100.00	100.00	100.00	100.00	100.00
8	Sub-Total, NER	Hindus	64.10	-	-	66.39	64.82	81.52	48.57	45.91	61.79
		Muslims	21.00	-	-	19.40	20.53	8.57	4.45	4.56	3.90
		Christians	7.75	-	-	9.12	9.28	7.56	32.97	33.57	29.98
		Sikhs	0.08	-	-	0.09	0.04	0.51	0.08	0.04	0.28
		Buddhists	0.53	-	-	0.77	0.83	0.23	2.76	3.23	0.44
		Jains	0.07	-	-	0.08	0.03	0.55	0.05	0.001	0.24
		Others	3.68	-	-	4.12	4.44	1.06	10.95	12.53	3.15
		Religion not stated	2.79	-	-	0.03	0.03	0.00	0.17	0.16	0.22
		All Religions	100.00	-	-	100.00	100.00	100.00	100.00	100.00	100.00
9	Sikkim	Hindus	66.69	-	-	68.88	69.03	67.48	67.25	67.66	65.13
		Muslims	0.75	-	-	0.16	0.07	1.04	1.03	0.57	3.38
		Christians	1.74	-	-	0.79	0.65	2.20	2.22	1.93	3.73
		Sikhs	0.04	-	-	0.05	0.03	0.13	0.10	0.06	0.29
		Buddhists	30.76	-	-	29.84	29.92	29.07	28.71	29.03	27.10
		Jains	0.01	-	-	0.09	0.09	0.08	0.03	0.001	0.18
		Others	-	-	-	0.19	0.21	0.00	0.63	0.72	0.17
		Religion not stated	0.01	-	-	0.00	0.00	0.00	0.03	0.03	0.02
		All Religions	100.00	-	-	100.00	100.00	100.00	100.00	100.00	100.00

1	2	3	4	5	6	7	8	9	10	11	12
10	Grand-Total, NER	Hindus	64.12	-	-	66.42	64.86	81.37	49.42	46.90	61.93
		Muslims	20.78	-	-	19.20	20.31	8.49	4.29	4.38	3.88
		Christians	7.69	-	-	9.03	9.19	7.51	31.58	32.13	28.84
		Sikhs	0.08	-	-	0.09	0.04	0.51	0.08	0.04	0.28
		Buddhists	0.86	-	-	1.08	1.14	0.53	3.93	4.40	1.60
		Jains	0.07	-	-	0.08	0.03	0.54	0.05	0.001	0.24
		Others	3.64	-	-	4.07	4.39	1.05	10.49	11.99	3.02
		Religion not stated	2.76	-	-	0.03	0.04	0.00	0.16	0.16	0.21
		All Religions	100.00	-	-	100.00	100.00	100.00	100.00	100.00	100.00
11	India	Hindus	83.45	-	-	82.73	84.34	76.25	82.63	84.53	76.51
		Muslims	10.69	-	-	11.21	9.97	16.21	11.36	9.82	16.31
		Christians	2.44	-	-	2.60	2.43	3.26	2.43	2.26	2.99
		Sikhs	1.79	-	-	1.89	1.91	1.81	1.97	2.02	1.80
		Buddhists	0.74	-	-	0.70	0.65	0.88	0.71	0.63	0.96
		Jains	0.46	-	-	0.48	0.24	1.43	0.48	0.23	1.29
		Others	0.34	-	-	0.39	0.46	0.15	0.42	0.51	0.14
		Religion not stated	0.09	-	-	0.001	0.001	0.01	0.001	0.001	0.001
		All Religions	100.00	-	-	100.00	100.00	100.00	100.00	100.00	100.00

Note: - Means information not available.
Source: Percentage calculated from the relevant Appendices.

Appendix-4.7 (cont.)

State-wise Percentage Distribution of Different Religious Groups to Total of All Religious Groups with Rural-Urban Break-up in different Census Years

Sl. No.	Name of the States/ Region/India	Religious Communities	Percentage distribution in Census year								
			1991			2001			2011		
			Total	Rural	Urban	Total	Rural	Urban	Total	Rural	Urban
1	2	3	13	14	15	16	17	18	19	20	21
1	Arunachal Pradesh	Hindus	37.04	32.96	64.80	34.60	23.68	53.41	29.04	24.07	45.73
		Muslims	1.38	0.85	5.00	1.88	1.19	4.52	1.95	1.17	4.59
		Christians	10.30	11.20	4.15	18.72	21.07	9.75	30.26	32.75	21.92
		Sikhs	0.14	0.10	0.43	0.17	0.10	0.44	0.24	0.15	0.53
		Buddhists	12.88	14.11	4.52	13.03	15.21	4.70	11.77	13.48	6.01
		Jains	0.001	0.001	0.04	0.02	0.001	0.06	0.06	0.05	0.07
		Others	36.22	38.48	20.78	30.73	31.70	27.03	26.20	27.85	20.65
		Religion not stated	2.04	2.30	0.28	0.85	1.05	0.09	0.48	0.48	0.50
		All Religions	100.00	100.00	100.00	100.00	100.00	100.00	100.00	100.00	100.00
2	Assam	Hindus	67.13	65.08	83.58	64.89	62.36	81.95	61.46	58.57	79.14
		Muslims	28.43	30.29	13.55	30.92	33.23	15.30	34.22	36.85	18.24
		Christians	3.32	3.59	1.19	3.70	4.03	1.47	3.74	4.11	1.44

1	2	3	13	14	15	16	17	18	19	20	21
		Sikhs	0.07	0.03	0.46	0.08	0.03	0.43	0.07	0.03	0.28
		Buddhists	0.29	0.30	0.18	0.19	0.19	0.19	0.18	0.18	0.16
		Jains	0.09	0.02	0.65	0.09	0.02	0.59	0.08	0.01	0.52
		Others	0.62	0.69	0.06	0.09	0.09	0.04	0.09	0.09	0.04
		Religion not stated	0.05	0.001	0.33	0.04	0.05	0.03	0.16	0.16	0.18
		All Religions	100.00	100.00	100.00	100.00	100.00	100.00	100.00	100.00	100.00
3	Manipur	Hindus	57.67	48.83	80.96	46.01	36.84	71.32	41.38	31.89	64.39
		Muslims	7.27	7.08	7.77	8.81	8.52	9.63	8.40	7.74	10.00
		Christians	34.11	43.35	9.78	34.04	44.30	5.71	41.29	52.80	13.38
		Sikhs	0.07	0.03	0.18	0.07	0.05	0.14	0.05	0.04	0.10
		Buddhists	0.04	0.04	0.03	0.09	0.11	0.03	0.25	0.22	0.30
		Jains	0.07	0.001	0.26	0.07	0.001	0.24	0.06	0.02	0.16
		Others	0.77	0.67	1.02	10.86	10.13	12.88	8.19	6.92	11.26
		Religion not stated	0.001	0.001	0.001	0.05	0.05	0.05	0.38	0.37	0.41
		All Religions	100.00	100.00	100.00	100.00	100.00	100.00	100.00	100.00	100.00
4	Meghalaya	Hindus	14.67	10.12	34.59	13.27	9.73	27.82	11.53	8.02	25.50
		Muslims	3.46	3.70	2.42	4.28	4.67	2.68	4.40	4.85	2.58
		Christians	64.58	66.81	54.81	70.25	72.10	62.64	74.59	76.64	66.44
		Sikhs	0.15	0.01	0.73	0.14	0.05	0.49	0.10	0.03	0.41
		Buddhists	0.16	0.08	0.55	0.20	0.13	0.50	0.33	0.28	0.55
		Jains	0.02	0.001	0.12	0.03	0.02	0.10	0.02	0.01	0.06
		Others	16.82	19.16	6.55	11.53	12.96	5.64	8.71	9.81	4.30

1	2	3	13	14	15	16	17	18	19	20	21
		Religion not stated	0.14	0.12	0.23	0.30	0.34	0.13	0.32	0.36	0.16
		All Religions	100.00	100.00	100.00	100.00	100.00	100.00	100.00	100.00	100.00
5	Mizoram	Hindus	5.05	4.79	5.33	3.55	2.30	4.82	2.75	1.37	4.01
		Muslims	0.66	0.20	1.20	1.14	0.74	1.54	1.35	1.25	1.45
		Christians	85.73	80.24	92.16	86.97	81.01	93.03	87.16	79.82	93.91
		Sikhs	0.04	0.05	0.04	0.04	0.04	0.03	0.03	0.02	0.03
		Buddhists	7.83	14.32	0.25	7.93	15.50	0.25	8.51	17.34	0.40
		Jains	0.00	0.00	0.00	0.02	0.03	0.01	0.04	0.05	0.02
		Others	0.27	0.23	0.32	0.27	0.32	0.23	0.07	0.08	0.07
		Religion not stated	0.42	0.17	0.70	0.08	0.06	0.09	0.09	0.07	0.11
		All Religions	100.00	100.00	100.00	100.00	100.00	100.00	100.00	100.00	100.00
6	Nagaland	Hindus	10.13	6.11	29.42	7.70	4.45	23.30	8.75	4.47	19.29
		Muslims	1.71	1.24	3.94	1.76	1.01	5.36	2.47	1.64	4.55
		Christians	87.47	92.00	65.66	89.97	94.05	70.34	87.93	93.13	75.10
		Sikhs	0.06	0.02	0.25	0.06	0.04	0.16	0.10	0.08	0.13
		Buddhists	0.05	0.03	0.16	0.06	0.04	0.21	0.34	0.32	0.40
		Jains	0.10	0.001	0.57	0.10	0.001	0.58	0.13	0.03	0.39
		Others	0.48	0.59	0.00	0.31	0.37	0.02	0.16	0.21	0.04
		Religion not stated	0.001	0.01	0.00	0.04	0.04	0.03	0.12	0.12	0.10
		All Religions	100.00	100.00	100.00	100.00	100.00	100.00	100.00	100.00	100.00
7	Tripura	Hindus	86.50	84.67	96.62	85.62	83.56	95.70	83.40	79.94	93.14
		Muslims	7.13	7.91	2.81	7.95	8.92	3.24	8.60	9.94	4.83

1	2	3	13	14	15	16	17	18	19	20	21
		Christians	1.68	1.94	0.29	3.20	3.76	0.49	4.35	5.61	0.80
		Sikhs	0.03	0.03	0.01	0.04	0.03	0.10	0.03	0.03	0.04
		Buddhists	4.65	5.45	0.22	3.09	3.66	0.33	3.41	4.30	0.91
		Jains	0.01	0.001	0.05	0.02	0.001	0.05	0.02	0.01	0.05
		Others	0.00	0.00	0.00	0.04	0.04	0.03	0.04	0.05	0.03
		Religion not stated	0.00	0.00	0.00	0.04	0.03	0.06	0.15	0.12	0.20
		All Religions	100.00	100.00	100.00	100.00	100.00	100.00	100.00	100.00	100.00
8	Sub-Total, NER	Hindus	60.95	59.15	72.12	57.17	55.14	68.04	53.97	51.56	64.77
		Muslims	21.56	23.52	9.44	23.10	25.41	10.73	25.37	28.34	12.07
		Christians	13.64	13.27	15.87	16.24	16.04	17.33	17.34	16.85	19.56
		Sikhs	0.07	0.03	0.36	0.08	0.04	0.33	0.07	0.03	0.23
		Buddhists	1.15	1.28	0.31	0.97	1.08	0.39	1.02	1.12	0.55
		Jains	0.08	0.02	0.44	0.08	0.01	0.41	0.07	0.01	0.34
		Others	2.45	2.65	1.19	2.28	2.19	2.72	1.97	1.90	2.27
		Religion not stated	0.10	0.08	0.27	0.08	0.09	0.05	0.19	0.19	0.21
		All Religions	100.00	100.00	100.00	100.00	100.00	100.00	100.00	100.00	100.00
9	Sikkim	Hindus	68.37	68.45	67.54	60.93	60.37	65.42	57.76	56.52	61.46
		Muslims	0.95	0.61	4.31	1.42	1.02	4.64	1.62	0.80	4.04
		Christians	3.30	3.19	4.38	6.68	6.69	6.55	9.91	10.00	9.66
		Sikhs	0.09	0.08	0.23	0.22	0.23	0.15	0.30	0.36	0.13
		Buddhists	27.16	27.56	23.13	28.11	28.82	22.46	27.39	28.48	24.12
		Jains	0.001	0	0.11	0.03	0.01	0.21	0.05	0.03	0.11

1	2	3	13	14	15	16	17	18	19	20	21
		Others	0.09	0.08	0.2	2.39	2.63	0.43	2.67	3.45	0.35
		Religion not stated	0.04	0.03	0.1	0.22	0.23	0.14	0.30	0.36	0.13
		All Religions	100.00	100.00	100.00	100.00	100.00	100.00	100.00	100.00	100.00
10	Grand-Total, NER	Hindus	61.05	59.28	72.08	57.22	55.22	68.02	54.02	51.62	64.71
		Muslims	21.30	23.21	9.40	22.80	25.05	10.67	25.05	28.00	11.93
		Christians	13.50	13.14	15.78	16.11	15.90	17.22	17.25	16.76	19.38
		Sikhs	0.07	0.03	0.36	0.08	0.04	0.33	0.07	0.04	0.22
		Buddhists	1.48	1.63	0.50	1.35	1.49	0.60	1.37	1.46	0.98
		Jains	0.08	0.02	0.44	0.08	0.01	0.41	0.07	0.01	0.33
		Others	2.42	2.61	1.18	2.28	2.20	2.70	1.98	1.92	2.24
		Religion not stated	0.10	0.08	0.26	0.08	0.09	0.05	0.19	0.19	0.21
		All Religions	100.00	100.00	100.00	100.00	100.00	100.00	100.00	100.00	100.00
11	India	Hindus	82.00	83.96	76.35	80.46	82.33	75.60	79.80	82.05	74.82
		Muslims	12.12	10.53	16.70	13.43	11.96	17.27	14.23	12.41	18.23
		Christians	2.34	2.17	2.85	2.34	2.14	2.86	2.30	2.00	2.96
		Sikhs	1.94	2.00	1.76	1.87	1.90	1.79	1.72	1.79	1.57
		Buddhists	0.76	0.66	1.05	0.77	0.66	1.07	0.70	0.58	0.96
		Jains	0.40	0.16	1.09	0.41	0.13	1.12	0.36	0.11	0.94
		Others	0.39	0.48	0.13	0.65	0.81	0.22	0.65	0.86	0.20
		Religion not stated	0.05	0.04	0.07	0.07	0.07	0.07	0.24	0.20	0.32
		All Religions	100.00	100.00	100.00	100.00	100.00	100.00	100.00	100.00	100.00

Source: Percentage calculated from the relevant Appendices.

Appendix-4.8

State-wise Decadal Growth of different Religious Groups with Rural-Urban Break-up

Sl. No.	Name of the States/Region/India	Religious Communities	Decadal Growth in											
			1961-71						1971-81					
			Absolute			Per cent			Absolute			Per cent		
			Total	Rural	Urban	Total	Rural	Urban	Total	Rural	Urban	Total	Rural	Urban
1	2	3	4	5	6	7	8	9	10	11	12	13	14	15
1	Arunachal Pradesh	Hindus	77233	-	-	301.70	-	-	81900	66485	15415	79.64	73.39	125.99
		Muslims	(-)166	-	-	(-) 16.47	-	-	4231	2737	1494	502.49	523.33	468.34
		Christians	1971	-	-	115.06	-	-	23622	22586	1036	641.21	684.22	270.50
		Sikhs	510	-	-	68.46	-	-	(-)24	(-) 49	25	(-) 1.91	(-) 4.91	9.69
		Buddhists	55591	-	-	956.98	-	-	25083	24044	1039	40.85	39.98	82.20
		Jains	25	-	-	178.57	-	-	3	3	0	7.69	33.33	0.00
		Others	294890	-	-	16530	-	-	29326	24362	4964	9.88	8.29	177.35
		Religion not stated	(-)299101	-	-	(-) 99.74	-	-	187	20	0	23.82	2.55	0.00
		All Religions	130953	-	-	38.91	-	-	164328	140188	24140	35.15	31.14	139.63
2	Assam	Hindus	2719697	-	-	34.49	-	-	-	-	-	-	-	-
		Muslims	826615	-	-	29.89	-	-	-	-	-	-	-	-
		Christians	(-) 383543	-	-	(-) 50.16	-	-	-	-	-	-	-	-
		Sikhs	2234	-	-	23.06	-	-	-	-	-	-	-	-

1	2	3	4	5	6	7	8	9	10	11	12	13	14	15
		Buddhists	(-) 13948	-	-	(-) 38.20	-	-	-	-	-	-	-	-
		Jains	3449	-	-	36.43	-	-	-	-	-	-	-	-
		Others	-	-	-	-	-	-	-	-	-	-	-	-
		Religion not stated	-	-	-	-	-	-	-	-	-	-	-	-
		All Religions	2752381	-	-	23.18	-	-	-	-	-	-	-	-
3	Manipur	Hindus	151485	-	-	31.49	-	-	220583	44449	176134	34.87	8.67	147.20
		Muslims	22381	-	-	46.06	-	-	28358	7227	21131	39.96	10.43	1240.08
		Christians	127200	-	-	83.66	-	-	142459	107305	35154	51.02	40.16	291.95
		Sikhs	505	-	-	96.56	-	-	(-) 36	(-) 262	226	(-) 3.50	(-) 63.90	36.57
		Buddhists	170	-	-	52.31	-	-	(-) 22	(-) 160	138	(-) 4.44	(-) 35.63	300.00
		Jains	630	-	-	80.93	-	-	(-) 433	(-) 410	(-) 23	(-) 30.75	(-) 98.09	(-) 2.32
		Others	-	-	-	-	-	-	(-) 47677	(-) 46699	(-) 978	(-) 57.33	(-) 60.86	(-) 15.20
		Religion not stated	(-)92822	-	-	(-) 96.02	-	-	4968	2782	-	129.17	72.33	-
		All Religions	292716	-	-	37.53	-	-	348200	114232	233968	32.46	12.27	165.36
4	Meghalaya	Hindus	-	-	-	-	-	-	53691	25980	27711	28.69	22.43	38.86
		Muslims	-	-	-	-	-	-	15087	12177	2910	57.26	55.24	67.60
		Christians	-	-	-	-	-	-	227587	177971	49616	47.89	42.87	82.51
		Sikhs	-	-	-	-	-	-	412	278	134	32.65	222.40	11.78
		Buddhists	-	-	-	-	-	-	861	(-) 288	1149	45.85	(-) 21.97	202.65
		Jains	-	-	-	-	-	-	274	53	221	102.24	36.05	182.64
		Others	-	-	-	-	-	-	26047	13721	12326	8.19	4.45	128.52
		Religion not stated	-	-	-	-	-	-	161	65	96	11.76	4.79	800.00
		All Religions	-	-	-	-	-	-	324120	229957	94163	32.04	26.60	63.98

1	2	3	4	5	6	7	8	9	10	11	12	13	14	15
5	Mizoram	Hindus	-	-	-	-	-	-	14016	5559	8457	66.02	29.47	357.59
		Muslims	-	-	-	-	-	-	323	(-) 413	736	17.16	(-) 27.96	181.73
		Christians	-	-	-	-	-	-	127699	53227	74472	44.63	21.19	213.03
		Sikhs	-	-	-	-	-	-	(-) 6	(-) 182	176	(-) 1.41	(-) 43.33	2514.29
		Buddhists	-	-	-	-	-	-	17782	17712	70	78.52	78.29	304.35
		Jains	-	-	-	-	-	-	8	-	-	266.67	-	-
		Others	-	-	-	-	-	-	1545	1412	-	2532.79	2314.75	-
		Religion not stated	-	-	-	-	-	-	-	-	-	-	-	-
		All Religions	-	-	-	-	-	-	161367	77312	84055	48.55	26.24	222.61
6	Nagaland	Hindus	24[illegible]51	-	-	70.23	-	-	52235	36228	16007	88.49	117.89	56.56
		Muslims	2075	-	-	232.88	-	-	8840	5995	2845	298.04	488.19	163.69
		Christians	1492[illegible]0	-	-	76.29	-	-	276792	226918	49874	80.28	69.72	257.80
		Sikhs	132	-	-	169.41	-	-	56	194	(-) 138	8.15	222.99	(-) 23.00
		Buddhists	37	-	-	326.19	-	-	338	92	246	188.83	101.10	279.55
		Jains	[illegible]54	-	-	138.40	-	-	526	10	516	83.89	200.00	82.96
		Others	(-) 29285	-	-	(-) 21.31	-	-	(-) 80307	(-) 79797	(-) 510	(-) 74.25	(-) 74.26	(-) 72.86
		Religion not stated	-	-	-	-	-	-	-	-	-	-	-	-
		All Religions	147249	-	-	39.88	-	-	258481	189641	68840	50.05	40.78	133.95
7	Tripura	Hindus	525691			60.56	-	-	440529	379019	61510	31.61	30.64	39.29
		Muslims	(-) 126040	-	-	(-) 54.80	-	-	34567	33433	1134	33.25	33.86	21.70
		Christians	5674	-	-	56.52	-	-	9159	8901	258	58.29	57.59	100.78
		Sikhs	269	-	-	548.98	-	-	(-) 33	(-) 100	67	(-) 10.38	(-) 34.72	223.33

1	2	3	4	5	6	7	8	9	10	11	12	13	14	15
		Buddhists	8569	-	-	25.42	-	-	12521	12336	185	29.61	29.27	127.59
		Jains	180	-	-	92.31	-	-	(-) 78	(-) 114	36	(-) 20.80	(-) 53.02	22.50
		Others	-	-	-	-	-	-	-	-	-	-	-	-
		Religion not stated	-	-	-	-	-	-	-	-	-	-	-	-
		All Religions	414337	-	-	36.28	-	-	496716	433508	63208	31.92	31.10	38.93
8	Sub-Total, NER	Hindus	3706829	-	-	39.88	-	-	*	*	*	*	*	*
		Muslims	753094	-	-	24.72	-	-	*	*	*	*	*	*
		Christians	661920	-	-	58.89	-	-	*	*	*	*	*	*
		Sikhs	5639	-	-	50.09	-	-	*	*	*	*	*	*
		Buddhists	75044	-	-	98.22	-	-	*	*	*	*	*	*
		Jains	4916	-	-	45.87	-	-	*	*	*	*	*	*
		Others	272910	-	-	51.17	-	-	*	*	*	*	*	*
		Religion not stated	(-) 398627	-	-	(-) 98.52	-	-	*	*	*	*	*	*
		All Religions	5081725	-	-	35.04	-	-	*	*	*	*	*	*
9	Sikkim	Hindus	36379	-	-	33.63	-	-	68236	48235	20001	47.21	36.74	150.69
		Muslims	(-) 872	-	-	(-) 72.25	-	-	2906	1382	1524	867.46	1054.96	747.06
		Christians	(-) 1150	-	-	(-) 40.88	-	-	5352	3881	1471	321.83	315.27	340.51
		Sikhs	22	-	-	30.56	-	-	228	103	125	242.55	151.47	480.77
		Buddhists	12723	-	-	25.50	-	-	28231	20106	8125	45.08	35.34	142.12
		Jains	172	-	-	905.26	-	-	(-) 83	(-) 159	76	(-) 43.46	(-) 90.86	475.00
		Others	-	-	-	-	-	-	1588	1503	-	397.99	376.69	-
		Religion not stated	-	-	-	-	-	-	-	-	-	-	-	-
		All Religions	47654	-	-	29.38	-	-	106542	75126	31416	50.77	39.50	159.73

1	2	3	4	5	6	7	8	9	10	11	12	13	14	15
10	Grand-Total, NER	Hindus	3743208	-	-	39.81	-	-	*	*	*	*	*	*
		Muslims	752222	-	-	24.69	-	-	*	*	*	*	*	*
		Christians	660770	-	-	58.64	-	-	*	*	*	*	*	*
		Sikhs	5661	-	-	49.96	-	-	*	*	*	*	*	*
		Buddhists	87767	-	-	69.49	-	-	*	*	*	*	*	*
		Jains	5088	-	-	47.39	-	-	*	*	*	*	*	*
		Others	273309	-	-	51.25	-	-	*	*	*	*	*	*
		Religion not stated	(-) 398646	-	-	(-) 98.52	-	-	*	*	*	*	*	*
		All Religions	5129379	-	-	34.98	-	-	*	*	*	*	*	*
11	India	Hindus	86765220	-	-	23.67	-	-	96432631	58975856	37456775	21.27	15.93	45.03
		Muslims	14477135	-	-	30.84	-	-	14153580	6122844	8030736	23.04	14.00	45.41
		Christians	3495296	-	-	32.58	-	-	1951116	792050	1159066	13.72	7.43	32.59
		Sikhs	2532882	-	-	32.28	-	-	2699349	1842609	856740	26.01	21.93	43.36
		Buddhists	556289	-	-	17.08	-	-	907575	360579	546996	23.81	12.66	56.80
		Jains	577365	-	-	28.48	-	-	587926	108768	479158	22.57	10.39	30.75
		Others	685661	-	-	45.74	-	-	581729	529939	51790	26.63	26.21	31.79
		Religion not stated	(-)374810	-	-	(-) 91.22	-	-	24134	19533	4601	66.88	78.08	41.58
		All Religions	108715038	-	-	24.75	-	-	117338040	68752178	48585862	21.41	15.67	44.54

Note: - means information not available.

* means information of Assam for 1981 census not included, as Census was not conducted there in that year.

Appendix-4.8 (*cont.*)

State-wise Decadal Growth of different Religious Groups with Rural-Urban Break-up

Sl. No.	Name of the States/ Region/ India	Religious Communities	Decadal Growth in											
			1981-91 (for Assam & NER, it is 1971-91)						1991-2001					
			Absolute			Per cent			Absolute			Per cent		
			Total	Rural	Urban	Total	Rural	Urban	Total	Rural	Urban	Total	Rural	Urban
1	2	3	16	17	18	19	20	21	22	23	24	25	26	27
1	Arunachal Pradesh	Hindus	135480	91438	44042	73.34	58.21	159.28	59723	9705	50018	18.65	3.90	69.77
		Muslims	6849	3135	3714	135.01	96.17	204.85	8753	3974	4779	73.42	62.14	86.47
		Christians	61707	58532	3175	225.98	226.11	223.75	116535	98919	17616	130.92	117.18	383.46
		Sikhs	(-) 26	(-) 219	193	(-) 2.11	(-) 23.10	68.20	660	135	525	54.77	18.52	110.29
		Buddhists	24889	22198	2691	28.78	26.37	116.85	31656	25945	5711	28.42	24.39	114.36
		Jains	22	5	17	52.38	41.67	56.67	152	69	83	237.50	405.88	176.60
		Others	(-) 12882	(-) 28113	15231	(-)3.95	(-) 8.83	196.20	24281	(-) 14326	38607	7.75	(-) 4.94	167.90
		Religion not stated	16680	16543	137	1716.05	2055.03	82.04	(-) 8350	(-) 8264	(-) 86	(-) 47.30	(-) 47.64	(-) 28.29
		All Religions	232719	163519	69200	36.83	27.70	167.04	233410	116157	117253	27.00	15.41	105.99
2	Assam	Hindus	4442675	3478239	964436	41.89	36.65	86.50	2249162	1510107	739055	14.95	11.64	35.54
		Muslims	2781080	2588479	192601	77.42	75.08	133.26	1867407	1678547	188860	29.30	27.81	56.02

1	2	3	16	17	18	19	20	21	22	23	24	25	26	27
		Christians	363357	346289	17068	95.37	93.99	135.86	242222	221272	20950	32.54	30.96	70.70
		Sikhs	4572	43	4529	38.36	0.84	66.51	6027	2481	3546	36.54	48.15	31.27
		Buddhists	41443	39061	2382	183.66	190.85	113.54	(-) 12979	(-) 14982	2003	(-) 20.28	(-) 25.17	44.71
		Jains	7731	(-) 180	7911	59.87	(-) 3.84	96.22	3312	(-) 909	4221	16.04	(-) 20.15	26.16
		Others	-	-	-	-	-	-	(-) 115231	(-) 115238	7	(-) 83.36	(-) 84.21	0.51
		Religion not stated	-	-	-	-	-	-	1286	8483	(-) 7197	12.75	465.84	(-) 87.11
		All Religions	7789169	6590597	1198572	53.26	49.42	92.97	4241206	3289761	951445	18.92	16.51	38.24
3	Manipur	Hindus	206290	92714	113576	24.18	16.63	38.40	(-) 62576	(-) 63988	1412	(-) 5.91	(-) 9.84	0.34
		Muslims	34208	17744	16464	34.44	23.20	72.10	57404	41258	16146	42.99	43.78	41.09
		Christians	204967	202714	2253	48.60	54.13	4.77	110909	127452	(-) 16543	17.70	22.08	(-) 33.45
		Sikhs	309	270	39	31.15	182.43	4.62	352	425	(-) 73	27.06	101.67	(-) 8.27
		Buddhists	238	272	(-) 34	50.32	94.12	(-) 18.48	1215	1207	8	170.89	215.15	5.33
		Jains	362	19	343	37.13	237.50	35.47	124	65	59	9.27	240.74	4.50
		Others	(-) 21424	(-) 21119	(-) 305	(-) 60.37	(-) 70.32	(-) 5.59	221214	152187	69027	1572.69	1707.28	1339.81
		Religion not stated	-	-	-	-	-	-	997	710	287	1661.67	2840.00	820.00
		All Religions	416196	286011	130185	29.29	27.36	34.67	329639	259316	70323	17.94	19.48	13.91
4	Meghalaya	Hindus	19475	4332	15143	8.07	3.05	15.29	47516	35322	12194	18.25	24.17	10.68
		Muslims	20028	19251	777	48.34	56.26	10.77	37707	33551	4156	61.35	62.75	52.00
		Christians	443238	372083	71155	63.06	62.74	64.83	482894	379330	103564	42.13	39.30	57.25
		Sikhs	938	(-) 197	1135	56.03	(-) 48.88	89.30	498	670	(-) 172	19.07	325.24	(-) 7.15
		Buddhists	195	80	115	7.12	7.82	6.70	1769	1328	441	60.29	120.40	24.09
		Jains	(-) 97	(-) 151	54	(-) 17.90	(-) 75.50	15.79	327	291	36	73.48	593.88	9.09

1	2	3	16	17	18	19	20	21	22	23	24	25	26	27
		Others	(-) 45749	(-) 45435	(-) 314	(-) 13.29	(-) 14.10	(-) 1.43	(-) 31221	(-) 35244	4023	(-) 10.46	(-) 12.73	18.62
		Religion not stated	931	282	649	60.85	19.83	600.93	4554	4732	(-) 178	185.05	277.70	(-) 23.51
		All Religions	438959	350245	88714	32.86	32.00	36.76	544044	419980	124064	30.65	29.07	37.59
5	Mizoram	Hindus	(-) 457	(-) 6598	6141	(-) 1.20	(-) 27.02	56.75	(-) 3226	(-) 7535	4309	(-) 9.27	(-) 42.27	25.40
		Muslims	2333	(-) 332	2665	105.80	(-) 31.20	233.57	5561	2586	2975	122.54	353.28	78.17
		Christians	177502	(-) 6072	183574	42.89	(-) 1.99	167.75	181467	64216	117251	30.69	21.52	40.02
		Sikhs	(-) 122	(-) 59	(-) 63	(-) 28.98	(-) 24.79	(-) 34.43	27	13	14	9.03	7.26	11.67
		Buddhists	13595	12898	697	33.63	31.98	749.46	16470	16151	319	30.49	30.34	40.38
		Jains	-	-	-	-	-	-	-	-	-	-	-	-
		Others	253	(-) 628	881	15.75	(-) 42.63	662.41	584	597	(-) 13	31.41	70.65	(-) 1.28
		Religion not stated	-	-	-	-	-	-	(-) 2241	(-) 405	(-)1836	(-) 77.22	(-) 61.55	(-) 81.82
		All Religions	195999	(-) 133	196132	39.70	(-) 0.04	161.01	198817	75757	123060	28.82	20.38	38.70
6	Nagaland	Hindus	11207	(-) 5752	16959	10.07	(-) 8.59	38.28	30689	12092	18597	25.06	19.76	30.35
		Muslims	8836	5215	3621	74.84	72.20	79.01	14363	4194	10169	69.58	33.72	123.95
		Christians	436350	368855	67495	70.20	66.78	97.51	732409	627996	104413	69.23	68.17	76.37
		Sikhs	(-) 11	(-) 61	50	(-) 1.48	(-) 21.71	10.82	420	395	25	57.38	179.55	4.88
		Buddhists	64	65	(-) 1	12.38	35.52	(-) 0.30	775	408	367	133.39	164.52	110.21
		Jains	49	(-) 3	52	4.25	(-) 20.00	4.57	891	97	794	74.13	808.33	66.72
		Others	(-) 21982	(-) 21794	(-) 188	(-) 78.92	(-) 78.79	(-) 98.95	238	157	81	4.05	2.68	4050.00
		Religion not stated	-	-	-	-	-	-	705	587	118	665.09	559.05	11800.00
		All Religions	434616	346627	87989	56.08	52.94	73.18	780490	645926	134564	64.53	64.51	64.62

1	2	3	16	17	18	19	20	21	22	23	24	25	26	27
7	Tripura	Hindus	550716	183306	189410	30.02	11.34	86.86	354376	239554	114822	14.86	12.11	28.18
		Muslims	57966	52478	5488	41.84	39.71	86.29	57947	52101	5846	29.49	28.22	49.34
		Christians	21600	20907	693	86.84	85.83	134.82	56017	54555	1462	120.54	120.52	121.13
		Sikhs	455	504	(-) 49	159.65	268.09	(-) 50.52	442	(-) 79	521	59.73	(-) 11.42	1085.42
		Buddhists	73454	72847	607	134.03	133.72	183.94	(-) 29338	(-) 30175	837	(-) 22.87	(-) 23.70	89.33
		Jains	4	(-) 16	20	1.35	(-) 15.84	10.20	176	105	71	58.47	123.53	32.87
		Others	-	-	-	-	-	-	-	-	-	-	-	-
		Religion not stated	-	-	-	-	-	-	-	-	-	-	-	-
		All Religions	704147	507994	196153	34.30	27.80	86.96	441998	317969	124029	16.03	13.61	29.41
8	Sub-Total, NER*	Hindus	6228340	4573399	1654941	47.91	39.78	109.93	2675664	1735257	940407	13.91	10.80	29.76
		Muslims	3002706	2747126	255580	79.04	75.45	161.53	2049142	1816211	232931	30.13	28.43	56.29
		Christians	2516039	1960216	555823	140.89	119.08	397.91	1922453	1573740	348713	44.69	43.64	50.14
		Sikhs	6484	160	6324	38.37	2.15	66.85	8426	4040	4386	36.04	53.18	27.79
		Buddhists	210441	201157	9284	138.95	136.64	219.43	9568	(-) 118	9686	2.64	(-) 0.03	71.67
		Jains	8364	(-) 787	9151	53.50	(-) 14.34	90.20	5157	(-) 148	5305	21.49	(-) 3.15	27.49
		Others	(-) 34620	(-) 67245	32625	(-) 4.29	(-) 8.55	167.08	101140	(-) 10760	111900	13.11	(-) 1.50	214.57
		Religion not stated	27263	15672	11591	454.23	261.64	96591.6 7	(-) 1946	6644	(-) 8590	(-) 5.85	30.67	(-) 74.03
		All Religions	11965017	9429698	2535319	61.10	53.17	137.29	6769604	5124866	1644738	21.46	18.87	37.53
9	Sikkim	Hindus	65101	73382	(-) 8281	30.60	40.88	(-) 24.89	51667	37496	14171	18.59	14.83	56.70
		Muslims	608	739	(-) 131	18.76	48.84	(-) 7.58	3844	2661	1183	99.87	118.16	74.08
		Christians	6398	6678	(-) 280	91.20	130.63	(-) 14.71	22702	20402	2300	169.25	173.04	141.71

1	2	3	16	17	18	19	20	21	22	23	24	25	26	27
		Sikhs	53	119	(-) 66	16.46	69.59	(-) 43.71	801	794	7	213.60	273.79	8.24
		Buddhists	19523	24806	(-) 5283	21.49	32.21	(-) 38.17	41671	36785	4886	37.76	36.13	57.09
		Jains	-	-	-	-	-	-	-	-	-	-	-	-
		Others	(-) 1613	(-) 1601	(-) 12	(-) 81.18	(-) 84.17	(-) 14.12	12552	12367	185	3356.15	4108.64	253.42
		Religion not stated	70	43	27	83.33	57.33	300.00	1014	968	46	658.44	820.34	127.78
		All Religions	90072	104150	(-) 14078	28.47	39.26	(-) 27.56	134394	111530	22864	33.06	30.19	61.78
10	Grand-Total, NER*	Hindus	6361677	4695016	1666661	48.39	40.38	109.74	2727331	1772753	954578	13.98	10.86	29.97
		Muslims	3006220	2749247	256973	79.12	75.51	162.20	2052986	1818872	234114	30.17	28.46	56.36
		Christians	2527789	1970775	557014	141.41	119.63	397.54	1945155	1594142	351013	45.08	44.06	50.35
		Sikhs	6765	382	6383	39.82	5.09	67.29	9227	4834	4393	38.84	61.29	27.68
		Buddhists	258195	246069	12126	120.61	120.55	121.89	51239	36667	14572	10.85	8.14	66.01
		Jains	8213	(-) 962	9175	51.90	(-) 16.98	90.30	5300	(-) 91	5391	22.05	(-) 1.94	27.88
		Others	(-) 34645	(-) 67343	32698	(-) 4.30	(-) 8.56	167.46	113692	1607	112085	14.73	0.22	214.62
		Religion not stated	27417	15790	-	456.80	263.61	-	(-) 932	7612	(-) 8544	(-) 2.79	34.95	(-) 73.41
		All Religions	12161631	9608974	2552657	61.45	53.60	136.77	6903998	5236396	1667602	21.61	19.02	37.74
11	India	Hindus	137922004	93810004	44112000	25.09	21.86	36.57	139932147	88366670	51565477	20.35	16.90	31.30
		Muslims	26024543	15707898	10316645	34.44	31.51	40.12	36592183	23231049	13361134	36.02	35.43	37.08
		Christians	3465786	2026535	1439251	21.43	17.69	30.52	4439732	2408697	2031035	22.61	17.86	33.00
		Sikhs	3181598	2228083	953515	24.33	21.75	33.66	2955986	1633051	1322935	18.18	13.09	34.94
		Buddhists	1667600	917628	749972	35.33	28.59	49.67	1567707	766126	801581	24.54	18.56	35.47
		Jains	160134	(-) 157456	317590	5.02	(-) 3.63	15.59	872347	11629	860718	26.02	1.17	36.55

1	2	3	16	17	18	19	20	21	22	23	24	25	26	27
		Others	503070	430026	73044	18.19	16.85	34.02	3370271	3020836	349435	103.09	101.31	121.45
		Religion not stated	355352	225928	129424	590.12	507.12	826.15	312019	256257	55762	75.08	94.74	38.43
		All Religions	173280087	115188646	58091441	26.05	22.69	36.84	190042392	119694315	70348077	22.66	19.22	32.60

Note: - means information not available

* for Assam and NER, position is of 1971-91, as Census was not conducted in Assam in 1981.

Appendix-4.8 (*cont.*)

State-wise Decadal Growth of different Religious Groups with Rural-Urban Break-up

Sl. No.	Name of the States/ Region/ India	Religious Communities	Decadal Growth in 2001-11						Growth during 1971-2011 (i.e. within a period of 40 years)						Growth during 1961-2011 (i.e. within a period of 50 years)	
			Absolute			Per cent			Absolute			Per cent			Total	
			Total	Rural	Urban	Total	Rural	Urban	Total	Rural	Urban	Total	Rural	Urban	Absolute	Per cent
1	2	3	28	29	30	31	32	33	34	35	36	37	38	39	40	41
1	Arunachal Pradesh	Hindus	21941	(-) 1498	23439	5.77	(-) 0.58	19.26	299044	166130	132914	290.81	183.37	1086.34	376277	1469.89
		Muslims	6370	2119	4251	30.81	20.44	41.25	26203	11965	14238	3112.00	2287.76	4463.32	26037	2583.04
		Christians	213184	165842	47342	103.71	90.46	213.16	415048	345879	69169	11266.23	10478.01	18059.79	417019	24344.37
		Sikhs	1422	723	699	76.25	83.68	69.83	2032	590	1442	161.91	59.18	558.91	2542	341.21
		Buddhists	19787	11403	8384	13.83	8.62	78.32	101415	83590	17825	165.17	139.00	1410.21	157006	2702.81
		Jains	555	475	80	256.94	552.32	61.54	732	552	180	1876.92	6133.33	600.00	757	5407.14
		Others	25154	21223	3931	7.46	7.70	6.38	65879	3146	62733	22.21	1.07	2241.26	360769	20222.48
		Religion not stated	(-) 2654	(-) 4016	1362	(-) 28.53	(-) 44.21	624.77	5863	4283	1580	746.88	545.61	-	(-) 293238	(-) 97.78
		All Religions	285759	196271	89488	26.03	22.56	39.27	916216	616135	300081	195.98	136.85	1735.78	1047169	311.14
2	Assam	Hindus	1884304	1221905	662399	10.89	8.44	23.50	8576141	6210251	2365890	80.87	65.44	212.19	11295838	143.26
		Muslims	2438734	2162599	276135	29.59	28.03	52.50	7087221	6429625	657596	197.30	186.50	454.99	7913836	286.16
		Christians	179278	166707	12571	18.17	17.81	24.85	784857	734268	50589	205.99	199.29	402.68	401314	52.49

1	2	3	28	29	30	31	32	33	34	35	36	37	38	39	40	41
		Sikhs	(-) 1847	608	(-) 2455	(-) 8.20	7.96	(-) 16.49	8752	3132	5620	73.42	61.29	82.53	10986	113.42
		Buddhists	3964	3186	778	7.77	7.15	12.00	32428	27265	5163	143.71	133.21	246.09	18480	50.61
		Jains	1992	(-) 745	2737	8.31	(-) 20.68	13.45	13035	(-) 1834	14869	100.94	(-) 39.09	180.84	16481	174.07
		Others	4119	3935	184	17.91	18.21	13.23	-	-	-	-	-	-	(-) 366971	(-) 93.12
		Religion not stated	39504	32551	6953	347.47	315.91	652.86	-	-	-	-	-	-	42840	533.30
		All Religions	4550048	3590746	959302	17.07	15.47	27.89	16580423	13471104	3109319	113.37	101.01	241.18	19332804	162.83
3	Manipur	Hindus	184982	58637	126345	18.56	10.00	30.76	549279	131812	417467	86.83	25.70	348.88	700764	145.65
		Muslims	48897	20926	27971	25.61	15.44	50.45	168867	87155	81712	237.94	125.83	4795.31	191248	393.61
		Christians	441465	362730	78735	59.85	51.47	239.28	899800	800201	99599	322.23	299.47	827.17	1027000	675.47
		Sikhs	(-) 126	(-) 108	(-) 18	(-) 7.62	(-) 12.81	(-) 2.22	499	325	174	48.54	79.27	28.16	1004	191.97
		Buddhists	5158	2819	2339	267.81	159.45	1480.38	6589	4138	2451	1331.11	921.60	5328.26	6759	2079.69
		Jains	231	276	(-) 45	15.81	300.00	(-) 3.29	284	(-) 50	334	20.17	(-) 11.96	33.74	914	117.48
		Others	(-) 1513	(-) 21235	19722	(-) 0.64	(-) 13.18	26.59	150600	63134	87466	181.08	82.28	1359.22	^	^
		Religion not stated	9912	6775	3137	937.75	921.77	974.22	7123	3664	-	185.21	95.27	-	(-) 85699	(-) 88.65
		All Religions	689006	430820	258186	31.80	27.08	44.83	1783041	1090379	692662	166.21	117.09	489.54	2075757	266.11
4	Meghalaya	Hindus	34256	8785	25471	11.13	4.84	20.16	154938	74419	80519	82.79	64.24	112.93	-	-
		Muslims	31230	28020	3210	31.49	32.20	26.42	104052	92999	11053	394.93	421.92	256.75	-	-
		Christians	584041	472904	111137	35.85	35.17	39.07	1737760	1402288	335472	365.64	337.79	557.86	-	-
		Sikhs	(-) 65	(-) 263	198	(-) 2.09	(-) 30.02	8.86	1783	488	1295	141.28	390.40	113.90	-	-
		Buddhists	5161	4116	1045	109.74	169.31	45.99	7986	5236	2750	425.24	399.39	485.01	-	-
		Jains	(-) 145	(-) 67	(-) 78	(-) 18.78	(-) 19.71	(-) 18.06	359	126	233	133.96	85.71	192.56	-	-

1	2	3	28	29	30	31	32	33	34	35	36	37	38	39	40	41
		Others	(-) 8974	(-) 8960	(-) 14	(-) 3.36	(-) 3.71	(-) 0.05	(-) 59897	(-) 75918	-6021	(-) 18.82	(-) 24.60	167.04	-	-
		Religion not stated	2563	2193	370	36.54	34.07	63.90	8209	7272	937	599.63	535.89	7808.33	-	-
		All Religions	648067	506728	141339	27.95	27.17	31.12	1955190	1506910	448280	193.26	174.30	304.60	-	-
5	Mizoram	Hindus	(-) 1426	(-) 3096	1670	(-) 4.52	(-) 30.09	7.85	8907	(-) 11670	20577	41.96	(-) 61.86	870.06	-	-
		Muslims	4733	3231	1502	46.87	97.38	22.15	12950	5072	7878	688.10	343.40	1945.18	-	-
		Christians	183522	56845	126677	23.75	15.68	30.88	670190	168216	501974	234.22	66.97	1435.89	-	-
		Sikhs	(-) 40	(-) 104	64	(-) 12.27	(-) 54.17	47.76	(-) 141	(-) 332	191	(-) 33.02	(-) 79.05	2728.57	-	-
		Buddhists	22917	21727	1190	32.51	31.31	107.30	70764	68488	2276	312.47	302.72	9895.65	-	-
		Jains	197	126	71	110.06	94.03	157.78	373	257	-	12433.33	8566.67	-	-	-
		Others	(-) 1635	(-) 1008	(-) 627	(-) 66.93	(-) 69.90	(-) 62.64	747	373	-	1224.59	611.48	-	-	-
		Religion not stated	365	147	218	55.22	58.10	53.43	-	-	-	-	-	-	-	-
		All Religions	208633	77868	130765	23.48	17.40	29.65	764816	230804	534012	230.10	78.34	1414.26	-	-
6	Nagaland	Hindus	19892	(-) 10365	30257	12.99	(-) 14.14	37.89	114023	32203	81820	193.16	104.79	289.12	138377	399.05
		Muslims	13958	6375	7583	39.87	38.33	41.27	45997	21779	24218	1550.81	1773.53	1393.44	48072	5395.29
		Christians	(-) 50698	(-) 238383	187685	(-) 2.83	(-) 15.39	77.84	1394853	985386	409467	404.54	302.77	2116.55	1544063	789.45
		Sikhs	738	501	237	64.06	81.46	44.13	1203	1029	174	175.11	1182.76	29.00	1635	641.18
		Buddhists	5403	3822	1581	398.45	582.62	225.86	6580	4387	2193	3675.98	4820.88	2492.05	6717	15992.86
		Jains	562	312	250	26.85	286.24	12.60	2028	416	1612	323.44	8320.00	259.16	2392	909.51
		Others	(-) 2894	(-) 3028	134	(-) 47.38	(-) 50.26	161.45	(-) 104945	(-)104462	(-) 483	(-) 97.03	(-) 97.21	(-) 69.00	(-)134230	(-) 97.66
		Religion not stated	1505	1053	452	185.57	152.17	379.83	-	-	-	-	-	-	2276	5690.00

1	2	3	28	29	30	31	32	33	34	35	36	37	38	39	40	41
		All Religions	(-) 11534	(-) 239713	228179	(-) 0.58	(-) 14.55	66.57	1462053	942481	519572	283.10	202.66	1010.96	1609302	435.89
7	Tripura	Hindus	324593	(-) 48630	373223	11.85	(-) 2.19	71.46	1670214	931249	738965	119.84	75.27	472.05	2195905	252.98
		Muslims	61600	32873	28727	24.21	13.89	162.35	212080	170885	41195	204.00	173.07	788.27	86040	37.41
		Christians	57393	52350	5043	56.00	52.44	188.95	144169	136713	7456	917.51	884.47	2912.50	149843	1492.61
		Sikhs	(-) 112	120	(-) 232	(-) 9.48	19.58	(-) 40.77	752	445	307	236.48	154.51	1023.33	1021	2083.67
		Buddhists	26463	19460	7003	26.75	20.03	394.76	83100	74468	8632	196.52	176.72	5953.10	91669	271.89
		Jains	383	231	152	80.29	121.58	52.96	485	206	279	129.33	95.81	174.38	665	341.03
		Others	237	117	120	18.56	10.57	70.59	-	-	-	-	-	-	-	-
		Religion not stated	4157	2490	1667	376.54	310.47	551.99	-	-	-	-	-	-	-	-
		All Religions	474714	59011	415703	14.84	2.22	76.17	2117575	1318482	799093	136.06	94.58	492.17	2531912	221.71
8	Sub-Total, NER	Hindus	2468542	1225738	1242804	11.27	6.88	30.31	11372546	7534394	3838152	87.47	65.54	254.96	15079375	162.24
		Muslims	2605522	2256143	349379	29.44	27.50	54.02	7657370	6819480	837890	201.56	187.30	529.55	8410464	276.12
		Christians	1608185	1038995	569190	25.84	20.06	54.51	6046677	4572951	1473726	338.59	277.79	1055.04	6708597	596.88
		Sikhs	(-) 30	1477	(-) 1507	(-) 0.09	12.69	(-) 7.47	14880	5677	9203	88.06	76.33	97.28	20519	182.26
		Buddhists	88853	66533	22320	23.92	19.10	96.20	308862	267572	41290	203.94	181.75	975.89	383906	502.46
		Jains	3775	608	3167	12.95	13.35	12.87	17296	(-) 327	17623	110.63	(-) 5.96	173.71	22212	207.24
		Others	14494	(-) 8956	23450	1.66	(-) 1.26	14.29	81014	(-) 86961	167975	10.05	(-) 11.05	860.26	353924	66.36
		Religion not stated	55352	41193	14159	176.74	145.53	469.93	80669	63509	17160	1344.04	1060.25	143000.00	(-)317958	(-)78.58
		All Religions	6844693	4621731	2222962	17.86	14.31	36.88	25579314	19176295	6403019	130.62	108.12	346.73	30661039	211.48
9	Sikkim	Hindus	23114	(-) 32104	55218	7.01	(-) 11.06	140.99	208118	127009	81109	143.98	96.75	611.08	244497	226.04
		Muslims	2174	(-) 1255	3429	28.26	(-) 25.54	123.35	9532	3527	6005	2845.37	2692.37	2943.63	8660	717.48

1	2	3	28	29	30	31	32	33	34	35	36	37	38	39	40	41
		Christians	24407	13486	10921	67.58	41.89	278.38	58859	44447	14412	3539.33	3610.64	3336.11	57709	2051.51
		Sikhs	692	588	104	58.84	54.24	113.04	1774	1604	170	1887.23	2358.82	653.85	1796	2494.44
		Buddhists	15174	(-) 8423	23597	9.98	(-) 6.08	175.51	104599	73274	31325	167.05	128.78	547.93	117322	235.14
		Jains	131	82	49	71.58	143.86	38.89	123	(-) 36	159	64.40	(-) 20.57	993.75	295	1552.63
		Others	3374	3097	277	26.10	24.45	107.36	15901	15366	-	3985.21	3851.13	-	-	-
		Religion not stated	660	547	113	56.51	50.37	137.80	-	-	-	-	-	-	-	-
		All Religions	69726	(-) 23982	93708	12.89	(-) 4.99	156.52	400734	266824	133910	190.97	140.30	680.85	448388	276.46
10	Grand-Total, NER	Hindus	2491656	1193634	1298022	11.21	6.60	31.35	11580664	7661403	3919261	88.09	65.89	258.07	15323872	162.98
		Muslims	2607696	2254888	352808	29.44	27.47	54.32	7666902	6823007	843895	201.79	187.39	532.65	8419124	276.29
		Christians	1632592	1052481	580111	26.08	20.19	55.35	6105536	4617398	1488138	341.56	280.28	1062.08	6766306	600.52
		Sikhs	662	2065	(-) 1403	2.01	16.23	(-) 6.92	16654	7281	9373	98.02	97.02	98.81	22315	196.95
		Buddhists	104027	58110	45917	19.87	11.94	125.30	413461	340846	72615	193.15	166.98	729.95	501228	396.86
		Jains	3906	690	3216	13.31	14.96	13.01	17419	(-) 363	17782	110.07	(-) 6.41	175.00	22507	209.62
		Others	17868	(-) 5859	23727	2.02	(-) 0.81	14.44	96915	(-) 71595	168510	12.01	(-) 9.10	863.00	370224	69.42
		Religion not stated	56012	41740	14272	172.41	142.01	461.13	82497	65142	17355	1374.49	1087.51	144625.00	(-) 316149	(-) 78.13
		All Religions	6914419	4597749	2316670	17.79	14.03	38.06	25980048	19443119	3536929	131.26	108.46	350.25	31109427	212.17
11	India	Hindus	138678485	72830656	65847829	16.76	11.91	30.44	512965267	313983186	193982081	113.16	84.83	239.21	599730487	163.63
		Muslims	34056918	14709995	19346923	24.65	16.57	39.17	110827224	59771786	51055438	180.45	136.67	288.69	125304359	266.94
		Christians	3739572	763107	2976465	15.53	4.80	36.36	13596206	5990389	7605817	95.59	56.16	213.84	17091502	159.32
		Sikhs	1617386	824311	793075	8.42	5.84	15.52	10454319	6528054	3926265	100.73	77.69	198.69	12987201	165.53
		Buddhists	487765	(-) 78761	566526	6.13	(-) 1.61	18.50	4630647	1965572	2665075	121.47	68.98	276.73	5186936	159.30

1	2	3	28	29	30	31	32	33	34	35	36	37	38	39	40	41
		Jains	226700	(-) 104538	331238	5.37	(-) 10.36	10.30	1847107	(-) 141597	1988704	70.92	(-) 13.53	127.63	2424472	119.59
		Others	1298108	1196539	101569	19.55	19.93	15.94	5753178	5177340	575838	263.36	256.09	353.52	6438839	429.57
		Religion not stated	2139715	1116904	1022811	294.08	212.04	509.24	2831220	1618622	1212598	7846.41	6469.83	10958.86	2456410	597.82
		All Religions	182244649	91258213	90986436	17.72	12.29	31.80	662905168	394893352	268011816	120.98	89.98	245.67	771620206	175.67

Source: Calculated from the relevant Appendices.

– means information not available.

5
Literacy

Literacy is one of the most important characteristics of human beings. It defines the ability of a person to read and write. And the literacy rate is also one of the key indicators of human development. That means, higher the literacy rate—higher the number of educated persons, which is very much essential for the socio-economic development of a state or of a country.

Most of the North Eastern States are hilly and were lacking in many respects. It was really a challenging task to develop and establish the basic infrastructure, like Road, Electricity, Medical Institutions, Schools etc. in many of the remote areas. These basic necessities are very much essential for human development and expansion of education. However, with the starting of planning era, concerted efforts were taken up and gradually the situation started improving.

From Appendix–5, it can be seen that, even in 1961, the states like Arunachal Pradesh, Sikkim and Nagaland, were very much lacking in education. The literacy rate in Arunachal Pradesh was only 7.13 per cent, in Sikkim, it was 12.33 per cent and in Nagaland, it was 17.91 per cent. However, over the years, the literacy rate started increasing and by 2011, the literacy rate in Arunachal Pradesh reached to 66.95 per cent, in Sikkim, it touched to the height of 82.20 per cent and in Nagaland, it reached to 80.11 per cent. That indicates that, the literacy was increasing with a faster pace in Sikkim and within a period of 50 (fifty) years, i.e. from 1961 to 2011, there was an absolute increase of literacy rate by 59.82 per cent in Arunachal Pradesh, 69.87 per cent in Sikkim and 62.20 per cent in Nagaland.

The position of Tripura, Meghalaya and Manipur was slightly better. In 1961, the literacy rate in Tripura was 20.24 per cent, in Meghalaya, it was 26.92 per cent and in Manipur, it was 30.42 per cent. But it is seen that, literacy was increasing with a faster pace in Tripura and the rate touched the height of 87.75 per cent by 2011. In Meghalaya, the literacy rate reached to 75.48 per cent and in Manipur, it increased to 79.85 per cent by 2011. In last 50 (fifty) years, i.e. from 1961 to 2011, the absolute increase was also more in Tripura. It was 67.51 per cent in Tripura, 48.56 per cent in Meghalaya and 49.43 per cent in Manipur.

Amongst all the North Eastern States, the literacy position was comparatively better in Assam and Mizoram. In 1961, the literacy rate was 32.95 per cent in Assam and in Mizoram, it was much higher to the extent of 44.01 per cent. By 2011, the literacy rate reached to 73.18 per cent in Assam and in Mizoram, it reached to the height of 91.58 per cent, which is the second highest of our country. However, the absolute increase of literacy rate within a period of 50 (fifty) years starting with 1961, was 40.23 per cent in Assam and 47.57 per cent in Mizoram.

It is seen from the last population census, the overall literacy position of the country is better than some of the NE States *viz.* Arunachal Pradesh and Assam. In 1961, the overall literacy rate of the country was though 23.95 per cent, but it reached to 74.04 per cent by 2011. And within a period of last 50 (fifty) years, i.e. from 1961 to 2011, the absolute increase was 50.09 per cent, which is also more than many of the North Eastern States.

Further, it is seen that, the literacy rate for Males is higher than the literacy rate for Females in all the NE States as well as in the country as a whole. In the beginning of sixties, the literacy gap between Males and Females was though more, but over the years, this gap narrowed down in all the States except Arunachal Pradesh. In 1961, the literacy gap in Arunachal Pradesh was 10.83 per cent, which increased to 14.12 per cent in 2011. This indicates that, the education of Girl Child is lagging behind or in other words, Girls are not coming forward for education, as the Boys are, in Arunachal Pradesh.

On the other hand, the literacy gap between Males and Females in Meghalaya was the lowest. In 1961, it was 11.17 per cent, which came down to 3.39 per cent in 2011. In Mizoram, the literacy gap in 1961 was though quite high to the extent of 18.71 per cent, but it came down very rapidly and reached to 4.32 per cent in 2011. In Nagaland also, the literacy gap reduced at a faster pace. In 1961, the literacy gap was 12.70 per cent, which narrowed down to 6.60 per cent in 2011.

The Male-Female literacy gap is reasonably high in the States of Tripura, Sikkim, Assam and Manipur. In Tripura, the gap was 19.42 per cent in 1961, which has come down to 9.03 per cent in 2011, in

Sikkim, it was 15.37 per cent, which has reduced to 10.86 per cent by 2011 and in Assam the gap was 11.54 per cent. Amongst all the NE States, literacy gap was the highest in Manipur. In 1961, it was 29.19 per cent and it has come down to 13.32 per cent in 2011. The literacy gap in the country as a whole was also quite high. In 1961, it was 21.47 per cent, which has reduced to 16.68 per cent by 2011.

It is a fact that, in urban areas, educational facilities are more. Moreover, Government Offices, Business Establishment, Industry and other economic activities are more in urban and therefore, the number of educated persons are comparatively more in urban areas. That means, the literacy rate is normally more in urban than in rural. Amongst the North Eastern States, the Rural-Urban literacy gap is more in Arunachal Pradesh, Nagaland, Meghalaya and Tripura. In 1971, the Rural-Urban literacy gap in Arunachal Pradesh was 40.67 per cent and even in 2001, it remained at a high of 30.43 per cent. The Rural-Urban literacy gap in Nagaland was 40.30 per cent in 1961, which however narrowed down to 21.95 per cent in 2001. In Meghalaya, the gap was 40.13 per cent in 1961 and it remained at a high of 30.01 per cent in 2001. The position of Tripura was slightly better. In 1961, the literacy gap was 35.05 per cent, which reduced to 19.49 per cent in 2001.

The position of Manipur, Mizoram and Sikkim is comparatively better. The Rural-Urban literacy gap in Manipur was 22.29 per cent in 1961 and it narrowed down to 11.99 per cent in 2001. In case of Mizoram, it was 23.30 per cent in 1961 and in 2001, it reduced to 14.86 per cent. The Rural-Urban literacy gap in Sikkim was 29.52 per cent in 1961 and it came down to 17.09 per cent in 2001. In Assam, even in 2001, the gap was quite high at 25.61 per cent.

The position of the Rural-Urban literacy gap of the country as a whole is comparatively better than the position of many of the North Eastern States. It was 28.04 per cent in 1961 and it came down to 21.18 per cent in 2001 and further reduced to 16.07 per cent in 2011. Further details can be seen from the Appendix-5.

Appendix-5

State-wise Percentage Distribution of Literacy with sex and Rural-Urban Break-up in different Census years

Sl. No.	Name of the State/ India	Total/ Rural/ Urban	Percentage Distribution of Literacy in the Census Year																	
			1961			1971			1981			1991			2001			2011**		
			Person	Male	Female	Person	Male	Female	Person	Male	Female	Person	Male	Female	Person	Male	Female	Person	Male	Female
1	2	3	4	5	6	7	8	9	10	11	12	13	14	15	16	17	18	19	20	21
1	Arunachal Pradesh	T	7.13	12.25	1.42	11.29	17.82	3.71	20.79	28.94	11.32	41.59	51.45	29.69	54.34	63.83	43.53	66.95	73.69	59.57
		R	7.13	12.25	1.42	9.79	15.77	3.00	18.51	26.36	9.60	37.02	47.00	25.31	47.83	57.65	36.95	61.59	68.79	53.78
		U	*	*	*	50.46	59.28	31.18	53.22	60.80	41.18	71.59	77.99	62.23	78.26	85.19	69.49	84.57	89.45	79.04
2	Assam	T	32.95	-	-	33.94	-	-	-	-	-	52.89	61.87	43.03	63.25	71.28	54.61	73.18	78.81	67.27
		R	-	-	-	-	-	-	-	-	-	49.32	58.66	39.19	59.73	68.22	50.70	70.44	76.51	64.09
		U	-	-	-	-	-	-	-	-	-	79.39	84.37	73.32	85.34	89.74	80.24	88.88	91.84	85.71
3	Manipur	T	30.42	45.12	15.93	32.91	46.04	19.53	41.35	53.29	29.06	59.89	71.63	47.60	70.53	80.33	60.53	79.85	86.49	73.17
		R	28.48	42.69	14.54	29.83	43.04	16.35	37.37	49.33	25.06	55.79	67.64	43.26	67.29	77.31	56.95	77.15	84.14	69.95
		U	50.77	70.35	30.88	53.24	65.80	40.43	52.44	64.30	40.20	70.53	82.11	58.67	79.28	88.71	70.01	85.98	92.05	80.21
4	Meghalaya	T	26.92	32.32	21.15	29.49	34.12	24.56	34.08	37.89	30.08	49.10	53.12	44.85	62.56	65.43	59.61	75.48	77.17	73.78
		R	20.79	25.26	16.19	23.40	27.68	18.94	27.45	30.83	23.96	41.05	44.83	37.12	56.29	59.24	53.24	71.15	72.83	69.45
		U	60.92	67.36	52.50	65.22	69.93	59.69	64.12	68.90	58.82	81.74	85.72	77.32	86.30	89.05	83.50	91.33	93.17	89.49

1	2	3	4	5	6	7	8	9	10	11	12	13	14	15	16	17	18	19	20	21
5	Mizoram	T	44.01	53.41	34.70	53.79	60.49	46.71	59.88	64.46	54.91	82.27	85.61	78.60	88.80	90.72	86.75	91.58	93.72	89.40
		R	42.76	52.30	33.39	51.39	58.29	44.10	55.24	60.19	49.92	72.47	77.35	67.03	81.27	84.93	77.26	84.31	88.35	80.04
		U	66.06	71.49	59.80	72.53	77.55	67.18	74.06	77.26	70.47	93.45	95.15	91.61	96.13	96.43	95.80	98.10	98.67	97.54
6	Nagaland	T	17.91	24.04	11.34	27.40	35.02	18.65	42.57	50.06	33.89	61.65	67.62	54.75	66.59	71.16	61.46	80.11	83.29	76.69
		R	15.82	21.39	9.96	23.71	30.51	16.39	38.59	46.09	30.25	57.23	63.42	50.36	62.79	67.58	57.52	75.86	79.49	72.01
		U	56.12	64.30	43.11	60.79	66.13	49.47	64.23	69.26	56.91	83.10	85.94	79.10	84.74	87.44	81.42	90.21	92.11	88.10
7	Tripura	T	20.24	29.61	10.19	30.98	40.20	21.19	42.12	51.70	32.00	60.44	70.58	49.65	73.19	81.02	64.91	87.75	92.18	83.15
		R	17.08	26.38	7.16	27.13	36.43	17.27	38.23	43.24	27.64	56.08	67.07	44.33	69.72	78.40	60.50	85.58	90.86	80.06
		U	52.13	61.33	41.74	64.01	72.42	55.03	73.66	79.95	67.09	83.09	89.00	76.93	89.21	93.21	85.03	93.61	95.80	91.38
9	Sikkim	T	12.33	19.63	4.26	17.74	25.37	8.90	34.05	43.95	22.20	56.94	65.74	46.69	68.81	76.04	60.40	82.20	87.29	76.43
		R	11.08	18.25	3.22	14.80	22.11	6.53	30.05	40.25	18.24	54.38	63.49	43.98	66.82	74.45	58.01	79.82	85.42	73.42
		U	40.60	48.29	30.37	46.17	53.48	35.43	54.86	61.44	45.42	80.89	85.19	74.94	83.91	87.81	79.16	89.26	92.94	85.19
11	India	T	23.95	34.37	12.90	29.48	39.52	18.70	36.23	46.89	24.82	52.21	64.13	39.29	64.84	75.26	53.67	74.04	82.14	65.46
		R	18.83	28.89	8.42	23.69	33.76	13.08	29.65	40.79	17.96	44.69	57.87	30.62	58.74	70.70	46.13	68.91	78.57	58.75
		U	46.87	57.43	34.41	52.37	61.24	42.05	57.40	65.83	47.82	73.08	81.09	64.05	79.92	86.27	72.86	84.98	89.67	79.92

Source: Occasional Paper No. 1 of 1987 on Literacy Trends & web-site, Registrar General and Census Commissioner, New Delhi.

* entire Arunachal Pradesh was treated as Rural, ** Provisional, - information not available.

6
Workers and Non-Workers

The population of a state or of a country can be classified into 2 (two) main groups *viz*. Workers and Non-workers. Workers ordinarily means, persons engaged in any kind of economic activities (paid or unpaid). Workers are generally of 2 (two) types, e.g. Main workers and Marginal workers. Main workers are those, who work for the major part of the year (i.e. 6 months or more of the year). Whereas, Marginal workers are those, who do not work for the major part of the year (i.e. less than 6 months of the year). And the Non-workers are those, who do not do any economic activity. The Non-workers occupy the major portion of the population as it includes children, students, pensioners, old aged people, rentiers, beggars etc.

It is a known fact that, the economy of a state or of a country depends on the skill and educational level of its workers. Therefore, it is always desirable that, more number of people should be engaged in economic activities and they have their requisite qualification and expertise. In other words, it can be said that, lesser the number of Non-workers—better the economic condition of the state or of the country. But that is always not feasible, as children and students, who occupy a very big portion of population, are considered as Non-workers. However, a complete picture of the Workers and Non-workers of each of the Northern states as well of the country as a whole, as per 1971 to 2011 census, can be seen from the Appendix–6.1 to Appendix–6.6.

It is seen that, the proportion of Workers was much less than the proportion of Non-workers in all the North Eastern States except Arunachal Pradesh. In seventies and eighties, Arunachal Pradesh had a unique character in this regard, which however, changed in later years. In 1971, the percentage of Main workers was quite high at 57.65 and that of Non-workers was 42.35. In 1981, this was changed to 49.61 per cent and 47.37 per cent respectively. That means, the proportion of

Main workers decreased by (–) 8.04 per cent, whereas, the proportion of Non-workers increased by (+) 5.02 per cent.

From 1991, the situation reversed and the proportion of Main workers reduced to 45.22 per cent whereas the proportion of Non-workers increased to 53.76 per cent. This shows that, in the decade of 1981–91, the proportion of Main workers decreased by (–) 4.39 per cent whereas, in case of Non-workers, it increased by (+) 6.39 per cent. In 2001, the proportion of Main workers further reduced to 37.80 per cent, but the proportion of Non-workers increased to 56.02 per cent. In 2011, these two proportions became 34.60 per cent and 57.53 per cent respectively, and the decadal change in case of Main workers was (–) 7.42 per cent in 1991–2001 and (–) 3.20 per cent in 2001–11, but in case of Non-workers, it was (+) 2.26 per cent and (+) 1.51 per cent respectively. Moreover, it is seen that, within a period of 40 (forty) years, i.e. from 1971 to 2011, the proportion of Main workers decreased by (–) 23.05 per cent, whereas the proportion of Marginal workers increased by (+) 4.84 per cent and the proportion of Non-workers also increased by (+) 15.18 per cent.

The position of Nagaland was more or less similar to Arunachal Pradesh. In seventies, the proportion of Main workers was more than the proportion of Non-workers in Nagaland. It is seen that, the proportion of Main workers was 50.75 per cent and that of Non-workers was 49.25 per cent in 1971. But in 1981, the situation changed, and the proportion of Main workers reduced to 47.53 per cent whereas the proportion of Non-workers increased to 51.77 per cent. In 1991, these two proportions became 42.29 per cent and 57.32 per cent respectively. That means, the decadal change in case of Main workers was (–) 3.22 per cent in 1971–81 and (–) 5.24 per cent in 1981–91, but in case of Non-workers, it was (+) 2.52 per cent and (+) 5.55 per cent respectively in these two decades.

From 2001, the population of Nagaland started showing a different trend. As usual the proportion of Main workers was declining at a faster pace, but the proportion of Marginal workers was increasing considerably. In 2001, the proportion of Main workers was 35.38 per cent, the proportion of Marginal workers was 7.22 per cent and the proportion of Non-workers was 57.40 per cent. In 2011, these three proportions became 37.46 per cent, 11.78 per cent and 50.76 per cent respectively. That indicates that, in the decade of 1991-2001, the proportion of Main workers decreased by (–) 6.91 per cent, Marginal workers increased by (+) 6.83 per cent and Non-workers also increased marginally by (+) 0.08 per cent. But in the decade of 2001–11, there was a change. The proportion of Main workers increased by (+) 2.08 per cent, Marginal workers also increased by (+) 4.56 per cent whereas, the proportion of Non-workers decreased by (–) 6.64 per cent. However, within a period of 40 (forty) years, i.e. from 1971 to 2011, the proportion of Main workers decreased by (–) 13.29 per cent, but the proportion of Marginal workers increased by (+) 11.08 per cent and the proportion of Non-workers also increased by (+) 1.51 per cent.

The position of Meghalaya, Mizoram and Sikkim was more or less similar. In seventies and eighties, the proportion of Main workers was considerably high. But over the years, it was decreasing and at the same time the proportion of Marginal workers was increasing. It is seen that, in Meghalaya, the proportion of Main workers was 44.17 per cent in 1971, but it came down to 43.44 per cent in 1981, 40.32 per cent in 1991, 32.65 per cent in 2001 and then to 31.06 per cent in 2011. Whereas, the proportion of Marginal workers, which was 2.49 per cent in 1981 and 2.35 per cent in 1991, increased to 9.19 per cent in 2001 and then to a bit less of 8.90 per cent in 2011. And the proportion of Non-workers, which was 55.83 per cent in 1971, decreased slightly and became 54.08 per cent in 1981. After that, it started increasing again and reached to 57.33 per cent in 1991, 58.16 per cent in 2001 and finally to 60.04 per cent in 2011.

However, the decadal change in respect of Main workers was (–) 0.73 per cent in 1971–81, (–) 3.12 per cent in 1981–91, (–) 7.67 per cent in 1991-2001 and (–) 1.59 per cent in 2001-11 and within a period of 40 (forty) years, it decreased by (–) 13.11 per cent. The decadal change of Marginal workers shows some ups and downs. During 1981–91, it decreased slightly by (–) 0.14 per cent and then it increased by (+) 6.84 per cent during 1991-2001 and again it decreased slightly by (–) 0.29 per cent in 2001–11. However, within a period of 30 (thirty) years, it increased by (+) 6.41 per cent. In case of Non-workers, the decadal change was though negative by (–) 1.75 per cent during 1971–81, but it increased by (+) 3.25 per cent in 1981–91, (+) 0.83 per cent in 1991-2001 and (+) 1.88 per cent during 2001–11. But within a period of 40 (forty) years, it increased by (+) 4.21 per cent.

The information on Workers and Non-workers of seventies and eighties for the State of Mizoram was not available. However, from the information of later years, it is seen that, the proportion of Main workers was 42.09 per cent in 1991, which decreased to 40.79 per cent in 2001 and finally to 37.83 per cent in 2011. But the decadal change was (–) 1.30 per cent in 1991-2001 and (–) 2.96 per cent in 2001–11 and within a period of 20 (twenty) years, i.e. from 1991 to 2011, the proportion of Main workers decreased by (–) 4.26 per cent. The proportion of Marginal workers however, showed some ups and downs. In 1991, the proportion of Marginal workers was 6.82 per cent, which increased to 11.78 per cent in 2001 and then again came down to 6.53 per cent in 2011. The decadal change was (+) 4.96 per cent in 1991-2001 and (–) 5.25 per cent in 2001–11 and within a period of 20 (twenty) years, the proportion of Marginal workers decreased slightly by (–) 0.29 per cent.

The proportion of Non-workers also showed some ups and downs. In 1991, the proportion of Non-workers was 51.09 per cent, which came down to 47.43 per cent in 2001 and again increased to 55.64 per cent in 2011. The decadal change was (–) 3.66 per cent in 1991-2001, but it increased to (+) 8.21 per cent in 2001–11 and within a period of 20 (twenty) years, the proportion of Non-workers increased by (+) 4.55 per cent.

In case of Sikkim, the proportion of Main workers and Marginal workers showed a unique trend. That means, the proportion of Main workers was continuously decreasing and the proportion of Marginal workers was increasing whereas, the proportion of Non-workers was showing some ups and downs. It is seen that, the proportion of Main workers was 46.60 per cent in 1981, which came down to 40.45 per cent in 1991, 39.36 per cent in 2001 and finally to 37.73 per cent in 2011. And the decadal change was (–) 6.15 per cent in 1981–91, (–) 1.09 per cent in 1991-2001, (–) 1.63 per cent in 2001–11 and within a period of 30 (thirty) years, i.e. from 1981 to 2011, the proportion of Main workers decreased by (–) 8.87 per cent.

The proportion of Marginal workers, which was 1.70 per cent in 1981, though slightly decreased to 1.07 per cent in 1991, but again it increased to a high of 9.27 per cent in 2001 and then to 12.73 per cent in 2011. The decadal change was though negative with a small amount of (–) 0.63 per cent during 1981–91, but it increased to (+) 8.20 per cent during 1991-2001 and then to (+) 3.46 per cent during 2001–11 and within a period of 30 (thirty) years, the proportion of Marginal workers increased by (+) 11.03 per cent.

In case of Non-workers, the proportion was 51.70 per cent in 1981, which increased to 58.48 per cent in 1991 and then again came down to 51.37 per cent in 2001 and finally to 49.54 per cent in 2011. And the decadal change was (+) 6.78 per cent in 1981–91, (–) 7.11 per cent in 1991-2001 and (–) 1.83 per cent in 2011, but within a period of 30 (thirty) years, the proportion of Non-workers decreased by (–) 2.16 per cent.

In Manipur, the proportion of Main workers was comparatively less in early seventies and in eighties and thereafter, though it increased slightly, but again started declining. The proportion of Marginal workers was also less in eighties, but later on, it started increasing. However, the proportion of Non-workers was comparatively high and it also showed some ups and downs.

It is seen that, the proportion of Main workers was 34.57 per cent in 1971 and it increased to 40.35 per cent in 1981. But in 1991, it came down to 38.55 per cent and then to 30.43 per cent in 2001 and again it increased to 34.11 per cent in 2011. The decadal change was (+) 5.78 per cent in 1971–81, (–) 1.80 per cent in 1981–91, (–) 8.12 per cent in 1991-2001 and (+) 3.68 per cent in 2001–11. And within a period of 40 (forty) years, i.e. from 1971 to 2011, the proportion of Main workers decreased by (–) 0.46 per cent.

The proportion of Marginal workers was 2.85 per cent in 1981 and then it increased to 3.63 per cent in 1991 and to 13.19 per cent in 2001 and finally to 11.57 per cent in 2011. The decadal change was (+) 0.78 per cent in 1981–91, (+) 9.56 per cent in 1991-2001 and (–) 1.62 per cent in 2001–11, but within a period of 40 (forty) years, the proportion of Marginal workers increased by (+) 8.72 per cent.

The proportion of Non-workers was comparatively high at 65.43 per cent in 1971, which came down to 56.80 per cent in 1981 and then increased slightly to 57.82 per cent in 1991 and again decreased to 56.38 per cent in 2001 and finally to 54.32 per cent in 2011. The decadal change was (–) 8.63 per cent in 1971–81, (+) 1.02 per cent in 1981–91, (–) 1.44 per cent in 1991-2001 and (–) 2.06 per cent in 2001-11. But within a period of 40 (forty) years, the proportion of Non-workers decreased by (–) 11.11 per cent.

It is seen that, amongst all the North Eastern States, the proportion of Main workers was comparatively low and it was more or less the same in both the States of Assam and Tripura. And it maintained almost a steady value over the years. In case of Marginal workers, the proportion was also very low and there was no much difference in the values of these two States over the years. However, the proportion of Non-workers maintained a very high value in Assam as well as in Tripura from 1971 to 2011.

In Assam, the proportion of Main workers was 28.99 per cent in

1971, which increased a bit and reached to 31.19 per cent in 1991 and then again came down to 26.69 per cent in 2001 and finally reached to 27.84 per cent in 2011. The decadal change was (–) 4.50 per cent in 1991-2001 and (+) 1.15 per cent in 2001–11. But within a period of 40 (forty) years, i.e. from 1971 to 2011, the proportion of Main workers decreased by (–) 1.15 per cent. The proportion of Marginal workers was only 4.89 per cent in 1991, which increased to 9.10 per cent in 2001 and then to 10.52 per cent in 2011. The decadal change was (+) 4.21 per cent in 1991-2001 and (+) 1.42 per cent in 2001-11 and within a period of 20 (twenty) years, i.e. from 1991 to 2011, the proportion of Marginal workers increased by (+) 5.63 per cent.

The proportion of Non-workers was quite high at 73.28 per cent in 1971, which came down to 63.92 per cent in 1991. It slightly increased and reached to 64.21 per cent in 2001 and thereafter reduced to 61.64 per cent in 2011. The decadal change was (+) 0.29 per cent during 1991-2001 and (–) 2.57 per cent during 2001–11 and within a period of 40 (forty) years, the proportion of Non-workers decreased by (–) 11.64 per cent.

In Tripura, the proportion of Main workers was 27.79 per cent in 1971, which increased slightly to 29.64 per cent in 1981 and then reduced, 29.09 per cent in 1991, 28.52 per cent in 2001 and again increased to 29.32 per cent in 2011. The decadal change was (+) 1.85 per cent in 1971–81, (–) 0.55 per cent in 1981–91, (–) 0.57 per cent in 1991-2001, and (+) 0.80 per cent in 2001–11. But within a period of 40 (forty) years, i.e. from 1971 to 2011, the proportion of Main workers increased by (+) 1.53 per cent.

The proportion of Marginal workers was 2.62 per cent in 1981, which came down to 2.05 per cent in 1991 and thereafter increased to 7.73 per cent in 2001 and to 10.68 per cent in 2011. The decadal change was though negative by a small amount of (–) 0.57 per cent in 1981–91, but it increased to (+) 5.68 per cent in 1991-2001 and then to (+) 2.95 per cent in 2001–11. And within a period of 40 (forty) years, the proportion of Marginal workers increased by (+) 8.06 per cent.

The proportion of Non-workers showed some ups and downs. In 1971, it was 72.21 per cent and in 1981, it came down to 67.73 per cent and then again went up to 68.86 per cent in 1991 and again reduced to 63.75 per cent in 2001 and finally to 60.00 per cent in 2011. The decadal change was (–) 4.48 per cent in 1971–81, (+) 1.13 per cent in 1981–91, (–) 5.11 per cent in 1991-2001 and (–) 3.75 per cent in 2001–11. But within a period of 40 (forty) years, the proportion of Non-workers decreased by (–) 12.21 per cent.

The position of the country as a whole was slightly different from the position of the North Eastern States. It is seen that, the proportion of workers of the country as a whole was comparatively less than the proportion of workers of each of the States of NE Region except Assam and Tripura. It is found that, in early seventies, not even one third of the total population of our country was workers. The proportion of Main workers was though increased slightly in eighties, but again, it started declining. The proportion of Marginal workers was also very less in eighties, which was of course, started increasing in subsequent years. However, the proportion of Non-workers was quite high in seventies and eighties, but in later years, it was showing a declining trend.

It is seen that, the proportion of Main workers of the country was 32.92 per cent in 1971, which increased to 36.77 per cent in 1981 and then came down to 34.10 per cent in 1991, 30.43 per cent in 2001 and finally to 29.94 per cent in 2011. The decadal change was (+) 3.85 per cent in 1971–81, (–) 2.67 per cent in 1981–91, (–) 3.67 per cent in 1991-2001 and (–) 0.49 per cent in 2001–11. And within a period of 40 (forty) years, i.e. from 1971 to 2011, the proportion of Main workers decreased by (–) 2.98 per cent.

The proportion of Marginal workers was 3.32 per cent in 1981, which increased slightly to 3.36 per cent in 1991 and then to 8.67 per cent in 2001 and finally to 9.86 per cent in 2011. The decadal change was (+) 0.04 per cent in 1981–91, (+) 5.31 per cent in 1991-2001 and (+) 1.19 per cent in 2001–11 and within a period of 30 (thirty) years, the proportion of Marginal workers increased by (+) 6.54 per cent.

The proportion of Non-workers was quite high at 67.08 per cent in 1971 and thereafter, it showed a declining trend and came down to 63.23 per cent in 1981, 62.54 per cent in 1991, 60.90 per cent in 2001 and then to 60.20 per cent in 2011. The decadal change was (–) 3.85 per cent in 1971–81, (–) 0.69 per cent in 1981–91, (–) 1.64 per cent in 1991-2001 and (–) 0.70 per cent in 2001–11. However, within a period of 40 (forty) years, i.e. from 1971 to 2011, the proportion of Non-workers of the country decreased by (–) 6.88 per cent.

Further, it is seen that, in case of Main workers, the proportion of Males was more than the proportion of Females in all the North Eastern States and also in the country as a whole in all the years from 1971 to 2011. However, it is also evident that, in some of the tribal dominated States, like Arunachal Pradesh, Meghalaya, Mizoram, Nagaland, Manipur and Sikkim, the proportion of Female Main workers was quite high and in many cases, there was no much difference between the values of the proportion of Male Main workers and the proportion of Female Main workers. It is a known fact that, Tribal Females are more active and they take equal part in Agricultural and other economic activities. And it is also a fact that, the proportion of Female Main workers is generally high in Rural areas.

However, it is evident that, the proportion of Male Main workers of the NE States did not show any uniform trend between Rural and Urban. In some of the States like, Arunachal Pradesh, Assam and Sikkim, the proportion of Male Main workers was comparatively more in Urban in all these years. But in the States of Manipur, Meghalaya and Mizoram, the proportion of Male Main workers was comparatively more in Rural in all these years. However, in the States of Nagaland and Tripura, the position was different. In seventies and eighties, though it was more in Rural, but in later years, the proportion of Male Main workers did not follow any rule. Sometimes it was more in Rural, sometimes in Urban. But, in most of the cases, the difference between the values of the proportion of Rural and Urban was not much.

The position of the country as a whole was slightly different from the position of the NE States. It is seen that, the proportion of Male Main workers was much higher than the proportion of Female Main workers both in Rural as well as in Urban in all these years, i.e. from 1971 to 2011. However, it is seen that, the proportion of Female Main workers was always more in Rural than in Urban, all the times. Further, it is also seen that, the proportion of Male Main workers did not follow any pattern. In seventies and eighties, it was more in Rural and in later years, it was more in Urban, though the difference between the values of the proportion of Rural and Urban, was not much at any point of time.

The Marginal workers however, showed a unique trend in all the NE States. It is seen that, the proportion of Female Marginal workers was higher than the proportion of Male Marginal workers in most of the cases, both in Rural and Urban. It is also seen that, the proportion of Female Marginal workers was higher in Rural than Urban with a few exceptions. The position of the country as a whole was also similar to North Eastern States. It is seen that the proportion of Female Marginal workers of the country was always higher than the proportion of the Male Marginal workers in Rural as well as in Urban. Moreover, the proportion of Female Marginal workers was also higher in Rural than Urban in all the years from 1981 to 2011. From this it is evident that, compared to Males, more number of Females, particularly Rural Females, are going for the job of Marginal worker.

The Non-workers play completely a different role. It occupies the major portion of the population of the State or of the country. In some cases, it is seen that, almost three fourth of the population are Non-workers. Further, it is seen that, the Non-workers are more in Urban areas than Rural areas. However, the proportion of Female Non-workers was always much higher than the proportion of Male Non-workers, both in Rural as well as in Urban.

In the North Eastern Region, the States like, Assam and Tripura, were having maximum number of Non-workers. It is seen that, in early seventies, the overall proportion of Non-workers in Assam, was 73.28 per cent, which however reduced to 63.92 per cent in 1991. But it increased slightly and reached to 64.21 per cent in 2001 and again came down to 61.64 per cent in 2011. However, in 1971, the proportion of Non-workers was higher in Rural to the extent of 73.44 per cent, but in later years, the proportion of Non-workers was higher in Urban. In 1991, it was 69.08 per cent and thereafter it decreased slightly and reached to 66.80 per cent in 2001 and finally to 63.59 per cent in 2011. The proportion of Urban Female Non-workers was as high as 99.21 per cent in 1971, which however, showed a declining trend and reached to 92.48 per cent in 1991, 89.38 per cent in 2001 and 85.14 per cent in 2011.

The position of Tripura was similar to Assam. The overall proportion of Non-workers was 72.21 per cent in 1971, but it reduced to 67.73 per cent in 1981, but it increased slightly and reached to 68.86 per cent in 1991 and again came down to 63.75 per cent in 2001 and finally to 60.00 per cent in 2011. In Tripura also, the proportion of Urban Non-workers was more. It was 75.75 per cent in 1971 and after that, it showed a declining trend. It came down to 72.40 per cent in 1981, 71.11 per cent in 1991, 67.54 per cent in 2001 and finally to 63.24 per cent in 2011. The proportion of Urban Female Non-workers was as high as 94.57 per cent in 1971, which however, decreased to 91.27 per cent in 1981, 90.73 per cent in 1991, 87.56 per cent in 2001 and to 84.00 per cent in 2011.

The proportion of Non-workers was comparatively high in the States of Manipur and Meghalaya. In Manipur, the overall proportion of Non-workers was 65.43 per cent in 1971 and after that, it showed some ups and downs. It was 56.80 per cent in 1981, 57.82 per cent in 1991, 56.38 per cent in 2001 and 54.32 per cent in 2011. The proportion of Urban Non-workers was as high as 73.44 per cent in 1971, but it came down to 64.48 per cent in 1981 and then increased slightly and reached to 65.82 per cent in 1991 and thereafter reduced to 61.44 per cent in 2001 and finally to 58.59 per cent in 2011. The proportion of Urban Female Non-workers was also quite high to the extent of 85.13 per cent in 1971, which however, decreased to 71.39 per cent in 1981 and again increased slightly to 72.12 per cent in 1991 and thereafter reduced to 67.75 per cent in 2001 and finally to 66.83 per cent in 2011.

In case of Meghalaya, the overall proportion of Non-workers was 55.83 per cent in 1971 and then it reduced slightly and became 54.08 per cent in 1981. After that, it started showing an increasing trend. It reached to 57.33 per cent in 1991, 58.16 per cent in 2001 and to 60.04 per cent in 2011. The proportion of Urban Non-workers was quite high and it showed almost a steady position. It was 67.66 per cent in 1971, 67.37 per cent in 1981, 67.70 per cent in 1991, 67.49 per cent in 2001 and finally decreased to 64.37 per cent in 2011. The proportion of Urban Female Non-workers was also quite high, but it showed a declining trend. It was 86.64 per cent in 1971, 83.88 per cent in 1981, 82.77 per cent in 1991, 79.02 per cent in 2001 and 76.41 per cent in 2011.

In other States like Arunachal Pradesh, Mizoram, Nagaland and Sikkim, though the proportion of Non-workers was comparatively lower in seventies and eighties, but later on, it is seen that, more than half of their population was Non-workers. In Arunachal Pradesh, the overall proportion of Non-workers was 42.35 per cent in 1971, but it increased to 47.37 per cent in 1981, 53.76 per cent in 1991, 56.02 per cent in 2001 and finally reached to 57.53 per cent in 2011. The proportion of Non-workers was also higher in Urban areas of Arunachal Pradesh. It was 48.43 per cent in 1971, 58.53 per cent in 1981, 63.61 per cent in 1991, 64.50 per cent in 2001 and 63.03 per cent in 2011. The proportion of Urban Female Non-workers was also quite high. It was 89.42 per cent in 1971, but it showed a declining trend and became 88.38 per cent in 1981, 88.05 per cent in 1991, 82.85 per cent in 2001 and finally to 78.68 per cent in 2011.

The information of Mizoram in respect of seventies and eighties was not available. However, it is seen that, the overall proportion of Non-workers was 51.09 per cent in 1991, which though decreased slightly and became 47.43 per cent in 2001, but again increased and reached to 55.64 per cent in 2011. The proportion of Non-workers was also higher in Urban areas. It was 53.77 per cent in 1991, 52.13 per cent in 2001 and 59.02 per cent in 2011. The proportion of Urban Female Non-workers was 60.63 per cent in 1991, 59.48 per cent in 2001 and 68.95 per cent in 2011.

In Nagaland, the overall proportion of Non-workers was though 49.25 per cent in 1971, but it increased to 51.77 per cent in 1981, 57.32 per cent in 1991, 57.40 per cent in 2001 and then decreased a bit and reached to 50.76 per cent in 2011. The proportion of Urban Non-workers was also high. It was though 49.62 per cent in 1971, but it increased to 65.03 per cent in 1981, 67.28 per cent in 1991, 68.97 per cent in 2001 and then reduced to 62.56 per cent in 2011. The proportion of Urban Female Non-workers was also high to the extent of 90.89 per cent in 1971, which however, came down to 89.07 per cent in 1981, 87.91 per cent in 1991, 84.39 per cent in 2001 and to 74.13 per cent in 2011.

The overall proportion of Non-workers in Sikkim was 51.70 per cent in 1981, 58.48 per cent in 1991, 51.37 per cent in 2001 and 49.54 per cent in 2011. Like other states, the proportion of Non-workers was higher in Urban areas. It was 58.19 per cent in 1981, 60.80 per cent in 1991, 59.85 per cent in 2001 and 58.10 per cent in 2011. The proportion of Urban Female Non-workers was also quite high. It was 84.42 per cent in 1981, which however showed a declining trend and reached to 81.25 per cent in 1991, 78.33 per cent in 2001 and finally to 75.20 per cent in 2011.

The position of the country as a whole was somewhat different from the position of the North Eastern States. It is seen that, the proportion of Non-workers of the country was higher than the proportion of Non-workers of many of the NE States, both in Rural as well as in Urban. The proportion of Female Non-workers was also higher in many cases.

It is seen that the overall proportion of Non-workers of the country was as high as 67.08 per cent in 1971, which however showed a declining trend and reached to 63.23 per cent in 1981, 62.54 per cent in 1991, 60.90 per cent in 2001 and finally to 60.20 per cent in 2011. Similar to NE States, the proportion of Non-workers of the country was higher in Urban areas. It was quite high to the extent of 70.67 per cent in 1971, but after that, it started declining. It became 70.00 per cent in 1981, 69.83 per cent in 1991, 67.75 per cent in 2001 and finally to 64.69 per cent in 2011. In case of Urban Female Non-workers, the proportion was as high as 93.39 per cent in 1971, which however decreased to 91.68 per cent in 1981, 90.83 per cent in 1991, 88.12 per cent in 2001 and finally reached to 84.56 per cent in 2011.

The children are considered as Non-workers. They occupy a considerable portion of population of the State or of the country. However, their proportion, though vary from state to state and time to time, but not to a large extent. Generally, the proportion of children is higher in Rural areas than in Urban areas. Moreover, the proportion of Girls is higher than the proportion of Boys in many of the North Eastern States. This is also true both in Rural as well as in Urban with a few exceptions. It is also a fact that, the proportion of children is showing a declining trend over a period of 40 (forty) years from 1971 to 2011, both in Rural and Urban.

It is seen that, amongst all the North Eastern States, Assam was having the highest proportion of children of the age group (0–4) years. Their overall proportion was 17.39 per cent in 1971, but it came down to 10.30 per cent in 2011. The proportion was more in Rural to the extent of 17.84 per cent in 1971, which reduced to 10.82 per cent in 2011. The proportion of Rural Girls, which was quite high to the extent of 18.82 per cent in 1971, also came down to 10.86 per cent in 2011. The proportion of children of the age group (0–4) years in Assam was comparatively much less in Urban. It was 12.79 per cent in 1971, but it reduced considerably and became 7.11 per cent in 2011.

The proportion of children of the age group (0–4) years was also high in Meghalaya. In 1971, the overall proportion was 15.90 per cent and it came down to 13.69 per cent in 2011. In Rural areas, the proportion was higher to the extent of 16.50 per cent in 1971 and it reduced to 14.82 per cent in 2011. In Urban, the proportion was comparatively less. It was 12.40 per cent in 1971, which reduced considerably and became 9.18 per cent in 2011. The proportion of Rural Girls was high at 16.60 per cent in 1971 and it became 14.75 per cent in 2011.

The proportion of children of the age group (0–4) years in Arunachal Pradesh, Manipur, Mizoram and Tripura was more or less similar. The overall proportion was ranging from 14.85 per cent of Arunachal Pradesh to 8.78 per cent of Tripura, within a period of 40 (forty) years from 1971. In all these States, the proportion of children was higher in Rural than Urban. In Rural, it was in the range of 14.93 per cent of Arunachal Pradesh to 9.22 per cent of Manipur. Whereas, in Urban, it was 13.53 per cent of Mizoram to 6.71 per cent of Tripura. The proportion of Girl child was varying from the highest of 20.55 per cent in Urban of Arunachal Pradesh to the lowest of 6.63 per cent in Urban of Tripura during the above mentioned period.

The proportion of children of the age group (0–4) years in Nagaland and Sikkim was comparatively less. During the period from 1971 to 2011, the overall proportion was in the range of 12.52 per cent of Nagaland to 6.93 per cent of Sikkim. The proportion of children of this age group was also high in Rural in both the States. It was within 12.54 per cent of Nagaland to 7.09 per cent of Sikkim. And in Urban, it was also within 12.32 per cent of Nagaland to 6.48 per cent of Sikkim. The proportion of Girl child was in the range of 19.53 per cent in Urban areas of Nagaland to 6.56 per cent in Urban areas of Sikkim.

The position of the country as a whole was similar to the North Eastern States. The proportion of children of the age group (0–4) years was higher in Rural than Urban, but in both the cases, it was showing a declining trend from 1971 to 2011. The overall proportion was 14.52 per cent in 1971, which decreased to 9.32 per cent in 2011. The Rural proportion was slightly higher at 14.92 per cent and it came down to 9.95 per cent. Whereas, the Urban proportion was slightly lower at 12.92 per cent and it came down to 7.91 per cent during this period of 40 (forty) years. The proportion of Girl child of the age group (0–4) years, which was high at 15.19 per cent in Rural in 1971, became 7.83 per cent in Urban in 2011.

It is significant to note that, though the proportion of Girl Child was comparatively higher than the proportion of Boys in all the North Eastern States in seventies and eighties, but in 2001 and 2011, particularly in the States of Manipur, Meghalaya and Mizoram, the situation was different. In these States and specifically in 2011, the proportion of Girl Child was lower than the proportion of Boys of the age group (0–4) years. Similar is the case of the country as a whole. The proportion of Girl child was lower than the proportion of Boys, both in Rural and in Urban in 2011. Further details can be seen from the Appendix–6.1 to Appendix–6.6.

Appendix-6.1

State-wise Distribution of Workers and Non-Workers and Children in the age group (0-4) years and their Percentage with Rural-Urban Break-up in different Census Years

Sl. No.	Name of the State/NER/India	Total/ Rural/ Urban	Census Year, 1971								
			Total Main Workers (I-IX)			Total Marginal Workers			Total Non-Workers		
			Person	Male	Female	Person	Male	Female	Person	Male	Female
1	2	3	4	5	6	7	8	9	10	11	12
1	Arunachal Pradesh	T	269542	158623	110919	-	-	-	197969	92608	105361
		R	260626	150281	110345	-	-	-	189597	89088	100509
		U	8916	8342	574	-	-	-	8372	3520	4852
2	Assam	T	4240112	3854543	385569	-	-	-	10717430	4030521	6686909
		R	3836809	3473828	362981	-	-	-	9793752	3652625	6141127
		U	403303	380715	22588	-	-	-	923678	377896	545782
3	Manipur	T	370863	245435	125428	-	-	-	701890	296240	405650
		R	333288	218277	115011	-	-	-	597973	251954	346019
		U	37575	27158	10417	-	-	-	103917	44286	59631
4	Meghalaya	T	446828	277186	169642	-	-	-	564871	243781	321090
		R	399232	238638	160594	-	-	-	465297	202895	262402
		U	47596	38548	9048	-	-	-	99574	40886	58688
5	Mizoram*	T	-	-	-	-	-	-	-	-	-
		R	-	-	-	-	-	-	-	-	-
		U	-	-	-	-	-	-	-	-	-

1	2	3	4	5	6	7	8	9	10	11	12
6	Nagaland	T	262114	153374	108740	-	-	-	254335	122710	131625
		R	236220	128982	107238	-	-	-	228835	112189	116646
		U	25894	24392	1502	-	-	-	25500	10521	14979
7	Tripura	T	432463	395958	36505	-	-	-	1123879	405168	718711
		R	393092	360849	32243	-	-	-	1000890	356378	644512
		U	39371	35109	4262	-	-	-	122989	48790	74199
8	Sub-Total, NER	T	6021922	5085119	936803	-	-	-	13560374	5191028	8369346
		R	5459267	4570855	888412	-	-	-	12276344	4665129	7611215
		U	562655	514264	48391	-	-	-	1284030	525899	758131
9	Sikkim	T	-	-	-	-	-	-	-	-	-
		R	-	-	-	-	-	-	-	-	-
		U	-	-	-	-	-	-	-	-	-
10	Total, NER	T	6021922	5085119	936803	-	-	-	13560374	5191028	8369346
		R	5459267	4570855	888412	-	-	-	12276344	4665129	7611215
		U	562655	514264	48391	-	-	-	1284030	525899	758131
11	India	T	180373399	149075136	31298263	-	-	-	367576410	134861478	232714932
		R	148374590	120408312	27966278	-	-	-	290480910	104810672	185670238
		U	31998809	28666824	3331985	-	-	-	77095500	30050806	47044694

Source: Primary Census Abstract, 1971, Registrar General & Census Commissioner, India, New Delhi.
* information included in Assam, - information not available.
\- means information not available.

Appendix-6.1 (*cont.*)

State-wise Distribution of Workers and Non-Workers and Children in the age group (0-4) years and their Percentage with Rural-Urban Break-up in different Census Years

Sl. No.	Name of the State/NER/India	Total/ Rural/ Urban	Census Year, 1971														
			Total Children in the age group (0-4) years			Percentage (to Total Population) of											
						Total Main Workers			Total Marginal Workers			Total Non-Workers			Total Children in the age group (0-4) years		
			Person	Male	Female	Person	Male	Female	Person	Male	Female	Person	Male	Female	Person	Male	Female
1	2	3	13	14	15	16	17	18	19	20	21	22	23	24	25	26	27
1	Arunachal Pradesh	T	69426	34165	35261	57.65	63.14	51.28	-	-	-	42.35	36.86	48.72	14.85	13.60	16.30
		R	67206	33060	34146	57.89	62.78	52.33	-	-	-	42.11	37.22	47.67	14.93	13.81	16.19
		U	2220	1105	1115	51.57	70.33	10.58	-	-	-	48.43	29.67	89.42	12.84	9.32	20.55
2	Assam	T	2543997	1266059	1277938	28.99	49.97	5.58	-	-	-	73.28	52.25	96.76	17.39	16.41	18.49
		R	2379073	1182111	1196962	28.77	49.80	5.71	-	-	-	73.44	52.37	96.55	17.84	16.95	18.82
		U	164924	83948	80976	31.28	51.51	4.11	-	-	-	71.65	51.13	99.21	12.79	11.36	14.72
3	Manipur	T	154908	77272	77636	34.57	45.31	23.62	-	-	-	65.43	54.69	76.38	14.44	14.27	14.62
		R	136288	68025	68263	35.79	46.42	24 95	-	-	-	64.21	53.58	75.05	14.63	14.47	14.81
		U	18620	9247	9373	26.56	38.01	14 87	-	-	-	73.44	61.99	85.13	13.16	12.94	13.38
4	Meghalaya	T	160866	81364	79502	44.17	53.21	34.57	-	-	-	55.83	46.79	65.43	15.90	15.62	16.20
		R	142619	72402	70217	46.18	54.05	37.97	-	-	-	53.82	45.95	62.03	16.50	16.40	16.60
		U	18247	8962	9285	32.34	48.53	13.36	-	-	-	67.66	51.47	86.64	12.40	11.28	13.71

1	2	3	13	14	15	16	17	18	19	20	21	22	23	24	25	26	27
5	Mizoram	T	-	-	-	-	-	-	-	-	-		-	-	-	-	-
		R	-	-	-	-	-	-	-	-	-		-	-	-	-	-
		U	-	-	-	-	-	-	-	-	-		-	-	-	-	-
6	Nagaland	T	64643	32248	32395	50.75	55.55	45.24	-	-	-	49.25	44.45	54.76	12.52	11.68	13.48
		R	58313	29137	29176	50.79	53.48	47.90	-	-	-	49.21	46.52	52.10	12.54	12.08	13.03
		U	6330	3111	3219	50.38	69.87	9.11	-	-	-	49.62	30.13	90.89	12.32	8.91	19.53
7	Tripura	T	224347	113570	110777	27.79	49.43	4.83	-	-	-	72.21	50.57	95.17	14.42	14.18	14.67
		R	205454	104064	101390	28.20	50.31	4.76	-	-	-	71.80	49.69	95.24	14.74	14.51	14.98
		U	18893	9506	9387	24.25	41.85	5.43	-	-	-	75.75	58.15	94.57	11.64	11.33	11.96
8	Sub-Total, NER	T	3218187	1604678	1613509	30.75	49.48	10.07	-	-	-	69.25	50.52	89.93	16.43	15.62	17.34
		R	2988953	1488799	1500154	30.78	49.49	10.45	-	-	-	69.22	50.51	89.55	16.85	16.12	17.65
		U	229234	115879	113355	30.47	49.44	6.00	-	-	-	69.53	50.56	94.00	12.41	11.14	14.05
9	Sikkim	T	25744	12457	13287	-	-	-	-	-	-	-	-	-	12.27	11.06	13.67
		R	23200	11128	12072	-	-	-	-	-	-	-	-	-	12.20	11.02	13.53
		U	2544	1329	1215	-	-	-	-	-	-	-	-	-	12.93	11.36	15.25
10	Total, NER	T	3243931	1617135	1626796	30.43	48.95	9.96	-	-	-	68.51	49.97	89.00	16.39	15.57	17.30
		R	3012153	1499927	1512226	30.45	48.95	10.34	-	-	-	68.48	49.96	88.62	16.80	16.06	17.61
		U	231778	117208	114570	30.15	48.89	5.94	-	-	-	68.80	50.00	93.08	12.42	11.14	14.07
11	India	T	79559516	40203916	39355600	32.92	52.50	11.85	-	-	-	67.08	47.50	88.15	14.52	14.16	14.91
		R	65460804	33008240	32452564	33.81	53.46	13.09	-	-	-	66.19	46.54	86.91	14.92	14.66	15.19
		U	14098712	7195676	6903036	29.33	48.82	6.61	-	-	-	70.67	51.18	93.39	12.92	12.25	13.78

Note: means information not available.

Percentage calculated on the basis of the information of relevant Appendices.

Appendix-6.2

State-wise Distribution of Workers and Non-Workers and Children in the age group (0-4) years and their Percentage with Rural-Urban Break-up in different Census Years

Sl. No.	Name of the State/NER/India	Total/Rural/ Urban	Census Year, 1981								
			Total Main Workers (I-IX)			Total Marginal Workers			Total Non-Workers		
			Person	Male	Female	Person	Male	Female	Person	Male	Female
1	2	3	4	5	6	7	8	9	10	11	12
1	Arunachal Pradesh	T	313435	194831	118604	19120	4125	14995	299284	140366	158918
		R	296392	179579	116813	18982	4055.00	14927	275037	130252	144785
		U	17043	15252	1791	138	70	68	24247	10114	14133
2	Assam*	T	-	-	-	-	-	-	-	-	-
		R	-	-	-	-	-	-	-	-	-
		U	-	-	-	-	-	-	-	-	-
3	Manipur	T	573339	331242	242097	40469	6200	34269	807145	383564	423581
		R	453210	253079	200131	27250	3878	23372	565033	273374	291659
		U	120129	78163	41966	13219	2322	10897	242112	110190	131922
4	Meghalaya	T	580220	363164	217056	33221	5799	27422	722378	314747	407631
		R	502350	303175	199175	32348	5516	26832	559788	248267	311521
		U	77870	59989	17881	873	283	590	162590	66480	96110

1	2	3	4	5	6	7	8	9	10	11	12
5	Mizoram	T	-	-	-	-	-	-	-	-	-
		R	-	-	-	-	-	-	-	-	-
		U	-	-	-	-	-	-	-	-	-
6	Nagaland	T	368321	215904	152417	5433	2762	2671	401176	197244	203932
		R	326685	179426	147259	5029	2559	2470	322982	162714	160268
		U	41636	36478	5158	404	203	201	78194	34530	43664
7	Tripura	T	608589	519291	89298	53860	15620	38240	1390609	519935	870674
		R	548066	467866	80200	52132	14426	37706	1227292	457266	770026
		U	60523	51425	9098	1728	1194	534	163317	62669	100648
8	Sub-Total, NER	T	2443904	1624432	819472	152103	34506	117597	3620592	1555856	2064736
		R	2126703	1383125	743578	135741	30434	105307	2950132	1271873	1678259
		U	317201	241307	75894	16362	4072	12290	670460	283983	386477
9	Sikkim	T	147436	97508	49928	5378	1164	4214	163571	73768	89803
		R	126308	79571	46737	5150	1014	4136	133843	61756	72087
		U	21128	17937	3191	228	150	78	29728	12012	17716
10	Total, NER	T	2591340	1721940	869400	157481	35670	121811	3784163	1629624	2154539
		R	2253011	1462696	790315	140891	31448	109443	3083975	1333629	1750346
		U	338329	259244	79085	16590	4222	12368	700188	295995	404193
11	India	T	244604986	181080212	63524774	22088412	3536806	18551606	420682863	162850211	257832652
		R	197308289	139920487	57387802	20874399	3089582	17784817	310299389	120133533	190165856
		U	47296697	41159725	6136972	1214013	447224	766789	110383474	42716678	67666796

Source: Primary Census Abstract, 1981, Registrar General & Census Commissioner, India, New Delhi.

* Census was not conducted in Assam, - information not available.

Appendix-6.2 (*cont.*)

State-wise Distribution of Workers and Non-Workers and Children in the age group (0-4) years and their Percentage with Rural-Urban Break-up in different Census Years

Sl. No.	Name of the State/NER/India	Total/ Rural/ Urban	Census Year, 1981														
			Total Children in the age group (0-4) years			Percentage (to Total Population) of											
						Total Main Workers			Total Marginal Workers			Total Non-Workers			Total Children in the age group (0-4) years		
			Person	Male	Female	Person	Male	Female	Person	Male	Female	Person	Male	Female	Person	Male	Female
1	2	3	13	14	15	16	17	18	19	20	21	22	23	24	25	26	27
1	Arunachal Pradesh	T	90101	44880	45221	49.61	57.42	40.55	3.03	1.22	5.13	47.37	41.37	54.33	14.26	13.23	15.46
		R	84568	42084	42484	50.20	57.21	42.24	3.22	1.29	5.40	46.58	41.50	52.36	14.32	13.41	15.36
		U	5533	2796	2737	41.14	59.96	11.20	0.33	0.28	0.43	58.53	39.76	88.38	13.36	10.99	17.11
2	Assam	T	-	-	-	-	-	-	-	-	-	-	-	-	-	-	-
		R	-	-	-	-	-	-	-	-	-	-	-	-	-	-	-
		U	-	-	-	-	-	-	-	-	-	-	-	-	-	-	-
3	Manipur	T	182528	91680	90848	40.35	45.94	34.59	2.85	0.86	4.90	56.80	53.20	60.52	12.85	12.72	12.98
		R	133180	66850	66330	43.35	47.72	38.85	2.61	0.73	4.54	54.04	51.55	56.62	12.74	12.61	12.88
		U	49348	24830	24518	32.00	40.99	22.71	3.52	1.22	5.90	64.48	57.79	71.39	13.14	13.02	13.27
4	Meghalaya	T	196553	98498	98055	43.44	53.12	33.29	2.49	0.85	4.21	54.08	46.04	62.51	14.71	14.41	15.04
		R	166595	83507	83088	45.90	54.43	37.05	2.96	0.99	4.99	51.15	44.58	57.95	15.22	14.99	15.46
		U	29958	14991	14967	32.27	47.33	15.61	0.36	0.22	0.51	67.37	52.45	83.88	12.41	11.83	13.06

1	2	3	13	14	15	16	17	18	19	20	21	22	23	24	25	26	27
5	Mizoram	T	70746	35486	35260	-	-	-	-	-	-	-	-	-	14.33	13.79	14.91
		R	54268	27270	26998	-	-	-	-	-	-	-	-	-	14.59	14.14	15.08
		U	16478	8216	8262	-	-	-	-	-	-	-	-	-	13.53	12.76	14.38
6	Nagaland	T	90602	45476	45126	47.53	51.91	42.45	0.70	0.66	0.74	51.77	47.42	56.80	11.69	10.93	12.57
		R	75167	37719	37448	49.90	52.05	47.50	0.77	0.74	0.80	49.33	47.20	51.70	11.48	10.94	12.08
		U	15435	7757	7678	34.63	51.23	10.52	0.34	0.29	0.41	65.03	48.49	89.07	12.84	10.89	15.66
7	Tripura	T	237895	120136	117759	29.64	49.23	8.95	2.62	1.48	3.83	67.73	49.29	87.22	11.59	11.39	11.80
		R	217676	109974	107702	29.99	49.80	9.03	2.85	1.54	4.25	67.16	48.67	86.72	11.91	11.70	12.13
		U	20219	10162	10057	26.83	44.61	8.25	0.77	1.04	0.48	72.40	54.36	91.27	8.96	8.81	9.12
8	Sub-Total, NER	T	868425	436156	432269	9.19	11.65	6.47	0.57	0.25	0.93	13.61	11.16	16.30	3.26	3.13	3.41
		R	731454	367404	364050	9.08	11.35	6.61	0.58	0.25	0.94	12.59	10.44	14.92	3.12	3.01	3.24
		U	136971	68752	68219	10.00	13.78	5.34	0.52	0.23	0.86	21.13	16.21	27.19	4.32	3.93	4.80
9	Sikkim	T	44178	22365	21813	46.60	56.55	34.69	1.70	0.68	2.93	51.70	42.78	62.39	13.96	12.97	15.15
		R	37894	19203	18691	47.61	55.90	38.01	1.94	0.71	3.36	50.45	43.39	58.63	14.28	13.49	15.20
		U	6284	3162	3122	41.36	59.59	15.21	0.45	0.50	0.37	58.19	39.91	84.42	12.30	10.51	14.88
10	Total, NER	T	912603	458521	454082	9.62	12.20	6.79	0.58	0.25	0.95	14.06	11.55	16.82	3.39	3.25	3.54
		R	769348	386607	382741	9.51	11.86	6.95	0.59	0.26	0.96	13.01	10.82	15.40	3.25	3.14	3.37
		U	143255	71914	71341	10.49	14.55	5.48	0.51	0.24	0.86	21.72	16.61	28.02	4.44	4.04	4.95
11	India	T	83509808	42227767	41282041	36.77	52.65	19.77	3.32	1.03	5.77	63.23	47.35	80.23	12.55	12.28	12.85
		R	65411621	33053559	32358062	38.87	53.80	23.18	4.11	1.19	7.18	61.13	46.20	76.82	12.89	12.71	13.07
		U	18098187	9174208	8923979	30.00	49.07	8.32	0.77	0.53	1.04	70.00	50.93	91.68	11.48	10.94	12.09

Note: Since the data of 1981 census of Assam is not included, the percentage total of the relevant columns is not coming as 100 in some cases, particularly in sub-total and total of NER.

\- means information not available.

Percentage calculated on the basis of the information of relevant Appendices.

Appendix-6.3

State-wise Distribution of Workers and Non-Workers and Children in the age group (0-4) years and their Percentage with Rural-Urban Break-up in different Census Years

Sl. No.	Name of the State/NER/ India	Total/ Rural/ Urban	Census Year, 1991								
			Total Main Workers (I-IX)			Total Marginal Workers			Total Non-Workers		
			Person	Male	Female	Person	Male	Female	Person	Male	Female
1	2	3	4	5	6	7	8	9	10	11	12
1	Arunachal Pradesh	T	390976	248876	142100	8806	1117	7689	464776	215011	249765
		R	350893	214238	136655	8627	1058	7569	394410	185670	208740
		U	40083	34638	5445	179	59	120	70366	29341	41025
2	Assam	T	6992056	5640187	1351869	1096879	124213	972666	14325387	5893589	8431798
		R	6236035	4960283	1275752	1083673	120153	963520	12606819	5223725	7383094
		U	756021	679904	76117	13206	4060	9146	1718568	669864	1048704
3	Manipur	T	708283	414812	293471	66621	9958	56663	1062245	513589	548656
		R	555727	314245	241482	46343	7302	39041	729434	360848	368586
		U	152556	100567	51989	20278	2656	17622	332811	152741	180070
4	Meghalaya	T	715587	449625	265962	41735	4844	36891	1017456	453218	564238
		R	611164	370511	240653	39567	4447	35120	794000	359907	434093
		U	104423	79114	25309	2168	397	1771	223456	93311	130145

1	2	3	4	5	6	7	8	9	10	11	12
5	Mizoram	T	290317	178011	112306	47028	15370	31658	352411	165597	186814
		R	169337	99722	69615	21010	7048	13962	181463	87644	93819
		U	120980	78289	42691	26018	8322	17696	170948	77953	92995
6	Nagaland	T	511497	299437	212060	4740	1078	3662	693309	340767	352542
		R	443459	242107	201352	4647	1059	3588	553217	279069	274148
		U	68038	57330	10708	93	19	74	140092	61698	78394
7	Tripura	T	802063	666287	135776	56454	7897	48557	1898688	743746	1154942
		R	682098	564238	117860	54579	7237	47342	1598807	631054	967753
		U	119965	102049	17916	1875	660	1215	299881	112692	187189
8	Sub-Total, NER	T	10410779	7897235	2513544	1322263	164477	1157786	19814272	8325517	11488755
		R	9048713	6765344	2283369	1258446	148304	1110142	16858150	7127917	9730233
		U	1362066	1131891	230175	63817	16173	47644	2956122	1197600	1758522
9	Sikkim	T	164392	109994	54398	4329	937	3392	237736	105496	132240
		R	150299	98734	51565	3915	663	3252	215237	95880	119357
		U	14093	11260	2833	414	274	140	22499	9616	12883
10	Total, NER	T	10575171	8007229	2567942	1326592	165414	1161178	20052008	8431013	11620995
		R	9199012	6864078	2334934	1262361	148967	1113394	17073387	7223797	9849590
		U	1376159	1143151	233008	64231	16447	47784	2978621	1207216	1771405
11	India	T	285932493	221658584	64273909	28198877	2705223	25493654	524436566	210844351	313592215
		R	222289579	166293608	55995971	26739365	2305136	24434229	373767380	152672461	221094919
		U	63642914	55364976	8277938	1459512	400087	1059425	150669186	58171890	92497296

Source: Census of India, 1991, Economic Tables, Part III-B Series, Volume-I, Registrar General & Census Commissioner, New Delhi.

Appendix-6.3 (*cont.*)

State-wise Distribution of Workers and Non-Workers and Children in the age group (0-4) years and their Percentage with Rural-Urban Break-up in different Census Years

Sl. No.	Name of the State/ NER/India	Total/ Rural/ Urban	Census Year, 1991														
			Total Children in the age group (0-4) years			Percentage (to Total Population) of											
						Total Main Workers			Total Marginal Workers			Total Non-Workers			Total Children in the age group (0-4) years		
			Person	Male	Female	Person	Male	Female	Person	Male	Female	Person	Male	Female	Person	Male	Female
1	2	3	13	14	15	16	17	18	19	20	21	22	23	24	25	26	27
1	Arunachal Pradesh	T	126453	63073	63380	45.22	53.52	35.57	1.02	0.24	1.92	53.76	46.24	62.51	14.63	13.56	15.86
		R	112033	55748	56285	46.54	53.43	38.72	1.14	0.26	2.14	52.32	46.31	59.14	14.86	13.90	15.95
		U	14420	7325	7095	36.23	54.09	11.69	0.16	0.09	0.26	63.61	45.82	88.05	13.03	11.44	15.23
2	Assam	T	3012405	1522786	1489619	31.19	48.38	12.57	4.89	1.07	9.04	63.92	50.55	78.39	13.44	13.06	13.85
		R	2773528	1401013	1372515	31.30	48 14	13.26	5.44	1.16	10.01	63.26	50.70	76.73	13.92	13.60	14.26
		U	238877	121773	117104	30.39	50.22	6.71	0.53	0.30	0.81	69.08	49.48	92.48	9.60	8.99	10.33
3	Manipur	T	204225	103478	100747	38.55	44.21	32.65	3.63	1.06	6.30	57.82	54.73	61.05	11.12	11.03	11.21
		R	151452	76511	74941	41.74	46.05	37.20	3.48	1.07	6.02	54.78	52.88	56.78	11.37	11.21	11.55
		U	52773	26967	25806	30.17	39.29	20.82	4.01	1.04	7.06	65.82	59.67	72.12	10.44	10.54	10.34
4	Meghalaya	T	280960	141152	139808	40.32	49.54	30.68	2.35	0.53	4.25	57.33	49.93	65.07	15.83	15.55	16.12
		R	240126	120393	119733	42.30	50.42	33.90	2.74	0.61	4.95	54.96	48.97	61.15	16.62	16.38	16.87
		U	40834	20759	20075	31.64	45.78	16.10	0.66	0.23	1.13	67.70	53.99	82.77	12.37	12.01	12.77
5	Mizoram	T	90711	45806	44905	42.09	49.59	33.95	6.82	4.28	9.57	51.09	46.13	56.48	13.15	12.76	13.58
		R	50632	25543	25089	45.54	51.23	39.24	5.65	3.63	7.87	48.81	45.08	52.89	13.62	13.14	14.14
		U	40079	20263	19816	38.05	47.57	27.83	8.18	5.06	11.54	53.77	47.37	60.63	12.61	12.31	12.92

1	2	3	13	14	15	16	17	18	19	20	21	22	23	24	25	26	27
6	Nagaland	T	139737	69658	70079	42.29	46.69	37.32	0.39	0.17	0.64	57.32	53.14	62.04	11.55	10.86	12.33
		R	113770	56527	57243	44.29	46.36	42.03	0.46	0.20	0.75	55.25	53.44	57.22	11.36	10.82	11.95
		U	25967	13131	12836	32.68	48.16	12.01	0.04	0.02	0.08	67.28	51.82	87.91	12.47	11.03	14.39
7	Tripura	T	336226	170600	165626	29.09	46.99	10.14	2.05	0.56	3.63	68.86	52.45	86.23	12.19	12.03	12.37
		R	297886	151174	146712	29.21	46.92	10.40	2.34	0.60	4.18	68.45	52.48	85.42	12.75	12.57	12.95
		U	38340	19426	18914	28.45	47.38	8.68	0.44	0.31	0.59	71.11	52.31	90.73	9.09	9.02	9.17
8	Sub-Total, NER	T	4190717	2116553	2074164	33.00	48.19	16.58	4.19	1.00	7.64	62.81	50.81	75.78	13.28	12.92	13.68
		R	3739427	1886909	1852518	33.31	48.18	17.40	4.63	1.06	8.46	62.06	50.76	74.14	13.77	13.44	14.12
		U	451290	229644	221646	31.08	48.25	11.30	1.46	0.69	2.34	67.46	51.06	86.36	10.30	9.79	10.88
9	Sikkim	T	51406	26161	25245	40.45	50.82	28.63	1.07	0.43	1.78	58.48	48.75	69.59	12.65	12.09	13.28
		R	47930	24347	23583	40.68	50.56	29.61	1.06	0.34	1.87	58.26	49.10	68.52	12.97	12.47	13.54
		U	3476	1814	1662	38.08	53.24	17.87	1.12	1.30	0.88	60.80	45.46	81.25	9.39	8.58	10.48
10	Total, NER	T	4242123	2142714	2099409	33.10	48.23	16.73	4.15	1.00	7.56	62.75	50.77	75.71	13.28	12.91	13.68
		R	3787357	1911256	1876101	33.41	48.21	17.56	4.58	1.05	8.37	62.01	50.74	74.07	13.75	13.42	14.11
		U	454766	231458	223308	31.14	48.30	11.35	1.46	0.69	2.33	67.40	51.01	86.32	10.29	9.78	10.88
11	India	T	102378032	52360652	50017380	34.10	50.93	15.93	3.36	0.62	6.32	62.54	48.45	77.75	12.21	12.03	12.40
		R	79341384	40506575	38834809	35.69	51.76	18.57	4.29	0.72	8.10	60.02	47.52	73.33	12.74	12.61	12.88
		U	23036648	11854077	11182571	29.49	48.59	8.13	0.68	0.35	1.04	69.83	51.06	90.83	10.68	10.40	10.98

Source: Census of India, 1991, A Study Report in the Analytical Study Report Series on the 1991 Census Data, Registrar General, India, New Delhi.

Percentage calculated on the basis of the information of relevant Appendices.

Appendix-6.4

State-wise Distribution of Workers and Non-Workers and Children in the age group (0-6) years and their Percentage with Rural-Urban Break-up in different Census Years

Sl. No.	Name of the State/NER/India	Total/Rural/ Urban	Census Year, 2001								
			Total Main Workers (I-IX)			Total Marginal Workers			Total Non-Workers		
			Person	Male	Female	Person	Male	Female	Person	Male	Female
1	2	3	4	5	6	7	8	9	10	11	12
1	Arunachal Pradesh	T	415007	267384	147623	67895	26228	41667	615066	286329	328737
		R	340027	207110	132917	61983	23210	38773	468077	224360	243717
		U	74980	60274	14706	5912	3018	2894	146989	61969	85020
2	Assam	T	7114097	5849032	1265065	2424494	1021928	1402566	17116937	6906077	10210860
		R	6050639	4926395	1124244	2346130	972809	1373321	14819519	6040741	8778778
		U	1063458	922637	140821	78364	49119	29245	2297418	865336	1432082
3	Manipur	T	659364	430227	229137	285849	96989	188860	1221575	568418	653157
		R	494747	320432	174315	228340	77942	150398	867733	410579	457154
		U	164617	109795	54822	57509	19047	38462	353842	157839	196003
4	Meghalaya	T	757011	485694	271317	213135	82797	130338	1348676	607596	741080
		R	626538	393364	233174	195993	74731	121262	1042180	478904	563276
		U	130473	92330	38143	17142	8066	9076	306496	128692	177804

1	2	3	4	5	6	7	8	9	10	11	12
5	Mizoram	T	362450	225428	137022	104709	37580	67129	421414	196101	225313
		R	201599	120662	80937	54445	18193	36252	191523	93871	97652
		U	160851	104766	56085	50264	19387	30877	229891	102230	127661
6	Nagaland	T	703977	424811	279166	143819	64157	79662	1142240	558173	584067
		R	608335	348972	259363	133104	57887	75217	905810	452857	452953
		U	95642	75839	19803	10715	6270	4445	236430	105316	131114
7	Tripura	T	912292	742054	170238	247269	89292	157977	2039642	810879	1228763
		R	747822	606103	141719	234625	81379	153246	1671006	676156	994850
		U	164470	135951	28519	12644	7913	4731	368636	134723	233913
8	Sub-Total, NER	T	10924198	8424630	2499568	3487170	1418971	2068199	23905550	9933573	13971977
		R	9069707	6923038	2146669	3254620	1306151	1948469	19965848	8377468	11588380
		U	1854491	1501592	352899	232550	112820	119730	3939702	1556105	2383597
9	Sikkim	T	212904	146541	66363	50139	19175	30964	277808	122768	155040
		R	190656	129679	60977	48346	17881	30465	241979	108214	133765
		U	22248	16862	5386	1793	1294	499	35829	14554	21275
10	Total, NER	T	11137102	8571171	2565931	3537309	1438146	2099163	24183358	10056341	14127017
		R	9260363	7052717	2207646	3302966	1324032	1978934	20207827	8485682	11722145
		U	1876739	1518454	358285	234343	114114	120229	3975531	1570659	2404872
11	India	T	313004983	240147813	72857170	89229741	34866663	54363078	626375604	257142296	369233308
		R	229186552	169101251	60085301	80769518	29737902	51031616	432534569	182763521	249771048
		U	83818431	71046562	12771869	8460223	5128761	3331462	193841035	74378775	119462260

Source: Registrar General & Census Commissioner, India, New Delhi.

Appendix-6.4 (*cont.*)

State-wise Distribution of Workers and Non-Workers and Children in the age group (0-6) years and their Percentage with Rural-Urban Break-up in different Census Years

Sl. No.	Name of the State/NER/India	Total/ Rural/ Urban	Census Year, 2001														
			Total Children in the age group (0-6) years*			Percentage (to Total Population) of											
						Total Main Workers			Total Marginal Workers			Total Non-Workers			Total Children in the age group (0-6) years*		
			Person	Male	Female	Person	Male	Female	Person	Male	Female	Person	Male	Female	Person	Male	Female
1	2	3	13	14	15	16	17	18	19	20	21	22	23	24	25	26	27
1	Arunachal Pradesh	T	205871	104833	101038	37.80	46.11	28.50	6.18	4.52	8.04	56.02	49.37	63.46	18.75	18.08	19.50
		R	169029	86230	82799	39.08	45.55	32.00	7.12	5.10	9.33	53.80	49.35	58.67	19.43	18.96	19.93
		U	36842	18603	18239	32.90	48.12	14.33	2.60	2.41	2.82	64.50	49.47	82.85	16.17	14.85	17.77
2	Assam	T	4498075	2289116	2208959	26.69	42.45	9.82	9.10	7.42	10.89	64.21	50.13	79.29	16.87	16.62	17.15
		R	4104407	2086499	2017908	26.06	41.26	9.97	10.11	8.15	12.18	63.83	50.59	77.85	17.68	17.47	17.90
		U	393668	202617	191051	30.92	50.22	3.79	2.28	2.68	1.83	66.80	47.10	89.38	11.45	11.03	11.92
3	Manipur	T	308585	157682	150903	30.43	39.27	21.39	13.19	8.85	17.63	56.38	51.88	60.98	14.24	14.39	14.09
		R	233675	119486	114189	31.10	39.61	22.29	14.35	9.63	19.24	54.55	50.76	58.47	14.69	14.77	14.60
		U	74910	38196	36714	28.58	38.30	18.95	9.98	6.64	13.30	61.44	55.06	67.75	13.01	13.32	12.69
4	Meghalaya	T	467979	237215	230764	32.65	41.30	23.74	9.19	7.04	11.41	58.16	51.66	64.85	20.18	20.17	20.19
		R	400563	202981	197582	33.60	41.54	25.41	10.51	7.89	13.21	55.89	50.57	61.38	21.48	21.43	21.53
		U	67416	34234	33182	28.73	40.30	16.95	3.78	3.52	4.03	67.49	56.18	79.02	14.85	14.94	14.75

1	2	3	13	14	15	16	17	18	19	20	21	22	23	24	25	26	27
5	Mizoram	T	143734	73176	70558	40.79	49.10	31.91	11.78	8.19	15.63	47.43	42.71	52.46	16.18	15.94	16.43
		R	80466	40947	39519	45.04	51.85	37.67	12.16	7.82	16.87	42.80	40.33	45.46	17.98	17.59	18.39
		U	63268	32229	31039	36.47	46.28	26.13	11.40	8.56	14.39	52.13	45.16	59.48	14.35	14.24	14.46
6	Nagaland	T	289678	147524	142154	35.38	40.57	29.61	7.22	6.13	8.45	57.40	53.30	61.94	14.56	14.09	15.08
		R	241197	122519	118678	36.93	40.59	32.93	8.08	6.73	9.55	54.99	52.68	57.52	14.64	14.25	15.07
		U	48481	25005	23476	27.90	40.46	12.75	3.13	3.35	2.86	68.97	56.19	84.39	14.14	13.34	15.11
7	Tripura	T	436446	222002	214444	28.52	45.19	10.93	7.73	5.44	10.15	63.75	49.37	78.92	13.64	13.52	13.77
		R	383177	194660	188517	28.18	44.45	10.99	8.84	5.97	11.88	62.98	49.58	77.13	14.44	14.28	14.62
		U	53269	27342	25927	30.14	48.80	10.67	2.32	2.84	1.77	67.54	48.36	87.56	9.76	9.81	9.70
8	Sub-Total, NER	T	6350368	3231548	3118820	28.51	42.60	13.48	9.10	7.17	11.16	62.39	50.23	75.36	16.57	16.34	16.82
		R	5612514	2853322	2759192	28.09	41.69	13.69	10.08	7.87	12.42	61.83	50.44	73.89	17.38	17.18	17.59
		U	737854	378226	359628	30.77	47.36	12.36	3.86	3.56	4.19	65.37	49.08	83.45	12.24	11.93	12.59
9	Sikkim	T	78195	39842	38353	39.36	50.80	26.30	9.27	6.65	12.27	51.37	42.55	61.43	14.46	13.81	15.20
		R	72017	36627	35390	39.64	50.70	27.08	10.05	6.99	13.53	50.31	42.31	59.39	14.97	14.32	15.71
		U	6178	3215	2963	37.16	51.55	19.83	2.99	3.96	1.84	59.85	44.49	78.33	10.32	9.83	10.91
10	Total, NER	T	6428563	3271390	3157173	28.66	42.72	13.65	9.10	7.16	11.17	62.24	50.12	75.18	16.54	16.30	16.80
		R	5684531	2889949	2794582	28.26	41.83	13.88	10.08	7.85	12.44	61.66	50.32	73.68	17.35	17.14	17.57
		U	744032	381441	362591	30.83	47.40	12.43	3.85	3.56	4.17	65.32	49.04	83.40	12.22	11.91	12.58
11	India	T	163819614	84999203	78820411	30.43	45.13	14.68	8.67	6.55	10.95	60.90	48.32	74.37	15.93	15.97	15.88
		R	126470497	65407648	61062849	30.87	44.31	16.65	10.88	7.80	14.14	58.25	47.89	69.21	17.03	17.14	16.92
		U	37349117	19591555	17757562	29.29	47.19	9.42	2.96	3.41	2.46	67.75	49.40	88.12	13.05	13.01	13.10

Source: Web-site, Registrar General of India, New Delhi.

Percentage calculated on the basis of the information of relevant Appendices.

* Classification of the Children in the age group (0–4) years was not available.

Appendix-6.5

State-wise Distribution of Workers and Non-Workers and Children in the age group (0-4) years and their Percentage with Rural-Urban Break-up in different Census Years

Sl. No.	Name of the State/ NER/India	Total/Rural/ Urban	Census Year, 2011								
			Total Main Workers (I-IX)			Total Marginal Workers			Total Non-Workers		
			Person	Male	Female	Person	Male	Female	Person	Male	Female
1	2	3	4	5	6	7	8	9	10	11	12
1	Arunachal Pradesh	T	478721	301109	177612	108936	49164	59772	796070	363639	432431
		R	377388	223929	153459	92927	40861	52066	596043	281221	314822
		U	101333	77180	24153	16009	8303	7706	200027	82418	117609
2	Assam	T	8687123	7034642	1652481	3282567	1506918	1775649	19235886	7397883	11838003
		R	7311015	5880174	1430841	3057268	1377678	1679590	16438751	6421137	10017614
		U	1376108	1154468	221640	225299	129240	96059	2797135	976746	1820389
3	Manipur	T	974163	615135	359028	330447	124273	206174	1551184	699178	852006
		R	713482	442482	271000	245679	91603	154076	1062479	492799	569680
		U	260681	172653	88028	84768	32670	52098	488705	206379	282326
4	Meghalaya	T	921575	585520	336055	264044	118189	145855	1781270	788123	993147
		R	730959	455430	275529	242499	106382	136117	1397981	632448	765533
		U	190616	130090	60526	21545	11807	9738	383289	155675	227614
5	Mizoram	T	415030	263305	151725	71675	27435	44240	610501	264599	345902
		R	217824	134888	82936	34558	10203	24355	273053	124044	149009
		U	197206	128417	68789	37117	17232	19885	337448	140555	196893

1	2	3	4	5	6	7	8	9	10	11	12
6	Nagaland	T	741179	442204	298975	232943	105153	127790	1004380	477292	527088
		R	567674	316384	251290	192686	87528	105158	647176	321560	325616
		U	173505	125820	47685	40257	17625	22632	357204	155732	201472
7	Tripura	T	1077019	887881	189138	392502	157445	235057	2204396	829050	1375346
		R	776583	637023	139560	339493	130744	208749	1596388	619406	976982
		U	300436	250858	49578	53009	26701	26308	608008	209644	398364
8	Sub-Total, NER	T	13294810	10129796	3165014	4683114	2088577	2594537	27183687	10819764	16363923
		R	10694925	8090310	2604615	4205110	1844999	2360111	22011871	8892615	13119256
		U	2599885	2039486	560399	478004	243578	234426	5171816	1927149	3244667
9	Sikkim	T	230397	160513	69884	77741	33845	43896	302439	128712	173727
		R	173682	119014	54668	70103	29172	40931	213214	94611	118603
		U	56715	41499	15216	7638	4673	2965	89225	34101	55124
10	Total, NER	T	13525207	10290309	3234898	4760855	2122422	2638433	27486126	10948476	16537650
		R	10868607	8209324	2659283	4275213	1874171	2401042	22225085	8987226	13237859
		U	2656600	2080985	575615	485642	248251	237391	5261041	1961250	3299791
11	India	T	362565571	273209976	89355595	119323297	58729899	60593398	728966109	291330383	437635726
		R	245868421	178095330	67773091	102874671	48741683	54132988	485005760	200944045	284061715
		U	116697150	95114646	21582504	16448626	9988216	6460410	243960349	90386338	153574011

Source: website of the Registrar General & Census Commissioner, India, New Delhi.

Appendix-6.5 (cont.)

State-wise Distribution of Workers and Non-Workers and Children in the age group (0-4) years and their Percentage with Rural-Urban Break-up in different Census Years

Sl. No.	Name of the State/NER/India	Total/ Rural/ Urban	Census Year, 2011														
			Total Children in the age group (0-4) years			Percentage (to Total Population) of											
						Total Main Workers			Total Marginal Workers			Total Non-Workers			Total Children in the age group (0-4) years		
			Person	Male	Female	Person	Male	Female	Person	Male	Female	Person	Male	Female	Person	Male	Female
1	2	3	13	14	15	16	17	13	19	20	21	22	23	24	25	26	27
1	Arunachal Pradesh	T	142879	72464	70415	34.60	42.18	26.52	7.87	6.89	8.92	57.53	50.93	64.56	10.33	10.15	10.51
		R	115773	58593	57180	35.39	41.01	29.49	8.71	7.49	10.01	55.90	51.50	60.50	10.86	10.73	10.99
		U	27106	13871	13235	31.93	45.97	16.16	5.04	4.95	5.16	63.03	49.08	78.68	8.54	8.26	8.85
2	Assam	T	3212833	1634922	1577911	27.84	44.13	10.82	10.52	9.45	11.64	61.64	46.42	77.54	10.30	10.26	10.34
		R	2900310	1474612	1425698	27.28	42.99	10.90	11.40	10.07	12.79	61.32	46.94	76.31	10.82	10.78	10.86
		U	312523	160310	152213	31.29	51.07	10.37	5.12	5.72	4.49	63.59	43.21	85.14	7.11	7.09	7.12
3	Manipur	T	256682	133160	123522	34.11	42.76	25.33	11.57	8.64	14.55	54.32	48.60	60.12	8.99	9.26	8.72
		R	186405	97094	89311	35.29	43.09	27.24	12.15	8.92	15.49	52.56	47.99	57.27	9.22	9.46	8.98
		U	70277	36066	34211	31.25	41.94	20.34	10.16	7.94	12.33	58.59	50.12	66.83	8.42	8.76	8.10
4	Meghalaya	T	406154	205846	200308	31.06	39.25	22.78	8.90	7.92	9.89	60.04	52.83	67.33	13.69	13.80	13.58
		R	351463	177831	173632	30.82	38.13	23.41	10.23	8.91	11.56	58.95	52.96	65.03	14.82	14.89	14.75
		U	54691	28015	26676	32.01	43.72	20.32	3.62	3.97	3.27	64.37	52.31	76.41	9.18	9.41	8.96
5	Mizoram	T	121233	61541	59692	37.83	47.41	28.00	6.53	4.94	8.16	55.64	47.65	63.84	11.05	11.08	11.02
		R	66972	34077	32895	41.46	50.12	32.36	6.58	3.79	9.50	51.96	46.09	58.14	12.75	12.66	12.83
		U	54261	27464	26797	34.49	44.87	24.09	6.49	6.02	6.96	59.02	49.11	68.95	9.49	9.60	9.38

1	2	3	13	14	15	16	17	18	19	20	21	22	23	24	25	26	27
6	Nagaland	T	197262	101291	95971	37.46	43.16	31.34	11.78	10.26	13.40	50.76	46.58	55.26	9.97	9.89	10.06
		R	147261	75981	71280	40.33	43.61	36.84	13.69	12.07	15.42	45.98	44.32	47.74	10.46	10.47	10.45
		U	50001	25310	24691	30.39	42.06	17.54	7.05	5.89	8.33	62.56	52.05	74.13	8.76	8.46	9.08
7	Tripura	T	322566	164505	158061	29.32	47.37	10.51	10.68	8.40	13.06	60.00	44.23	76.43	8.78	8.78	8.78
		R	258020	131384	126636	28.63	45.92	10.53	12.52	9.43	15.75	58.85	44.65	73.72	9.51	9.47	9.56
		U	64546	33121	31425	31.25	51.49	10.45	5.51	5.48	5.55	63.24	43.03	84.00	6.71	6.80	6.63
8	Sub-Total, NER	T	4659609	2373729	2285880	29.44	43.97	14.31	10.37	9.07	11.73	60.19	46.96	73.96	10.32	10.30	10.33
		R	4026204	2049572	1976632	28.97	42.97	14.40	11.39	9.80	13.05	59.64	47.23	72.55	10.91	10.89	10.93
		U	633405	324157	309248	31.51	48.44	13.87	5.79	5.79	5.80	62.70	45.77	80.33	7.68	7.70	7.66
9	Sikkim	T	42336	21685	20651	37.73	49.68	24.31	12.73	10.48	15.27	49.54	39.84	60.42	6.93	6.71	7.18
		R	32382	16541	15841	38.00	49.02	25.52	15.34	12.01	19.11	46.66	38.97	55.37	7.09	6.81	7.40
		U	9954	5144	4810	36.93	51.70	20.76	4.97	5.82	4.04	58.10	42.48	75.20	6.48	6.41	6.56
10	Total, NER	T	4701945	2395414	2306531	29.55	44.05	14.43	10.40	9.09	11.77	60.05	46.86	73.80	10.27	10.25	10.29
		R	4058586	2066113	1992473	29.08	43.05	14.53	11.44	9.83	13.12	59.48	47.12	72.35	10.86	10.83	10.89
		U	643359	329301	314058	31.61	48.50	14.00	5.78	5.79	5.77	62.61	45.71	80.23	7.66	7.68	7.64
11	India	T	112806778	58632074	54174704	29.94	43.83	15.21	9.86	9.43	10.31	60.20	46.74	74.48	9.32	9.41	9.22
		R	82986660	43036377	39950283	29.49	41.63	16.69	12.34	11.39	13.33	58.17	46.98	69.98	9.95	10.06	9.84
		U	29820118	15595697	14224421	30.95	48.65	11.88	4.36	5.11	3.56	64.69	46.24	84.56	7.91	7.98	7.83

Source: Web-site, Registrar General of India, New Delhi.

Note: Children have been classified in (0-4) years group in all the Census years from 1971 to 2011 except 2001 wherein it was (0-6) years.

Percentage calculated on the basis of the information of relevant Appendices.

Appendix-6.6

State-wise Decadal change in the percentage [increased (+), decreased (-)] of Main Workers, Marginal Workers, Non-Workers and Children in the age group (0-4) years with Rural-Urban Break-up

Sl. No.	Name of the State/NER/India	Total/ Rural/ Urban	Decadal change in the percentage of											
			During 1961-71				During 1971-81				During 1981-91 (for Assam & NER, it is 1971-91)			
			Main workers	Marginal workers	Non-workers	Children in the age group (0-4) years	Main workers	Marginal workers	Non-workers	Children in the age group (0-4) years	Main workers	Marginal workers	Non-workers	Children in the age group (0-4) years
1	2	3	4	5	6	7	8	9	10	11	12	13	14	15
1	Arunachal Pradesh	T	-	-	-	-	(-) 8.04	-	(+) 5.02	(-) 0.59	(-) 4.39	(-) 2.01	(+) 6.39	(+) 0.37
		R	-	-	-	-	(-) 7.69	-	(+) 4.47	(-) 0.61	(-) 3.66	(-) 2.08	(+) 5.74	(+) 0.54
		U	-	-	-	-	(-)10.43	-	(+) 10.10	(+) 0.52	(-) 4.91	(-) 0.17	(+) 5.08	(-) 0.33
2	Assam	T	-	-	-	-	-	-	-	-	(+) 2.20	-	(-) 9.36	(-) 3.95
		R	-	-	-	-	-	-	-	-	(+) 2.53	-	(-) 10.18	(-) 3.92
		U	-	-	-	-	-	-	-	-	(-) 0.89	-	(-) 2.57	(-) 3.19
3	Manipur	T	-	-	-	-	(+) 5.78	-	(-) 8.63	(-) 1.59	(-) 1.80	(+) 0.78	(+) 1.02	(-) 1.73
		R	-	-	-	-	(+) 7.56	-	(-) 10.17	(-) 1.89	(-) 1.61	(+) 0.87	(+) 0.74	(-) 1.37
		U	-	-	-	-	(+) 5.44	-	(-) 8.96	(-) 0.02	(-) 1.83	(+) 0.49	(+) 1.34	(-) 2.70
4	Meghalaya	T	-	-	-	-	(-) 0.73	-	(-) 1.75	(-) 1.19	(-) 3.12	(-) 0.14	(+) 3.25	(+) 1.12
		R	-	-	-	-	(-) 0.28	-	(-) 2.67	(-) 1.28	(-) 3.60	(-) 0.22	(+) 3.81	(+) 1.40
		U	-	-	-	-	(-) 0.07	-	(-) 0.29	(+) 0.01	(-) 0.63	(+) 0.30	(+) 0.33	(-) 0.04

1	2	3	4	5	6	7	8	9	10	11	12	13	14	15
5	Mizoram	T	-	-	-	-	-	-	-	-	-	-	-	(-) 1.18
		R	-	-	-	-	-	-	-	-	-	-	-	(-) 0.97
		U	-	-	-	-	-	-	-	-	-	-	-	(-) 0.92
6	Nagaland	T	-	-	-	-	(-) 3.22	-	(+) 2.52	(-) 0.83	(-) 5.24	(-) 0.31	(+) 5.55	(-) 0.14
		R	-	-	-	-	(-) 0.89	-	(+) 0.12	(-) 1.06	(-) 5.61	(-) 0.31	(+) 5.92	(-) 0.12
		U	-	-	-	-	(-) 15.75	-	(+) 15.41	(+) 0.52	(-) 1.95	(-) 0.30	(+) 2.25	(-) 0.37
7	Tripura	T	-	-	-	-	(+) 1.85	-	(-) 4.48	(-) 2.83	(-) 0.55	(-) 0.57	(+) 1.13	(+) 0.60
		R	-	-	-	-	(+) 1.79	-	(-) 4.64	(-) 2.83	(-) 0.78	(-) 0.51	(+) 1.29	(+) 0.84
		U	-	-	-	-	(+) 2.58	-	(-) 3.35	(-) 2.68	(+) 1.62	(-) 0.33	(-) 1.29	(+) 0.13
8	Sub-Total, NER	T	-	-	-	-	-	-	-	-	(+) 2.25	-	(-) 6.44	(-) 3.15
		R	-	-	-	-	-	-	-	-	(+) 2.53	-	(-) 7.16	(-) 3.08
		U	-	-	-	-	-	-	-	-	(+) 0.61	-	(-) 2.07	(-) 2.11
9	Sikkim	T	-	-	-	-	-	-	-	(+) 1.69	(-) 6.15	(-) 0.63	(+) 6.78	(-) 1.31
		R	-	-	-	-	-	-	-	(+) 2.08	(-) 6.93	(-) 0.88	(+) 7.81	(-) 1.31
		U	-	-	-	-	-	-	-	(-) 0.63	(-) 3.28	(+) 0.67	(+) 2.61	(-) 2.91
10	Total, NER	T	-	-	-	-	-	-	-	-	(+) 2.67	-	(-) 5.76	(-) 3.11
		R	-	-	-	-	-	-	-	-	(+) 2.96	-	(-) 6.47	(-) 3.05
		U	-	-	-	-	-	-	-	-	(+) 0.99	-	(-) 1.40	(-) 2.13
11	India	T	-	-	-	-	(+) 3.85	-	(-) 3.85	(-) 1.97	(-) 2.67	(+) 0.04	(-) 0.69	(-) 0.34
		R	-	-	-	-	(+) 5.06	-	(-) 5.06	(-) 2.03	(-) 3.18	(+) 0.18	(-) 1.11	(-) 0.15
		U	-	-	-	-	(+) 0.67	-	(-) 0.67	(-) 1.44	(-) 0.51	(-) 0.09	(-) 0.17	(-) 0.80

- indicates information not available.

Appendix-6.6 (*cont.*)

State-wise Decadal change in the percentage [increased (+), decreased (-)] of Main Workers, Marginal Workers, Non-Workers and Children in the age group (0-4) years with Rural-Urban Break-up

Sl. No.	Name of the State/NER/India	Total/ Rural/ Urban	Decadal change in the percentage of											
			During 1991-2001				During 2001-11				During 1971-2011 (for Assam & Mizoram, it is 1991-2011) (i.e. within a period of 40/20 years)			
			Main workers	Marginal workers	Non-workers	Children in the age group (0-4) years	Main workers	Marginal workers	Non-workers	Children in the age group (0-4) years	Main workers	Marginal workers	Non-workers	Children in the age group (0-4) years
1	2	3	16	17	18	19	20	21	22	23	24	25	26	27
1	Arunachal Pradesh	T	(-) 7.42	(+) 5.16	(+) 2.26	(+) 4.12	(-) 3.20	(+) 1.69	(+) 1.51	(-) 8.42	(-) 23.05	(+) 4.84	(+) 15.18	(-) 4.52
		R	(-) 7.46	(+) 5.98	(+) 1.48	(+) 4.57	(-) 3.69	(+) 1.59	(+) 2.10	(-) 8.57	(-) 22.50	(+) 5.49	(+) 13.79	(-) 4.07
		U	(-) 3.33	(+) 2.44	(+) 0.89	(+) 3.14	(-) 0.97	(+) 2.44	(-) 1.47	(-) 7.63	(-) 19.64	(+) 4.71	(+) 14.60	(-) 4.30
2	Assam	T	(-) 4.50	(+) 4.21	(+) 0.29	(+) 3.43	(+) 1.15	(+) 1.42	(-) 2.57	(-) 6.57	(-) 1.15	(+) 5.63	(-) 11.64	(-) 7.09
		R	(-) 5.24	(+) 4.67	(+) 0.57	(+) 3.76	(+) 1.22	(+) 1.29	(-) 2.51	(-) 6.86	(-) 1.49	(+) 5.96	(-) 12.12	(-) 7.02
		U	(+) 0.53	(+) 1.75	(-) 2.28	(+) 1.85	(+) 0.37	(+) 2.84	(-) 3.21	(-) 4.34	(+) 0.01	(+) 4.59	(-) 8.06	(-) 5.68
3	Manipur	T	(-) 8.12	(+) 9.56	(-) 1.44	(+) 3.12	(+) 3.68	(-) 1.62	(-) 2.06	(-) 5.25	(-) 0.46	(+) 8.72	(-) 11.11	(-) 5.45
		R	(-) 10.64	(+) 10.87	(-) 0.23	(+) 3.32	(+) 4.19	(-) 2.20	(-) 1.99	(-) 5.47	(-) 0.50	(+) 9.54	(-) 11.65	(-) 5.41
		U	(-) 2.59	(+) 5.97	(-) 4.38	(+) 2.57	(+) 2.67	(+) 0.18	(-) 2.85	(-) 4.59	(+) 4.69	(+) 6.64	(-) 14.85	(-) 4.74

1	2	3	16	17	18	19	20	21	22	23	24	25	26	27
4	Meghalaya	T	(-) 7.67	(+) 6.84	(+) 0.83	(+) 4.35	(-) 1.59	(-) 0.29	(+) 1.88	(-) 6.49	(-) 13.11	(+) 6.41	(+) 4.21	(-) 2.21
		R	(-) 8.70	(+) 7.77	(+) 0.93	(+) 4.86	(-) 2.78	(-) 0.28	(+) 3.06	(-) 6.66	(-) 15.36	(+) 7.27	(+) 5.13	(-) 1.68
		U	(-) 2.91	(+) 3.12	(-) 0.21	(+) 2.48	(+) 3.28	(-) 0.16	(-) 3.12	(-) 5.67	(-) 0.33	(+) 3.26	(-) 3.29	(-) 3.22
5	Mizoram	T	(-) 1.30	(+) 4.96	(-) 3.66	(+) 3.03	(-) 2.96	(-) 5.25	(+) 8.21	(-) 5.13	(-) 4.26	(-) 0.29	(+) 4.55	(-) 2.10
		R	(-) 0.50	(+) 6.51	(-) 6.01	(+) 4.36	(-) 3.58	(-) 5.58	(+) 9.16	(-) 5.23	(-) 4.08	(+) 0.93	(+) 3.15	(-) 0.87
		U	(-) 1.58	(+) 3.22	(-) 1.64	(+) 1.74	(-) 1.98	(-) 4.91	(+) 6.89	(-) 4.86	(-) 3.56	(-) 1.69	(+) 5.25	(-) 3.12
6	Nagaland	T	(-) 6.91	(+) 6.83	(+) 0.08	(+) 3.01	(+) 2.08	(+) 4.56	(-) 6.64	(-) 4.59	(-) 13.29	(+) 11.08	(+) 1.51	(-) 2.55
		R	(-) 7.36	(+) 7.62	(-) 0.26	(+) 3.28	(+) 3.40	(+) 5.61	(-) 9.01	(-) 4.18	(-) 10.46	(+) 12.92	(-) 3.23	(-) 2.08
		U	(-) 4.78	(+) 3.09	(+) 1.69	(+) 1.67	(+) 2.49	(+) 3.92	(-) 6.41	(-) 5.38	(-) 19.99	(+) 6.71	(+) 12.94	(-) 3.56
7	Tripura	T	(-) 0.57	(+) 5.68	(-) 5.11	(+) 1.45	(+) 0.80	(+) 2.95	(-) 3.75	(-) 4.86	(+) 1.53	(+) 8.06	(-) 12.21	(-) 5.63
		R	(-) 1.03	(+) 6.50	(-) 5.47	(+) 1.69	(+) 0.45	(+) 3.68	(-) 4.13	(-) 4.93	(+) 0.43	(+) 9.67	(-) 12.95	(-) 5.23
		U	(+) 1.69	(+) 1.88	(-) 3.57	(+) 0.67	(+) 1.11	(+) 3.19	(-) 4.30	(-) 3.05	(+) 7.00	(+) 4.74	(-) 12.51	(-) 4.93
8	Sub-Total, NER	T	(-) 4.49	(+) 4.91	(-) 0.42	(+) 3.29	(+) 0.93	(+) 1.27	(-) 2.20	(-) 6.25	(-) 1.31	(+) 9.80	(-) 9.06	(-) 6.11
		R	(-) 5.22	(+) 5.45	(-) 0.23	(+) 3.61	(+) 0.88	(+) 1.31	(-) 2.19	(-) 6.47	(-) 1.81	(+) 10.81	(-) 9.58	(-) 5.94
		U	(-) 0.31	(+) 2.40	(-) 2.09	(+) 1.94	(+) 0.74	(+) 1.93	(-) 2.67	(-) 4.56	(+) 1.04	(+) 5.27	(-) 6.83	(-) 4.73
9	Sikkim	T	(-) 1.09	(+) 8.20	(-) 7.11	(+) 1.81	(-) 1.63	(+) 3.46	(-) 1.83	(-) 7.53	(-) 8.87	(+) 11.03	(-) 2.16	(-) 5.34
		R	(-) 1.04	(+) 8.99	(-) 7.95	(+) 2.00	(-) 1.64	(+) 5.29	(-) 3.65	(-) 7.88	(-) 9.61	(+) 13.40	(-) 3.79	(-) 5.11
		U	(-) 0.92	(+) 1.87	(-) 0.95	(+) 0.93	(-) 0.23	(+) 1.98	(-) 1.75	(-) 3.84	(-) 4.43	(+) 4.52	(-) 0.09	(-) 6.45
10	Total, NER	T	(-) 4.44	(+) 4.95	(-) 0.51	(+) 3.26	(+) 0.89	(+) 1.30	(-) 2.19	(-) 6.27	(-) 0.88	(+) 9.82	(-) 8.46	(-) 6.12
		R	(-) 5.15	(+) 5.50	(-) 0.35	(+) 3.60	(+) 0.82	(+) 1.36	(-) 2.18	(-) 6.49	(-) 1.37	(+) 10.85	(-) 9.00	(-) 5.94
		U	(-) 0.31	(+) 2.39	(-) 2.08	(+) 1.93	(+) 0.78	(+) 1.93	(-) 2.71	(-) 4.56	(+) 1.46	(+) 5.27	(-) 6.19	(-) 4.76
11	India	T	(-) 3.67	(+) 5.31	(-) 1.64	(+) 3.72	(-) 0.49	(+) 1.19	(-) 0.70	(-) 6.61	(-) 2.98	(+) 6.54	(-) 6.88	(-) 5.20
		R	(-) 4.82	(+) 6.59	(-) 1.77	(+) 4.29	(-) 1.38	(+) 1.46	(-) 0.08	(-) 7.08	(-) 4.32	(+) 8.23	(-) 8.02	(-) 4.97
		U	(-) 0.20	(+) 2.28	(-) 2.08	(+) 2.37	(+) 1.66	(+) 1.40	(-) 3.06	(-) 5.14	(+) 1.62	(+) 3.59	(-) 5.98	(-) 5.01

Source: Percentage changes were calculated from the relevant Appendices.

7
Marital Status

During population Census, for collecting information on Marital status, people are generally classified under 4 (four) main groups *viz.* (i) Never Married, (ii) Married, (iii) Widowed, and iv. Divorced or Separated. Further, if any person or persons cannot be classified under any of the above mentioned 4 (four) groups, they are being recorded as Unspecified. It is seen that, from 1961 to 1991 Census, a sizable population of all the States of North Eastern Region as well as of the Country, were recorded as Unspecified both in Rural and in Urban areas. The details of Marital status of the people of all the NE States and of the Country from the Census year—1961 to 2011, can be seen from the Appendix–7.1 to Appendix–7.6.

It is seen that, in the States like Arunachal Pradesh, Meghalaya and Nagaland, more than half of the population were Never Married and there was an increasing trend in their percentage over the years with some ups and downs. In case of Arunachal Pradesh, though the overall percentage of Never Married people was 46.53 in 1961, but it increased to 51.86 per cent in 1971, 54.43 per cent in 1981, 55.09 per cent in 1991, 56.36 per cent in 2001 and finally it came down to 55.35 per cent in 2011. And within a period of 50 (fifty) years from 1961 to 2011, there was an absolute increase of (+) 8.82 per cent in the percentage of Never Married persons. Further it is seen that, the proportion of Male Never Married persons was higher than the proportion of Female Never Married persons in all these years.

As a natural phenomenon, i.e. due to increase in the percentage of Never Married people, the percentage of Married people started declining. It is seen that, though the overall percentage of Married people was 50.14 in 1961, but it came down to 43.25 per cent in 1971, 41.64 per cent in 1981 and then again it increased slightly and reached to 42.04 per cent in 1991. In 2001, it came down to 40.10 per cent and then increased slightly and reached to 41.14 per cent in 2011. But, within a period of 50 (fifty) years, the percentage of Married people decreased by (–) 9.00 per cent. However, in this case, though the proportion of Married Male was a bit higher in 1961, but in later years, the proportion of Married Female was always higher.

The percentage of Widowed and Divorced or Separated people was not much in Arunachal Pradesh. The percentage of Widowed was ranging from 1.86 per cent to 4.55 per cent. But, within a period of 50 (fifty) years from 1961, there was an absolute increase in the percentage of Widowed persons by (+) 1.15 per cent. However, the proportion of Widowed Female was always higher and it was ranging from 3.36 per cent to 7.01 per cent. The overall percentage of Divorced or Separated people was very less. It was not even one per cent of the population of the State. But the proportion of Divorced or Separated Women was comparatively higher. It was ranging from 0.31 per cent to 1.05 per cent in this period.

In Meghalaya, the overall percentage of Never Married people was 57.50 in 1971, which increased to 58.63 per cent in 1981, 59.52 per cent in 1991, 60.50 per cent in 2001 and then decreased slightly and came down to 58.98 per cent in 2011. And within a period of 40 (forty) years from 1971, there was an absolute increase in the overall percentage of Never Married people by (+) 1.48 per cent. Further, it is seen that the proportion of Never Married Males was higher than the proportion of Never Married Females in all these years.

In Meghalaya, Married people were comparatively less and their percentage showed a declining trend over the years with some ups and downs. The overall percentage of Married people was 37.19 per cent in 1971, which came down to 36.31 per cent in 1981 and then increased to 36.77 per cent in 1991 and again came down to 34.93 per cent in 2001 and finally reached to 36.06 per cent in 2011. But, within a period of 40 (forty) years, the percentage of Married people decreased by (–) 1.13 per cent.

The Widowed people in Meghalaya, was not very less. It is seen that, more than three per cent of the people were Widowed, which however showed a declining trend. The overall percentage of Widowed was ranging from 3.50 per cent to 2.60 per cent. In case of Widowed, it is seen that, the proportion of Females was much higher than the proportion of Males in all these years. The percentage of Divorced or Separated people was much less, but there was an increasing trend. The overall percentage of Divorced or Separated people was ranging from

1.10 per cent to 1.54 per cent. In this case also, the proportion of Divorced or Separated Females was higher than the proportion of Males in this period.

In Nagaland, it is seen that, much more than half of the people were Never Married and there was an increasing trend over the years. The overall percentage of Never Married people was 56.46 per cent in 1961, which increased to 58.73 per cent in 1971, 61.18 per cent in 1981, 63.34 per cent in 1991, 63.95 per cent in 2001 and finally decreased to 60.26 per cent in 2011. But, within a period of 50 (fifty) years from 1961, there was an absolute increase in the percentage of Never Married people by (+) 3.80 per cent. In case of Never Married people, the proportion of Males was higher than the proportion of Females.

Married people are comparatively less in Nagaland and it showed a declining trend The overall percentage of Married people was 38.11 per cent in 1961, which reduced to 37.90 per cent in 1971, 36.35 per cent in 1981, 34.84 per cent in 1991, 33.80 per cent in 2001 and finally increased slightly and reached to 36.44 per cent in 2011. However, the overall percentage of Married people decreased by (–) 1.67 per cent from 1961 to 2011. But in case of Married people, the proportion of Females was higher than the proportion of Males in all these years.

The Widowed people were not much in Nagaland and there was a declining trend over the years. The overall percentage of Widowed people was ranging from 4.63 per cent to 1.57 per cent in this period. However, the proportion of Widowed Females was higher than the proportion of Widowed Males. The Divorced or Separated people were very less, not even one per cent of the population of the State, but it was showing an increasing trend. The overall percentage of Divorced or Separated people was in the range of 0.23 per cent to 0.75 per cent. In this case also, the proportion of Females was higher than the proportion of Males in all these years.

In all other North Eastern States, it is seen that, the overall percentage of Never Married people was showing a decreasing trend and on the other hand, the overall percentage of Married people was showing an increasing trend, with slight ups and downs in their percentages. That means, more and more people were getting married over the years. In Assam, the overall percentage of Never Married people was 57.12 in 1961, but it increased to 58.92 per cent in 1971 and then came down to 58.05 per cent in 1991, 55.48 per cent in 2001 and finally to 50.85 per cent in 2011. And within a period of 50 (fifty) years, i.e. from 1961 to 2011, the overall percentage of Never Married people decreased by (–) 6.27 per cent. In this case, the proportion of Never Married Males was higher than the proportion of Never Married Females.

The overall percentage of Married people was 38.56 per cent in 1961 and though it came down to 36.29 per cent in 1971, but it increased to 38.17 per cent in 1991, 40.15 per cent in 2001 and finally reached to 44.25 per cent in 2011. The absolute increase in the percentage of Married persons was (+) 5.69 per cent from 1961 to 2011. However, in this case, the proportion of Married Females was higher than the proportion of Married Males.

The Widowed persons in Assam were not very less. It was about four per cent of the population and it was showing an increasing trend. The overall percentage of Widowed persons was ranging from 3.52 per cent to 4.52 per cent. The proportion of Widowed Females was much higher than the proportion of Widowed Males in all these years. Divorced or Separated people were comparatively much less in Assam. Their overall percentage was ranging from 0.25 per cent to 0.43 per cent during this period. But, in this case also, the proportion of Females was higher than the proportion of Males.

In the State of Manipur, it is seen that, more than half of the people were Never Married. However, it was showing a declining trend with some ups and downs. The overall percentage of Never Married people was 55.26 in 1961, which increased to 59.42 per cent in 1971, 59.75 per cent in 1981 and then decreased to 59.19 per cent in 1991, 57.41 per cent in 2001 and finally to 54.19 per cent in 2011. But within a period of 50 (fifty) years, i.e. from 1961 to 2011, the percentage of Never Married persons decreased by (–) 1.07 per cent. In case of Never Married people, the proportion of Males was higher than the proportion of Females in all these years.

The percentage of Married people was comparatively less, but it was showing an increasing trend. In 1961, the overall percentage of Married people was 37.60 and though it came down to 35.80 per cent in 1971, but it increased to 36.06 per cent in 1981, 37.62 per cent in 1991, 38.63 per cent in 2001 and finally reached to 41.84 per cent in 2011. And within a period of 50 (fifty) years from 1961, there was an absolute increase in the percentage of Married people by (+) 4.24 per cent. But in this case, the proportion of Married Females was more than the proportion of Married Males, in almost all the years.

The Widowed persons in Manipur, was a bit high to the extent of

5.41 per cent in 1961. But in later years, it was little more than three per cent and was showing a declining trend. However, the percentage of Widowed Females was much higher than the percentage of Widowed Males in all these years. The Divorced or Separated people were comparatively less and their percentage was showing a declining trend. The percentage of Divorced or Separated people was ranging from 1.59 per cent to 0.49 per cent during this period. In this case also, the proportion of Females was higher than the proportion of Males.

For the State of Mizoram, the information of 1961 and 1971 was not available. However, from the information of later years, it is seen that, much more than half of the people of Mizoram were Never Married and their percentage was showing a declining trend over the years. The overall per cent of Never Married people was 60.14 per cent in 1981, which reduced to 60.12 per cent in 1991, 57.86 per cent in 2001 and finally to 54.64 per cent in 2011. And within a period of 30 (thirty) years, i.e. from 1981 to 2011, the percentage of Never Married people decreased by (–) 5.50 per cent. In case of Never Married people, the proportion of Males was higher than the proportion of Females in all these years.

The Married people in Mizoram were little more than one third of the population, and their percentage was showing an increasing trend. In 1981, the overall percentage of Married people was 34.55 per cent, which increased to 35.83 per cent in 1991, 36.86 per cent in 2001 and to 39.35 per cent in 2011. The absolute increase in the percentage of Married people from 1981 to 2011, was (+) 4.80 per cent. But in this case, sometimes the proportion of Males was higher and sometimes the proportion of Females was higher, but there was no much difference between the values of their proportions, at any of these years.

The Widowed and Divorced or Separated people were also not very less in Mizoram. However, the Widowed people were showing a declining trend and their percentage was ranging from 3.36 to 2.41. But on the other hand, the percentage of Divorced or Separated people was showing an increasing trend and it was ranging from 1.63 per cent to 2.66 per cent. In case of Divorced or Separated people, the proportion of Females was higher than the proportion of Males in all these years.

In Tripura, more than half of the people were Never Married, but their percentage showed a declining trend over the years with some ups and downs. It is seen that, the overall percentage of Never Married people was 50.99 per cent in 1961 and then it increased to 55.00 per cent in 1971, 55.69 per cent in 1981 and again came down to 54.72 per cent in 1991, 51.41 per cent in 2001 and finally to 45.04 per cent in 2011. And within a period of 50 (fifty) years, i.e. from 1961 to 2011, the percentage of Never Married people decreased by (–) 5.95 per cent. It is also seen that, the proportion of Never Married Males was higher than the proportion of Females in all these years.

In Tripura, Married people were comparatively more and their percentage was showing an increasing trend with certain variations. The overall percentage of Married people was 41.98 in 1961, which came down to 39.22 per cent in 1971, 38.70 per cent in 1981 and then increased to 40.57 per cent in 1991, 43.55 per cent in 2001 and finally to 49.03 per cent in 2011. But within a period of 50 (fifty) years, there was an absolute increase in the percentage of Married persons by (+) 7.05 per cent. In this case, the proportion of Married Females was higher than the proportion of Married Males in each of these years.

Number of Widowed people, were not less in Tripura, but their percentage was showing a declining trend. The percentage of Widowed persons was ranging from 6.32 per cent to 4.26 per cent during this period. In case of Widowed persons, the proportion of Females was much higher than the proportion of Males in each of these years. Divorced or Separated people were comparatively much less, not even one per cent of the population of the State and their percentage was showing a declining trend. The percentage of Divorced or Separated people was ranging from 0.68 per cent to 0.41 per cent during this period. In this case also, the proportion of Females was higher than the proportion of Males.

Like other NE States, more than half of the people of Sikkim were Never Married, but their percentage was showing a declining trend over the years with some ups and downs. In 1961, the overall percentage of Never Married people was 54.79 per cent, which increased to 57.49 per cent in 1971, 58.22 per cent in 1981, 59.13 per cent in 1991 and then came down to 56.15 per cent in 2001 and finally to 50.11 per cent in 2011. And within a period of 50 (fifty) years, i.e. from 1961 to 2011, the percentage of Never Married people decreased by (–) 4.68 per cent. In case of Never Married people, the proportion of Males was higher than the proportion of Females.

Married people in Sikkim were not much less and their percentage was showing an increasing trend with some ups and downs. The overall percentage of Married people was 41.14 per cent in 1961, but it came down to 37.30 per cent in 1971 and then increased to 37.76 per cent in 1981, 38.42 per cent in 1991, 40.15 per cent in 2001 and finally to

45.55 per cent in 2011. However, from 1961 to 2011, there was an absolute increase in the percentage of Married people by (+) 4.41 per cent. In this case, the proportion of Female was higher than the proportion of Males almost in all cases.

The Widowed people in Sikkim were not much less, but their percentage was showing a declining trend. The percentage of Widowed people was ranging from 3.52 per cent to 2.04 per cent during this period, and the proportion of Females was higher than the proportion of Males in each of these years. However, the number of Divorced or Separated people in Sikkim was comparatively less. But their percentage was showing an increasing trend. The percentage of Divorced or Separated people was within the range of 0.29 per cent to 1.05 per cent in this period. However, in this case, sometimes the proportion of Females was higher and sometimes the proportion of Males was higher.

The position of the country as a whole was more or less similar to many of the North Eastern States. It is seen that, about half of the people of the country were Never Married, but their percentage was showing a declining trend with some ups and downs. In 1961, though the overall percentage of Never Married people of the country was 47.79 per cent, but it increased to 50.43 per cent in 1971, 50.67 per cent in 1981 and then came down to 50.23 per cent in 1991, 49.84 per cent in 2001 and finally to 47.14 per cent in 2011. And within a period of 50 (fifty) years, i.e. from 1961 to 2011, the percentage of Never Married people decreased by a small margin of (–) 0.65 per cent. In case of Never Married people, the proportion of Males was higher than the proportion of Females in all these years.

The percentage of Married people of the country was however, showing an increasing trend with some variations over the years. In 1961, the overall percentage of Married people was 44.57 per cent, but it reduced to 43.39 per cent in 1971 and thereafter increased to 43.85 per cent in 1981, 45.37 per cent in 1991, 45.56 per cent in 2001 and finally to 47.87 per cent in 2011. Further, it is seen that, there was an absolute increase in the percentage of Married persons by (+) 3.30 per cent from 1961 to 2011. During this period, the proportion of Females was higher than the proportion of Males.

The number of Widowed people in the country were not less, but their percentage was showing a declining trend. The percentage of Widowed people was ranging from 7.15 per cent to 4.13 per cent. In this case, the proportion of Females was much higher than the percentage of Males in each of these years. The number of Divorced or Separated people was comparatively much less. It was not even half per cent of the population of the country, and was also showing a declining trend. The percentage of Divorced or Separated people was ranging from 0.45 per cent to 0.25 per cent and in this case also, the proportion of Females was higher than the proportion of Males in all these years.

It is seen that, the information on Marital Status of the population, collected during the Census of 1961 to 2011, with their residential status, did not show any particular pattern either in the North Eastern State or in the country as a whole. However, in some of the States like Assam, Manipur and Sikkim, the proportion of Never Married people was always higher in the Rural areas than the Urban areas. In case of Married people, the proportion was always higher only in the Rural areas of Mizoram. But on the other hand, the proportion of Married people was always higher in the Urban areas of Arunachal Pradesh and Assam.

Further, it is seen that, the proportion of Widowed people was always higher in the Rural areas of Arunachal Pradesh, Nagaland and Sikkim. Whereas, it was always higher in the Urban areas of Manipur only. In case of Divorced or Separated people, the proportion was always higher in the Rural areas of Arunachal Pradesh, Meghalaya, Tripura and Sikkim. But it was always higher in the Urban areas of Manipur. In all other cases, the proportion did not follow any particular pattern. Sometimes, the proportion was higher in Rural and sometimes in Urban.

The position of the country as a whole was different. The proportion in respect of all kinds of Marital status except Divorced, did not follow any particular pattern. However, in case of Divorced people, the proportion was always higher in the Rural areas except 2011, where the proportion was higher in the Urban areas. Further details can be seen from the Appendix–7.1 to Appendix–7.6.

Appendix-7.1

State-wise Distribution of Population according to Marital Status with Rural-Urban Break-up in different Census Years

Sl. No.	Name of the States/Region/India	Total / Rural / Urban	As per 1961 Census								
			Total Population			Marital Status					
						Never Married			Married		
			Person	Male	Female	Person	Male	Female	Person	Male	Female
1	2	3	4	5	6	7	8	9	10	11	12
1	Arunachal Pradesh*	Total	38705	30580	8125	18011	14328	3683	19406	15355	4051
		Rural	38705	30580	8125	18011	14328	3683	19406	15355	4051
		Urban	-	-	-	-	-	-	-	-	-
2	Assam	Total	11872772	6328129	5544643	6782039	3809054	2972985	4577918	2348575	2229343
		Rural	10959744	5783675	5176069	6265270	3493879	2771391	4207113	2124322	2082791
		Urban	913028	544454	368574	516769	315175	201594	370805	224253	146552
3	Manipur	Total	780037	387058	392979	431033	231035	199998	293256	144858	148398
		Rural	712320	352937	359383	395011	210703	184308	267611	131950	135661
		Urban	67717	34121	33596	36022	20332	15690	25645	12908	12737
4	Meghalaya	Total	-	-	-	-	-	-	-	-	-
		Rural	-	-	-	-	-	-	-	-	-
		Urban	-	-	-	-	-	-	-	-	-
5	Mizoram	Total	-	-	-	-	-	-	-	-	-
		Rural	-	-	-	-	-	-	-	-	-
		Urban	-	-	-	-	-	-	-	-	-

1	2	3	4	5	6	7	8	9	10	11	12
6	Nagaland	Total	369200	191027	178173	208443	112306	96137	140700	72437	68263
		Rural	350043	179261	170782	197193	105464	91729	133449	67676	65773
		Urban	19157	11766	7391	11250	6842	4408	7251	4761	2490
7	Tripura	Total	1142005	591237	550768	582365	330931	251434	479369	240022	239347
		Rural	1039008	536580	502428	523313	296063	227250	442641	221486	221155
		Urban	102997	54657	48340	59052	34868	24184	36728	18536	18192
8	Sub-Total, NER	Total	14202719	7528031	6674688	8021891	4497654	3524237	5510649	2821247	2689402
		Rural	13099820	6883033	6216787	7398798	4120437	3278361	5070220	2560789	2509431
		Urban	1102899	644998	457901	623093	377217	245876	440429	260458	179971
9	Sikkim	Total	162189	85193	76996	88857	48272	40585	66721	35337	31384
		Rural	155341	81285	74056	85192	46155	39037	63905	33631	30274
		Urban	6848	3908	2940	3665	2117	1548	2816	1706	1110
10	Total, NER	Total	14364908	7613224	6751684	8110748	4545926	3564822	5577370	2856584	2720786
		Rural	13255161	6964318	6290843	7483990	4166592	3317398	5134125	2594420	2539705
		Urban	1109747	648906	460841	626758	379334	247424	443245	262164	181081
11	India	Total	438945918	226155101	212790817	209772012	119683701	90088311	195624160	97140678	98483482
		Rural	360009315	183365995	176643320	169361581	96054570	73307011	162150883	79283190	82867693
		Urban	78936603	42789106	36147497	40410431	23629131	16781300	33473277	17857488	15615789

Source: Census of India, 1961, Volume-I, Part II-C(i), Social and Cultural Tables, Registrar General & Census Commissioner, New Delhi.

* Entire Arunachal Pradesh (NEFA) was treated as Rural at that time. - information not available.

Appendix-7.1 (*cont.* 1)

State-wise Distribution of Population according to Marital Status with Rural-Urban Break-up in different Census Years

Sl. No.	Name of the States/Region/ India	Total / Rural / Urban	As per 1961 Census								
			Marital Status								
			Widowed			Divorced or Separated			Unspecified		
			Person	Male	Female	Person	Male	Female	Person	Male	Female
1	2	3	13	14	15	16	17	18	19	20	21
1	Arunachal Pradesh	Total	719	446	273	377	292	85	192	159	33
		Rural	719	446	273	377	292	85	192	159	33
		Urban	-	-	-	-	-	-	-	-	-
2	Assam	Total	452887	144495	308392	51401	21743	29658	8527	4262	4265
		Rural	431369	141110	290259	48104	20415	27689	7888	3949	3939
		Urban	21518	3385	18133	3297	1328	1969	639	313	326
3	Manipur	Total	42209	7580	34629	12458	3076	9382	1081	509	572
		Rural	37826	6985	30841	10791	2790	8001	1081	509	572
		Urban	4383	595	3788	1667	286	1381	0	0	0
4	Meghalaya	Total	-	-	-	-	-	-	-	-	-
		Rural	-	-	-	-	-	-	-	-	-
		Urban	-	-	-	-	-	-	-	-	-
5	Mizoram	Total	-	-	-	-	-	-	-	-	-
		Rural	-	-	-	-	-	-	-	-	-
		Urban	-	-	-	-	-	-	-	-	-

1	2	3	13	14	15	16	17	18	19	20	21
6	Nagaland	Total	17110	5040	12070	2684	1042	1642	263	202	61
		Rural	16546	4925	11621	2602	998	1604	253	198	55
		Urban	564	115	449	82	44	38	10	4	6
7	Tripura	Total	72154	16481	55673	7739	3609	4130	378	194	184
		Rural	65388	15384	50004	7321	3480	3841	345	167	178
		Urban	6766	1097	5669	418	129	289	33	27	6
8	Sub-Total, NER	Total	585079	174042	411037	74659	29762	44897	10441	5326	5115
		Rural	551848	168850	382998	69195	27975	41220	9759	4982	4777
		Urban	33231	5192	28039	5464	1787	3677	682	344	338
9	Sikkim	Total	5712	1171	4541	477	243	234	422	170	252
		Rural	5491	1089	4402	457	241	216	296	169	127
		Urban	221	82	139	20	2	18	126	1	125
10	Total, NER	Total	590791	175213	415578	75136	30005	45131	10863	5496	5367
		Rural	557339	169939	387400	69652	28216	41436	10055	5151	4904
		Urban	33452	5274	28178	5484	1789	3695	808	345	463
11	India	Total	31365574	8340690	23024884	1968736	882599	1086137	206436	98433	108003
		Rural	26604769	7157938	19446831	1717779	787182	930597	165303	74115	91188
		Urban	4760805	1182752	3578053	250957	95417	155540	41133	24318	16815

Source: Census of India, 1961, Volume-I, Part II-C(i), Social and Cultural Tables, Registrar General & Census Commissioner, New Delhi .

* Entire Arunachal Pradesh (NEFA) was treated as Rural at that time. - information not available.

Appendix-7.1 (*cont. 2*)

State-wise Percentage Distribution of Population according to Marital Status with Rural-Urban Break-up in different Census Years

Sl. No.	Name of the States/Region/ India	Total / Rural / Urban	As per 1961 Census														
			Marital Status in per cent (to total population)														
			Never Married			Married			Widowed			Divorced or Separated			Unspecified		
			Person	Male	Female	Person	Male	Female	Person	Male	Female	Person	Male	Female	Person	Male	Female
1	2	3	22	23	24	25	26	27	28	29	30	31	32	33	34	35	36
1	Arunachal Pradesh	Total	46.53	46.85	45.33	50.14	50.21	49.86	1.86	1.46	3.36	0.97	0.95	1.05	0.50	0.52	0.40
		Rural	46.53	46.85	45.33	50.14	50.21	49.86	1.86	1.46	3.36	0.97	0.95	1.05	0.50	0.52	0.40
		Urban	-	-	-	-	-	-	-	-	-	-	-	-	-	-	-
2	Assam	Total	57.12	60.19	53.62	38.56	37.11	40.21	3.81	2.28	5.56	0.43	0.34	0.53	0.07	0.07	0.08
		Rural	57.17	60.41	53.54	38.39	36.73	40.24	3.93	2.44	5.61	0.44	0.35	0.53	0.07	0.07	0.08
		Urban	56.60	57.89	54.70	40.61	41.19	39.76	2.36	0.62	4.92	0.36	0.24	0.53	0.07	0.06	0.09
3	Manipur	Total	55.26	59.69	50.89	37.60	37.43	37.76	5.41	1.96	8.8[illegible]	1.59	0.79	2.39	0.14	0.13	0.15
		Rural	55.46	59.70	51.28	37.57	37.40	37.76	5.31	1.98	8.58	1.52	0.79	2.23	0.14	0.13	0.15
		Urban	53.19	59.59	46.70	37.87	37.83	37.91	6.48	1.74	11.23	2.46	0.84	4.11	0.00	0.00	0.00
4	Meghalaya	Total	-	-	-	-	-	-	-	-	-	-	-	-	-	-	-
		Rural	-	-	-	-	-	-	-	-	-	-	-	-	-	-	-
		Urban	-	-	-	-	-	-	-	-	-	-	-	-	-	-	

1	2	3	22	23	24	25	26	27	28	29	30	31	32	33	34	35	36
5	Mizoram	Total	-	-	-	-	-	-	-	-	-	-	-	-	-	-	-
		Rural	-	-	-	-	-	-	-	-	-	-	-	-	-	-	-
		Urban	-	-	-	-	-	-	-	-	-	-	-	-	-	-	-
6	Nagaland	Total	56.46	58.79	53.96	38.11	37.92	38.31	4.63	2.64	6.77	0.73	0.55	0.92	0.07	0.10	0.04
		Rural	56.33	58.84	53.71	38.13	37.75	38.51	4.73	2.75	6.81	0.74	0.56	0.94	0.07	0.10	0.03
		Urban	58.73	58.15	59.64	37.85	40.46	33.69	2.94	0.98	6.07	0.43	0.36	0.52	0.05	0.05	0.08
7	Tripura	Total	50.99	55.97	45.65	41.98	40.60	43.46	6.32	2.79	10.11	0.68	0.61	0.75	0.03	0.03	0.03
		Rural	50.37	55.18	45.23	42.60	41.28	44.02	6.29	2.86	9.95	0.71	0.65	0.76	0.03	0.03	0.04
		Urban	57.33	63.79	50.03	35.66	33.91	37.63	6.57	2.01	11.73	0.41	0.24	0.60	0.03	0.05	0.01
8	Sub-Total, NER	Total	56.48	59.75	52.80	38.80	37.48	40.29	4.12	2.30	6.16	0.53	0.40	0.67	0.07	0.07	0.08
		Rural	56.48	59.86	52.73	38.70	37.20	40.37	4.21	2.45	6.16	0.54	0.42	0.66	0.07	0.07	0.08
		Urban	56.50	58.48	53.70	39.93	40.38	39.30	3.01	0.80	6.12	0.50	0.28	0.81	0.06	0.06	0.07
9	Sikkim	Total	54.79	56.66	52.71	41.14	41.48	40.76	3.52	1.37	5.90	0.29	0.29	0.30	0.26	0.20	0.33
		Rural	54.84	56.78	52.71	41.14	41.37	40.88	3.54	1.34	5.95	0.29	0.30	0.29	0.19	0.21	0.17
		Urban	53.52	54.17	52.65	41.12	43.65	37.76	3.23	2.10	4.73	0.29	0.05	0.61	1.84	0.03	4.25
10	Total, NER	Total	56.46	59.71	52.80	38.83	37.52	40.30	4.11	2.30	6.16	0.52	0.40	0.66	0.08	0.07	0.08
		Rural	56.46	59.83	52.73	38.73	37.25	40.37	4.20	2.44	6.16	0.53	0.41	0.66	0.08	0.07	0.08
		Urban	56.48	58.46	53.69	39.94	40.40	39.29	3.02	0.81	6.12	0.49	0.28	0.80	0.07	0.05	0.10
11	India	Total	47.79	52.92	42.34	44.57	42.95	46.28	7.15	3.69	10.82	0.45	0.40	0.51	0.05	0.04	0.05
		Rural	47.04	52.38	41.50	45.04	43.24	46.91	7.39	3.91	11.01	0.48	0.43	0.53	0.05	0.04	0.05
		Urban	51.19	55.22	46.42	42.41	41.73	43.20	6.03	2.76	9.90	0.32	0.23	0.43	0.05	0.06	0.05

Source: Percentage calculated on the basis of the information of the relevant Appendices.

- information not available.

Appendix-7.2

State-wise Distribution of Population (all ages) according to Marital Status with Rural-Urban Break-up in different Census Years

Sl. No.	Name of the States/Region/ india	Total / Rural / Urban	As per 1971 Census								
			Total Population			Marital Status					
						Never Married			Married		
			Person	Male	Female	Person	Male	Female	Person	Male	Female
1	2	3	4	5	6	7	8	9	10	11	12
1	Arunachal Pradesh	Total	467511	251231	216280	242441	137266	105175	202197	107166	95031
		Rural	450223	239369	210854	233965	131592	102373	193703	101141	92562
		Urban	17288	11862	5426	8476	5674	2802	8494	6025	2469
2	Assam	Total	14957542	7885064	7072478	8813730	4889468	3924262	5427415	2794246	2633169
		Rural	13630561	7126453	6504108	8036443	4426070	3610373	4930002	2511224	2418778
		Urban	1326981	758611	568370	777287	463398	313889	497413	283022	214391
3	Manipur	Total	1072753	541675	531078	637390	335552	301838	384034	195209	188825
		Rural	931261	470231	461030	558481	293383	265098	330859	167629	163230
		Urban	141492	71444	70048	78909	42169	36740	53175	27580	25595
4	Meghalaya	Total	1011699	520967	490732	581682	314160	267522	376267	191185	185082
		Rural	864529	441533	422996	491372	263591	227781	325290	163768	161522
		Urban	147170	79434	67736	90310	50569	39741	50977	27417	23560

1	2	3	4	5	6	7	8	9	10	11	12
5	Mizoram*	Total	-	-	-	-	-	-	-	-	-
		Rural	-	-	-	-	-	-	-	-	-
		Urban	-	-	-	-	-	-	-	-	-
6	Nagaland	Total	516449	276084	240365	303335	166041	137294	195722	104556	91166
		Rural	465055	241171	223884	276683	148693	127990	172043	87584	84459
		Urban	51394	34913	16481	26652	17348	9304	23679	16972	6707
7	Tripura	Total	1556342	801126	755216	855978	476251	379727	610439	305389	305050
		Rural	1393982	717227	676755	760381	422305	338076	552531	276580	275951
		Urban	162360	83899	78461	95597	53946	41651	57908	28809	29099
8	Sub-Total, NER	Total	19582296	10276147	9306149	11434556	6318738	5115818	7196074	3697751	3498323
		Rural	17735611	9235984	8499627	10357325	5685634	4671691	6504428	3307926	3196502
		Urban	1846685	1040163	806522	1077231	633104	444127	691646	389825	301821
9	Sikkim	Total	209843	112662	97181	120633	65636	54997	78272	41977	36295
		Rural	190175	100959	89216	109987	59305	50682	70120	37036	33084
		Urban	19668	11703	7965	10646	6331	4315	8152	4941	3211
10	Total, NER	Total	19792139	10388809	9403330	11555189	6384374	5170815	7274346	3739728	3534618
		Rural	17925786	9336943	8588843	10467312	5744939	4722373	6574548	3344962	3229586
		Urban	1866353	1051866	814487	1087877	639435	448442	699798	394766	305032
11	India	Total	548159652	284049276	264110376	276421580	155950676	120470904	237856473	118796176	119060297
		Rural	439045675	225319943	213725732	218124075	122353060	95771015	192719958	95036662	97683296
		Urban	109113977	58729333	50384644	58297505	33597616	24699889	45136515	23759514	21377001

Source: Census of India, 1971, Series - 1, Part II-C (ii), Registrar General & Census Commissioner, New Delhi.

* - Information of Mizoram included in Assam.

Appendix-7.2 (*cont.* 1)

State-wise Distribution of Population (all ages) according to Marital Status with Rural-Urban Break-up in different Census Years

Sl. No.	Name of the States/ Region/India	Total/Rural/ Urban	As per 1971 Census								
			Marital Status								
			Widowed			Divorced or Separated			Unspecified		
			Person	Male	Female	Person	Male	Female	Person	Male	Female
1	2	3	13	14	15	16	17	18	19	20	21
1	Arunachal Pradesh	Total	21271	6114	15157	1602	685	917	-	-	-
		Rural	21009	5978	15031	1546	658	888	-	-	-
		Urban	262	136	126	56	27	29	-	-	-
2	Assam	Total	649599	174854	474745	60260	22514	37746	6538	3982	2556
		Rural	601330	164902	436428	57502	21389	36113	5284	2868	2416
		Urban	48269	9952	38317	2758	1125	1633	1254	1114	140
3	Manipur	Total	40136	7956	32180	10526	2803	7723	667	155	512
		Rural	33014	6793	26221	8296	2312	5984	611	114	497
		Urban	7122	1163	5959	2230	491	1739	56	41	15
4	Meghalaya	Total	35372	8113	27259	15228	5619	9609	3150	1890	1260
		Rural	31424	7404	24020	13509	5096	8413	2934	1674	1260
		Urban	3948	709	3239	1719	523	1196	216	216	0

1	2	3	13	14	15	16	17	18	19	20	21
5	Mizoram*	Total	-	-	-	-	-	-	-	-	-
		Rural	-	-	-	-	-	-	-	-	-
		Urban	-	-	-	-	-	-	-	-	-
6	Nagaland	Total	13706	3846	9860	2825	1102	1723	861	539	322
		Rural	13251	3690	9561	2531	898	1633	547	306	241
		Urban	455	156	299	294	204	90	314	233	81
7	Tripura	Total	83243	16570	66673	6295	2716	3579	387	200	187
		Rural	74712	15564	59148	6041	2636	3405	317	142	175
		Urban	8531	1006	7525	254	80	174	70	58	12
8	Sub-Total, NER	Total	843327	217453	625874	96736	35439	61297	11603	6766	4837
		Rural	774740	204331	570409	89425	32989	56436	9693	5104	4589
		Urban	68587	13122	55465	7311	2450	4861	1910	1662	248
9	Sikkim	Total	6738	2359	4379	2213	1070	1143	1987	1620	367
		Rural	6217	2160	4057	2136	1026	1110	1715	1432	283
		Urban	521	199	322	77	44	33	272	188	84
10	Total, NER	Total	850065	219812	630253	98949	36509	62440	13590	8386	5204
		Rural	780957	206491	574466	91561	34015	57546	11408	6536	4872
		Urban	69108	13321	55787	7388	2494	4894	2182	1850	332
11	India	Total	31752479	8340554	23411925	1727488	700659	1026829	401632	261211	140421
		Rural	26490137	7182518	19307619	1497368	622387	874981	214137	125316	88821
		Urban	5262342	1158036	4104306	230120	78272	151848	187495	135895	51600

Source: Census of India, 1971, Series - 1, Part II-C (ii), Registrar General & Census Commissioner, New Delhi.

* - Information of Mizoram included in Assam.

Appendix-7.2 (cont. 2)

State-wise Percentage Distribution of Population (all ages) according to Marital Status with Rural-Urban Break-up in different Census Years

Sl. No.	Name of the States/ Region/India	Total / Rural / Urban	As per 1971 Census														
			Marital Status in per cent (to total population)														
			Never Married			Married			Widowed			Divorced or Separated			Unspecified		
			Person	Male	Female	Person	Male	Female	Person	Male	Female	Person	Male	Female	Person	Male	Female
1	2	3	22	23	24	25	26	27	28	29	30	31	32	33	34	35	36
1	Arunachal Pradesh	Total	51.86	52.38	48.63	43.25	42.66	43.94	4.55	2.43	7.01	0.34	0.27	0.42	-	-	-
		Rural	51.97	54.97	48.55	43.02	42.26	43.90	4.67	2.50	7.13	0.34	0.27	0.42	-	-	-
		Urban	49.03	47.83	51.65	49.13	50.79	45.50	1.52	1.15	2.32	0.32	0.23	0.53	-	-	-
2	Assam	Total	58.92	62.01	55.49	36.29	35.44	37.23	4.35	2.21	6.71	0.40	0.29	0.53	0.04	0.05	0.04
		Rural	58.96	62.11	55.51	36.17	35.24	37.19	4.41	2.31	6.70	0.42	0.30	0.56	0.04	0.04	0.04
		Urban	58.58	61.09	55.23	37.48	37.31	37.72	3.64	1.30	6.74	0.21	0.15	0.29	0.09	0.15	0.02
3	Manipur	Total	59.42	61.95	56.83	35.80	36.04	35.56	3.74	1.46	6.06	0.98	0.52	1.45	0.06	0.03	0.10
		Rural	59.96	62.39	57.50	35.53	35.65	35.40	3.55	1.45	5.69	0.89	0.49	1.30	0.07	0.02	0.11
		Urban	55.77	59.02	52.45	37.58	38.60	36.54	5.03	1.63	8.51	1.58	0.69	2.48	0.04	0.06	0.02
4	Meghalaya	Total	57.50	60.30	54.51	37.19	36.70	37.72	3.50	1.56	5.55	1.50	1.08	1.96	0.31	0.36	0.26
		Rural	56.84	59.70	53.85	37.63	37.09	38.13	3.63	1.68	5.68	1.56	1.15	1.98	0.34	0.38	0.30
		Urban	61.36	63.66	58.67	34.64	34.52	34.73	2.68	0.89	4.78	1.17	0.66	1.77	0.15	0.27	0.00

1	2	3	22	23	24	25	26	27	28	29	30	31	32	33	34	35	36
5	Mizoram	Total	-	-	-	-	-	-	-	-	-	-	-	-	-	-	-
		Rural	-	-	-	-	-	-	-	-	-	-	-	-	-	-	-
		Urban	-	-	-	-	-	-	-	-	-	-	-	-	-	-	-
6	Nagaland	Total	58.73	60.14	57.12	37.90	37.87	37.93	2.65	1.39	4.10	0.55	0.40	0.72	0.17	0.20	0.13
		Rural	59.49	61.65	57.17	36.99	36.32	37.72	2.86	1.53	4.27	0.54	0.37	0.73	0.12	0.13	0.11
		Urban	51.86	49.69	56.45	46.07	48.61	40.70	0.89	0.45	1.81	0.57	0.58	0.55	0.61	0.67	0.49
7	Tripura	Total	55.00	59.45	50.28	39.22	38.12	40.39	5.35	2.07	8.83	0.41	0.34	0.48	0.02	0.02	0.02
		Rural	54.55	58.88	49.95	39.64	38.56	40.78	5.36	2.17	8.74	0.43	0.37	0.50	0.02	0.02	0.03
		Urban	58.88	64.30	53.08	35.67	34.34	37.09	5.25	1.20	9.59	0.16	0.10	0.22	0.04	0.06	0.02
8	Sub-Total, NER	Total	58.39	61.49	54.97	36.75	35.98	37.59	4.31	2.12	6.73	0.49	0.34	0.66	0.06	0.07	0.05
		Rural	58.40	61.56	54.97	36.68	35.81	37.61	4.37	2.21	6.71	0.50	0.36	0.66	0.05	0.06	0.05
		Urban	58.33	60.86	55.07	37.45	37.48	37.42	3.72	1.26	6.88	0.40	0.24	0.60	0.10	0.16	0.03
9	Sikkim	Total	57.49	58.26	56.59	37.30	37.26	37.35	3.21	2.09	4.51	1.05	0.95	1.18	0.95	1.44	0.37
		Rural	57.84	58.74	56.81	36.87	36.68	37.08	3.27	2.14	4.55	1.12	1.02	1.24	0.90	1.42	0.32
		Urban	54.13	54.10	54.18	41.45	42.22	40.31	2.65	1.70	4.04	0.39	0.38	0.41	1.38	1.60	1.06
10	Total, NER	Total	58.38	61.45	54.99	36.76	36.00	37.59	4.29	2.12	6.70	0.50	0.35	0.66	0.07	0.08	0.06
		Rural	58.39	61.53	54.98	36.68	35.83	37.60	4.36	2.21	6.69	0.51	0.36	0.67	0.06	0.07	0.06
		Urban	58.29	60.79	55.06	37.50	37.53	37.45	3.70	1.27	6.85	0.40	0.24	0.60	0.11	0.17	0.04
11	India	Total	50.43	54.90	45.61	43.39	41.82	45.08	5.79	2.94	8.86	0.32	0.25	0.39	0.07	0.09	0.06
		Rural	49.68	54.30	44.81	43.90	42.18	45.70	6.03	3.18	9.03	0.34	0.28	0.41	0.05	0.06	0.05
		Urban	53.43	57.21	49.02	41.37	40.46	42.43	4.82	1.97	8.15	0.21	0.13	0.30	0.17	0.23	0.10

Source: Percentage calculated on the basis of the information of the relevant Appendices.

Appendix-7.3

State-wise Distribution of Population according to Marital Status with Rural-Urban Break-up in different Census Years

Sl. No.	Name of the States/ Region/India	Total / Rural / Urban	As per 1981 Census								
			Total Population			Marital Status					
						Never Married			Married		
			Person	Male	Female	Person	Male	Female	Person	Male	Female
1	2	3	4	5	6	7	8	9	10	11	12
1	Arunachal Pradesh	Total	631839	339322	292517	343904	194877	149027	263072	137101	125971
		Rural	590411	313886	276525	320819	180358	140461	245251	126335	118916
		Urban	41428	25436	15992	23085	14519	8566	17821	10766	7055
2	Assam	Total	-	-	-	-	-	-	-	-	-
		Rural	-	-	-	-	-	-	-	-	-
		Urban	-	-	-	-	-	-	-	-	-
3	Manipur	Total	1420953	721006	699947	849080	453203	395877	512340	255907	256433
		Rural	1045493	530331	515162	626220	333633	292587	377766	188056	189710
		Urban	375460	190675	184785	222860	119570	103290	134574	67851	66723
4	Meghalaya	Total	1335819	683710	652109	783210	423841	359369	485096	243771	241325
		Rural	1094486	556958	537528	638022	344662	293360	398813	198310	200503
		Urban	241333	126752	114581	145188	79179	66009	86283	45461	40822

1	2	3	4	5	6	7	8	9	10	11	12
5	Mizoram	Total	493757	257239	236518	296901	159387	137514	170594	90905	79689
		Rural	371943	192874	179069	222728	119406	103322	129029	67946	61083
		Urban	121814	64365	57449	74173	39981	34192	41565	22959	18606
6	Nagaland	Total	774930	415910	359020	474083	261986	212097	281713	148302	133411
		Rural	654696	344699	309997	400625	218326	182299	236067	121101	114966
		Urban	120234	71211	49023	73458	43660	29798	45646	27201	18445
7	Tripura	Total	2053058	1054846	998212	1143378	637779	505599	794522	395395	399127
		Rural	1827490	939558	887932	1015185	566341	448844	709157	353195	355962
		Urban	225568	115288	110280	128193	71438	56755	85365	42200	43165
8	Sub-Total, NER	Total	6710356	3472033	3238323	3890556	2131073	1759483	2507337	1271381	1235956
		Rural	5584519	2878306	2706213	3223599	1762726	1460873	2096083	1054943	1041140
		Urban	1125837	593727	532110	666957	368347	298610	411254	216438	194816
9	Sikkim	Total	316385	172440	143945	184158	104064	80094	119482	62696	56786
		Rural	265301	142341	122960	155380	86761	68619	98555	50433	48122
		Urban	51084	30099	20985	28778	17303	11475	20927	12263	8664
10	Total, NER	Total	7026741	3644473	3382268	4074714	2235137	1839577	2626819	1334077	1292742
		Rural	5849820	3020647	2829173	3378979	1849487	1529492	2194638	1105376	1089262
		Urban	1176921	623826	553095	695735	385650	310085	432181	228701	203480
11	India	Total	665287849	343930423	321357426	337077763	190057835	147019928	291756700	144617526	147139174
		Rural	507607678	260054020	247553658	253407214	142328718	111078496	224930996	109930001	115000995
		Urban	157680171	83876403	73803768	83670549	47729117	35941432	66825704	34687525	32138179

Source: Census of India, 1981, Social and Cultural Tables, Part-IV A, Registrar General & Census Commissioner, New Delhi.

- Census was not conducted.

Appendix-7.3 (cont. 1)

State-wise Distribution of Population according to Marital Status with Rural-Urban Break-up in different Census Years

Sl. No.	Name of the States/ Region/India	Total / Rural / Urban	As per 1981 Census								
			Marital Status								
			Widowed			Divorced or Separated			Unspecified		
			Person	Male	Female	Person	Male	Female	Person	Male	Female
1	2	3	13	14	15	16	17	18	19	20	21
1	Arunachal Pradesh	Total	22590	6383	16207	2138	369	1269	135	92	43
		Rural	22145	6263	15832	2075	850	1225	121	80	41
		Urban	445	120	325	63	19	44	14	12	2
2	Assam *	Total	-	-	-	-	-	-	-	-	-
		Rural	-	-	-	-	-	-	-	-	-
		Urban	-	-	-	-	-	-	-	-	-
3	Manipur	Total	48608	9291	39317	10251	2411	7840	674	194	480
		Rural	34310	6911	27399	6692	1584	5108	505	147	358
		Urban	14298	2380	11918	3559	827	2732	169	47	122
4	Meghalaya	Total	45862	9207	36655	19328	6648	12680	2323	243	2080
		Rural	38741	8022	30719	16656	5767	10889	2254	197	2057
		Urban	7121	1185	5936	2672	881	1791	69	46	23

1	2	3	13	14	15	16	17	18	19	20	21
5	Mizoram	Total	16607	4323	12284	9536	2551	6985	119	73	46
		Rural	12956	3534	9422	7159	1943	5216	71	45	26
		Urban	3651	789	2862	2377	608	1769	48	28	20
6	Nagaland	Total	16117	4396	11721	2718	1075	1643	299	151	148
		Rural	15258	4180	11078	2498	974	1524	248	118	130
		Urban	859	216	643	220	101	119	51	33	18
7	Tripura	Total	103469	17788	85681	11383	3764	7619	306	120	186
		Rural	92127	16340	75787	10736	3571	7165	285	111	174
		Urban	11342	1448	9894	647	193	454	21	9	12
8	Sub-Total, NER	Total	253253	51388	201865	55354	17318	38036	3856	873	2983
		Rural	215537	45250	170287	45816	14689	31127	3484	698	2786
		Urban	37716	6138	31578	9538	2629	6909	372	175	197
9	Sikkim	Total	10505	4426	6079	2166	1203	963	74	51	23
		Rural	9384	4041	5343	1916	1062	854	66	44	22
		Urban	1121	385	736	250	141	109	8	7	1
10	Total, NER	Total	263758	55814	207944	57520	18521	38999	3930	924	3006
		Rural	224921	49291	175630	47732	15751	31981	3550	742	2808
		Urban	38837	6523	32314	9788	2770	7018	380	182	198
11	India	Total	34130270	8363010	25767260	2151711	795402	1356309	171405	96650	74755
		Rural	27353314	7051579	20301735	1806327	686503	1119824	109827	57219	52608
		Urban	6776956	1311431	5465525	345384	108899	236485	61578	39431	22147

Source: Census of India, 1981, Social and Cultural Tables, Part - IV A, Registrar General & Census Commissioner, New Delhi.

* - Census was not conducted.

Appendix-7.3 (*cont.* 2)

State-wise Percentage Distribution of Population according to Marital Status with Rural-Urban Break-up in different Census Years

Sl. No.	Name of the States/Region/ India	Total / Rural / Urban	As per 1981 Census														
			Marital Status in per cent (to total population)														
			Never Married			Married			Widowed			Divorced or Separated			Unspecified		
			Person	Male	Female	Person	Male	Female	Person	Male	Female	Person	Male	Female	Person	Male	Female
1	2	3	22	23	24	25	26	27	28	29	30	31	32	33	34	35	36
1	Arunachal Pradesh	Total	54.43	57.43	50.95	41.64	40.40	43.07	3.57	1.88	5 54	0.34	0.26	0.43	0.02	0.03	0.01
		Rural	54.34	57.46	50.80	41.54	40.24	43.00	3.75	2.00	5 75	0.35	0.27	0.44	0.02	0.03	0.01
		Urban	55.72	57.08	53.56	43.02	42.33	44.12	1.08	0.47	2 03	0.15	0.07	0.28	0.03	0.05	0.01
2	Assam*	Total	-	-	-	-	-	-	-	-	-	-	-	-	-	-	-
		Rural	-	-	-	-	-	-	-	-	-	-	-	-	-	-	-
		Urban	-	-	-	-	-	-	-	-	-	-	-	-	-	-	-
3	Manipur	Total	59.75	62.86	56.56	36.06	35.49	36.64	3.42	1.29	5 62	0.72	0.33	1.12	0.05	0.03	0.06
		Rural	59.90	62.91	56.80	36.13	35.46	36.83	3.28	1.30	5 32	0.64	0.30	0.98	0.05	0.03	0.07
		Urban	59.36	62.71	55.90	35.84	35.58	36.11	3.81	1.25	6 45	0.95	0.44	1.47	0.05	0.02	0.07
4	Meghalaya	Total	58.63	61.99	55.11	36.31	35.65	37.01	3.43	1.35	5 62	1.45	0.97	1.94	0.17	0.04	0.32
		Rural	58.29	61.88	54.58	36.44	35.61	37.30	3.54	1.43	5.71	1.52	1.04	2.03	0.21	0.04	0.38
		Urban	60.16	62.47	57.61	35.75	35.86	35.63	2.95	0.93	5.18	1.11	0.70	1.56	0.03	0.04	0.02

1	2	3	22	23	24	25	26	27	28	29	30	31	32	33	34	35	36
5	Mizoram	Total	60.14	61.96	58.14	34.55	35.34	33.69	3.36	1.68	5.19	1.93	0.99	2.96	0.02	0.03	0.02
		Rural	59.88	61.91	57.70	34.69	35.23	34.11	3.49	1.83	5.26	1.92	1.01	2.92	0.02	0.02	0.01
		Urban	60.89	62.12	59.52	34.12	35.67	32.39	3.00	1.23	4.98	1.95	0.94	3.08	0.04	0.04	0.03
6	Nagaland	Total	61.18	62.98	59.08	36.35	35.66	37.16	2.08	1.06	3.26	0.35	0.26	0.46	0.04	0.04	0.04
		Rural	61.19	63.34	58.81	36.06	35.13	37.09	2.33	1.22	3.57	0.38	0.28	0.49	0.04	0.03	0.04
		Urban	61.10	61.31	60.78	37.97	38.20	37.63	0.71	0.30	1.31	0.18	0.14	0.24	0.04	0.05	0.04
7	Tripura	Total	55.69	60.46	50.65	38.70	37.48	39.98	5.05	1.69	8.59	0.55	0.36	0.76	0.01	0.01	0.02
		Rural	55.55	60.28	50.55	38.80	37.59	40.09	5.04	1.74	8.53	0.59	0.38	0.81	0.02	0.01	0.02
		Urban	56.83	61.96	51.46	37.84	36.60	39.15	5.03	1.26	8.97	0.29	0.17	0.41	0.01	0.01	0.01
8	Sub-Total, NER	Total	57.98	61.38	54.33	37.37	36.62	38.17	3.77	1.47	6.23	0.82	0.50	1.18	0.06	0.03	0.09
		Rural	57.73	61.24	53.98	37.53	36.65	38.47	3.86	1.57	6.29	0.82	0.52	1.16	0.06	0.02	0.10
		Urban	59.24	62.04	56.12	36.53	36.45	36.61	3.35	1.03	5.93	0.85	0.45	1.30	0.03	0.03	0.04
9	Sikkim	Total	58.22	60.35	55.64	37.76	36.36	39.45	3.32	2.56	4.22	0.68	0.70	0.67	0.02	0.03	0.02
		Rural	58.57	60.95	55.81	37.15	35.43	39.14	3.54	2.84	4.35	0.72	0.75	0.68	0.02	0.03	0.02
		Urban	56.33	57.49	54.68	40.97	40.74	41.29	2.19	1.28	3.51	0.49	0.47	0.52	0.02	0.02	0.00
10	Total, NER	Total	57.99	61.33	54.39	37.38	36.61	38.22	3.75	1.52	6.15	0.82	0.51	1.15	0.06	0.03	0.09
		Rural	57.76	61.23	54.06	37.52	36.59	38.50	3.84	1.63	6.21	0.82	0.52	1.13	0.06	0.03	0.10
		Urban	59.12	61.82	56.06	36.72	36.66	36.79	3.30	1.05	5.84	0.83	0.44	1.27	0.03	0.03	0.04
11	India	Total	50.67	55.26	45.75	43.85	42.05	45.79	5.13	2.43	8.02	0.32	0.23	0.42	0.03	0.03	0.02
		Rural	49.92	54.73	44.87	44.31	42.27	46.45	5.39	2.71	8.20	0.36	0.27	0.46	0.02	0.02	0.02
		Urban	53.06	56.90	48.70	42.38	41.36	43.55	4.30	1.56	7.40	0.22	0.13	0.32	0.04	0.05	0.03

Source : Percentage calculated on the basis of the information of the relevant Appendices.

* - Census was not conducted.

Appendix-7.4

State-wise Distribution of Population according to Marital Status with Rural-Urban Break-up in different Census Years

Sl. No.	Name of the States/Region/ India	Total / Rural / Urban	As per 1991 Census								
			Total Population			Marital Status					
						Never Married			Married		
			Person	Male	Female	Person	Male	Female	Person	Male	Female
1	2	3	4	5	6	7	8	9	10	11	12
1	Arunachal Pradesh	Total	864558	465004	399554	476267	267958	208309	363418	190477	172941
		Rural	753930	400966	352964	414628	231660	182968	315736	163053	152683
		Urban	110628	64038	46590	61639	36298	25341	47682	27424	20258
2	Assam	Total	22414322	11657989	10756333	13012532	7248632	5763900	8555014	4223385	4331629
		Rural	19926527	10304161	9622366	11628671	6445583	5183088	7530227	3686430	3843797
		Urban	2487795	1353828	1133967	1383861	803049	580812	1024787	536955	487832
3	Manipur	Total	1837149	938359	898790	1087427	578883	508544	691180	345687	345493
		Rural	1331504	682395	649109	793656	423849	369807	497462	248874	248588
		Urban	505645	255964	249681	293771	155034	138737	193718	96813	96905
4	Meghalaya	Total	1774778	907687	867091	1056417	566143	490274	652646	324843	327803
		Rural	1444731	734865	709866	857815	458652	399163	530486	261185	269301
		Urban	330047	172822	157225	198602	107491	91111	122160	63658	58502

1	2	3	4	5	6	7	8	9	10	11	12
5	Mizoram	Total	689756	358978	330778	414658	225015	189643	247106	125359	121747
		Rural	371810	194414	177396	223383	122038	101345	134201	67729	66472
		Urban	317946	164564	153382	191275	102977	88298	112905	57630	55275
6	Nagaland	Total	1209546	641282	568264	766112	417792	348320	421462	216644	204818
		Rural	1001323	522235	479088	639295	345219	294076	341992	170832	171160
		Urban	208223	119047	89176	126817	72573	54244	79470	45812	33658
7	Tripura	Total	2757205	1417930	1339275	1508681	839926	668755	1118613	555938	562675
		Rural	2335484	1202529	1132955	1286636	715261	571375	941240	467799	473441
		Urban	421721	215401	206320	222045	124665	97380	177373	88139	89234
8	Sub-Total, NER	Total	31547314	16387229	15160085	18322094	10144349	8177745	12049439	5982333	6067106
		Rural	27165309	14041565	13123744	15844084	8742262	7101822	10291344	5065902	5225442
		Urban	4382005	2345664	2036341	2478010	1402087	1075923	1758095	916431	841664
9	Sikkim	Total	406457	216427	190030	240350	132690	107660	156158	79415	76743
		Rural	369451	195277	174174	219108	120142	98966	140904	70961	69943
		Urban	37006	21150	15856	21242	12548	8694	15254	8454	6800
10	Total, NER	Total	31953771	16603656	15350115	18562444	10277039	8285405	12205597	6061748	6143849
		Rural	27534760	14236842	13297918	16063192	8862404	7200788	10432248	5136863	5295385
		Urban	4419011	2366814	2052197	2499252	1414635	1084617	1773349	924885	848464
11	India*	Total	838567936	435208158	403359778	421214411	238136093	183078318	380418921	187816546	192602375
		Rural	622796324	321271205	301525119	309476999	174522414	134954585	284562282	139160806	145401476
		Urban	215771612	113936953	101834659	111737412	63613679	48123733	95856639	48655740	47200899

Source: Census of India, 1991, Series 1, Registrar General & Census Commissioner, New Delhi.

* excluding the information of Jammu & Kashmir, as 1991 Census was not conducted there.

Appendix-7.4 (*cont. 1*)

State-wise Distribution of Population according to Marital Status with Rural-Urban Break-up in different Census Years

Sl. No.	Name of the States/Region/India	Total / Rural/ Urban	As per 1991 Census								
			Marital Status								
			Widowed			Divorced or Separated			Unspecified		
			Person	Male	Female	Person	Male	Female	Person	Male	Female
1	2	3	13	14	15	16	17	18	19	20	21
1	Arunachal Pradesh	Total	22813	5768	17045	1994	752	1242	66	49	17
		Rural	21686	5527	16159	1825	687	1138	55	39	16
		Urban	1127	241	386	169	65	104	11	10	1
2	Assam	Total	787469	169548	617921	56917	14954	41963	2390	1470	920
		Rural	712911	157584	555327	52738	13364	39374	1980	1200	780
		Urban	74558	11964	62594	4179	1590	2589	410	270	140
3	Manipur	Total	49508	11251	38257	8764	2398	6366	270	140	130
		Rural	34268	7952	26316	5937	1615	4322	181	105	76
		Urban	15240	3299	11941	2827	783	2044	89	35	54
4	Meghalaya	Total	45983	10467	35516	19575	6126	13449	157	108	49
		Rural	39408	9507	29901	16899	5435	11464	123	86	37
		Urban	6575	960	5615	2676	691	1985	34	22	12

1	2	3	13	14	15	16	17	18	19	20	21
5	Mizoram	Total	16612	4932	11680	11298	3627	7671	82	45	37
		Rural	9029	2929	6100	5138	1684	3454	59	34	25
		Urban	7583	2003	5580	6160	1943	4217	23	11	12
6	Nagaland	Total	19028	5602	13426	2714	1066	1648	230	178	52
		Rural	17437	5154	12283	2488	966	1522	111	64	47
		Urban	1591	448	1143	226	100	126	119	114	5
7	Tripura	Total	117434	18432	99002	12092	3335	8757	385	299	86
		Rural	96397	16166	80231	10886	3045	7841	325	258	67
		Urban	21037	2266	18771	1206	290	916	60	41	19
8	Sub-Total, NER	Total	1058847	226000	832847	113354	32258	81096	3580	2289	1291
		Rural	931136	204819	726317	95911	26796	69115	2834	1786	1048
		Urban	127711	21181	106530	17443	5462	11981	746	503	243
9	Sikkim	Total	8271	3432	4839	1621	855	766	57	35	22
		Rural	7856	3324	4532	1534	820	714	49	30	19
		Urban	415	108	307	87	35	52	8	5	3
10	Total, NER	Total	1067118	229432	837686	114975	33113	81862	3637	2324	1313
		Rural	938992	208143	730849	97445	27616	69829	2883	1816	1067
		Urban	128126	21289	106837	17530	5497	12033	754	508	246
11	India*	Total	34638686	8433568	26205118	2119340	692640	1426700	176578	129311	47267
		Rural	26943627	6937075	20006552	1704705	572367	1132338	108711	78543	30168
		Urban	7695059	1496493	6198566	414635	120273	294362	67867	50768	17099

Source: Census of India, 1991, Series 1, Registrar General & Census Commissioner, New Delhi.

* - excluding the information of Jammu & Kashmir, as 1991 Census was not conducted there.

Appendix-7.4 (*cont.* 2)

State-wise Percentage Distribution of Population according to Marital Status with Rural-Urban Break-up in different Census Years

Sl. No.	Name of the States/Region/ India	Total/ Rural/ Urban	As per 1991 Census														
			Marital Status in per cent (to total population)														
			Never Married			Married			Widowed			Divorced or Separated			Unspecified		
			Person	Male	Female	Person	Male	Female	Person	Male	Female	Person	Male	Female	Person	Male	Female
1	2	3	22	23	24	25	26	27	28	29	30	31	32	33	34	35	36
1	Arunachal Pradesh	Total	55.09	57.62	52.14	42.04	40.96	43.28	2.63	1.25	4.27	0.23	0.16	0.31	0.01	0.01	0.00
		Rural	55.00	57.78	51.84	41.88	40.67	43.26	2.87	1.37	4.58	0.24	0.17	0.32	0.01	0.01	0.00
		Urban	55.72	56.68	54.39	43.10	42.82	43.48	1.02	0.38	1.90	0.15	0.10	0.23	0.01	0.02	0.00
2	Assam	Total	58.05	62.18	53.59	38.17	36.23	40.27	3.52	1.45	5.74	0.25	0.13	0.39	0.01	0.01	0.01
		Rural	58.36	62.55	53.87	37.79	35.78	39.95	3.58	1.53	5.76	0.26	0.13	0.41	0.01	0.01	0.01
		Urban	55.63	59.32	51.22	41.19	39.66	43.02	3.00	0.88	5 52	0.16	0.12	0.23	0.02	0.02	0.01
3	Manipur	Total	59.19	61.69	56.58	37.62	36.84	38.44	2.69	1.20	4 26	0.49	0.26	0.71	0.01	0.01	0.01
		Rural	59.61	62.11	56.97	37.36	36.47	38.30	2.57	1.17	4.05	0.45	0.23	0.67	0.01	0.02	0.01
		Urban	58.10	60.57	55.57	38.31	37.82	38.81	3.01	1.29	4.78	0.56	0.31	0.82	0.02	0.01	0.02
4	Meghalaya	Total	59.52	62.37	56.54	36.77	35.79	37.80	2.60	1.16	4.10	1.10	0.67	1.55	0.01	0.01	0.01
		Rural	59.38	62.41	56.23	36.72	35.54	37.94	2.73	1.29	4.21	1.16	0.75	1.61	0.01	0.01	0.01
		Urban	60.17	62.20	57.95	37.01	36.83	37.21	1.99	0.56	3.57	0.82	0.40	1.26	0.01	0.01	0.01

1	2	3	22	23	24	25	26	27	28	29	30	31	32	33	34	35	36
5	Mizoram	Total	60.12	62.68	57.33	35.83	34.92	36.81	2.41	1.37	3.53	1.63	1.02	2.32	0.01	0.01	0.01
		Rural	60.08	62.77	57.13	36.09	34.84	37.47	2.43	1.50	3.44	1.38	0.87	1.95	0.02	0.02	0.01
		Urban	60.16	62.58	57.57	35.51	35.02	36.04	2.38	1.22	3.64	1.94	1.17	2.74	0.01	0.01	0.01
6	Nagaland	Total	63.34	65.15	61.30	34.84	33.78	36.04	1.57	0.87	2.36	0.23	0.17	0.29	0.02	0.03	0.01
		Rural	63.85	66.10	61.38	34.15	32.71	35.73	1.74	0.99	2.56	0.25	0.19	0.32	0.01	0.01	0.01
		Urban	60.90	60.96	60.83	38.17	38.48	37.74	0.76	0.38	1.28	0.11	0.08	0.14	0.06	0.10	0.01
7	Tripura	Total	54.72	59.24	49.93	40.57	39.21	42.01	4.26	1.30	7.39	0.44	0.23	0.66	0.01	0.02	0.01
		Rural	55.09	59.48	50.43	40.30	38.90	41.79	4.13	1.34	7.08	0.47	0.26	0.69	0.01	0.02	0.01
		Urban	52.65	57.88	47.20	42.06	40.92	43.25	4.99	1.05	9.10	0.29	0.13	0.44	0.01	0.02	0.01
8	Sub-Total, NER	Total	58.08	61.90	53.94	38.19	36.51	40.02	3.36	1.38	5.49	0.36	0.20	0.54	0.01	0.01	0.01
		Rural	58.32	62.26	54.11	37.88	36.08	39.82	3.43	1.46	5.53	0.36	0.19	0.53	0.01	0.01	0.01
		Urban	56.55	59.77	52.84	40.12	39.07	41.33	2.91	0.90	5.23	0.40	0.24	0.59	0.02	0.02	0.01
9	Sikkim	Total	59.13	61.31	56.65	38.42	36.69	40.38	2.04	1.58	2.56	0.40	0.40	0.40	0.01	0.02	0.01
		Rural	59.31	61.52	56.82	38.14	36.34	40.16	2.12	1.70	2.60	0.42	0.42	0.41	0.01	0.02	0.01
		Urban	57.40	59.33	54.83	41.22	39.97	42.89	1.12	0.51	1.94	0.24	0.17	0.33	0.02	0.02	0.01
10	Total, NER	Total	58.09	61.90	53.98	38.20	36.51	40.02	3.34	1.38	5.46	0.36	0.20	0.53	0.01	0.01	0.01
		Rural	58.34	62.25	54.15	37.89	36.08	39.82	3.41	1.47	5.50	0.35	0.19	0.52	0.01	0.01	0.01
		Urban	56.56	59.77	52.85	40.12	39.08	41.34	2.90	0.90	5.21	0.40	0.23	0.59	0.02	0.02	0.01
11	India	Total	50.23	54.72	45.39	45.37	43.16	47.75	4.13	1.94	6.50	0.25	0.15	0.35	0.02	0.03	0.01
		Rural	49.69	54.32	44.76	45.69	43.32	48.22	4.33	2.16	6.64	0.27	0.18	0.37	0.02	0.02	0.01
		Urban	51.79	55.83	47.26	44.43	42.70	46.35	3.57	1.31	6.09	0.18	0.12	0.28	0.03	0.04	0.02

Source: Percentage calculated on the basis of the information of the relevant Appendices.

Appendix-7.5

State-wise Distribution of Population according to Marital Status with Rural-Urban Break-up in different Census Years

Sl. No.	Name of the States/Region/ India	Total / Rural / Urban	As per 2001 Census								
			Total Population			Marital Status					
						Never Married			Married		
			Person	Male	Female	Person	Male	Female	Person	Male	Female
1	2	3	4	5	6	7	8	9	10	11	12
1	Arunachal Pradesh	Total	1097968	579941	518027	618772	338401	280371	440422	231235	209187
		Rural	870087	454680	415407	491737	268072	223665	344195	177210	166985
		Urban	227881	125261	102620	127035	70329	56706	96227	54025	42202
2	Assam	Total	26655528	13777037	12878491	14788804	8225259	6563545	10703437	5326115	5377322
		Rural	23216288	11939945	11276343	13020783	7211307	5809476	9172778	4524847	4647931
		Urban	3439240	1837092	1602148	1768021	1013952	754069	1530659	801268	729391
3	Manipur	Total	2166788	1095634	1071154	1243970	656732	587238	837091	420702	416389
		Rural	1590820	808953	781867	923635	489549	434086	609437	306691	302746
		Urban	575968	286681	289287	320335	167183	153152	227654	114011	113643
4	Meghalaya	Total	2318822	1176087	1142735	1402873	747717	655156	810013	405965	404048
		Rural	1864711	946999	917712	1131554	605478	526076	647638	322460	325178
		Urban	454111	229088	225023	271319	142239	129080	162375	83505	78870

1	2	3	4	5	6	7	8	9	10	11	12
5	Mizoram	Total	888573	459109	429464	514121	276552	237569	327518	169177	158341
		Rural	447567	232726	214841	259396	140702	118694	166409	85339	81070
		Urban	441006	226383	214623	254725	135850	118875	161109	83838	77271
6	Nagaland	Total	1990036	1047141	942895	1272698	689774	582924	672651	345204	327447
		Rural	1647249	859716	787533	1064900	573956	490944	543858	275028	268830
		Urban	342787	187425	155362	207798	115818	91980	128793	70176	58617
7	Tripura	Total	3199203	1642225	1556978	1644753	916824	727929	1393171	701322	691849
		Rural	2653453	1363638	1289815	1388860	772708	616152	1133470	569878	563592
		Urban	545750	278587	267163	255893	144116	111777	259701	131444	128257
8	Sub-Total, NER	Total	38316918	19777174	18539744	21485991	11851259	9634732	15184303	7599720	7584583
		Rural	32290175	16606657	15683518	18280865	10061772	8219093	12617785	6261453	6356332
		Urban	6026743	3170517	2856226	3205126	1789487	1415639	2566518	1338267	1228251
9	Sikkim	Total	540851	288484	252367	303669	166569	137100	217164	114268	102896
		Rural	480981	255774	225207	271799	148785	123014	190814	99795	91019
		Urban	59870	32710	27160	31870	17784	14086	26350	14473	11877
10	Total, NER	Total	38857769	20065658	18792111	21789660	12017828	9771832	15401467	7713988	7687479
		Rural	32771156	16862431	15908725	18552664	10210557	8342107	12808599	6361248	6447351
		Urban	6086613	3203227	2883386	3236996	1807271	1429725	2592868	1352740	1240128
11	India	Total	1028610328	532156772	496453556	512667639	289619359	223048280	468593016	231820399	236772617
		Rural	742490639	381602674	360887965	370531390	208231522	162299868	336894950	164990657	171904293
		Urban	286119689	150554098	135565591	142136249	81387837	60748412	131698066	66829742	64868324

Source: Website, Registrar General and Census Commissioner, India.

Appendix-7.5 (*cont. 1*)

State-wise Distribution of Population according to Marital Status with Rural-Urban Break-up in different Census Years

Sl. No.	Name of the States/Region/India	Total / Rural / Urban	As per 2001 Census								
			Marital Status								
			Widowed			Divorced or Separated			Unspecified		
			Person	Male	Female	Person	Male	Female	Person	Male	Female
1	2	3	13	14	15	16	17	18	19	20	21
1	Arunachal Pradesh	Total	34216	8577	25639	4558	1728	2830	0	0	0
		Rural	30312	7940	22372	3843	1458	2385	0	0	0
		Urban	3904	637	3267	715	270	445	0	0	0
2	Assam	Total	1072556	203551	869005	90731	22112	68619	0	0	0
		Rural	942034	185013	757021	80693	18778	61915	0	0	0
		Urban	130522	18538	111984	10038	3334	6704	0	0	0
3	Manipur	Total	74345	14886	59459	11382	3314	8068	0	0	0
		Rural	49756	10253	39503	7992	2460	5532	0	0	0
		Urban	24589	4633	19956	3390	854	2536	0	0	0
4	Meghalaya	Total	72469	12865	59604	33467	3540	23927	0	0	0
		Rural	57309	10829	46480	28210	3232	19978	0	0	0
		Urban	15160	2036	13124	5257	1308	3949	0	0	0

1	2	3	13	14	15	16	17	18	19	20	21
5	Mizoram	Total	26293	5920	20373	20641	7460	13181	0	0	0
		Rural	12802	3340	9462	8960	3345	5615	0	0	0
		Urban	13491	2580	10911	11681	4115	7566	0	0	0
6	Nagaland	Total	34874	8358	26516	9813	3805	6008	0	0	0
		Rural	30119	7487	22632	8372	3245	5127	0	0	0
		Urban	4755	871	3884	1441	560	881	0	0	0
7	Tripura	Total	144403	20586	123817	16876	3493	13383	0	0	0
		Rural	116476	17896	98580	14647	3156	11491	0	0	0
		Urban	27927	2690	25237	2229	337	1892	0	0	0
8	Sub-Total, NER	Total	1459156	274743	1184413	187468	51452	136016	0	0	0
		Rural	1238808	242758	996050	152717	40674	112043	0	0	0
		Urban	220348	31985	188363	34751	10778	23973	0	0	0
9	Sikkim	Total	15474	5469	10005	4544	2178	2366	0	0	0
		Rural	14157	5141	9016	4211	2053	2158	0	0	0
		Urban	1317	328	989	333	125	208	0	0	0
10	Total, NER	Total	1474630	280212	1194418	192012	53630	138382	0	0	0
		Rural	1252965	247899	1005066	156928	42727	114201	0	0	0
		Urban	221665	32313	189352	35084	10903	24181	0	0	0
11	India	Total	44018648	9728919	34289729	3331025	988095	2342930	0	0	0
		Rural	32580523	7634502	24946021	2483776	745993	1737783	0	0	0
		Urban	11438125	2094417	9343708	847249	242102	605147	0	0	0

Source: Website, Registrar General of India, New Delhi.

Appendix-7.5 (cont. 2)

State-wise Percentage Distribution of Population according to Marital Status with Rural-Urban Break-up in different Census Years

Sl. No.	Name of the States/Region/ India	Total / Rural / Urban	As per 2001 Census														
			Marital Status in per cent (to total population)														
			Never Married			Married			Widowed			Divorced or Separated			Unspecified		
			Person	Male	Female	Person	Male	Female	Person	Male	Female	Person	Male	Female	Person	Male	Female
1	2	3	22	23	24	25	26	27	28	29	30	31	32	33	34	35	36
1	Arunachal Pradesh	Total	56.36	58.35	54.12	40.10	39.87	40.38	3.12	1.48	4.95	0.42	0.30	0.55	0	0	0
		Rural	56.52	58.96	53.84	39.56	38.97	40.20	3.48	1.75	5.39	0.44	0.32	0.57	0	0	0
		Urban	55.75	56.15	55.27	42.23	43.13	41.12	1.71	0.51	3.18	0.31	0.21	0.43	0	0	0
2	Assam	Total	55.48	59.70	50.97	40.15	38.66	41.75	4.02	1.48	6.75	0.35	0.16	0.53	0	0	0
		Rural	56.08	60.40	51.52	39.51	37.90	41.22	4.06	1.55	6.71	0.35	0.15	0.55	0	0	0
		Urban	51.41	55.19	47.07	44.51	43.62	45.53	3.80	1.01	6.99	0.28	0.18	0.41	0	0	0
3	Manipur	Total	57.41	59.94	54.82	38.63	38.40	38.87	3.43	1.36	5.56	0.53	0.30	0.75	0	0	0
		Rural	58.06	60.52	55.52	38.31	37.91	38.72	3.13	1.27	5.05	0.50	0.30	0.71	0	0	0
		Urban	55.62	58.32	52.94	39.53	39.76	39.28	4.27	1.62	6.90	0.58	0.30	0.88	0	0	0
4	Meghalaya	Total	60.50	63.58	57.33	34.93	34.52	35.36	3.13	1.09	5.22	1.44	0.81	2.09	0	0	0
		Rural	60.68	63.94	57.32	34.73	34.05	35.43	3.07	1.14	5.07	1.52	0.87	2.18	0	0	0
		Urban	59.75	62.09	57.36	35.75	36.45	35.05	3.34	0.89	5.83	1.16	0.57	1.76	0	0	0

1	2	3	22	23	24	25	26	27	28	29	30	31	32	33	34	35	36
5	Mizoram	Total	57.86	60.24	55.32	36.86	36.85	36.87	2.96	1.29	4.74	2.32	1.62	3.07	0	0	0
		Rural	57.96	60.46	55.25	37.18	36.67	37.73	2.86	1.44	4.40	2.00	1.43	2.62	0	0	0
		Urban	57.76	60.01	55.39	36.53	37.03	36.00	3.06	1.14	5.08	2.65	1.82	3.53	0	0	0
6	Nagaland	Total	63.95	65.87	61.82	33.80	32.97	34.73	1.76	0.80	2.81	0.49	0.36	0.64	0	0	0
		Rural	64.65	66.76	62.34	33.02	31.99	34.14	1.83	0.87	2.87	0.50	0.38	0.65	0	0	0
		Urban	60.62	61.79	59.20	37.57	37.45	37.73	1.39	0.46	2.50	0.42	0.30	0.57	0	0	0
7	Tripura	Total	51.41	55.83	46.75	43.55	42.71	44.44	4.51	1.25	7.95	0.53	0.21	0.86	0	0	0
		Rural	52.34	56.67	47.77	42.72	41.79	43.70	4.39	1.31	7.64	0.55	0.23	0.89	0	0	0
		Urban	46.89	51.73	41.84	47.59	47.18	48.01	5.12	0.97	9.45	0.40	0.12	0.70	0	0	0
8	Sub-Total, NER	Total	56.07	59.92	51.97	39.63	38.43	40.91	3.81	1.39	6.39	0.49	0.26	0.73	0	0	0
		Rural	56.61	60.59	52.41	39.08	37.70	40.53	3.84	1.46	6.35	0.47	0.25	0.71	0	0	0
		Urban	53.18	56.44	49.57	42.58	42.21	43.00	3.66	1.01	6.59	0.58	0.34	0.84	0	0	0
9	Sikkim	Total	56.15	57.74	54.33	40.15	39.61	40.77	2.86	1.90	3.96	0.84	0.75	0.94	0	0	0
		Rural	56.51	58.17	54.62	39.67	39.02	40.42	2.94	2.01	4.00	0.88	0.80	0.96	0	0	0
		Urban	53.23	54.37	51.86	44.01	44.25	43.73	2.20	1.00	3.64	0.56	0.38	0.77	0	0	0
10	Total, NER	Total	56.08	59.89	52.00	39.64	38.44	40.91	3.79	1.40	6.36	0.49	0.27	0.73	0	0	0
		Rural	56.62	60.55	52.44	39.08	37.72	40.53	3.82	1.47	6.32	0.48	0.26	0.71	0	0	0
		Urban	53.18	56.42	49.58	42.60	42.23	43.01	3.64	1.01	6.57	0.58	0.34	0.84	0	0	0
11	India	Total	49.84	54.42	44.93	45.56	43.56	47.69	4.28	1.83	6.91	0.32	0.19	0.47	0	0	0
		Rural	49.90	54.56	44.97	45.37	43.24	47.63	4.39	2.00	6.92	0.34	0.20	0.48	0	0	0
		Urban	49.68	54.06	44.81	46.02	44.39	47.85	4.00	1.39	6.89	0.30	0.16	0.45	0	0	0

Source: Calculated from the relevant Appendices.

Appendix-7.6

State-wise Distribution of Population according to Marital Status with Rural-Urban Break-up in different Census Years

Sl. No.	Name of the States/Region/India	Total/ Rural/Urban	As per 2011 Census								
			Total Population			Marital Status					
						Never Married			Married		
			Person	Male	Female	Person	Male	Female	Person	Male	Female
1	2	3	4	5	6	7	8	9	10	11	12
1	Arunachal Pradesh	Total	1383727	713912	669815	765934	410829	355105	569238	290314	278924
		Rural	1066358	546011	520347	595506	319912	275594	430209	215137	215072
		Urban	317369	167901	149468	170428	90917	79511	139029	75177	63852
2	Assam	Total	31205576	15939443	15266133	15868475	8820415	7048060	13807668	6834718	6972950
		Rural	26807034	13678989	13128045	13828784	7665773	6163011	11681533	5764465	5917068
		Urban	4398542	2260454	2138088	2039691	1154642	885049	2126135	1070253	1055882
3	Manipur	Total	2855794	1438586	1417208	1547572	817403	730169	1194813	595143	599670
		Rural	2021640	1026884	994756	1126032	598268	527764	823898	411031	412867
		Urban	834154	411702	422452	421540	219135	202405	370915	184112	186803
4	Meghalaya	Total	2966889	1491832	1475057	1749728	932373	817355	1069842	530185	539657
		Rural	2371439	1194260	1177179	1409921	753342	656579	848178	416624	431554
		Urban	595450	297572	297878	339807	179031	160776	221664	113561	108103

1	2	3	4	5	6	7	8	9	10	11	12
5	Mizoram	Total	1097206	555339	541867	599506	318194	281312	431768	217637	214131
		Rural	525435	269135	256300	289853	156210	133643	207899	103941	103958
		Urban	571771	286204	285567	309653	161984	147669	223869	113696	110173
6	Nagaland	Total	1978502	1024649	953853	1192160	639157	553003	720923	368633	352290
		Rural	1407536	725472	682064	855567	458725	396842	504056	253725	250331
		Urban	570966	299177	271789	336593	180432	156161	216867	114908	101959
7	Tripura	Total	3673917	1874376	1799541	1654782	934172	720610	1801171	905826	895345
		Rural	2712464	1387173	1325291	1261990	708263	553727	1297628	652191	645437
		Urban	961453	487203	474250	392792	225909	166883	503543	253635	249908
8	Sub-Total, NER	Total	45161611	23038137	22123474	23378157	12872543	10505614	19595423	9742456	9852967
		Rural	36911906	18827924	18083982	19367653	10660493	8707160	15793401	7817114	7976287
		Urban	8249705	4210213	4039492	4010504	2212050	1798454	3802022	1925342	1876680
9	Sikkim	Total	610577	323070	287507	305986	168021	137965	278114	145422	132692
		Rural	456999	242797	214202	231048	127477	103571	205212	107243	97969
		Urban	153578	80273	73305	74938	40544	34394	72902	38179	34723
10	Total, NER	Total	45772188	23361207	22410981	23684143	13040564	10643579	19873537	9887878	9985659
		Rural	37368905	19070721	18298184	19598701	10787970	8810731	15998613	7924357	8074256
		Urban	8403283	4290486	4112797	4085442	2252594	1832848	3874924	1963521	1911403
11	India	Total	1210854977	623270258	587584719	570833969	322870527	247963442	579584783	286507311	293077472
		Rural	833748852	427781058	405967794	398897685	224507507	174390178	393025961	193130143	199895818
		Urban	377106125	195489200	181616925	171936284	98363020	73573264	186558822	93377168	93181654

Source: Website, Registrar General and Census Commissioner, India.

Appendix-7.6 (cont. 1)

State-wise Distribution of Population according to Marital Status with Rural-Urban Break-up in different Census Years

Sl. No.	Name of the States/Region/ India	Total/Rural/ Urban	As per 2011 Census								
			Marital Status								
			Widowed			Divorced or Separated			Unspecified		
			Person	Male	Female	Person	Male	Female	Person	Male	Female
1	2	3	13	14	15	16	17	18	19	20	21
1	Arunachal Pradesh	Total	41619	9832	31787	6936	2937	3999	0	0	0
		Rural	35261	8707	26554	5382	2255	3127	0	0	0
		Urban	6358	1125	5233	1554	682	872	0	0	0
2	Assam	Total	1409905	253863	1156042	119528	30447	89081	0	0	0
		Rural	1196150	225051	971099	100567	23700	76867	0	0	0
		Urban	213755	28812	184943	18961	6747	12214	0	0	0
3	Manipur	Total	97460	19470	77990	15949	6570	9379	0	0	0
		Rural	61085	12881	48204	10625	4704	5921	0	0	0
		Urban	36375	6589	29786	5324	1866	3458	0	0	0
4	Meghalaya	Total	101448	16623	84825	45871	12651	33220	0	0	0
		Rural	76637	13826	62811	36703	10468	26235	0	0	0
		Urban	24811	2797	22014	9168	2183	6985	0	0	0

5	Mizoram	Total	36719	8150	28569	29213	11358	17855	0	0	0
		Rural	16384	4274	12110	11299	4710	6589	0	0	0
		Urban	20335	3876	16459	17914	6648	11266	0	0	0
6	Nagaland	Total	50404	10908	39496	15015	5951	9064	0	0	0
		Rural	37382	8898	28484	10531	4124	6407	0	0	0
		Urban	13022	2010	11012	4484	1827	2657	0	0	0
7	Tripura	Total	194023	29054	164969	23941	5324	18617	0	0	0
		Rural	135119	22586	112533	17727	4133	13594	0	0	0
		Urban	58904	6468	52436	6214	1191	5023	0	0	0
8	Sub-Total, NER	Total	1931578	347900	1583678	256453	75238	181215	0	0	0
		Rural	1558018	296223	1261795	192834	54094	138740	0	0	0
		Urban	373560	51677	321883	63619	21144	42475	0	0	0
9	Sikkim	Total	20327	6610	13717	6150	3017	3133	0	0	0
		Rural	15836	5586	10250	4903	2491	2412	0	0	0
		Urban	4491	1024	3467	1247	526	721	0	0	0
10	Total, NER	Total	1951905	354510	1597395	262603	78255	184348	0	0	0
		Rural	1573854	301809	1272045	197737	56585	141152	0	0	0
		Urban	378051	52701	325350	64866	21670	43196	0	0	0
11	India	Total	55538707	12277229	43261478	4897518	1615191	3282327	0	0	0
		Rural	38592341	9073427	29518914	3232865	1069981	2162884	0	0	0
		Urban	16946366	3203802	13742564	1664653	545210	1119443	0	0	0

Source: Website of the Registrar General of India, New Delhi.

Appendix-7.6 (*cont. 2*)

State-wise Percentage Distribution of Population according to Marital Status with Rural-Urban Break-up in different Census Years

Sl. No.	Name of the States/Region of India	Total/ Rural/ Urban	As per 2011 Census														
			Marital Status in per cent (to total population)														
			Never Married			Married			Widowed			Divorced or Separated			Unspecified		
			Person	Male	Female	Person	Male	Female	Person	Male	Female	Person	Male	Female	Person	Male	Female
1	2	3	22	23	24	25	26	27	28	29	30	31	32	33	34	35	36
1	Arunachal Pradesh	Total	55.35	57.55	53.02	41.14	40.67	41.64	3.01	1.37	4.74	0.50	0.41	0.60	0	0	0
		Rural	55.84	58.59	52.96	40.34	39.40	41.33	3.32	1.59	5.11	0.50	0.42	0.60	0	0	0
		Urban	53.70	54.15	53.20	43.81	44.77	42.72	2.00	0.67	3.50	0.49	0.41	0.58	0	0	0
2	Assam	Total	50.85	55.34	46.17	44.25	42.88	45.68	4.52	1.59	7.57	0.38	0.19	0.58	0	0	0
		Rural	51.59	56.04	46.95	43.58	42.14	45.07	4.46	1.65	7.40	0.37	0.17	0.58	0	0	0
		Urban	46.37	51.08	41.39	48.34	47.35	49.38	4.86	1.27	8.65	0.43	0.30	0.58	0	0	0
3	Manipur	Total	54.19	56.82	51.52	41.84	41.37	42.31	3.41	1.35	5.50	0.56	0.46	0.67	0	0	0
		Rural	55.70	58.26	53.05	40.75	40.03	41.50	3.02	1.25	4.85	0.53	0.46	0.60	0	0	0
		Urban	50.54	53.23	47.91	44.47	44.72	44.22	4.36	1.60	7.05	0.63	0.45	0.82	0	0	0
4	Meghalaya	Total	58.98	62.50	55.41	36.06	35.54	36.59	3.42	1.11	5.75	1.54	0.85	2.25	0	0	0
		Rural	59.45	63.08	55.78	35.77	34.89	36.66	3.23	1.16	5.33	1.55	0.87	2.23	0	0	0
		Urban	57.07	60.16	53.97	37.23	38.16	36.29	4.17	0.94	7.39	1.53	0.74	2.35	0	0	0

1	2	3	22	23	24	25	26	27	28	29	30	31	32	33	34	35	36
5	Mizoram	Total	54.64	57.30	51.92	39.35	39.19	39.52	3.35	1.47	5.26	2.66	2.04	3.30	0	0	0
		Rural	55.16	58.04	52.14	39.57	38.62	40.56	3.12	1.59	4.72	2.15	1.75	2.58	0	0	0
		Urban	54.16	56.60	51.71	39.15	39.73	38.58	3.56	1.35	5.76	3.13	2.32	3.95	0	0	0
6	Nagaland	Total	60.26	62.38	57.98	36.44	35.98	36.93	2.55	1.06	4.14	0.75	0.58	0.95	0	0	0
		Rural	60.78	63.23	58.18	35.81	34.97	36.70	2.66	1.23	4.18	0.75	0.57	0.94	0	0	0
		Urban	58.95	60.31	57.46	37.98	38.41	37.51	2.28	0.67	4.05	0.79	0.61	0.98	0	0	0
7	Tripura	Total	45.04	49.84	40.04	49.03	48.33	49.75	5.28	1.55	9.18	0.65	0.28	1.03	0	0	0
		Rural	46.53	51.06	41.78	47.84	47.02	48.70	4.98	1.62	8.49	0.65	0.30	1.03	0	0	0
		Urban	40.85	46.37	35.19	52.37	52.06	52.70	6.13	1.33	11.06	0.65	0.24	1.05	0	0	0
8	Sub-Total, NER	Total	51.77	55.87	47.49	43.38	42.29	44.54	4.28	1.51	7.15	0.57	0.33	0.82	0	0	0
		Rural	52.47	56.62	48.15	42.79	41.52	44.11	4.22	1.57	6.98	0.52	0.29	0.76	0	0	0
		Urban	48.61	52.54	44.52	46.09	45.73	46.46	4.53	1.23	7.97	0.77	0.50	1.05	0	0	0
9	Sikkim	Total	50.11	52.01	47.99	45.55	45.01	46.15	3.33	2.05	4.77	1.01	0.93	1.09	0	0	0
		Rural	50.56	52.50	48.35	44.90	44.17	45.74	3.47	2.30	4.79	1.07	1.03	1.12	0	0	0
		Urban	48.79	50.51	46.92	47.47	47.56	47.37	2.93	1.28	4.73	0.81	0.65	0.98	0	0	0
10	Total, NER	Total	51.74	55.82	47.49	43.42	42.33	44.56	4.26	1.52	7.13	0.58	0.33	0.82	0	0	0
		Rural	52.45	56.57	48.15	42.81	41.55	44.13	4.21	1.58	6.95	0.53	0.30	0.77	0	0	0
		Urban	48.62	52.50	44.56	46.11	45.76	46.47	4.50	1.23	7.92	0.77	0.51	1.05	0	0	0
11	India	Total	47.14	51.80	42.20	47.87	45.97	49.88	4.59	1.97	7.36	0.40	0.26	0.56	0	0	0
		Rural	47.84	52.48	42.96	47.14	45.15	49.24	4.63	2.12	7.27	0.39	0.25	0.53	0	0	0
		Urban	45.59	50.32	40.51	49.47	47.77	51.31	4.49	1.64	7.56	0.45	0.27	0.62	0	0	0

Source: Percentage calculated on the basis of the information of relevant Appendices.

8
Fertility

In Demography, 'Fertility' refers to the actual birth performance of the group of women or to the relative frequency with which the births occur in the total population or in the population involved in it. It is actually the result of 'Fecundity', i.e. the physiological capacity to reproduce. But, it is also a fact that, a fecund woman may not release her potential fecundity into actual reproduction because, the child-bearing process depends on the fertility of both male and female. Deficiency in one normally affects the other which results in sterility to the one capable of reproduction.

The child bearing period or the child bearing span for female is normally from 15 to 49 years of age and for male it is from 15 to 51 years of age. And marriage is a social and sacred bonding between a male and a female which has a direct bearing on the process of reproduction. Further, fertility depends on the period of fecundity which marriage provides to the eligible couple. Marriage taking place at an early age means, a longer period of fertility and the scope of having more number of children. Late marriage on the other hand means, a smaller period of fertility and the scope of having lesser number of children.

However, for a healthy and happy family life, there should be adequate difference, in terms of age, between the children. The modern means of 'Family Planning' has given the scope and freedom to the people of deciding the timing of having children and limiting their family size. But, in olden days, there was no much scope of maintaining the gap between children and in addition to that, there were so many social taboos. Even now, there are people, who believe that, children are the gift of God and preventing birth by artificial means is against the social system. Moreover, ladies having no children, are always blamed, even cursed for that. Many people do not understand or try to understand that, male partner is also equally responsible for child birth and if he is having any deficiency, a female cannot give birth to a child of her own.

However, things are changing and people are gradually becoming aware about the utility of Family Planning and coming forward for adopting family planning methods and the fertility scenario started changing. The state-wise fertility indicators e.g., birth rate, total fertility rate along with death rate and natural growth rate etc. from 1971 onwards, of the NE States, can be seen from the Appendix-3.2. Further, the Appendix-8.1, Appendix–8.2 and Appendix–8.3 will give an idea about the number of Children, the Females are having, according to 1991, 2001 and 2011 Censuses, in different States of North Eastern Region as well as, in the Country as a whole.

From above mentioned Appendices, it can be seen that, amongst all the NE States, except Tripura, the proportion of ever married women (all ages) was comparatively low and it was not even fifty per cent of the total women (all ages) of the respective states in the Census year of 1991 and 2001. In case of Nagaland, it was not even forty per cent in these two periods. However, in case of Tripura, the percentage of ever married women was 50.06 in 1991 and it increased to 53.25 per cent in 2001 and than to 59.96 per cent in 2011.

Moreover, it is seen that, the proportion of married women, having no children, was quite high, in almost all the NE States, according to all these 3 (three) Census years. It was ranging from the lowest of 11.18 per cent of Tripura to the highest of 28.07 per cent of Arunachal Pradesh in 1991. In 2001, it was the lowest of 11.66 per cent of Mizoram to the highest of 21.20 per cent of Nagaland. And in 2011, it was the lowest of 12.82 per cent of Tripura to the highest of 19.34 per cent of Arunachal Pradesh. It is also seen that, amongst all the surviving children, the proportion of males was slightly higher than the proportion of females, both in Rural as well as in Urban, in all the NE States and in all these Census years. The proportion of male children was more than 50 to 52 per cent and in case of female children, it was more than 47 to 49 per cent.

Further, it is seen that, in the States like Nagaland, Meghalaya, Mizoram, Manipur and Assam, the proportion of ever married women having more number of children, was quite high. In case of Nagaland, it is seen that, according to 1991 Census, 28.37 per cent of the ever married women were having 5 or more children, 11.69 per cent were having 4 children, 12.19 per cent were having 3 children, 12.19 per cent were having 2 children and 10.16 per cent were having 1 child. According to 2001 Census, the percentage was 31.68, 12.86, 12.92, 11.75 and 9.59 respectively. And according to 2011 Census, it was 25.51, 14.15, 15.36, 15.89 and 13.24 per cent respectively.

In Meghalaya, according to 1991 Census, 24.96 per cent of the ever married women were having 5 or more children, 11.85 per cent were having 4 children, 13.90 per cent were having 3 children, 14.98 per cent were having 2 children and 13.88 per cent were having 1 child. According to 2001 Census, the percentage was 25.39, 11.76, 13.58, 14.58 and 14.09 per cent respectively. And according to 2011 Census, it was 23.47, 11.33, 13.68, 15.90 and 16.49 per cent respectively.

In Mizoram, Manipur and Assam, though the proportion of ever married women having 5 or more children was high but, it was showing a declining trend over the years. In case of Mizoram, it can be seen that, according to 1991 Census, 25.85 per cent of the ever married women were having 5 or more children, 13.53 per cent were having 4 children, 13.45 per cent were having 3 children, 12.52 per cent were having 2 children and 11.31 per cent were having 1 child. As per 2001 Census, the percentage was 24.18, 15.99, 18.51, 15.80 and 13.86 per cent respectively. And according to 2011 Census, it was 17.63, 15.32, 19.90, 18.14 and 15.71 per cent respectively.

In Manipur, according to 1991 Census, 26.91 per cent of the ever married women were having 5 or more children, 12.18 per cent were having 4 children, 12.46 per cent were having 3 children, 11.59 per cent were having 2 children and 10.77 per cent were having 1 child. According to 2001 Census, the percentage was 22.71, 13.50, 15.34, 15.28 and 13.16 per cent respectively. And according to 2011 Census, it was 17.69, 12.35, 16.15, 18.58 and 16.54 per cent respectively.

In Assam, according to 1991 Census, 25.59 per cent of the ever married women were having 5 or more children, 13.62 per cent were having 4 children, 16.12 per cent were having 3 children, 16.13 per cent were having 2 children and 14.49 per cent were having 1 child. According to 2001 Census, the percentage was 20.05, 13.06, 16.93, 18.31 and 15.52 per cent respectively. And according to 2011 Census, it was 14.86, 11.15, 16.41, 21.95 and 19.00 per cent respectively.

In Sikkim, Tripura and Arunachal Pradesh, the proportion of ever married women having 5 or more children was comparatively low and it was also showing a declining trend over the years. In Sikkim, according to 1991 Census, 22.84 per cent of the ever married women were having 5 or more children, 11.52 per cent were having 4 children,

14.22 per cent were having 3 children, 15.56 per cent were having 2 children and 13.08 per cent were having 1 child. According to 2001 Census, the percentage was 20.40, 11.79, 15.96, 20.44 and 16.26 per cent respectively. And as per 2011 Census, it was 14.57, 9.56, 14.81, 23.53 and 21.02 per cent respectively.

In Tripura, according to 1991 Census, 22.44 per cent of the ever married women were having 5 or more children, 13.71 per cent were having 4 children, 16.91 per cent were having 3 children, 17.94 per cent were having 2 children and 16.18 per cent were having 1 child. According to 2001 Census, the percentage was 16.15, 12.54, 17.61, 21.85 and 18.39 per cent respectively. And as per 2011 Census, it was 11.01, 9.77, 15.92, 26.48 and 24.00 per cent respectively.

The State of Arunachal Pradesh showed more or less a unique characteristic. The proportion of ever married women having 5 or more children was comparatively much lower, and also there was no much difference in the values of the proportion of ever married women having different numbers of children. According to 1991 Census, only 16.70 per cent of the ever married women were having 5 or more children, 10.59 per cent were having 4 children, 13.82 per cent were having 3 children, 15.74 per cent were having 2 children and 15.06 per cent were having 1 child. According to 2001 Census, the percentage was 19.69, 13.36, 16.69, 18.10 and 15.70 per cent respectively. And as per 2011 Census, it was 17.05, 12.96, 16.53, 18.71 and 15.41 per cent respectively.

The Rural-Urban situation was slightly different. It is seen that, in the States like Assam, Manipur, Nagaland, Tripura and Sikkim, the proportion of ever married women was higher in Urban than Rural in all these three Census years. Not only this, in Urban areas, the proportion was showing an increasing trend over the years. According to 1991 Census, it was ranging from the lowest of 39.17 per cent of Nagaland to the highest of 52.79 per cent of Tripura. As per 2001 Census, it was ranging from the lowest of 40.80 per cent of Nagaland to the highest of 58.16 per cent of Tripura. And according to 2011 Census, it was again from the lowest of 42.54 per cent of Nagaland to the highest of 64.81 per cent of Tripura. From this, it appears that, married women in Nagaland were comparatively less, but in Tripura, it was comparatively muoh more.

In other States *viz.*, Arunachal Pradesh, Meghalaya and Mizoram, the proportion of ever married women was higher in Rural areas in all these States in the Census year of 1991 and 2001, but as per 2011

Census, the proportion was slightly higher in Urban areas of Meghalaya and Mizoram. But there was no much difference between the values of the proportion of Rural and of Urban in any of the Census year. According to 1991 Census, the proportion of ever married women in the Rural areas was ranging from the lowest of 42.86 per cent of Mizoram to the highest of 48.16 per cent of Arunachal Pradesh. As per 2001 Census, it was the lowest of 42.68 per cent of Meghalaya to the highest of 46.16 per cent of Arunachal Pradesh. And as per 2011 Census, the Rural proportion was ranging from the lowest of 44.22 per cent of Meghalaya to the highest of 47.86 per cent of Mizoram.

In case of children, it is seen that, the proportion of ever married women having 5 or more children was higher in the Rural areas of all the NE States in all the three Census years of 1991, 2001 and 2011. However, this was showing a declining trend over the years, both in Rural as well as in Urban. According to 1991 Census, the proportion of ever married women having 5 or more children in the Rural areas was ranging from the highest of 29.84 per cent of Nagaland to the lowest of 17.07 per cent of Arunachal Pradesh. As per 2001 Census, it was ranging from the highest of 34.29 per cent of Nagaland to the lowest of 17.50 per cent of Tripura. And according to 2011 Census, it was again the highest of 28.51 per cent of Nagaland to the lowest of 12.46 per cent of Tripura.

In Urban areas, the proportion of ever married women having 5 or more children, as per 1991 Census, was the highest of 24.25 per cent of Manipur to the lowest of 13.82 per cent of Arunachal Pradesh. As per 2001 Census, it was the highest of 20.87 per cent of Manipur to the lowest of 10.28 per cent of Tripura. And as per 2011 Census, it was the highest of 18.09 per cent of Nagaland to the lowest of 7.32 per cent of Sikkim.

From the overall position of the North Eastern Region, it can be seen that, the proportion of ever married women, on two occasions, i.e. having 2 children and having 5 or more children, was comparatively higher. According to 1991 Census, the percentage of ever married women having 2 children was 15.78 and having 5 or more children was 25.15. Thereafter, the situation started changing. As per 2001 Census, the percentage of ever married women having 2 children increased to 17.98, but having 5 or more children decreased to 20.67. In subsequent years, the same trend continued. And according to 2011 Census, it can be seen that, the percentage of ever married women having 2 children, further increased to 21.47, but having 5 or more children further decreased to 15.63.

Further, it is seen that, the proportion of ever married women was more in Urban than Rural, and it was showing an increasing trend, both in Urban as well as in Rural over the years. However, in case of children, it can be seen that, the proportion of women having 5 or more children was more in the Rural areas, but in case of women having 2 children, it was more in the Urban areas. It can also be seen that, the proportion of ever married women having 5 or more children was showing a declining trend, both in Urban as well as in Rural, over the years. In Rural areas, the percentage of ever married women having 5 or more children, was the highest of 25.95 in 1991 and it came down to 17.01 per cent in 2011. And in Urban areas, it came down from 20.18 per cent to 9.89 per cent during this period. In case of ever married women having 2 children, the percentage increased from 18.51 to 25.69 in Urban areas, and in Rural areas, the increase was from 15.35 per cent to 20.46 per cent during the Census period of 1991 to 2011.

Moreover, it is seen that, the decline in the proportion of ever married women having 5 or more children, showed a noticeable increasing trend in the proportion of ever married women having 2 children, in the subsequent years. In other words, it can be said that, for the decrease in the proportion of ever married women having 5 or more children, the increase was the most in the proportion of ever married women having 2 children, in the subsequent years in the North Eastern Region. From these two situations, it can be concluded that, in present days, the idea of having more number of children is changing, rather, most of the people are preferring 2-child family norm.

The position of the country as a whole was not much different from the position of the North Eastern Region. Similar to NER, the proportion of women having 5 or more children was though higher in Rural, but it was slightly lower than the NE Region, both in Rural as well as in Urban, in all the Census years of 1991, 2001 and 2011. In case of Rural, the proportion of ever married women having 5 or more children, which was 19.47 per cent in 1991, came down to 14.23 per cent in 2011. And in case of Urban, it came down from 17.56 per cent to 8.56 per cent during this period.

However, in case of ever married women having 2 children, the proportion was more than the proportion of the NE Region, both in Rural as well as in Urban and in all these Census years. But, similar to the NER, the proportion was higher in Urban and it was also increasing both in Urban and Rural, over the years. In case of Urban, the proportion of ever married women having 2 children increased from 19.92 per cent to 28.92 per cent. And in Rural, it increased from 16.79 per cent to 23.67 per cent, during the period from 1991 to 2011.

From above, it can be seen that, in the country as a whole, the number of ever married women having 5 or more children was proportionately less, both in Rural as well as in Urban. But, the number of ever married women having 2 children was proportionately more, both in Rural as well as in Urban, in all these Census years of 1991, 2001 and 2011. That means, compared to the position of the North Eastern Region, proportionately, less number of ever married women were having 5 or more children but, more number of ever married women were having 2 children. However, from the position of the country as a whole, it is also very much clear that, in the present days, people are changing the idea of having more number of children rather, most of them are going for 2-child family norm. Further details can be seen from the Appendix-8.1, Appendix-8.2 and Appendix-8.3.

Appendix-8.1

Number of Women and ever married Women (all ages) and Number of Surviving Children and total Surviving Children by sex according to different Census Years

Sl. No.	State / NER / India	Total/ Rural/ Urban	Census year, 1991											
			Total Women	Total ever married Women	No. of Surviving Children / No. of ever married Women					Total Surviving Children				
					0	1	2	3	4	5+	Not Stated	Total	Male	Female
1	2	3	4	5	6	7	8	9	10	11	12	13	14	15
1	Arunachal Pradesh	T	399554	191228 (47.86)	53678 (28.07)	28796 (15.06)	30093 (15.74)	26421 (13.82)	20248 (10.59)	31958 (16.70)	34 (0.02)	444096	231305 (52.08)	212791 (47.92)
		R	352964	169980 (48.16)	50084 (29.46)	24951 (14.68)	25509 (15.01)	22557 (13.27)	17826 (10.49)	29023 (17.07)	30 (0.02)	392266	204339 (52.09)	187927 (47.91)
		U	46590	21248 (45.61)	3594 (16.91)	3845 (18.10)	4584 (21.57)	3864 (18.19)	2422 (11.40)	2935 (13.82)	4 (0.01)	51830	26966 (52.03)	24864 (47.97)
2	Assam	T	10756333	4991513 (46.41)	700877 (14.04)	723171 (14.49)	805159 (16.13)	804713 (16.12)	679762 (13.62)	1277361 (25.59)	470 (0.01)	15500756	8178484 (52.76)	7322272 (47.24)
		R	9622366	4438498 (46.13)	623405 (14.05)	632734 (14.26)	695228 (15.66)	708333 (15.96)	608548 (13.71)	1169790 (26.35)	460 (0.01)	13949376	7364606 (52.80)	6584770 (47.20)
		U	1133967	553015 (48.77)	77472 (14.01)	90437 (16.35)	109931 (19.88)	96380 (17.43)	71214 (12.88)	107571 (19.45)	10 (0.00)	1551380	813878 (52.46)	737502 (47.54)
3	Manipur	T	898790	390116 (43.40)	92869 (23.81)	42000 (10.77)	45220 (11.59)	48590 (12.46)	47519 (12.18)	104991 (26.91)	8927 (2.28)	1135243	592517 (52.19)	542726 (47.81)
		R	649109	279226 (43.02)	63741 (22.83)	29665 (10.62)	32360 (11.59)	34605 (12.39)	34053 (12.20)	78107 (27.97)	6695 (2.40)	832268	436415 (52.44)	395853 (47.56)
		U	249681	110890 (44.41)	29128 (26.27)	12335 (11.12)	12860 (11.60)	13985 (12.61)	13466 (12.14)	26884 (24.25)	2232 (2.01)	302975	156102 (51.52)	146873 (48.48)

1	2	3	4	5	6	7	8	9	10	11	12	13	14	15
4	Meghalaya	T	867091	376768 (43.45)	59859 (15.89)	52303 (13.88)	56423 (14.98)	52352 (13.90)	44636 (11.85)	94066 (24.96)	17129 (4.54)	1103533	560156 (50.76)	543377 (49.24)
		R	709866	310666 (43.76)	52167 (16.79)	42514 (13.68)	45033 (14.50)	42182 (13.58)	36325 (11.69)	79316 (25.53)	13129 (4.23)	913104	463242 (50.73)	449862 (49.27)
		U	157225	66102 (42.04)	7692 (11.64)	9789 (14.81)	11390 (17.23)	10170 (15.39)	8311 (12.57)	14750 (22.31)	4000 (6.05)	190429	96914 (50.89)	93515 (49.11)
5	Mizoram	T	330778	141098 (42.66)	31794 (22.53)	15959 (11.31)	17666 (12.52)	18977 (13.45)	19096 (13.53)	36463 (25.85)	1143 (0.81)	416541	211623 (50.80)	204918 (49.20)
		R	177396	76026 (42.86)	19131 (25.16)	7872 (10.36)	8857 (11.65)	8708 (11.46)	9499 (12.49)	21160 (27.83)	799 (1.05)	225643	115472 (51.17)	110171 (48.83)
		U	153382	65072 (42.42)	12663 (19.46)	8087 (12.43)	8809 (13.54)	10269 (15.78)	9597 (14.75)	15303 (23.52)	344 (0.52)	190898	96151 (50.37)	94747 (49.63)
6	Nagaland	T	568264	219892 (38.70)	52503 (23.88)	22352 (10.16)	26794 (12.19)	26802 (12.19)	25714 (11.69)	62392 (28.37)	3335 (1.52)	661658	347039 (52.45)	314619 (47.55)
		R	479088	184965 (38.61)	45103 (24.38)	17710 (9.57)	21096 (11.41)	21511 (11.63)	21232 (11.48)	55187 (29.84)	3126 (1.69)	566852	297732 (52.52)	269120 (47.48)
		U	89176	34927 (39.17)	7400 (21.19)	4642 (13.29)	5698 (16.31)	5291 (15.15)	4482 (12.83)	7205 (20.63)	209 (0.60)	94806	49307 (52.01)	45499 (47.99)
7	Tripura	T	1339275	670434 (50.06)	74967 (11.18)	108453 (16.18)	120298 (17.94)	113366 (16.91)	91906 (13.71)	150465 (22.44)	10979 (1.64)	1978856	1044349 (52.78)	934507 (47.22)
		R	1132955	561513 (49.56)	63011 (11.22)	87622 (15.60)	96057 (17.11)	95293 (16.97)	79437 (14.15)	130957 (23.32)	9136 (1.63)	1684386	889624 (52.82)	794762 (47.18)
		U	206320	108921 (52.79)	11956 (10.98)	20831 (19.12)	24241 (22.26)	18073 (16.59)	12469 (11.45)	19508 (17.91)	1843 (1.69)	294470	154725 (52.54)	139745 (47.46)

1	2	3	4	5	6	7	8	9	10	11	12	13	14	15
8	Sub-Total, NER	T	15160085	6981049 (46.05)	1066547 (15.28)	993034 (14.22)	1101653 (15.78)	1091221 (15.63)	928881 (13.31)	1757696 (25.18)	42017 (0.60)	21240683	11165473 (52.57)	10075210 (47.43)
		R	13123744	6020874 (45.88)	916642 (15.22)	843068 (14.00)	924140 (15.36)	933189 (15.50)	806920 (13.40)	1563540 (25.97)	33375 (0.55)	18563895	9771430 (52.64)	8792465 (47.36)
		U	2036341	960175 (47.15)	149905 (15.61)	149966 (15.62)	177513 (18.49)	158032 (16.46)	121961 (12.70)	194156 (20.22)	8642 (0.90)	2676788	1394043 (52.08)	1282745 (47.92)
9	Sikkim	T	190030	82348 (43.33)	17149 (20.83)	10773 (13.08)	12810 (15.56)	11708 (14.22)	9490 (11.52)	18808 (22.84)	1610 (1.95)	230026	119279 (51.85)	110747 (48.15)
		R	174174	75189 (43.17)	15511 (20.63)	9742 (12.96)	11309 (15.04)	10588 (14.08)	8744 (11.63)	17759 (23.62)	1536 (2.04)	213162	110555 (51.86)	102607 (48.14)
		U	15856	7159 (45.15)	1638 (22.88)	1031 (14.40)	1501 (20.97)	1120 (15.65)	746 (10.42)	1049 (14.65)	74 (1.03)	16864	8724 (51.73)	8140 (48.27)
10	Total, NER	T	15350115	7063397 (46.02)	1083696 (15.34)	1003807 (14.22)	1114463 (15.78)	1102929 (15.61)	938371 (13.28)	1776504 (25.15)	43627 (0.62)	21470709	11284752 (52.56)	10185957 (47.44)
		R	13297918	6096063 (45.84)	932153 (15.28)	852810 (13.99)	935449 (15.35)	943777 (15.48)	815664 (13.38)	1581299 (25.95)	34911 (0.57)	18777057	9881985 (52.63)	8895072 (47.37)
		U	2052197	967334 (47.14)	151543 (15.67)	150997 (15.61)	179014 (18.51)	159152 (16.45)	122707 (12.68)	195205 (20.18)	8716 (0.90)	2693652	1402767 (52.08)	1290885 (47.92)
11	India	T	403359778	220234192 (54.60)	38156174 (17.33)	30938655 (14.05)	38662069 (17.55)	37978333 (17.25)	29013820 (13.17)	41846188 (19.00)	3638953 (1.65)	591997524	315780363 (53.34)	276217161 (46.66)
		R	301525119	166540366 (55.23)	30064243 (18.05)	23054250 (13.84)	27964946 (16.79)	28374968 (17.04)	22209900 (13.34)	32420362 (19.47)	2451697 (1.47)	448999268	239731676 (53.39)	209267592 (46.61)
		U	101834659	53693826 (52.73)	8091931 (15.07)	7884405 (14.68)	10697123 (19.92)	9603365 (17.89)	6803920 (12.67)	9425826 (17.56)	1187256 (2.21)	142998256	76048687 (53.18)	66949569 (46.82)

Source: website of the Registrar General of India, New Delhi.

Note: Figure within bracket indicates percentage.

Appendix-8.2

Number of Women and ever married Women (all ages) and Number of Surviving Children and total Surviving Children by sex according to different Census Years

Sl. No.	State / NER / India	Total/ Rural/ Urban	Census year, 2001										
			Total Women	Total ever married Women	No. of Surviving Children / No. of ever married Women						Total Surviving Children		
					0	1	2	3	4	5+	Total	Male	Female
1	2	3	4	5	6	7	8	9	10	11	12	13	14
1	Arunachal Pradesh	T	518027	237656 (45.88)	39130 (16.46)	37308 (15.70)	43020 (18 10)	39664 (16.69)	31737 (13.36)	46797 (19.69)	654090	336313 (51.42)	317777 (48.58)
		R	415407	191742 (46.16)	30759 (16.04)	29254 (15.26)	32533 (16 97)	31318 (16.33)	26387 (13.76)	41491 (21.64)	547056	282177 (51.58)	264879 (48.42)
		U	102620	45914 (44.74)	8371 (18.23)	8054 (17.54)	10487 (22 84)	8346 (18.18)	5350 (11.65)	5306 (11.56)	107034	54136 (50.58)	52898 (49.42)
2	Assam	T	12878491	6314946 (49.03)	1018734 (16.13)	980361 (15.52)	1156310 (18 31)	1068856 (16.93)	8245[illegible]7 (13.06)	1266168 (20.05)	17591595	9289405 (52.81)	8302190 (47.19)
		R	11276343	5466867 (48.48)	861934 (15.77)	818193 (14.97)	952904 (17.43)	927127 (16.96)	738257 (13.50)	1168452 (21.37)	15661777	8265929 (52.78)	7395848 (47.22)
		U	1602148	848079 (52.93)	156800 (18.49)	162168 (19.12)	203406 (23.98)	141729 (16.72)	86260 (10.17)	97716 (11.52)	1929818	1023476 (53.03)	906342 (46.97)
3	Manipur	T	1071154	483916 (45.18)	96844 (20.01)	63673 (13.16)	73956 (15.28)	74262 (15.34)	65306 (13.50)	109875 (22.71)	1372364	709709 (51.71)	662655 (48.29)
		R	781867	347781 (44.48)	72832 (20.94)	43765 (12.59)	50784 (14.60)	52041 (14.96)	46895 (13.43)	81464 (23.43)	991285	514690 (51.92)	476595 (48.08)
		U	289287	136135 (47.06)	24012 (17.64)	19908 (14.62)	23172 (17.02)	22221 (16.32)	18411 (13.53)	28411 (20.87)	381079	195019 (51.18)	186060 (48.82)

1	2	3	4	5	6	7	8	9	10	11	12	13	14
4	Meghalaya	T	1142735	487579 (42.67)	100457 (20.60)	68691 (14.09)	71078 (14.58)	66223 (13.58)	57333 (11.76)	123797 (25.39)	1433078	720828 (50.30)	712250 (49.70)
		R	917712	391636 (42.68)	82346 (21.03)	53803 (13.74)	53872 (13.76)	51477 (13.14)	45953 (11.73)	104185 (26.60)	1170308	588406 (50.28)	581902 (49.72)
		U	225023	95943 (42.64)	18111 (18.88)	14888 (15.52)	17206 (17.93)	14746 (15.37)	11380 (11.86)	19612 (20.44)	262770	132422 (50.39)	130348 (49.61)
5	Mizoram	T	429464	191895 (44.68)	22377 (11.66)	26595 (13.86)	30317 (15.80)	35527 (18.51)	30688 (15.99)	46391 (24.18)	604470	305392 (50.52)	299078 (49.48)
		R	214841	96147 (44.75)	10962 (11.40)	12645 (13.15)	13850 (14.40)	15764 (16.40)	14975 (15.58)	27951 (29.07)	322640	164561 (51.00)	158079 (49.00)
		U	214623	95748 (44.61)	11415 (11.92)	13950 (14.57)	16467 (17.20)	19763 (20.64)	15713 (16.41)	18440 (19.26)	281830	140831 (49.97)	140999 (50.03)
6	Nagaland	T	942895	359971 (38.18)	76303 (21.20)	34507 (9.59)	42282 (11.75)	46501 (12.92)	46325 (12.86)	114053 (31.68)	1180616	615447 (52.13)	565169 (47.87)
		R	787533	296589 (37.66)	61202 (20.64)	26417 (8.91)	32313 (10.89)	36715 (12.38)	38229 (12.89)	101713 (34.29)	1014438	529684 (52.21)	484754 (47.79)
		U	155362	63382 (40.80)	15101 (23.83)	8090 (12.76)	9969 (15.73)	9786 (15.44)	8096 (12.77)	12340 (19.47)	166178	85763 (51.61)	80415 (48.39)
7	Tripura	T	1556978	829049 (53.25)	111667 (13.47)	152434 (18.39)	181118 (21.85)	146013 (17.61)	103955 (12.54)	133862 (16.15)	2172141	1130244 (52.03)	1041897 (47.97)
		R	1289815	673663 (52.23)	89647 (13.31)	113424 (16.84)	139386 (20.69)	122798 (18.23)	90524 (13.43)	117884 (17.50)	1829381	952169 (52.05)	877212 (47.95)
		U	267163	155386 (58.16)	22020 (14.17)	39010 (25.11)	41732 (26.86)	23215 (14.94)	13431 (8.64)	15978 (10.28)	342760	178075 (51.95)	164685 (48.05)
8	Sub-Total, NER	T	18539744	8905012 (48.03)	1465512 (16.46)	1363569 (15.31)	1598081 (17.95)	1477046 (16.59)	1159861 (13.02)	1840943 (20.67)	25008354	13107338 (52.41)	11901016 (47.59)
		R	15683518	7464425 (47.59)	1209682 (16.21)	1097501 (14.70)	1275642 (17.09)	1237240 (16.58)	1001220 (13.41)	1643140 (22.01)	21536885	11297616 (52.46)	10239269 (47.54)
		U	2856226	1440587 (50.44)	255830 (17.76)	266068 (18.47)	322439 (22.38)	239806 (16.65)	158641 (11.01)	197803 (13.73)	3471469	1809722 (52.13)	1661747 (47.87)

1	2	3	4	5	6	7	8	9	10	11	12	13	14
9	Sikkim	T	252367	115267 (45.67)	17461 (15.15)	18745 (16.26)	23557 (20.44)	18399 (15.96)	13591 (11.79)	23514 (20.40)	324932	165506 (50.94)	159426 (49.06)
		R	225207	102193 (45.38)	15219 (14.89)	16079 (15.73)	20158 (19.73)	16283 (15.93)	12367 (12.10)	22087 (21.62)	295372	150430 (50.93)	144942 (49.07)
		U	27160	13074 (48.14)	2242 (17.15)	2666 (20.39)	3339 (26.00)	2116 (16.18)	1224 (9.36)	1427 (10.91)	29560	15076 (51.00)	14484 (49.00)
10	Total, NER	T	18792111	9020279 (48.00)	1482973 (16.44)	1382314 (15.32)	1621638 (17.98)	1495445 (16.58)	1173452 (13.0[illegible])	1864457 (20.67)	25333286	13272844 (52.39)	12060442 (47.61)
		R	15908725	7566618 (47.56)	1224901 (16.19)	1113580 (14.72)	1295800 (17.13)	1253523 (16.57)	1013537 (13.40)	1665227 (22.01)	21832257	11448046 (52.44)	10384211 (47.56)
		U	2883386	1453661 (50.42)	258072 (17.75)	268734 (18.49)	325838 (22.41)	241922 (16.64)	159865 (11.00)	199230 (13.71)	3501029	1824798 (52.12)	1676231 (47.88)
11	India	T	496453556	273405276 (55.07)	43398254 (15.87)	39674889 (14.51)	57308198 (20.96)	51450650 (18.82)	36023842 (13.18)	45549443 (16.66)	728243671	385154199 (52.89)	343089472 (47.11)
		R	360887965	198588097 (55.03)	31164587 (15.69)	27383089 (13.79)	39038142 (19.66)	37679586 (18.97)	27506838 (13.85)	35815855 (18.04)	544811891	287785399 (52.82)	257026492 (47.18)
		U	135565591	74817179 (55.19)	12233667 (16.35)	12291800 (16.43)	18270056 (24.42)	13771064 (18.41)	8517034 (11.38)	9733588 (13.01)	183431780	97368800 (53.08)	86062980 (46.92)

Source: website of the Registrar General of India, New Delhi.

Note: Figure within bracket indicates percentage.

Appendix-8.3

Number of Women and ever married Women (all ages) and Number of Surviving Children and total Surviving Children by sex according to different Census Years

Sl. No.	State / NER / India	Total/ Rural/ Urban	Census year, 2011										
			Total Women	Total ever married Women	No. of Surviving Children / No. of ever married Women						Total Surviving Children		
					0	1	2	3	4	5+	Total	Male	Female
1	2	3	4	5	6	7	8	9	10	11	12	13	14
1	Arunachal Pradesh	T	669815	314710 (46.98)	60862 (19.34)	48497 (15.41)	58883 (18.71)	52035 (16.53)	40793 (12.96)	53640 (17.05)	804470	419910 (52.20)	384560 (47.80)
		R	520347	244753 (47.04)	46400 (18.96)	35636 (14.56)	42751 (17.47)	40102 (16.38)	33071 (13.51)	46793 (19.12)	653048	342099 (52.38)	310949 (47.62)
		U	149468	69957 (46.80)	14462 (20.67)	12861 (18.38)	16132 (23.06)	11933 (17.06)	7722 (11.04)	6847 (9.79)	151422	77811 (51.39)	73611 (48.61)
2	Assam	T	15266133	8218073 (53.83)	1366761 (16.63)	1561421 (19.00)	1803915 (21.95)	1348323 (16.41)	916625 (11.15)	1221028 (14.86)	20271838	10719830 (52.88)	9552008 (47.12)
		R	13128045	6965034 (53.05)	1144275 (16.43)	1260640 (18.10)	1461063 (20.98)	1162196 (16.69)	815834 (11.70)	1121026 (16.10)	17732374	9372021 (52.85)	8360353 (47.15)
		U	2138088	1253039 (58.61)	222486 (17.76)	300781 (24.00)	342852 (27.36)	186127 (14.85)	100791 (8.05)	100002 (7.98)	2539464	1347809 (53.07)	1191655 (46.93)
3	Manipur	T	1417208	687039 (48.48)	128400 (18.69)	113649 (16.54)	127651 (18.58)	110972 (16.15)	84850 (12.35)	121517 (17.69)	1771541	921978 (52.04)	849563 (47.96)
		R	994756	466992 (46.95)	90251 (19.33)	71203 (15.25)	80109 (17.15)	74405 (15.94)	60031 (12.85)	90993 (19.48)	1241817	648719 (52.24)	593098 (47.76)
		U	422452	220047 (52.09)	38149 (17.34)	42446 (19.29)	47542 (21.61)	36567 (16.62)	24819 (11.28)	30524 (13.86)	529724	273259 (51.59)	256465 (48.41)

1	2	3	4	5	6	7	8	9	10	11	12	13	14
4	Meghalaya	T	1475057	657702 (44.59)	125828 (19.13)	108423 (16.49)	104592 (15.90)	89962 (13.68)	74519 (11.33)	154378 (23.47)	1869767	955304 (51.09)	914463 (48.91)
		R	1177179	520600 (44.22)	103981 (19.97)	82519 (15.85)	76164 (14.63)	68067 (13.07)	59089 (11.36)	130780 (25.12)	1512987	773860 (51.15)	739127 (48.85)
		U	297878	137102 (46.03)	21847 (15.93)	25904 (18.89)	28428 (20.74)	21895 (15.97)	15430 (11.25)	23598 (17.22)	356780	181444 (50.86)	175336 (49.14)
5	Mizoram	T	541867	260555 (48.08)	34644 (13.30)	40928 (15.71)	47264 (18.14)	51846 (19.90)	39919 (15.32)	45954 (17.63)	726734	369737 (50.88)	356997 (49.12)
		R	256300	122657 (47.86)	15477 (12.62)	17932 (14.62)	20354 (16.59)	21876 (17.84)	19335 (15.76)	27683 (22.57)	370275	189594 (51.20)	180681 (48.80)
		U	285567	137898 (48.29)	19167 (13.90)	22996 (16.68)	26910 (19.51)	29970 (21.73)	20584 (14.93)	18271 (13.25)	356459	180143 (50.54)	176316 (49.46)
6	Nagaland	T	953853	400850 (42.02)	63552 (15.85)	53024 (13.24)	63713 (15.89)	61586 (15.36)	56728 (14.15)	102247 (25.51)	1209223	624133 (51.61)	585090 (48.39)
		R	682064	285222 (41.82)	44665 (15.66)	34614 (12.14)	41177 (14.44)	41962 (14.71)	41477 (14.54)	81327 (28.51)	900413	466653 (51.83)	433760 (48.17)
		U	271789	115628 (42.54)	18887 (16.33)	18410 (15.92)	22536 (19.49)	19624 (16.98)	15251 (13.19)	20920 (18.09)	308810	157480 (51.00)	151330 (49.00)
7	Tripura	T	1799541	1078931 (59.96)	138345 (12.82)	258983 (24.00)	285677 (26.48)	171759 (15.92)	105412 (9.77)	118755 (11.01)	2467596	1290323 (52.29)	1177273 (47.71)
		R	1325291	771564 (58.22)	99371 (12.88)	166014 (21.52)	195052 (25.28)	131246 (17.01)	83693 (10.85)	96188 (12.46)	1852056	968593 (52.30)	883463 (47.70)
		U	474250	307367 (64.81)	38974 (12.68)	92969 (30.25)	90625 (29.48)	40513 (13.18)	21713 (7.07)	22567 (7.34)	615540	321730 (52.27)	293810 (47.73)

1	2	3	4	5	6	7	8	9	10	11	12	13	14
8	Sub-Total, NER	T	22123474	11617860 (52.51)	1918392 (16.51)	2184925 (18.81)	2491695 (21.45)	1886483 (16.24)	1318846 (11.35)	1817519 (15.64)	29121169	15301215 (52.54)	13819954 (47.46)
		R	18083982	9376822 (51.85)	1544420 (16.47)	1668558 (17.79)	1916670 (20.44)	1539854 (16.42)	1112530 (11.86)	1594790 (17.02)	24262970	12761539 (52.60)	11501431 (47.40)
		U	4039492	2241038 (55.48)	373972 (16.69)	516367 (23.04)	575025 (25.66)	346629 (15.46)	206316 (9.21)	222729 (9.94)	4858199	2539676 (52.28)	2318523 (47.72)
9	Sikkim	T	287507	149542 (52.01)	24691 (16.51)	31440 (21.02)	35183 (23.53)	22142 (14.81)	14294 (9.56)	21792 (14.57)	361544	186299 (51.53)	175245 (48.47)
		R	214202	110631 (51.65)	17673 (15.97)	21296 (19.25)	24488 (22.14)	16770 (15.16)	11459 (10.36)	18945 (17.12)	285530	146904 (51.45)	138626 (48.55)
		U	73305	38911 (53.08)	7018 (18.04)	10144 (26.07)	10695 (27.48)	5372 (13.81)	2835 (7.28)	2847 (7.32)	76014	39395 (51.83)	36619 (48.17)
10	Total, NER	T	22410981	11767402 (52.51)	1943083 (16.51)	2216365 (18.83)	2526878 (21.47)	1908625 (16.23)	1333140 (11.33)	1839311 (15.63)	29482713	15487514 (52.53)	13995199 (47.47)
		R	18298184	9487453 (51.85)	1562093 (16.46)	1689854 (17.81)	1941158 (20.46)	1556624 (16.41)	1123989 (11.85)	1613735 (17.01)	24548500	12908443 (52.58)	11640057 (47.42)
		U	4112797	2279949 (55.44)	380990 (16.71)	526511 (23.09)	585720 (25.69)	352001 (15.44)	209151 (9.18)	225576 (9.89)	4934213	2579071 (52.27)	2355142 (47.73)
11	India	T	587584719	339621277 (57.80)	54482587 (16.04)	55823796 (16.44)	86065258 (25.34)	62275797 (18.34)	38761066 (11.41)	42212773 (12.43)	819694674	435169066 (53.09)	384525608 (46.91)
		R	405967794	231577616 (57.04)	35558931 (15.36)	34866346 (15.06)	54815046 (23.67)	44238355 (19.10)	29135441 (12.58)	32963497 (14.23)	588620646	312012570 (53.01)	276608076 (46.99)
		U	181616925	108043661 (59.49)	18923656 (17.52)	20957450 (19.40)	31250212 (28.92)	18037442 (16.69)	9625625 (8.91)	9249276 (8.56)	231074028	123156496 (53.30)	107917532 (46.70)

Source: website of the Registrar General of India, New Delhi.

Note: Figure within bracket indicates percentage.

9
Migration

Migration is one of the main factors of population change. It affects the size of population mainly in 2 (two) ways, i.e. In-Migration and Out-Migration. But, there is no particular time, place or reason for Migration. It may be due to natural calamities, wars, fire, drought, political extremism, education, employment, marriage, business and other economic activities etc. Therefore, it is really very difficult to get such information at different points of time. However, during population Census, information on Migration is being collected following certain guidelines and norms and basing on the past experience, the nature and scope of collection of information are being extended, improved or modified for the future.

The North East India, particularly the States of Assam, Tripura and Meghalaya suffered from the problem of Migration at different points of times and with different reasons. The history of Migration in India actually dates back to 1905, while Lord Curzon was the Governor-General and Viceroy of India. It is a known fact that, Lord Curzon was not very much fond of Indians, particularly—Bengali Hindus. Rather, he was fond of Muslims and wanted to provide a separate Province for them, where they would be in majority and need not have to oblige Hindus. Accordingly, he chalked out a plan with the help of his lieutenant Sir Bamfylde Fuller to divide the then Bengal Presidency into 2 (two) parts. Accordingly, the western part, comprising the Presidency and Burdwan divisions together with Bihar, Chhota Nagpur and Orissa formed the part of Bengal and the eastern part of the Presidency together with Assam formed the part of the Province of Eastern Bengal and Assam. Finally, the partition of Bengal came into being in 1905, in spite of vehement opposition and protest from many quarters and from many political leaders, and Sir Bamfylde Fuller became the Governor of the new Province of Eastern Bengal and

Assam, with its capital in Dacca.[1] That was the foundation stone of innumerable and inhumane problems like riots, arson, looting, rapes and murders, blood baths and the like, that had been witnessed, by the people of this region.

In first 15 (fifteen) years of partition, the Presidency witnessed some reforms, changes and revolutions. According to Shri Tathagata Roy, "The period between 1905 and 1920 was a period of disquiet for the whole of subcontinent. There were the Morley-Minto administrative reforms in 1910, the repeal of the partition of Bengal in 1911, and moving the capital of British India from Calcutta to Delhi with the inauguration of New Delhi in the same year with a royal visit. Meanwhile armed rebellion as an expression of nationalism gained ground in Bengal."[2]

The country then witnessed the Khilafat Movement, due to which thousands of Hindus had to loss their lives at different points of times. Shri Roy mentioned that, there was widespread forcible conversion of Hindus and desecration as well as destruction of Hindu temples. Some three years later, in September 1924 and again in 1926 and 1929, terrible anti-Hindu riots broke out in different parts of India and several hundreds of Hindus died.[3] After that came the Government of India Act 1935, which received royal assent on 4th August, 1935. Shri Roy indicated that, this Act "enlarged the scope of popular representation subject to the paramountcy of the British. It put an end to the Dyarchy of the Montagu-Chelmsford Reforms and introduced the federal principle with the corollary of provincial autonomy and the principle of popular responsible government in the provinces."[4] This Act finally paved the way for division of some of the provinces and also the formation of some new provinces. And at the same time, Round Table Conferences were held and Provincial elections took place, wherein political parties could show their strengths and weaknesses in different places.[5]

Shri Tathagata Roy mentioned that, the Communal Award of 1932, the Government of India Act, 1935 and the taking office of Fazlul Haq's coalition ministry in 1937, all are momentous events.[6] In this connection, Shri Roy mentioned about Nirad C. Chaudhuri. Shri Choudhuri said, "Let me begin with the political situation in the strict sense. The starkly obvious feature was that, under the provincial constitution imposed on Bengal by the Government of India Act, 1935, Bengali Hindus were permanently debarred (italics his) from exercising any political power in their province.......except through the charity of the Muslims which was not likely to be bestowed......they were reduced to a permanent statutory minority, disenfranchised as to power, although given the franchise to elect members to the legislature."[7] Shri Roy further mentioned that, "this situation continued till the partition of the province (except for the brief interregnum of Fazlul Haq's ministry, 1941-43) till the province was partitioned and Hindu-majority West Bengal came into being."[8]

In the meanwhile, the Province had to pass through the unbelievable trauma of three macro-horrors within a period of four years. These were the Bengal Famine of 1943, Calcutta Killings of August 1946 and the Noakhali Carnage of October of the same year. And finally, the country got independence on 15th August, 1947 and Bengal got portioned with the new name of East Bengal and West Bengal.[9]

The Indian independence was not a very happy occasion, rather, it was tainted with many pre- and post-independence carnages, rapes, murders, burning of houses, conversions, evictions etc. which gave rise to large scale Migration of Hindus, Buddhists and Christians from East Bengal, the then East Pakistan, time to time.

On 24th October, 1948, the *Ananda Bazar Patrika* reported that, "Hindus were leaving East Pakistan in hordes". According to Dr. B.C. Roy, their number was around 15,00,000. According to Suresh Chandra Banerjee, a Congress leader of West Bengal, the number exceeded 20,00,000.[10]

The violence of 1950 affected the Sylhet District very much. According to A.J. Kamra, "During the months of November and December 1949 and January 1950, an alarming situation was developing in East Bengal. Persistent propaganda by Pakistan radio and press, inflammatory speeches by responsible Muslim leaders, official connivance at mob violence and lawlessness against Hindus—all these resulted in mob violence against the non-Muslims in Bianibazar and Barlekha P.S. of Sylhet district, Putia in Rajshahi, Bhandaria in Barisal, Bagerhat in Khulna, Kalashkatti in Barisal, Nachole in Rajshahi, Habiganj in Sylhet, Comilla in Tipperah, and Feni in Noakhali district."[11] Shri Kamra further mentioned that, "Refugees keep on arriving daily by the thousands in Karimganj (Assam) and relief organisations find it difficult to cope with the situation."[12]

Regarding attitude towards refugee, Shri A.J. Kamra mentioned about the observation of Shri Rohini Kumar Choudhury and stated, "Mr. Choudhury regretted that, in Gauhati it has not been possible to handle the situation satisfactorily. The authorities there, he alleged, were unwilling to give relief to the refugees unless border camp certificates were produced by the latter, whereas on investigation, Shri Choudhury had found that no agency had so far been set up for issuing any such border certificates."[13]

The violence in Feni was also very severe. It is stated that, on 13th February, 1950, "in broad daylight all parts of the town were attacked by Muslims. Hindu houses were set on fire and Hindus stabbed and killed."[14] It was further mentioned that, "persons trying to shift to the neighbouring Tripura State are intimidated, looted on the way and assaulted."[15] And finally about 5,000 persons have been able to flock to Belonia (Tripura) from Feni and neighbouring villages. Further, it was mentioned on 5th and 6th April, 1950 that, 1,10,000 refugees entered Karimganj from East Pakistan's Sylhet district till April 2, and 2,00,000 refugees from East Bengal had arrived in Tripura during the last one month.[16]

Then came the Genocide of 1964, the history of which was famous for the anti-Indian policy of Pakistan. The Pakistan Government chalked out a plan to divert the seething discontent of the Bengali Muslims of East Pakistan against systematic and ruthless exploitation of her by West Pakistan and her people, by turning the political movement of East Pakistan into a communal and anti-Indian movement. Accordingly, the government and the press in Pakistan started campaign of hatred and vilification against the Government of India.[17] And in no time, they achieved their goal.

Shri Kamra mentioned that, "Riots of unprecedented havoc and ferocity started in Dhaka and Narayanganj in the month of January, 1964. Atrocities committed in this riot surpassed all others of the past in this part of Pakistan."[18] According to Mr. Lahiry, "the ravage of the 1964 riot surpassed all the previous records in devastation and the non-Muslims of all categories and denominations began to flee the country to India for safety, security and honour."[19]

The history of Gory 1971—no one can forget. Yahya Khan announced an election in December, 1970. Accordingly election was held, and resulted in a landslide victory for Mujib's Awami League. But there was no way for Pakistan to accept it, and for East Pakistan to compromise on it.[20] Meanwhile, Zulfiqar Ali Bhutto made an effort to negotiate with Sheikh Mujibur Rahaman, but it went in vain. Finally, on 25th and 26th March, 1971, the Pakistan Army cracked down on unarmed citizens.[21] Shri Roy mentioned that, "The murder and mayhem took place throughout the length and breadth of East Pakistan, and it is as a result of this that more than ten million—one crore—East Pakistanis sought refuge in India. This time the refugees had a substantial number of Muslims among them."[22] Finally, Bangladesh got its independence through the bloody holocaust of 1971, followed by military action by the Indian Army, assisted by the Mukti Bahini and Sheik Mujibur Rahaman became the Prime Minister.[23]

In this connection, Shri Kamra mentioned that, according to Dr. Sujit Dhar, millions of Bangladeshi Muslims have crossed over from Bangladesh and settled in Bengal, Assam, Tripura and in many cities and provinces in India.[24] Shri Kamra further mentioned that, "The Bangladeshi Muslims infiltration continues day after day. When partition took place in 1947 one section of the educated and the affluent class of Muslims left for Pakistan, leaving behind the uneducated and unskilled mass of Muslim humanity in India."[25]

The life of Hindus, even after the independence of Bangladesh, was not very peaceful. However, the first five years of independence, was relatively good for Hindus, and it was average till late nineties of the Awami League rule. After that, many changes took place in Bangladesh and during the reign of Ziaur Rahaman, Khaleda Zia and Ershad, the life of Hindus was not good.[26] Intolerance, atrocities on women, desecration and destruction of temples and properties of Hindus etc. was taking place and Hindus had to leave Bangladesh, time to time.[27]

Though, some Writers, Scholars and Political leaders mentioned about the number of Migrants at different points of time, but it was not easy to get the correct position on this. Actually, the Migrants who came to India and registered their name in different Relief Camps, for them, there was a record, but, there was no record for those who did not go to the Camps, rather, they preferred to stay with their relatives. Moreover, it was a continuous process over the years, and was not possible to keep track, particularly on those, for whom, the authority was not having any knowledge.

However, the Population Census is playing a very vital role in collecting the detailed information on Migration, though, proper information is not available even for 1961. The 1971 Census was also conducted in a limited way and without the reason of Migration. During the Census of 1971, the information on Migration was collected taking into consideration of Sex, Place of last Residence and Duration of Residence. The information further classified under different groups i.e. **A**—Last residence elsewhere in India. This has 2 (two) components—**I**. Last residence within the State of enumeration, i.e. State Migrants, which again has 2 (two) components—(i) residence elsewhere in the same District, and (ii) residence in other District of the State. **II**. Last residence in States/Uts in India beyond the State of enumeration. The information was also collected for those whose last residence was **B**—i.e. Countries in Asia beyond India and **C**—i.e. in other countries. From 1981 Census onwards, the reasons for Migration was also taken into consideration and information collected accordingly. From 1991 Census onwards, some modification has been made for indicating outside Migration. According to that, **B**—shows total Migration from outside India, **C**—shows total Migration from Countries in Asian beyond India, and **D**—shows total Migration from other Countries. The detailed position of Migration of each of the North Eastern States according to 1971 Census to 2001 Census, can be seen from the Appendix-9.1 to Appendix-9.5.

These Appendices show the position of In-Migration only and there is no record of Out-Migration in it. The Decennial Census data generally refers the position as on 1st March of that Census Year. Therefore, in case of collection of Migration data in last Censuses, a person was considered as In-Migrant in a particular place, if it was found that, his last residence was elsewhere, at any point of time, during last 10 (ten) years, preceding the date of Census in the present location. That means, each Appendix shows the total number of In-Migrants within a period of 10 (ten) years, under different categories with reasons. The Appendices further show clearly the position of State Migrants, who are mostly the local people, under item **I**, outside Migrants from India, under item **II**, and the Migrants from other Countries at **B**, with further classification of Migrants from Asian Countries beyond India at **C**, and from other Countries at **D**. The Migrants shown under item **II** and under **B** together, generally gives the total number of outside Migrants in a State in a particular Census year. However, some inconsistencies are there in some of the Appendices.

From these Appendices, 2 (two) things are very clear. (i) item **II** shows the number of In-Migrants to a particular State, from other States/Uts of India, and (ii) item **B** or **C** shows the number of In-Migrants to that State, from the Countries in Asia beyond India, with the reasons of Migration. The neighbouring Countries in Asia beyond India are though Nepal, Bhutan, China and Myanmar, but in the context of Migration, it was primarily East Bengal/Bangladesh, as it is evident from the unprecedented happenings, as mentioned above, due to which, people were forced to leave that country and had to take shelter in the neighbouring North Eastern States, time to time. From Appendix-9.1 to Appendix-9.5, it is seen that, Assam, Tripura and Meghalaya were the most affected States from outside Migrants.

The Appendix-9.5 will give an idea about the total number of Migrants in a particular State from outside in different Census years. Further, it will also show the reasons of Migration together with the absolute number and the percentage to total Migrants, under each category. In addition to that, an attempt has been made to show that, out of the total outside Migrants in a particular State, what was the percentage of Indian Migrants, and what was the percentage of Migrants from the Asian Countries beyond India, to that State, separately, indicating the primary reasons of Migration, in different Census years.

From Appendix-9.5, it can be seen that, the total number of outside Migrants to Assam in 1971 was 15,22,461, which was 10.18 per cent of the total population of the State. Out of these Migrants, 35.17 per cent was from other States of India and 64.80 per cent was from the Asian Countries beyond India. After that, the situation slightly changed. In 1991, the number of outside Migrants was 7,10,977, which was 3.17 per cent of the total population of the State. In this case, Migrants from other States of India was 68.60 per cent and the Migrants from Asian Countries was 30.82 per cent. Further it is seen that, out of the total Indian Migrants, 15.18 per cent came to Assam for Employment, 15.90 per cent for Business, 26.06 per cent due to Family moved and 15.79 per cent due to Other reasons. Whereas, out of the total Migrants from Asian Countries, 39.82 per cent came to Assam due to Family moved and 35.50 per cent due to Other reasons.

In 2001, the total number of outside Migrants was 5,38,107, which was 2.02 per cent of the total population of Assam. And out of these Migrants, 75.66 per cent was from other States of India and 24.30 per cent was from Asian Countries. Further it is seen that, out of the Indian Migrants, 16.06 per cent came to Assam for Employment, 14.20 per cent for Business, 24.35 per cent due to Family moved and 20.57 per cent due to Other reasons. Whereas, out of the total Asian Migrants, 42.30 per cent came to Assam due to Family moved and 35.74 per cent due to Other reasons.

In case of Tripura, it is seen that, in 1971, total number of outside Migrants was 5,55,467, which was 35.69 per cent of the total population of the State. And out of the total number of Migrants, only 4.52 per cent was from other States of India and 95.16 per cent was from Asian Countries. In 1981, the total number of outside Migrants was 86,517, which was 4.21 per cent of the total population of the State. Out of the total Migrants, 44.58 per cent was Indian Migrants and 55.42 per cent was from Asian Countries. Further it is seen that, out of the total Indian Migrants, 26.01 per cent came to Tripura for Employment, 39.15 per cent due to Family moved and 18.62 per cent due to Other reasons. Whereas, 22.01 per cent of the Asian Migrants came to Tripura due to Family moved and 70.09 per cent due to Other reasons.

In 1991, the total number of outside Migrants was 3,10,752, which was 11.27 per cent of the total population of the State. Out of the total number of Migrants, 13.30 per cent was from other States of India and 86.32 per cent was from Asian Countries. Further it is seen that, 22.06 per cent of Indian Migrants, came to Tripura for Employment, 32.54 per cent due to Family moved and 16.82 per cent was due to Other reasons. But in case of Asian Migrants, 35.71 per cent was due to Family moved and 50.36 per cent due to Other reasons.

In 2001, the total outside Migrants was 3,25,409, which was 10.17 per cent of the total population of Tripura. And out of the total Migrants, 19.60 per cent was Indian Migrants and 80.39 per cent was from Asian Countries. Further it is seen that, out of total Indian Migrants, 11.98 per cent came to Tripura for Employment, 23.96 per cent due to Family moved and 45.58 per cent due to Other reasons. Whereas, 44.19 per cent of the Asian Migrants came to Tripura due to Family moved and 39.71 per cent due to Other reasons.

In case of Meghalaya, the total number of outside Migrants in 1971 was 1,17,066, which was 11.57 per cent of the total population of the State. Out of the total Migrants, 46.61 per cent was from other States of India and 52.44 per cent was from Asian countries. After that, the situation slightly changed. In 1981, the total number of outside Migrants was 83,473 and that was 6.25 per cent of the total population of the State. Further, 91.62 per cent of the total Migrants, was from other States of India and 8.34 per cent was from Asian Countries. Out of the total Indian Migrants, 23.65 per cent came to Meghalaya for Employment, 34.03 per cent due to Family moved and 21.85 per cent due to Other reasons. But in case of Asian Migrants, 29.10 per cent came to Meghalaya for Employment, 27.44 per cent due to Family moved and 28.92 per cent due to Other reasons.

The total number of outside Migrants to Meghalaya in 1991 was 83,749, which was 4.72 per cent of the total population of the State. Out of the total Migrants, 83.96 per cent was from other States of India and 15.08 per cent was from Asian countries. In case of Indian Migrants, 19.79 per cent came to Meghalaya for Employment, 29.40 per cent due to Family moved and 13.35 per cent due to Other reasons. Whereas, out of the total Asian Migrants, 13.92 per cent came for Employment, 35.72 per cent due to Family moved and 29.23 per cent due to Other reasons.

In 2001, the total number of outside Migrants in Meghalaya was 92,704, which was 4.00 per cent of the total population of the State. And out of the total Migrants, 89.62 per cent was from other States of India and 10.33 per cent was from Asian Countries. Further it is seen that, out of the total Indian Migrants, 22.30 per cent came to Meghalaya for Employment, 19.60 per cent due to Family moved and 27.02 per cent due to Other reasons. But in case of Asian Migrants, 15.25 per cent of them came to Meghalaya for Employment, 21.49 per cent due to Family moved and 47.72 per cent due to Other reasons.

Other States are comparatively less affected from the Migrants of Asian Countries. In 1971, total number of outside Migrants in Arunachal Pradesh was 69,820, which was 14.93 per cent of the total population of the State. Out of these Migrants, 63.50 per cent was from other States of India and 36.50 per cent was from the Asian Countries. In 1981, the total number of outside Migrants was 83,683 and it was 13.24 per cent of the total population. Further, it can be seen that, out of total Migrants, 87.34 per cent was Indian Migrants and 12.65 per cent was from Asian Countries. And out of total Indian Migrants, 34.90 per cent of them came to Arunachal Pradesh for Employment, 37.52 per cent due to Family moved and 20.17 per cent due to Other reasons. Whereas, in case of Migrants from Asian Countries, 34.25 per cent came due to Family moved and 24.40 per cent due to Other reasons.

In 1991, the Migrants were, mostly from other States of India. The total number of Migrants was 98,966, which was 11.45 per cent of the total population of the State. Out of these Migrants, 99.68 per cent was from other States of India and only 0.31 per cent was from Asian Countries. Out of the Indian Migrants, 30.26 per cent came for Employment, 35.59 per cent due to Family moved and 11.74 per cent due to Other reasons.

The total number of Migrants to Arunachal Pradesh in 2001 was 1,53,624 and it was 13.99 per cent of the total population of the State.

Out of total Migrants, 88.56 per cent was Indian Migrants and 11.40 per cent was from Asian Countries beyond India. Amongst the Indian Migrants, 35.32 per cent of them came for Employment, 28.24 per cent due to Family moved and 17.88 per cent due to Other reasons. In case of Asian Migrants, 25.19 per cent came due to Family moved and 40.98 per cent due to Other reasons.

In Manipur, the total number of outside Migrants in 1971 was 37,547, which was 3.50 per cent of the total population of the State. Out of these Migrants, 66.76 per cent was from other States of India and 33.18 per cent was from Asian Countries. In 1981, the total number of outside Migrants was 27,294 and it was 1.92 per cent of the total population of the State. Out of the total Migrants, 95.67 per cent was Indian Migrants and only 4.32 per cent was from Asian Countries. Further, it is seen that, 21.41 per cent of the Indian Migrants came to Manipur for Employment, 46.30 per cent due to Family moved and 16.89 per cent due to Other reasons. Whereas, 54.24 per cent of the Asian Migrants came to Manipur due to Family moved and 28.56 per cent due to Other reasons.

In 1991, total number of outside Migrants to Manipur was 16,719 and it was 0.91 per cent of the total population of the State. Out of these Migrants, 89.92 per cent was from other States of India and 9.40 per cent was from Asian Countries. In case of Indian Migrants, it is seen that, 15.04 per cent came to Manipur for Employment, 39.48 per cent due to Family moved and 14.17 per cent due to Other reasons. But, out of the Asian Migrants, 56.33 per cent came to Manipur due to Family moved and 18.97 per cent due to Other reasons.

The total number of outside Migrants to the State in 2001 was 16,201 and it was only 0.75 per cent of the total population of Manipur. Out of the total Migrants, 91.25 per cent was Indian Migrants and 8.58 per cent was from Asian countries. In case of Indian Migrants, 12.76 per cent came to Manipur for Employment, 24.65 per cent due to Family moved and 36.81 per cent due to Other reasons. And out of the Asian Migrants, 38.85 per cent came to Manipur due to Family moved and 30.65 per cent due to Other reasons.

In Mizoram, the total number of outside Migrants in 1981 was 20,125, which was 4.08 per cent of the total population of the State. Out of these Migrants, 98.39 per cent was from other states of India and only 1.60 per cent was from Asian Countries. Out of total Indian Migrants, 31.13 per cent came to Mizoram for Employment, 45.28 per cent due to Family moved and 19.31 per cent due to Other reasons. And in case of Asian Migrants, 43.17 per cent came to Mizoram for Employment, 20.50 per cent due to Family moved and 30.75 per cent due to Other reasons.

In 1991, the total number of outside Migrants to Mizoram was 11,309 and it was 1.64 per cent of the total population of the state. Out of total Migrants, 87.38 per cent was from other States of India and 12.18 per cent was from Asian Countries. In case of Indian Migrants, 27.19 per cent came to Mizoram for Employment, 40.24 per cent due to Family moved and 17.10 per cent due to Other reasons. Whereas, 58.42 per cent of the Asian Migrants came to Mizoram due to Family moved and 19.16 per cent due to Other reasons.

The total number of outside Migrants to Mizoram in 2001 was 50,780, which was 5.71 per cent of the total population of the State. Out of these Migrants, 69.50 per cent was from other States of India and 30.45 per cent was from Asian countries. In case of Indian Migrants, it is seen that, 36.34 per cent came to Mizoram for Employment, 33.62 per cent due to Family moved and 18.27 per cent due to Other reasons. Whereas, 18.67 per cent of the Asian Migrants came to Mizoram for Employment, 40.04 per cent due to Family moved and 26.38 per cent due to Other reasons.

In Nagaland, the total number of outside Migrants in 1971 was 49,515 and it was 9.59 per cent of the total population of the State. Out of these Migrants, 75.86 per cent was from other States of India and 23.84 per cent was from Asian Countries. In 1981, the number of outside Migrants was 63,522, which was 8.20 per cent of the total population of Nagaland. Out of these Migrants, 97.82 per cent Indian Migrants and only 2.18 per cent was from Asian Countries. It is seen that, 29.88 per cent of the Indian Migrants came to Nagaland for Employment, 32.46 per cent due to Family moved and 28.44 per cent due to Other reasons. Whereas, a high percentage to the tune of 43.38 per cent of the Asian Migrants came to Nagaland for Employment, 25.09 per cent due to Family moved and 24.15 per cent due to Other reasons.

In 1991, total number of outside Migrants to Nagaland was 46,438, which was 3.84 per cent of the total population of the State. Of these Migrants, 94.94 per cent was from other States of India and 5.02 per cent was from Asian Countries. Out of Indian Migrants, 27.38 per cent came to Nagaland for Employment, 27.10 per cent due to Family moved and 12.80 per cent due to Other reasons. But, 40.27 per cent of the Asian Migrants came to Nagaland for Employment, 21.90 per cent due to Family moved and 17.90 per cent due to Other reasons.

The total number of outside Migrants to Nagaland in 2001 was 88,370, which was 4.44 per cent of the total population of the State. Out of these Migrants, 92.31 per cent was Indian Migrants and 6.35 per cent was from Asian Countries. It is seen that, 28.69 per cent of the Indian Migrants came to Nagaland for Employment, 19.57 per cent due to Family moved and 27.31 per cent due to Other reasons. Whereas, 33.55 per cent of the Asian Migrants came to the State for Employment, 19.61 per cent due to Family moved and 30.05 per cent due to Other reasons.

In Sikkim, the total number of outside Migrants in 1971 was 21,056 and it was 10.03 per cent of the total population of the State. Of these Migrants, 53.88 per cent was Indian Migrants and 46.05 per cent was from Asian Countries. In 1981, the total number of outside Migrants was 32,418, which was 10.25 per cent of the total population of the State. Out of the total Migrants, 94.58 per cent was from other States of India and 5.40 per cent was from Asian Countries. In case of Indian Migrants, it is seen that, 33.59 per cent of them came to Sikkim for Employment, 27.52 per cent due to Family moved and 20.83 per cent due to Other reasons. Whereas, 27.36 per cent of the Asian Migrants came to the State for Employment, 29.81 per cent due to Family moved and 32.90 per cent due to Other reasons.

In 1991, the total number of outside Migrants to Sikkim was 29,032 and it was 7.14 per cent of the total population of the State. Out of these Migrants, 80.32 per cent was from other States of India and 19.09 per cent was from Asian countries. In case of Indian Migrants, it is seen that, 27.33 per cent of them came to Sikkim for Employment, 24.28 per cent due to Family moved and 14.21 per cent due to Other reasons. But, 21.25 per cent of the Asian Migrants came to Sikkim for Employment, 27.55 per cent due to Family moved and 26.38 per cent due to Other reasons.

The total number of outside Migrants to Sikkim in 2001 was 64,269 and it was 11.88 per cent of the total population of the State. Out of these Migrants, 71.62 per cent was from other states of India and 28.31 per cent was from the Countries of Asia beyond India. Of the Indian Migrants, 33.10 per cent came to Sikkim for Employment, 17.62 per cent due to Family moved and 18.91 per cent due to Other reasons. And of the Asian Migrants, 34.92 per cent came to Sikkim for Employment, 17.65 per cent due to Family moved and 20.30 per cent due to Other reasons. Further details can be seen from the Appendix-9.1 to Appendix-9.5.

Notes

1. *My People Uprooted,* A Saga of the Hindus of Eastern Bengal, by Tathagata Roy, p. 38.
2. *Ibid.*, p. 39.
3. *Ibid.*, p. 42.
4. *Ibid.*, p. 45.
5. *Ibid.*, pp. 45-46.
6. *Ibid.*, p. 48.
7. *Ibid.*, pp. 48-49.
8. *Ibid.*, p. 49.
9. *Ibid.*, p. 71.
10. *Ibid.*, p. 151.
11. *The Prolonged Partition and its Pogroms, Testimonies on Violence against Hindus in East Bengal 1946–64,* by A.J. Kamra, p. 56.
12. *Ibid.*, p. 61.
13. *Ibid.*, p. 136.
14. *Ibid.*, p. 71.
15. *Ibid.*, p. 71.
16. *Ibid.*, p. 136.
17. *Ibid.*, pp. 185-86.
18. *Ibid.*, p. 188.
19. *Ibid.*, p. 188.
20. *My People Uprooted*, *op. cit.*, p. 207.
21. *Ibid.*, p. 207.
22. *Ibid.*, p. 208.
23. *Ibid.*, p. 238.
24. *The Prolonged Partition and its Pogroms*, *op. cit.*, p. 228.
25. *Ibid.*, pp. 228-29.
26. *My People Uprooted*, *op. cit.*, p. 239.
27. *Ibid.*, pp. 246-47.

Appendix-9.1

Migration by Sex, Place of last Residence and Duration of Residence as per different Census Years

Sl No.	Name of the State	Last Residence		Rural/Urban/ Unclassified	Census Year, 1971								
					Enumerated in Rural or Urban Areas of								
					Total			Rural			Urban		
					Person	Male	Female	Person	Male	Female	Person	Male	Female
1	2	3		4	5	6	7	8	9	10	11	12	13
1	Arunachal Pradesh	A. Last residence elsewhere in India		R	426136	223107	203029	417836	216933	200903	8300	6174	2126
				U	15805	9843	5962	10012	6535	3477	5793	3308	2485
				UC	86	66	20	80	63	17	6	3	3
		I. Within the State of enumeration	i. Elsewhere in the district	R	97617	33813	63804	95245	32464	62781	2372	1349	1023
				U	2174	1297	877	2072	1259	813	102	38	64
				UC	-	-	-	-	-	-	-	-	-
			ii. In other district	R	7641	2047	1890	3704	1908	1796	233	139	94
				U	1408	413	332	663	375	288	82	38	44
				UC	-	-	-	-	-	-	-	-	-
		II. States/Uts in India beyond the State of enumeration		R	34900	25982	8918	29205	21296	7909	5695	4686	1009
				U	9350	6259	3091	7277	4901	2376	2073	1358	715
				UC	86	66	20	80	63	17	6	3	3

1	2	3		4	5	6	7	8	9	10	11	12	13
		B. Countries in Asia beyond India		T	25483	18214	7269	22295	15838	6457	3188	2376	812
		C. Other Countries		T	1	1	-	-	-	-	1	1	-
		Total Population		**T**	**467511**	**251231**	**216280**	**450223**	**239369**	**210854**	**17288**	**11862**	**5426**
2	Assam	**A**. Last residence elsewhere in India		R	130[illegible]0325	6831963	6178362	12696395	6631774	6064621	313930	200189	113741
				U	9[illegible]6950	492009	424941	129920	64410	65510	787030	427599	359431
				UC	43240	27230	16010	21140	12320	8820	22100	14910	7190
		I. Within the State of enumeration	i. Elsewhere in the district	R	2780469	1073476	1706993	2633279	995302	1637977	147190	78174	69016
				U	105622	48118	57504	61060	25510	35550	44562	22608	21954
				UC	11380	5440	5940	7460	2990	4470	3920	2450	1470
			ii. In other district	R	456960	251912	205048	403897	218309	185588	53063	33603	19460
				U	84204	43874	40330	36930	19130	17800	47274	24744	22530
				UC	6770	4105	2665	3730	2500	1230	3040	1605	1435
		II. States/Uts in India beyond the State of enumeration		R	432437	300812	131625	318760	212400	106360	113677	88412	25265
				U	77907	46599	31308	31930	19770	12160	45977	26829	19148
				UC	25090	17685	7405	9950	6830	3120	15140	10855	4285
		B. Countries in Asia beyond India		T	986552	533557	452995	782706	417669	365037	203846	115888	87958
		C. Other Countries		T	475	305	170	400	280	120	75	25	50
		Total Population		**T**	**14957542**	**7885064**	**7072478**	**13630561**	**7126453**	**6504108**	**1326981**	**758611**	**568370**
3	Manipur	**A**. Last residence elsewhere in India		R	920495	464011	456484	905475	456720	448755	15020	7291	7729
				U	138495	69318	69177	14212	6600	7612	124283	62718	61565
				UC	1283	657	626	558	205	353	725	452	273

1	2	3		4	5	6	7	8	9	10	11	12	13
		I. Within the State of enumeration	i. Elsewhere in the district	R	135933	53317	82616	125300	48720	76580	10633	4597	6036
				U	12103	4491	7612	10226	3785	6441	1877	706	1171
				UC	182	81	101	3	-	3	179	81	98
			ii. In other district	R	13198	7395	5803	11608	6480	5128	1590	915	675
				U	1946	1220	726	1590	1002	588	356	218	138
				UC	7	3	4	2	-	2	5	3	2
		II. States/Uts in India beyond the State of enumeration		R	19858	12846	7012	17061	11067	5994	2797	1779	1018
				U	4116	2892	1224	2396	1813	583	1720	1079	641
				UC	1094	573	521	553	205	348	541	368	173
		B. Countries in Asia beyond India		T	12458	7667	4791	10994	6684	4310	1464	983	481
		C. Other Countries		T	21	21	-	21	21	-	-	-	-
		Total Population		**T**	**1072753**	**541675**	**531078**	**931261**	**470231**	**461030**	**141492**	**71444**	**70048**
4	Meghalaya	**A.** Last residence elsewhere in India		R	827850	422034	405816	801366	406711	394655	26484	15323	11161
				U	115637	60502	55135	13985	8414	5571	101652	52088	49564
				UC	5709	3877	1832	2864	1841	1023	2845	2036	809
		I. Within the State of enumeration	i. Elsewhere in the district	R	170994	93544	77450	155865	86496	69369	15129	7048	8081
				U	9110	5226	3884	7593	4279	3314	1517	947	570
				UC	2583	1660	923	2248	1462	786	335	198	137
			ii. In other district	R	2461	1259	1202	2312	1164	1148	149	95	54
				U	1018	860	158	773	723	50	245	137	108
				UC	45	21	24	22	7	15	23	14	9

1	2	3	4	5	6	7	8	9	10	11	12	13
		II. States/Uts in India beyond the State of enumeration	R	31647	19502	12145	20441	11322	9119	11206	8180	3026
			U	19835	11690	8145	5619	3412	2207	14216	8278	5938
			UC	3081	2196	885	594	372	222	2487	1824	663
		B. Countries in Asia beyond India	T	61385	33575	27810	45276	23629	21647	16109	9946	6163
		C. Other Countries	T	1118	979	139	1038	938	100	80	41	39
		Total Population	**T**	**1011699**	**520967**	**490732**	**864529**	**441533**	**422996**	**147170**	**79434**	**67736**
5	Nagaland	**A**. Last residence elsewhere in India	R	478235	251553	226682	452615	231925	220690	25620	19628	5992
			U	25959	15266	10693	5111	3640	1471	20848	11626	9222
			UC	304	228	76	82	73	9	222	155	67
		I. Within the State of enumeration — i. Elsewhere in the district	R	33306	17613	15693	25885	13593	12292	7421	4020	3401
			U	1243	780	463	794	538	256	449	242	207
			UC	116	90	26	46	42	4	70	48	22
		ii. In other district	R	7462	4495	2967	5567	3340	2227	1895	1155	740
			U	823	482	341	459	280	179	364	202	162
			UC	39	28	11	4	3	1	35	25	10
		II States/Uts in India beyond the State of enumeration	R	28069	23640	4429	11765	9187	2578	16304	14453	1851
			U	9346	6689	2657	3858	2822	1036	5488	3867	1621
			UC	149	110	39	32	28	4	117	82	35
		B. Countries in Asia beyond India	T	11805	8896	2909	7102	5393	1709	4703	3503	1200
		C. Other Countries	T	46	141	5	145	140	5	1	1	-
		Total Population	**T**	**516449**	**276084**	**240365**	**465055**	**241171**	**223884**	**51394**	**34913**	**16481**

1	2	3	4	5	6	7	8	9	10	11	12	13
6	Tripura	**A.** Last residence elsewhere in India	R	925277	474210	451067	917140	469956	447184	8137	4254	3883
			U	99947	51575	48372	15543	8134	7409	84404	43441	40963
			UC	885	461	424	280	127	153	605	334	271
		I. Within the State of enumeration — i. Elsewhere in the district	R	142543	59973	82570	137471	57432	80039	5072	2541	2531
			U	8528	4171	4357	7125	3539	3586	1403	632	771
			UC	173	101	72	24	20	4	149	81	68
		ii. In other district	R	20276	9710	10566	19211	9168	10043	1065	542	523
			U	6779	3356	3423	4263	2124	2139	2516	1232	1284
			UC	57	29	28	31	15	16	26	14	12
		II. States/Uts in India beyond the State of enumeration	R	16658	10288	6370	14658	9117	5541	2000	1171	829
			U	7921	4286	3635	4155	2471	1684	3766	1815	1951
			UC	655	331	324	225	92	133	430	239	191
		B. Countries in Asia beyond India	T	528599	274092	254507	459387	238224	221163	69212	35868	33344
		C. Other Countries	T	1634	788	846	1632	786	846	2	2	-
		Total Population	**T**	**1556342**	**801126**	**755216**	**1393982**	**717227**	**676755**	**162360**	**83899**	**78461**
7	Sikkim	**A.** Last residence elsewhere in India	R	182477	96844	85633	180730	95827	84903	1747	1017	730
			U	11206	6386	4820	2040	1498	542	9166	4888	4278
			UC	6450	4341	2109	466	291	175	5984	4050	1934
		I. Within the State of enumeration — i. Elsewhere in the district	R	7220	3305	3915	5909	2575	3334	1311	730	581
			U	648	362	286	285	172	113	363	190	173
			UC	491	274	217	126	64	62	365	210	155

1	2	3	4	5	6	7	8	9	10	11	12	13
		ii. In other district	R	2696	984	1712	2264	701	1563	432	283	149
			U	1120	743	377	336	254	82	784	489	295
			UC	248	149	99	98	47	51	150	102	48
		II. States/Uts in India beyond the State of enumeration	R	4212	2883	1329	4208	2879	1329	4	4	-
			U	1422	1075	347	1419	1072	347	3	3	-
			UC	5711	3918	1793	242	180	62	5469	3738	1731
		B. Countries in Asia beyond India	T	9696	5082	4614	6934	3338	3596	2762	1744	1018
		C. Other Countries	T	15	10	5	5	5	-	10	5	5
		Total Population	**T**	**209843**	**112662**	**97181**	**190175**	**100959**	**89216**	**19668**	**11703**	**7965**

Source: Census of India, 1971, Migration Tables, Registrar General & Census Commissioner, New Delhi.

Note: information of Mizoram not available.

Appendix-9.2

Migration by Sex, Place of last Residence, Duration of Residence and Reason for Migration as per different Census Years

Sl. No.	Name of the State	Last Residence	Rural or Urban status of last Residence	Census Year, 1981											
				All duration of Residence											
				Total Migration		Reason for Migration									
				Male	Female	Employment		Education		Family moved		Marriage		Others	
						Male	Female	Male	Female	Male	Female	Male	Female	Male	Female
1	2	3	4	5	6	7	8	9	10	11	12	13	14	15	16
1	Arunachal Pradesh	A. Last residence elsewhere in India	T	128648	123622	48572	3693	7005	2466	40322	54491	1232	48891	31518	14080
			R	107619	111843	36503	2820	6447	2129	35722	46350	1174	47767	27774	12777
			U	20939	11702	12033	872	558	337	4564	8103	58	1097	3725	1293
		I. Within the State of enumeration: i. Elsewhere in the district	T	69090	88414	18580	1488	5569	1754	26107	32365	1026	43010	17809	9797
			R	64528	85863	15937	1320	5407	1675	24958	30545	1003	42765	17223	9558
			U	4520	2506	2635	167	162	80	1121	1799	23	224	579	236
		ii. In other district	T	12541	9136	6234	457	579	234	3442	5476	71	1935	2215	1033
			R	9620	7525	4452	334	469	191	2744	4231	63	1846	1891	923
			U	2915	1601	1779	124	110	43	698	1243	8	84	321	107
		II. States/Uts in India beyond the State of enumeration	T	47017	26072	23758	1748	857	478	10774	16650	135	3946	11494	3251
			R	33471	18455	16114	1166	570	263	8020	11574	107	3156	8660	2296
			U	13503	7595	7619	581	286	215	2745	5061	27	789	2825	950

1	2	3			4	5	6	7	8	9	10	11	12	13	14	15	16
		B. Countries in Asia beyond India			T	6360	4228	3240	260	56	24	1256	2370	29	759	1768	815
		C. Other Countries			T	6	9	3	-	-	-	-	8	1	-	2	1
		Total Migration			**T**	**135004**	**127859**	**51815**	**3953**	**7061**	**2490**	**41578**	**56869**	**1262**	**49650**	**33289**	**14896**
2	Manipur	**A.** Last residence elsewhere in India			T	78287	117757	12877	3005	2907	1984	43384	36374	1885	63846	17235	12748
					R	66067	102458	9487	2268	2397	1510	38696	32040	1601	55934	13885	10706
					U	11473	14639	3260	701	434	242	4391	4063	276	7673	3113	1960
		I. Within the State of enumeration	i.	Elsewhere in the district	T	47398	93317	5179	1487	1576	1142	27407	22863	1489	57450	11747	10375
					R	42708	83217	4093	1316	1438	1017	25506	21075	1274	50706	10396	9104
					U	4553	9865	1077	168	107	110	1844	1734	213	6612	1311	1241
			ii.	In other district	T	15385	13831	2869	757	836	438	9283	8113	233	3237	2163	1286
					R	12363	11732	1812	575	697	369	8103	7012	200	2852	1552	924
					U	2934	2008	1053	178	123	60	1134	1060	30	359	594	350
		II. States/Uts in India beyond the State of enumeration			T	15504	10609	4329	761	495	204	6694	5397	163	3159	3324	1087
					R	10996	7509	3582	377	262	124	5087	3953	127	2376	1938	679
					U	3986	2767	1130	355	204	72	1414	1268	32	702	1207	369
		B. Countries in Asia beyond India			T	711	469	92	19	7	3	370	270	6	76	236	101
		C. Other Countries			T	-	1	-	-	-	-	-	-	-	-	-	1
		Total Migration			**T**	**80737**	**119831**	**13220**	**3242**	**2936**	**1791**	**44983**	**37668**	**1901**	**64133**	**17697**	**12997**
3	Meghalaya	**A.** Last residence elsewhere in India			T	166341	125395	30934	6763	9544	7013	46699	58263	36380	23856	42784	29501
					R	130167	97537	18542	5090	7015	5545	36438	43758	34207	19429	33965	23715
					U	36068	27764	12359	1672	2529	1466	10241	14458	2160	4416	8780	5752
		I. Within the State of enumeration	i.	Elsewhere in the district	T	105801	79937	10349	3981	4958	4493	31035	36763	32124	13526	27335	21175
					R	91405	68284	7502	3374	4254	3925	29014	30864	30499	12268	23136	17853
					U	14357	11613	2813	607	704	569	5013	5882	1613	1255	4185	3300

1	2	3		4	5	6	7	8	9	10	11	12	13	14	15	16
			ii. In other district	T	16301	13217	3977	1356	1312	1079	4695	6440	2340	1299	4026	3043
				R	12174	10256	2210	1008	1001	839	3702	4843	2089	1037	3172	2529
				U	4102	2940	1709	347	312	239	989	1585	251	259	842	510
		II. States/Uts in India beyond the State of enumeration		T	44239	32240	16658	1426	3273	1440	10969	15059	1916	9031	11423	5284
				R	26587	18997	8829	708	1760	782	6722	8050	1620	6124	7656	3333
				U	17609	13211	7808	718	1513	658	4239	6990	296	2903	3753	1942
		B. Countries in Asia beyond India		T	4319	2642	1934	92	160	45	790	1120	47	760	1388	625
		C. Other Countries		T	15	18	3	2	1	1	4	3	-	1	7	11
		Total Migration		**T**	**184431**	**137229**	**35995**	**7253**	**9859**	**7131**	**51126**	**63307**	**37044**	**25878**	**50407**	**33660**
4	Mizoram	**A.** Last residence elsewhere in India		T	117839	107087	18497	2736	3689	2478	75035	77467	1038	9762	19580	14604
				R	101665	96487	12292	1938	3289	2159	69038	70699	871	8806	16175	12885
				U	15569	10167	6057	793	395	318	5770	6569	149	888	3198	1599
		I. Within the State of enumeration	i. Elsewhere in the district	T	96026	94396	10419	2154	3101	2098	66383	68261	812	8611	15311	13273
				R	88400	88000	8431	1691	2889	1927	62678	64296	717	8037	13685	12048
				U	7358	6153	1980	460	209	170	3540	3810	86	539	1543	1174
			ii. In other district	T	8158	6504	2180	316	405	242	4299	4595	125	725	1149	626
				R	5249	4605	832	153	302	167	3239	3315	93	526	782	445
				U	2853	1838	1335	163	101	76	1027	1260	30	175	361	164
		II. States/Uts in India beyond the State of enumeration		T	13655	6146	5898	266	184	138	4353	4612	100	427	3120	704
				R	8017	3882	3029	94	97	65	3121	3088	61	243	1708	392
				U	5357	2176	2741	169	85	72	1203	1499	34	174	1204	262
		B. Countries in Asia beyond India		T	261	61	133	6	-	-	36	30	1	17	91	8
		C. Other Countries		T	1	-	1	-	-	-	-	-	-	-	-	-
		Total Migration		**T**	**120378**	**108773**	**18849**	**2749**	**3720**	**2486**	**76215**	**78683**	**1073**	**9985**	**20520**	**14870**

1	2	3		4	5	6	7	8	9	10	11	12	13	14	15	16
5	Nagaland	**A.** Last residence elsewhere in India		T	113355	77569	38992	4689	10235	5739	29123	38530	862	13133	34143	15418
				R	83919	59108	27464	3390	8411	4656	21589	27958	688	10516	25767	12587
				U	29039	18236	11377	1285	1808	1140	7489	10489	169	2557	8195	2765
		I. Within the State of enumeration	i. Elsewhere in the district	T	52289	43448	14512	2412	6858	3834	14971	18788	452	7730	15495	10684
				R	42737	36903	11368	1973	6101	3339	12013	15250	390	6968	12865	9322
				U	9442	6449	3095	435	752	443	2939	3514	60	730	2596	1326
			ii. In other district	T	19187	13861	7077	1112	2238	1413	5788	7936	175	1601	3907	1799
				R	13251	9732	4829	748	1671	1027	3874	5273	139	1306	2739	1379
				U	5865	4084	2223	360	564	336	1908	2650	36	285	1135	403
		II. States/Uts in India beyond the State of enumeration		T	41879	20260	17403	1164	1139	552	8363	11806	235	3802	14740	2935
				R	27931	12472	11268	669	639	239	5702	7435	159	2243	10163	1887
				U	13731	7703	6060	490	493	312	2642	4325	73	1541	4463	1035
		B. Countries in Asia beyond India		T	954	429	580	20	12	4	92	255	5	81	265	69
		C. Other Countries		T	-	-	-	-	-	-	-	-	-	-	-	-
		Total Migration		**T**	**118834**	**80464**	**41325**	**4795**	**10329**	**5828**	**30039**	**40220**	**906**	**13569**	**36235**	**16051**
6	Tripura	**A.** Last residence elsewhere in India		T	178335	227106	35976	6233	3918	1702	88948	84052	5410	98562	44083	36557
				R	137341	185067	23094	4198	2632	1151	71169	64878	5116	85220	35330	29619
				U	39421	40403	12385	1955	1180	525	17158	18489	279	12783	8419	6651
		I. Within the State of enumeration	i. Elsewhere in the district	T	126860	176250	18381	3256	2610	1095	67776	61584	4740	81857	33353	28457
				R	108560	155504	14358	2568	2160	929	58479	52438	4587	74602	28967	24967
				U	17961	20180	3984	676	431	159	9087	8931	148	7014	4311	3400
			ii. In other district	T	30947	32817	9078	1461	766	371	13895	14647	561	11338	6647	5001
				R	19174	20937	4477	711	345	157	9340	9178	463	7620	4550	3271
				U	11680	11734	4573	742	415	211	4526	5415	96	3672	2069	1694

1	2	3	4	5	6	7	8	9	10	11	12	13	14	15	16
		II. States/Uts in India beyond the State of enumeration	T	20528	18039	8517	1516	542	236	7277	7821	110	5367	4083	3099
			R	9607	8626	4260	919	119	65	3350	3262	67	2998	1813	1381
			U	9780	8489	3828	537	333	155	3545	4143	35	2097	2038	1557
		B. Countries in Asia beyond India	T	24823	23126	687	101	287	102	4830	5722	26	2585	18993	14616
		C. Other Countries	T	-	-	-	-	-	-	-	-	-	-	-	-
		Total Migration	**T**	**356417**	**388407**	**39195**	**6901**	**4603**	**2028**	**126893**	**121840**	**5878**	**123664**	**179848**	**133975**
7	Sikkim	**A.** Last residence elsewhere in India	T	49153	49202	19149	2385	2009	819	15570	15672	673	24471	11752	5854
			R	34854	39612	11898	1487	1473	586	12218	11206	571	21759	8695	4575
			U	14193	9489	7206	893	535	233	3338	4449	100	2684	3015	1229
		I. Within the State of enumeration — i. Elsewhere in the district	T	20805	27918	5638	917	917	366	8896	7739	427	15621	4927	3275
			R	17605	25692	4340	755	761	320	7938	6590	396	15085	4171	2942
			U	3188	2204	1298	161	156	46	950	1147	31	529	744	321
		ii. In other district	T	9692	9279	4089	591	449	183	3019	3153	137	4331	1998	1021
			R	6614	7283	2518	377	342	135	2246	2199	108	3793	1401	778
			U	3069	1986	1566	211	108	48	772	953	29	533	594	241
		II. States/Uts in India beyond the State of enumeration	T	18655	12005	9423	877	643	270	3658	4780	109	4519	4827	1559
			R	10635	6637	5040	355	371	131	2034	2417	67	2880	3123	854
			U	7936	5299	4341	521	271	140	1608	2349	40	1622	1676	668
		B. Countries in Asia beyond India	T	1062	689	444	35	3	5	245	277	5	160	365	211
		C. Other Countries	T	1	3	-	1	-	-	-	2	-	-	-	-
		Total Migration	**T**	**60468**	**56455**	**23609**	**2907**	**2128**	**874**	**18346**	**18417**	**800**	**26904**	**15586**	**7352**

Source: Census of India, 1981, Migration Tables (Table D-3), Registrar General & Census Commissioner, New Delhi.

Note: Information of Assam is not available, as Census was not conducted there in 1981.

Appendix-9.3

Migration by Sex, Place of last Residence, Duration of Residence and Reason for Migration as per different Census Years

Sl. No.	Name of the State	Last Residence		Rural or Urban status of last Residence	Census Year, 1991											
					All duration of Residence											
					Total Migrantion			Reason for Migration								
					Person	Male	Female	Employment			Business			Education		
								Person	Male	Female	Person	Male	Female	Person	Male	Female
1	2	3		4	5	6	7	8	9	10	11	12	13	14	15	16
1	Arunachal Pradesh	A. Last residence elsewhere in India (I+II)		T	282197	142994	139203	60273	53810	6463	10874	10028	846	18844	12621	6223
				R	235200	115405	119795	44543	39853	4690	8165	7495	670	16765	11333	5432
				U	45780	26943	18837	15498	13745	1753	2663	2495	168	2053	1271	782
		I. Within the State of enumeration	i. Elsewhere in the district	T	147488	64623	82865	19731	17382	2349	2872	2436	436	14373	9593	4780
				R	136227	58069	78158	16135	14199	1936	2479	2089	390	13645	9163	4482
				U	11013	6433	4580	3568	3158	410	386	341	45	719	425	294
			ii. In other district	T	36056	19897	16159	10686	9287	1399	779	669	110	2723	1790	933
				R	25916	14002	11914	7057	6126	931	533	457	76	2046	1382	664
				U	9892	5768	4124	3592	3129	463	240	209	31	670	404	266

1	2	3	4	5	6	7	8	9	10	11	12	13	14	15	16
		II. States/Uts in India beyond the State of enumeration	T	98653	58474	40179	29856	27141	2715	7223	6923	300	1748	1238	510
			R	73057	43334	29723	21351	19528	1823	5153	4949	204	1074	788	286
			U	24875	14742	10133	8338	7458	880	2037	1945	92	664	442	222
		B. Last Residence outside India	T	313	186	127	81	76	5	12	9	3	4	4	-
		C. Countries in Asia beyond India	T	306	181	125	81	76	5	11	9	2	4	4	-
		D. Other Countries	T	7	5	2	-	-	-	1	-	1	-	-	-
		Total Migration	**T**	**291903**	**148564**	**143339**	**62931**	**56281**	**6650**	**11225**	**10333**	**892**	**19075**	**12772**	**6303**
2	Assam	**A.** Last residence elsewhere in India (I+II)	T	5152524	1939871	3212653	347260	305411	41849	175816	161668	14148	96551	64350	32201
			R	4600775	1678980	2921795	260761	227602	33159	132794	121046	11748	76671	51180	25491
			U	498532	239467	259065	82989	74759	8230	41042	38832	2210	19220	12770	6450
		I. Within the State of enumeration — i. Elsewhere in the district	T	3292098	1069993	2222105	126254	106257	19997	50614	43427	7187	50121	31600	18521
			R	3148804	1011572	2137232	111170	93083	18087	43574	37037	6537	45811	29030	16781
			U	118724	50591	68133	14214	12444	1770	6690	6130	560	4050	2400	1650
		ii. In other district	T	1372665	592906	779759	146964	131982	14982	47647	44322	3325	35810	25230	10580
			R	1113080	470919	642161	99543	89051	10492	32319	29714	2605	24950	17870	7080
			U	240334	113519	126815	46001	41691	4310	14908	14208	700	10620	7240	3380
		II. States/Uts in India beyond the State of enumeration	T	487761	276972	210789	74042	67172	6870	77555	73919	3636	10620	7520	3100
			R	338891	196489	142402	50048	45468	4580	56901	54295	2606	5910	4280	1630
			U	139474	75357	64117	22774	20624	2150	19444	18494	950	4550	3130	1420

1	2	3	4	5	6	7	8	9	10	11	12	13	14	15	16
		B. Lasr Residence outside India	T	223216	120237	102979	7843	6983	860	9422	8482	940	750	580	170
		C. Countries in Asia beyond India	T	219143	118417	100726	7613	6853	760	9242	8392	850	680	530	150
		D. Other Countries	T	4173	1870	2303	240	140	100	190	90	100	70	50	20
		Total Migration	**T**	**5407547**	**2077712**	**3329835**	**357363**	**314224**	**43139**	**186847**	**171429**	**15418**	**97691**	**65140**	**32551**
3	Manipur	A. Last residence elsewhere in India (I+II)	T	108002	41111	6689[illegible]	9384	7853	1531	4883	3848	1035	971	592	379
			R	86244	32368	53876	6860	5723	1137	2754	2116	638	756	454	302
			U	21180	8525	12655	2493	2109	384	2107	1719	388	205	131	74
		I. Within the State of enumeration — i. Elsewhere in the district	T	67512	21122	46390	4098	3355	743	1771	1228	543	551	313	238
			R	54481	17027	37454	3116	2554	562	959	595	364	435	243	192
			U	12826	4037	8789	981	800	181	809	632	177	115	69	46
		ii. In other district	T	25456	10636	14820	3025	2431	594	1069	782	287	337	221	116
			R	20916	8723	12193	2313	1838	475	674	493	181	268	175	93
			U	4376	1839	2537	706	590	116	392	287	105	63	43	20
		II. States/Uts in India beyond the State of enumeration	T	15034	9353	5681	2261	2067	194	2043	1838	205	83	58	25
			R	10847	6618	4229	1431	1331	100	1121	1028	93	53	36	17
			U	3978	2649	1329	806	719	87	906	800	106	27	19	8
		B. Last Residence outside India	T	1685	1018	667	137	120	17	146	106	40	3	-	3
		C. Countries in Asia beyond India	T	1571	961	610	137	120	17	141	106	35	3	-	3
		D. Other Countries	T	221	108	113	24	24	-	8	2	6	-	-	-
		Total Migration	**T**	**118009**	**49946**	**68063**	**13370**	**11739**	**1631**	**5087**	**3998**	**1089**	**982**	**596**	**386**

1	2	3	4	5	6	7	8	9	10	11	12	13	14	15	16
4	Meghalaya	**A.** Last residence elsewhere in India (I+II)	T	253182	140399	112783	31984	25616	6368	11611	9176	2436	12815	7249	5566
			R	201990	112210	89780	21514	16747	4767	8472	6448	2024	9708	5391	4317
			U	46248	25513	20735	9953	8431	1522	2959	2581	378	2898	1744	1154
		I. Within the State of enumeration — i. Elsewhere in the district	T	156563	86974	69589	13091	9486	3605	4715	2960	1755	7513	3848	3665
			R	136951	76512	60439	10620	7539	3081	4063	2490	1573	6358	3274	3084
			U	17023	9117	7906	2359	1866	493	603	437	166	1021	506	515
		ii. In other district	T	26301	14715	11586	4979	3756	1223	896	631	265	2175	1164	1011
			R	19481	10827	8654	2989	2214	775	587	407	180	1640	885	755
			U	5930	3392	2538	1907	1472	435	295	217	78	508	267	241
		II. States/Uts in India beyond the State of enumeration	T	70318	38710	31608	13914	12374	1540	6000	5585	415	3127	2237	890
			R	45558	24871	20687	7905	6994	911	3822	3551	271	1710	1232	478
			U	23295	13004	10291	5687	5093	594	2061	1927	134	1369	971	398
		B. Last Residence outside India	T	13431	7731	5700	1818	1605	213	826	659	167	250	183	67
		C. Countries in Asia beyond India	T	12629	7216	5413	1758	1559	199	811	646	165	229	167	62
		D. Other Countries	T	1033	642	391	88	71	17	29	26	3	25	18	7
		Total Migration	**T**	**266844**	**148257**	**118587**	**33830**	**27246**	**6584**	**12451**	**9848**	**2603**	**13069**	**7434**	**5635**
5	Mizoram	**A.** Last residence elsewhere in India	T	101227	47047	54180	15274	12457	2817	1912	1339	573	2508	1416	1092
			R	78302	34580	43722	9456	7647	1809	1207	789	418	1640	913	727
			U	22402	12205	10197	5731	4738	993	699	549	150	855	497	358

1	2	3		4	5	6	7	8	9	10	11	12	13	14	15	16
		I. Within the State of enumeration	i. Elsewhere in the district	T	82211	36238	45973	10509	8324	2185	1118	636	482	2003	1125	878
				R	67439	28819	38620	7295	5763	1532	873	496	377	1423	778	645
				U	14478	7298	7180	3195	2552	643	243	140	103	571	343	228
			ii. In other district	T	9134	4678	4456	2078	1708	370	160	124	36	324	185	139
				R	5688	2725	2963	958	774	184	85	59	26	163	100	63
				U	3348	1903	1445	1108	922	186	75	65	10	158	83	75
		II. States/Uts in India beyond the State of enumeration		T	9882	6131	3751	2687	2425	262	634	579	55	181	106	75
				R	5175	3036	2139	1203	1110	93	249	234	15	54	35	19
				U	4576	3004	1572	1428	1264	164	381	344	37	126	71	55
		B. Lasr Residence outside India		T	1427	667	760	139	101	38	52	25	27	5	3	2
		C. Countries in Asia beyond India		T	1378	644	734	134	97	37	39	25	14	5	3	2
		D. Other Countries		T	79	41	38	11	10	1	15	2	13	-	-	-
		Total Migration		**T**	**106530**	**49601**	**56929**	**15665**	**12730**	**2935**	**2072**	**1442**	**630**	**2561**	**1444**	**1117**
6	Nagaland	**A.** Last residence elsewhere in India		T	122789	72086	50703	30601	26369	4232	12019	10882	1137	7493	4421	3072
				R	87765	51189	36576	21248	18397	2851	7198	6467	731	5422	3266	2156
				U	34100	20378	13722	9186	7844	1342	4790	4387	403	2057	1142	915
		I. Within the State of enume-**ration**	i. Elsewhere in the district	T	51424	28183	23241	11101	9405	1696	2443	2031	412	4007	2312	1695
				R	40444	22129	18315	8685	7439	1246	1571	1286	285	3225	1864	1361
				U	10863	6008	4855	2401	1954	447	871	744	127	776	442	334

1	2	3		4	5	6	7	8	9	10	11	12	13	14	15	16
			ii. In other district	T	27277	15167	12110	7427	6022	1405	1005	847	158	2458	1435	1023
				R	19553	10847	8706	5152	4169	983	672	566	106	1594	1000	594
				U	7271	4065	3206	2249	1830	419	330	279	51	859	431	428
		II. States/Uts in India beyond the State of enumeration		T	44088	28736	15352	12073	10942	1131	8571	8004	567	1028	674	354
				R	27768	18213	9555	7411	6789	622	4955	4615	340	603	402	201
				U	15966	10305	5661	4536	4060	476	3589	3364	225	422	269	153
		B. Last Residence outside India		T	2350	1639	711	941	889	52	248	220	28	15	12	3
		C. Countries in Asia beyond India		T	2329	1629	700	938	887	51	242	217	25	14	11	3
		D. Other Countries		T	181	74	107	37	26	11	16	12	4	3	2	1
		Total Migration		**T**	**127904**	**75437**	**52467**	**32415**	**28068**	**4347**	**12501**	**11300**	**1201**	**7576**	**4479**	**3097**
7	Tripura	**A**. Last residence elsewhere in India		T	437661	168099	269562	44830	36489	8341	6008	5133	875	7580	5417	2163
				R	350323	129752	220571	30130	24287	5843	4104	3472	632	5949	4285	1664
				U	83657	36529	47128	14001	11621	2380	1779	1563	216	1581	1099	482
		I. Within the State of enume-ration	i. Else-where in the district	T	322945	117355	205590	23371	18903	4468	3428	2879	549	5269	3825	1444
				R	278030	98774	179256	18288	14716	3572	2742	2284	458	4554	3302	1252
				U	43946	18181	25765	4999	4120	879	678	588	90	698	514	184
			ii. In other district	T	73381	30959	42422	12341	10248	2093	1222	1071	151	1501	1033	468
				R	50384	20621	29763	7067	5798	1269	740	633	107	1048	728	320
				U	22473	10085	12388	5199	4387	812	468	428	40	449	301	148

1	2	3			4	5	6	7	8	9	10	11	12	13	14	15	16
		II. States/Uts in India beyond the State of enumeration			T	41335	19785	21550	9118	7338	1780	1358	1183	175	810	559	251
					R	21909	10357	11552	4775	3773	1002	622	555	67	347	255	92
					U	17238	8263	8975	3803	3114	689	633	547	86	434	284	150
		B. Last Residence outside India			T	269417	140459	128958	6614	5480	1134	1644	1277	367	759	573	186
		C. Countries in Asia beyond India			T	268235	139766	128469	6553	5450	1103	1593	1243	350	750	570	180
		D. Other Countries			T	1482	809	673	71	38	33	53	35	18	10	3	7
		Total Migration			**T**	**812139**	**362530**	**449609**	**54286**	**44216**	**10070**	**9061**	**7443**	**1618**	**8640**	**6194**	**2446**
8	Sikkim	**A.** Last residence elsewhere in India			T	111506	52886	58620	18859	15856	3003	4780	4221	559	3459	2142	1317
					R	84871	38219	46652	12251	10307	1944	3152	2752	400	2505	1535	970
					U	23506	13053	10453	6112	5136	976	1505	1363	142	853	550	303
		I. Within the State of enumeration	i.	Elsewhere in the district	T	70288	31307	38981	8581	6979	1602	1986	1637	349	2121	1281	840
					R	57512	24387	33125	6154	5023	1131	1243	980	263	1619	966	653
					U	11153	6127	5026	2279	1841	438	712	630	82	455	295	160
			ii.	In other district	T	17899	8512	9387	3905	3254	651	479	411	68	678	439	239
					R	13530	6105	7425	2635	2221	414	293	242	51	526	336	190
					U	3942	2211	1731	1209	986	223	177	162	15	138	95	43
		II. States/Uts in India beyond the State of enumeration			T	23319	13067	10252	6373	5623	750	2315	2173	142	660	422	238
					R	13829	7727	6102	3462	3063	399	1616	1530	86	360	233	127
					U	8411	4715	3696	2624	2309	315	616	571	45	260	160	100

1	2	3	4	5	6	7	8	9	10	11	12	13	14	15	16
		B. Last Residence outside India	T	5713	3216	2497	1192	1028	164	247	195	52	49	37	12
		C. Countries in Asia beyond India	T	5543	3130	2413	1178	1023	155	178	151	27	45	36	9
		D. Other Countries	T	292	154	138	38	26	12	92	66	26	7	3	4
		Total Migration	**T**	**124997**	**60786**	**64211**	**21785**	**18341**	**3444**	**5379**	**4671**	**708**	**3786**	**2401**	**1385**

Source: Census of India, 1991, Migration Tables Vol. 3 Registrar General & Census Commissioner, New Delhi.

Appendix-9.3 (*Cont.*)

Migration by Sex, Place of last Residence, Duration of Residence and Reason for Migration as per different Census Years

Sl. No.	Name of the State	Last Residence		Rural or Urban status of last Residence	Census Year, 1991											
					All duration of Residence											
					Reason for Migration											
					Family moved			Marriage			Natural Calamities			Others		
					Person	Male	Female	Person	Male	Female	Person	Male	Female	Person	Male	Female
1	2	3		4	17	18	19	20	21	22	23	24	25	26	27	28
1	Arunachal Pradesh	A. Last residence elsewhere in India		T	104187	40599	63588	52785	2130	50655	4364	3272	1092	30870	20534	10336
				R	85775	33851	51924	49185	1965	47220	4148	3120	1028	26619	17788	8831
				U	18010	6586	11424	3427	157	3270	201	141	60	3928	2548	1380
		I. Within the State of enumeration	i. Elsewhere in the district	T	53427	21721	31706	38239	1206	37033	2296	1672	624	16550	10613	5937
				R	48577	19789	28788	37485	1164	36321	2246	1635	611	15660	10030	5630
				U	4733	1878	2855	712	41	671	45	34	11	850	556	294
			ii. In other district	T	15646	5802	9844	3044	178	2866	438	355	83	2740	1816	924
				R	11016	4078	6938	2657	158	2499	412	339	73	2195	1462	733
				U	4586	1708	2878	357	19	338	21	12	9	426	287	139
		II. States/Uts in India beyond the State of enumeration		T	35114	13076	22038	11502	746	10756	1630	1246	385	11580	8105	3475
				R	26182	9984	16198	9043	643	8400	1490	1146	344	8764	6296	2468
				U	8691	3000	5691	2358	97	2261	135	95	40	2652	1705	947

1	2	3	4	17	18	19	20	21	22	23	24	25	26	27	28
		B. Last Residence outside India	T	117	44	73	28	2	26	-	-	-	71	51	20
		C. Countries in Asia beyond India	T	115	43	72	28	2	26	-	-	-	67	47	20
		D. Other Countries	T	2	1	1	-	-	-	-	-	-	4	4	-
		Total Migration	**T**	**107205**	**41611**	**65594**	**53769**	**2179**	**51590**	**4364**	**3272**	**1092**	**33334**	**22116**	**11218**
2	Assam	**A.** Last residence elsewhere in India	T	1230234	710983	519251	2337841	58280	2279561	277842	195412	82430	686980	443767	243213
			R	1086265	641156	445109	2171674	53906	2117768	271952	191692	80260	600658	392398	208260
			U	132516	63697	68819	147957	3854	144103	4080	2560	1520	70728	42995	27733
		I. Within the State of enumeration — i. Elsewhere in the district	T	744482	450534	293948	1708893	39757	1669136	178952	124860	54092	432782	273558	159224
			R	706918	430398	276520	1654598	38347	1616251	176642	123480	53162	410091	260197	149894
			U	32624	17256	15368	42245	1180	41065	1330	720	610	17571	10461	7110
		ii. In other district	T	358619	196377	162242	512726	13249	499477	93720	66972	26748	177179	114774	62405
			R	291779	165136	126643	435729	11405	424324	90880	65152	25728	137880	92591	45289
			U	63517	29521	33996	72697	1654	71043	2170	1460	710	30421	17745	12676
		II. States/Uts in India beyond the State of enumeration	T	127133	64072	63061	116222	5274	110948	5170	3580	1590	77019	55435	21584
			R	87568	45622	41946	81347	4154	77193	4430	3060	1370	52687	39610	13077
			U	36375	16920	19455	33015	1020	31995	580	380	200	22736	14789	7947
		B. Last Residence outside India	T	89360	51226	38134	37240	1370	35870	-	-	-	78601	51596	27005
		C. Countries in Asia beyond India	T	87270	50236	37034	36537	1260	35277	-	-	-	77801	51146	26655

1	2	3		4	17	18	19	20	21	22	23	24	25	26	27	28
		D. Other Countries		T	2100	1000	1100	743	120	623	-	-	-	830	470	360
		Total Migration		**T**	**1331297**	**767989**	**563308**	**2377931**	**59920**	**2318011**	**277842**	**195412**	**82430**	**778576**	**503598**	**274978**
3	Manipur	**A.** Last residence elsewhere in India		T	34965	19503	15462	44282	1541	42741	429	272	157	13088	7502	5586
				R	29754	16749	13005	35387	1251	34136	391	252	139	10342	5823	4519
				U	5067	2684	2383	8726	284	8442	38	20	18	2544	1578	966
		I. Within the State of enume-ration	i. Else-where in the district	T	19935	11032	8903	33363	1003	32360	184	78	106	7610	4113	3497
				R	17125	9526	7599	26660	821	25839	171	75	96	6015	3213	2802
				U	2769	1480	1289	6600	181	6419	13	3	10	1539	872	667
			ii. In other district	T	9094	4955	4139	8508	323	8185	75	45	30	3348	1879	1469
				R	7971	4372	3599	6831	256	6575	68	40	28	2791	1549	1242
				U	1103	571	532	1640	62	1578	7	5	2	465	281	184
		II. States/Uts in India beyond the State of enumeration		T	5936	3516	2420	2411	215	2196	170	149	21	2130	1510	620
				R	4658	2851	1807	1896	174	1722	152	137	15	1536	1061	475
				U	1195	633	562	486	41	445	18	12	6	540	425	115
		B. Last Residence outside India		T	950	536	414	134	21	113	-	-	-	315	235	80
		C. Countries in Asia beyond India		T	885	504	381	107	10	97	-	-	-	298	221	77
		D. Other Countries		T	93	52	41	73	11	62	1	1	-	22	18	4
		Total Migration		**T**	**36233**	**20191**	**16042**	**44639**	**1668**	**42971**	**432**	**275**	**157**	**17266**	**11479**	**5787**

1	2	3	4	17	18	19	20	21	22	23	24	25	26	27	28
4	Megha-laya	**A.** Last residence elsewhere in India	T	76068	32431	43637	64083	34873	29210	3409	2147	1262	53212	28907	24305
			R	60024	25995	34029	56249	32411	23838	3189	2018	1171	42834	23200	19634
			U	14931	5962	8969	7184	2100	5084	197	119	78	8126	4576	3550
		I. Within the State of enumer-ation: i. Else-where in the district	T	46851	20434	26417	44695	29531	15164	1066	607	459	38632	20108	18524
			R	40488	17704	22784	41681	27827	13854	980	561	419	32761	17117	15644
			U	5783	2484	3299	2685	1460	1225	77	43	34	4495	2321	2174
		ii. In other district	T	8542	3549	4993	4379	2666	1713	135	72	63	5195	2877	2318
			R	6553	2757	3796	3690	2334	1356	104	55	49	3918	2175	1743
			U	1799	697	1102	570	256	314	31	17	14	820	466	354
		II. States/Uts in India beyond the State of enumeration	T	20675	8448	12227	15009	2676	12333	2208	1468	740	9385	5922	3463
			R	12983	5534	7449	10878	2250	8628	2105	1402	703	6155	3908	2247
			U	7349	2781	4568	3929	384	3545	89	59	30	2811	1789	1022
		B. Last Residence out-side India	T	4697	2213	2484	1658	448	1210	-	-	-	4182	2623	1559
		C. Countries in Asia beyond India	T	4511	2093	2418	1629	440	1189	-	-	-	3691	2311	1380
		D. Other Countries	T	174	151	123	95	47	48	1	1	-	521	328	193
		Total Migration	**T**	**80853**	**34675**	**46178**	**65807**	**35360**	**30447**	**3410**	**2148**	**1262**	**57424**	**31546**	**25878**
5	Mizoram	**A.** Last residence elsewhere in India	T	57333	22966	34367	9681	928	8753	400	204	196	14119	7737	6382
			R	47601	19032	28569	7847	686	7161	355	191	164	10196	5322	4874
			U	9644	3895	5749	1762	219	1543	42	13	29	3669	2294	1375

1	2	3		4	17	18	19	20	21	22	23	24	25	26	27	28
		I. **Within** the State of enume-ration	i. Else-where in the district	T	48892	19500	29392	8093	712	7381	348	175	173	11248	5766	5482
				R	42144	16800	25344	6816	532	6284	310	164	146	8578	4286	4292
				U	6703	2682	4021	1221	158	1063	37	11	26	2508	1412	1096
			ii. In other district	T	4464	1919	2545	908	79	829	19	8	11	1181	655	526
				R	3053	1317	1736	631	60	571	14	7	7	784	408	376
				U	1387	590	797	268	19	249	3	1	2	349	223	126
		II. States/Uts in India beyond the State of enumeration		T	3977	1547	2430	680	137	543	33	21	12	1690	1316	374
				R	2404	915	1489	400	94	306	31	20	11	834	628	206
				U	1554	623	391	273	42	231	2	1	1	812	659	153
		B. Last Residence outside India		T	823	335	488	131	28	103	-	-	-	277	175	102
		C. Countries in Asia beyond India		T	805	325	480	131	28	103	-	-	-	264	166	98
		D. Other Countries		T	23	12	11	3	1	2	-	-	-	14	7	7
		Total Migration		**T**	**60185**	**24202**	**35983**	**10127**	**1000**	**9127**	**400**	**204**	**196**	**15520**	**8579**	**6941**
6	Nagaland	**A.** Last residence elsewhere in India		T	40433	17235	23198	12386	675	11711	861	508	353	18996	11996	7000
				R	30079	13132	16947	8935	538	8397	719	434	285	14164	8955	5209
				U	10201	4045	6156	3416	133	3283	137	71	66	4313	2756	1557
		I. Within the State of enume-	i. Else-where in the district	T	18032	8089	9943	5610	364	5246	354	189	165	9877	5793	4084
				R	14076	6376	7700	4627	309	4318	313	173	140	7947	4682	3265
				U	3912	1701	2211	978	55	923	40	16	24	1885	1096	789

1	2	3	4	17	18	19	20	21	22	23	24	25	26	27	28
		ration — ii. In other district	T	10452	4510	5942	2262	121	2141	198	121	77	3475	2111	1364
			R	7781	3423	4358	1779	92	1687	180	111	69	2395	1486	909
			U	2642	1076	1566	480	29	451	16	9	7	695	411	284
		II. States/Uts in India beyond the State of enumeration	T	11949	4636	7313	4514	190	4324	309	198	111	5644	4092	1552
			R	8222	3333	4889	2529	137	2392	226	150	76	3822	2787	1035
			U	3647	1268	2379	1958	49	1909	81	46	35	1733	1249	484
		B. Last Residence outside India	T	515	193	322	209	14	195	-	-	-	422	311	111
		C. Countries in Asia beyond India	T	510	192	318	208	14	194	-	-	-	417	308	109
		D. Other Countries	T	67	18	49	38	2	36	-	-	-	20	14	6
		Total Migration	**T**	**41734**	**17697**	**24037**	**12854**	**718**	**12136**	**862**	**509**	**353**	**19962**	**12666**	**7296**
7	Tripura	**A.** Last residence elsewhere in India	T	131188	68413	62775	161234	7155	154079	2373	1427	946	84448	44065	40383
			R	100269	53140	47129	137973	6689	131284	2084	1270	814	69814	36609	3320[illegible]
			U	29986	14792	15194	22496	435	22061	272	148	124	13542	6871	6671
		I. Within the State of enumeration — i. Elsewhere in the district	T	93607	49835	43772	129062	6053	123009	1822	1114	708	66386	34746	31640
			R	76775	41126	35649	115657	5787	109870	1681	1037	644	58333	30522	27811
			U	16653	8611	8042	13132	257	12875	138	75	63	7648	4016	3632
		ii. In other district	T	24129	11952	12177	22726	845	21881	352	189	163	11110	5621	5489
			R	16656	8532	8124	16756	737	16019	297	164	133	7820	4029	3791
			U	7352	3355	3997	5853	103	5750	53	24	29	3099	1487	1612

1	2	3	4	17	18	19	20	21	22	23	24	25	26	27	28
		II. States/Uts in India beyond the State of enumeration	T	13452	6626	6826	9446	257	9189	199	124	75	6952	3698	3254
			R	6838	3482	3356	5560	165	5395	106	69	37	3661	2058	1603
			U	5981	2826	3155	3511	75	3436	81	49	32	2795	1368	1427
		B. Last Residence outside India	T	96441	52024	44417	28635	756	27879	-	-	-	135324	80349	54975
		C. Countries in Asia beyond India	T	95799	51554	44245	28445	741	27704	-	-	-	135095	80208	54887
		D. Other Countries	T	695	495	200	296	18	278	3	3	-	354	217	137
		Total Migration	**T**	**244285**	**129093**	**115192**	**195917**	**8550**	**187367**	**2382**	**1435**	**947**	**297568**	**165599**	**131969**
8	Sikkim	**A.** Last residence elsewhere in India	T	27136	13609	13527	30703	1215	29488	508	310	198	26061	15533	10528
			R	20079	10474	9605	26628	1007	25621	432	267	165	19824	11877	7947
			U	6552	2880	3672	3560	182	3378	76	43	33	4848	2899	1949
		I. Within the State of enumeration — i. Elsewhere in the district	T	16316	8665	7651	20840	844	19996	382	232	150	20062	11669	8393
			R	13188	7192	5996	19120	743	18377	335	205	130	15853	9278	6575
			U	2919	1363	1556	1486	88	1398	47	27	20	3255	1883	1372
		ii. In other district	T	5158	2526	2632	4936	173	4763	58	33	25	2685	1676	1009
			R	3655	1844	1811	4296	137	4159	49	28	21	2076	1297	779
			U	1416	644	772	553	33	520	9	5	4	440	286	154
		II. States/Uts in India beyond the State of enumeration	T	5662	2418	3244	4927	198	4729	68	45	23	3314	2188	1126
			R	3236	1438	1798	3212	127	3085	48	34	14	1895	1302	593
			U	2217	873	1344	1521	61	1460	20	11	9	1153	730	423

1	2	3	4	17	18	19	20	21	22	23	24	25	26	27	28
		B. Last Residence outside India	T	1540	777	763	1178	50	1128	-	-	-	1507	1129	378
		C. Countries in Asia beyond India	T	1527	770	757	1153	44	1109	-	-	-	1462	1106	356
		D. Other Countries	T	31	17	14	60	7	53	4	2	2	60	33	27
		Total Migration	**T**	**30455**	**15236**	**15219**	**32954**	**1332**	**31622**	**517**	**315**	**202**	**30121**	**18490**	**11631**

Source: Census of India, 1991, Migration Tables, Volume -3, Registrar General & Census Commissioner, New Delhi.

Appendix-9.4

Migration by Sex, Place of last Residence, Duration of Residence and Reason for Migration as per different Census Years

Sl. No.	Name of the State	Last Residence	Rural or Urban status of last Residence	Census Year, 2001											
				All duration of Residence											
				Total Migration			Reason for Migration								
							Employment			Business			Education		
				Person	Male	Female	Person	Male	Female	Person	Male	Female	Person	Male	Female
1	2	3	4	5	6	7	8	9	10	11	12	13	14	15	16
1	Arunachal Pradesh	**A.** Last residence elsewhere in India	T	393866	205131	188735	95850	79847	16003	11821	10778	1043	12907	8000	4907
			R	271621	137594	134027	71697	59259	12438	8430	7665	765	10766	6775	3991
			U	67834	38540	29294	21826	18642	3184	3146	2903	243	1713	962	751
		I. Within the State of enumeration — i. Elsewhere in the district	T	193402	90056	103346	29235	23837	5398	2399	2032	367	7923	4895	3028
			R	135162	59596	75566	24128	19576	4552	1934	1630	304	7201	4459	2742
			U	19021	10314	8707	4411	3715	696	407	360	47	448	254	194
		ii. In other district	T	64414	34449	29965	18557	14803	3754	926	738	188	3972	2474	1498
			R	41390	21956	19434	12164	9505	2659	656	518	138	2999	1920	1079
			U	18155	9935	8220	6087	5070	1017	245	204	41	865	499	366
		II. States/Uts in India beyond the State of enumeration	T	136050	80626	55424	48058	41207	6851	8496	8008	488	1012	631	381
			R	95069	56042	39027	35405	30178	5227	5840	5517	323	566	396	170
			U	30658	18291	12367	11328	9857	1471	2494	2339	155	400	209	191

1	2	3	4	5	6	7	8	9	10	11	12	13	14	15	16
		B. Last Residence outside India	T	17574	10057	7517	4614	3879	735	221	186	35	88	75	13
		C. Countries in Asia beyond India	T	17516	10020	7496	4600	3867	733	217	183	34	87	75	12
		D. Other Countries	T	58	37	21	14	12	2	4	3	1	1	0	1
		Total Migration	**T**	**411440**	**215188**	**196252**	**100464**	**83726**	**16738**	**12042**	**10964**	**1078**	**12995**	**8075**	**4920**
2	Assam	**A.** Last residence elsewhere in India	T	6661860	2578503	4083357	370815	323750	47065	186950	174233	12717	46572	32103	14469
			R	4560771	1473660	3087111	278304	241993	36311	142251	132612	9639	34000	23601	10399
			U	679545	318903	360642	85615	76313	9302	41008	38426	2582	10712	7432	3280
		I. Within the State of enumeration — i. Elsewhere in the district	T	5090650	1875534	3215116	167235	141308	25927	79644	72441	7203	24065	15986	8079
			R	3419855	973966	2445889	132003	110945	21058	61140	55582	5558	19552	13136	6416
			U	375619	180586	195033	31574	27715	3859	16795	15472	1323	3573	2281	1292
		ii. In other district	T	1164069	478780	685289	138198	122162	16036	49493	45976	3517	18231	13131	5100
			R	874038	347371	526667	99681	87948	11733	37638	34933	2705	12285	8925	3360
			U	192728	83334	109394	36372	32414	3958	10935	10239	696	5249	3822	1427
		II. States/Uts in India beyond the State of enumeration	T	407141	224189	182952	65382	60280	5102	57813	55816	1997	4276	2986	1290
			R	266878	152323	114555	46620	43100	3520	43473	42097	1376	2163	1540	623
			U	111198	54983	56215	17669	16184	1485	13278	12715	563	1890	1329	561
		B. Last Residence outside India	T	130966	70254	60712	6328	5851	477	5275	4933	342	454	378	76
		C. Countries in Asia beyond India	T	130746	70129	60617	6291	5817	474	5268	4926	342	448	373	75
		D. Other Countries	T	220	125	95	37	34	3	7	7	0	6	5	1
		Total Migration	**T**	**6792826**	**2648757**	**4144069**	**377143**	**329601**	**47542**	**192225**	**179166**	**13059**	**47026**	**32481**	**14545**
3	Manipur	A. Last residence elsewhere in India	T	375641	154825	220816	13559	10180	3379	3857	2851	1006	3584	2184	1400
			R	190324	65087	125237	9688	7181	2507	2130	1557	573	2637	1620	1017
			U	46413	14610	31803	3323	2559	764	1590	1202	388	717	472	245

1	2	3		4	5	6	7	8	9	10	11	12	13	14	15	16
		I. Within the State of enumeration	i. Elsewhere in the district	T	301196	122409	178787	6580	4706	1874	1609	1082	527	1970	1203	767
				R	147644	48046	99598	4708	3382	1326	978	662	316	1482	891	591
				U	32970	9185	23785	1706	1217	489	558	377	181	391	254	137
			ii. In other district	T	59662	24140	35522	5093	3827	1266	983	674	309	1448	856	592
				R	34884	12974	21910	3841	2798	1043	597	404	193	1083	679	404
				U	9295	3131	6164	949	757	192	357	246	111	240	146	94
		II. States/Uts in India beyond the State of enumeration		T	14783	8276	6507	1886	1647	239	1265	1095	170	166	125	41
				R	7796	4067	3729	1139	1001	138	555	491	64	72	50	22
				U	4148	2294	1854	668	585	83	675	579	96	86	72	14
		B. Last Residence outside India		T	1418	790	628	157	124	33	124	92	32	16	13	3
		C. Countries in Asia beyond India		T	1390	776	614	147	122	25	124	92	32	15	12	3
		D. Other Countries		T	28	14	14	10	2	8	0	0	0	1	1	0
		Total Migration		**T**	**377059**	**155615**	**221444**	**13716**	**10304**	**3412**	**3981**	**2943**	**1038**	**3600**	**2197**	**1403**
4	Meghalaya	**A.** Last residence elsewhere in India		T	369570	198784	170786	34623	28101	6522	7140	6309	831	10737	6018	4719
				R	169792	92703	77089	21735	17062	4673	4312	3763	549	7408	4042	3366
				U	63115	34816	28299	11900	10287	1613	2590	2353	237	2981	1799	1182
		I. Within the State of enumeration	i. Elsewhere in the district	T	244916	130163	114753	9453	6874	2579	2042	1649	393	4175	2224	1951
				R	99344	54320	45024	6719	4649	2070	1247	957	290	3294	1703	1591
				U	28549	15661	12888	2465	2029	436	697	617	80	726	455	271
			ii. In other district	T	41572	22641	18931	6643	4596	2047	559	403	156	2605	1273	1332
				R	23878	12968	10910	4676	3100	1576	355	250	105	1953	956	997
				U	6925	3852	3073	1783	1376	407	193	147	46	568	276	292
		II. States/Uts in India beyond the State of enumeration		T	83082	45980	37102	18527	16631	1896	4539	4257	282	3957	2521	1436
				R	46570	25415	21155	10340	9313	1027	2710	2556	154	2161	1383	778
				U	27641	15303	12338	7652	6882	770	1700	1589	111	1687	1068	619

1	2	3		4	5	6	7	8	9	10	11	12	13	14	15	16
		B. Last Residence outside India		T	9622	5868	3754	1470	1355	115	236	190	46	170	122	48
		C. Countries in Asia beyond India		T	9579	5841	3738	1461	1349	112	235	189	46	168	120	48
		D. Other Countries		T	43	27	16	9	6	3	1	1	0	2	2	0
		Total Migration		**T**	**379192**	**204652**	**174540**	**36093**	**29456**	**6637**	**7376**	**6499**	**877**	**10907**	**6140**	**4767**
5	Mizoram	**A.** Last residence elsewhere in India		T	253445	133553	119892	46892	37097	9795	4388	2883	1505	10619	5871	4748
				R	166439	86115	80324	30002	23388	6614	2813	1768	1045	7445	4148	3297
				U	63165	35102	28063	15999	13038	2961	1530	1081	449	2998	1625	1373
		I. Within the State of enumeration	i. Elsewhere in the district	T	135693	68683	67010	16781	12603	4178	1615	955	660	4045	2228	1817
				R	92327	45961	46366	12149	9000	3149	1273	750	523	3028	1658	1370
				U	25338	13546	11792	4339	3412	927	327	194	133	958	536	422
			ii. In other district	T	82459	41963	40496	17285	13030	4255	1773	1055	718	5676	3175	2501
				R	52849	26768	26081	10853	8237	2616	1076	626	450	3894	2203	1691
				U	25645	13205	12440	6175	4613	1562	680	417	263	1685	917	768
		II. States/Uts in India beyond the State of enumeration		T	35293	22907	12386	12826	11464	1362	1000	873	127	898	468	430
				R	21263	13386	7877	7000	6151	849	464	392	72	523	287	236
				U	12182	8351	3831	5485	5013	472	523	470	53	355	172	183
		B. Last Residence outside India		T	15487	7887	7600	2889	1888	1001	654	349	305	94	62	32
		C. Countries in Asia beyond India		T	15465	7878	7587	2887	1886	1001	654	349	305	93	62	31
		D. Other Countries		T	22	9	13	2	2	0	0	0	0	1	0	1
		Total Migration		**T**	**268932**	**141440**	**127492**	**49781**	**38985**	**10796**	**5042**	**3232**	**1810**	**10713**	**5933**	**4780**
6	Nagaland	**A.** Last residence elsewhere in India		T	374016	207460	166556	54486	46048	8438	14497	13084	1413	8947	5323	3624
				R	166870	93956	72914	34941	29566	5375	7950	7137	813	5717	3451	2266
				U	84039	48026	36013	18387	15541	2846	6199	5640	559	2850	1632	1218

1	2	3		4	5	6	7	8	9	10	11	12	13	14	15	16
		I. Within the State of enumeration	i. Elsewhere in the district	T	220979	118459	102520	15093	12390	2703	3029	2565	464	3314	2041	1273
				R	84589	45502	39087	10609	8666	943	1687	1390	297	2331	1464	867
				U	33489	18597	14892	4109	3422	687	1240	1090	150	850	499	351
			ii. In other district	T	71460	37906	33554	15989	12664	3325	1883	1522	361	4668	2651	2017
				R	37254	19927	17327	9654	7741	1913	1096	882	214	2860	1642	1218
				U	22685	12049	10636	6026	4696	1330	761	622	139	1611	882	729
		II. States/Uts in India beyond the State of enumeration		T	81577	51095	30482	23404	20994	2410	9585	8997	588	965	631	334
				R	45027	28527	16500	14678	13159	1519	5167	4865	302	526	345	181
				U	27865	17380	10485	8252	7423	829	4198	3928	270	389	251	138
		B. Last Residence outside India		T	6793	4243	2550	1956	1768	188	327	272	55	66	45	21
		C. Countries in Asia beyond India		T	5610	3581	2029	1882	1699	183	310	256	54	53	36	17
		D. Other Countries		T	1186	664	522	74	69	5	17	16	1	13	9	4
		Total Migration		**T**	**380812**	**211705**	**169107**	**56442**	**47816**	**8626**	**14824**	**13356**	**1468**	**9013**	**5368**	**3645**
7	Tripura	**A.** Last residence elsewhere in India		T	700022	268937	431085	43192	35990	7202	6830	6222	608	7664	5321	2343
				R	452977	143516	309461	34510	28517	5993	5197	4719	478	6581	4567	2014
				U	63329	24960	38369	7816	6794	1022	1484	1381	103	904	636	268
		I. Within the State of enumeration	i. Elsewhere in the district	T	536875	198802	338073	24671	20416	4255	4662	4219	443	5639	3840	1799
				R	339409	97397	242012	21100	17406	3694	3774	3407	367	5032	3416	1616
				U	37284	13980	23304	3035	2590	445	775	716	59	467	335	132
			ii. In other district	T	99369	39631	59738	10880	9253	1627	1200	1112	88	1664	1220	444
				R	65721	23010	42711	8114	6873	1241	866	802	64	1366	1014	352
				U	14377	5698	8679	2580	2243	337	315	295	20	270	184	86
		II. States/Uts in India beyond the State of enumeration		T	63778	30504	33274	7641	6321	1320	968	891	77	361	261	100
				R	47847	23109	24738	5296	4238	1058	557	510	47	183	137	46
				U	11668	5282	6386	2201	1961	240	394	370	24	167	117	50

1	2	3	4	5	6	7	8	9	10	11	12	13	14	15	16
		B. Last Residence outside India	T	261631	134992	126639	8581	7455	1126	2313	2071	242	1146	947	199
		C. Countries in Asia beyond India	T	261602	134980	126622	8579	7454	1125	2312	2070	242	1145	947	198
		D. Other Countries	T	29	12	17	2	1	1	1	1	0	1	0	1
		Total Migration	**T**	**961653**	**403929**	**557724**	**51773**	**43445**	**8328**	**9143**	**8293**	**850**	**8810**	**6268**	**2542**
8	Sikkim	**A.** Last residence elsewhere in India	T	168751	79402	89349	35487	29817	5670	3819	3413	406	3797	2241	1556
			R	118250	52142	66108	27133	22731	4402	2581	2293	288	2836	1639	1197
			U	27938	15172	12766	7436	6336	1100	1126	1027	99	848	540	308
		I. Within the State of enumeration — i. Elsewhere in the district	T	90451	38913	51538	12468	10199	2269	1047	872	175	1905	1096	809
			R	63805	24994	38811	10472	8558	1914	759	611	148	1561	902	659
			U	9894	5175	4719	1605	1325	280	252	232	20	269	158	111
		ii. In other district	T	32267	14915	17352	7781	6440	1341	395	332	63	1121	645	476
			R	24503	10889	13614	6161	5103	1058	275	229	46	909	527	382
			U	5068	2709	2359	1400	1158	242	115	100	15	188	100	88
		II. States/Uts in India beyond the State of enumeration	T	46033	25574	20459	15238	13178	2060	2377	2209	168	771	500	271
			R	29942	16259	13683	10500	9070	1430	1547	1453	94	366	210	156
			U	12976	7288	5688	4431	3853	578	759	695	64	391	282	109
		B. Last Residence outside India	T	18236	9826	8410	6360	5308	1052	161	130	31	432	377	55
		C. Countries in Asia beyond India	T	18196	9812	8384	6354	5303	1051	157	127	30	431	376	55
		D. Other Countries	T	40	14	26	6	5	1	4	3	1	1	1	0
		Total Migration	**T**	**186987**	**89228**	**97759**	**41847**	**35125**	**6722**	**3980**	**3543**	**437**	**4229**	**2618**	**1611**

Source: Website, Registrar General and Census Commissioner, India.

Appendix-9.4 (*cont.*)

Migration by Sex, Place of last Residence, Duration of Residence and Reason for Migration as per different Census Years

Sl. No.	Name of the State	Last Residence		Rural or Urban status of last Residence	Census Year, 2001											
					All duration of Residence											
					Reason for Migration											
					Family moved			Marriage			Natural Calamities/Moved after Birth			Others		
					Person	Male	Female	Person	Male	Female	Person	Male	Female	Person	Male	Female
1	2	3		4	17	18	19	20	21	22	23	24	25	26	27	28
1	Arunachal Pradesh	**A.** Last residence elsewhere in India		T	109859	42315	67544	51294	987	50307	5369	2818	2551	106766	60386	46380
				R	80215	31130	49085	45640	871	44769	3253	1737	1516	51620	30157	21463
				U	24591	9068	15523	4135	83	4052	1879	956	923	10544	5926	4618
		I. Within the State of enumeration	i. Elsewhere in the district	T	47555	19460	28095	33555	692	32863	2735	1431	1304	70000	37709	32291
				R	37120	14933	22187	31684	636	31048	1747	925	822	31348	17437	13911
				U	7766	3329	4437	864	30	834	884	452	432	4241	2174	2067
			ii. In other district	T	23882	9000	14882	3959	125	3834	679	342	337	12439	6967	5472
				R	14930	5744	9186	3340	111	3229	426	226	200	6875	3932	2943

1	2	3		4	17	18	19	20	21	22	23	24	25	26	27	28
				U	81300	2918	5212	517	13	504	236	108	128	2075	1123	952
		II. States/Uts in India beyond the State of enumeration		T	38422	13855	24567	13780	170	13610	1955	1045	910	24327	15710	8617
				R	28165	10453	17712	10616	124	10492	1080	586	494	13397	8788	4609
				U	8695	2821	5874	2754	40	2714	759	396	363	4228	2629	1599
		B. Last Residence outside India		T	4426	1552	2874	978	30	948	49	27	22	7198	4308	2890
		C. Countries in Asia beyond India		T	4412	1545	2867	976	30	946	47	26	21	7177	4294	2883
		D. Other Countries		T	14	7	7	2	0	2	2	1	1	21	14	7
		Total Migration		**T**	**114285**	**43867**	**70418**	**52272**	**1017**	**51255**	**5418**	**2845**	**2573**	**113964**	**64694**	**49270**
2	Assam	**A.** Last residence elsewhere in India		T	969419	491257	478162	2462643	41797	2420846	69870	46705	23165	2555591	1468658	1086933
				R	775233	397755	377478	2247974	38303	2209671	45267	32445	12822	1037742	606951	430791
				U	159731	75806	83925	164041	2445	161596	21503	12291	9212	196935	106190	90745
		I. Within the State of enumeration	i. Elsewhere in the district	T	616897	322795	294102	1949819	32090	1917729	52143	35824	16319	2200847	1255090	945757
				R	508375	265698	242677	1834805	29918	1804887	35849	26298	9551	828131	472389	355742
				U	83995	44116	39879	75304	1343	73961	13960	8029	5931	150418	81630	68788
			ii. In other district	T	253384	124311	129073	421940	7069	414871	11824	7299	4525	270999	158832	112167
				R	203570	102612	100958	350405	6196	344209	6474	4240	2234	163985	102517	61468
				U	42591	18227	24364	62571	715	61856	4821	2731	2090	30189	15186	15003
		II. States/Uts in India beyond the State of enumeration		T	99138	44151	54987	90884	2638	88246	5903	3582	2321	83745	54736	29009
				R	63288	29445	33843	62764	2189	60575	2944	1907	1037	45626	32045	13581
				U	33145	13463	19682	26166	387	25779	2722	1531	1191	16328	9374	6954
		B. Last Residence outside		T	55366	28519	26847	15982	444	15538	761	513	248	46800	29616	17184

1	2	3		4	17	18	19	20	21	22	23	24	25	26	27	28
		India														
		C. Countries in Asia beyond India		T	55301	28495	26306	15959	443	15516	756	511	245	46723	29564	17159
		D. Other Countries		T	65	24	41	23	1	22	5	2	3	77	52	25
		Total Migration		**T**	**1024785**	**519776**	**505009**	**2478625**	**42241**	**2436384**	**70631**	**47218**	**23413**	**2602391**	**1498274**	**1104117**
3	Manipur	**A.** Last residence elsewhere in India		T	41395	20690	20705	95406	1432	93974	1375	706	669	216465	116782	99683
				R	32426	16297	16129	72760	1106	71654	1090	562	528	69593	36764	32829
				U	7150	3470	3680	20430	291	20139	236	122	114	12967	6494	6473
		I. Within the State of enumeration	i. Elsewhere in the district	T	25360	13039	12321	77468	1076	76392	1142	580	562	187067	100723	86344
				R	20006	10361	9645	59731	852	58879	1007	516	491	59732	31382	28350
				U	4298	2153	2145	16031	197	15834	100	48	52	9886	4939	4947
			ii. In other district	T	12391	5888	6503	15612	252	15360	179	89	90	23956	12554	11402
				R	9889	4647	5242	11416	176	11240	56	26	30	8002	4244	3758
				U	1842	898	944	3756	71	3685	112	60	52	2039	953	1086
		II. States/Uts in India beyond the State of enumeration		T	3644	1763	1881	2326	104	2222	54	37	17	5442	3505	1937
				R	2531	1289	1242	1613	78	1535	27	20	7	1859	1138	721
				U	1010	419	591	643	23	620	24	14	10	1042	602	440
		B. Last Residence outside India		T	542	276	266	134	3	131	6	4	2	439	278	161
		C. Countries in Asia beyond India		T	540	275	265	132	3	129	6	4	2	426	268	158
		D. Other Countries		T	2	1	1	2	0	2	0	0	0	13	10	3
		Total Migration		**T**	**41937**	**20966**	**20971**	**95540**	**1435**	**94105**	**1381**	**710**	**671**	**216904**	**117060**	**99844**

1	2	3			4	17	18	19	20	21	22	23	24	25	26	27	28
4	Meghalaya	**A.** Last residence elsewhere in India			T	40882	17565	23317	39629	16013	23616	6675	3413	3262	229884	121365	108519
					R	28321	12447	15874	30649	13769	16880	2184	1141	1043	75183	40479	34704
					U	10514	4194	6320	7622	1707	5915	4046	2047	1999	23462	12429	11033
		I. Within the State of enumera-tion	i. Else-where in the district		T	17476	8221	9255	18742	11291	7451	4834	2406	2428	188194	97498	90696
					R	12911	5984	6927	16321	10015	6306	1308	666	642	57544	30346	27198
					U	3439	1672	1767	1869	925	944	3177	1567	1610	16176	8396	7780
			ii. In other district		T	7122	2988	4134	4804	2773	2031	596	304	292	19243	10304	8939
					R	5403	2301	3102	3786	2270	1516	293	151	142	7412	3940	3472
					U	1396	550	846	837	397	440	257	136	121	1891	970	921
		II. States/Uts in India beyond the State of enumeration			T	16284	6356	9928	16083	1949	14134	1245	703	542	22447	13563	8884
					R	10007	4162	5845	10542	1484	9058	583	324	259	10227	6193	4034
					U	5679	1972	3707	4916	385	4531	612	344	268	5395	3063	2332
		B. Last Residence outside India			T	2066	985	1081	998	274	724	91	47	44	4591	2895	1696
		C. Countries in Asia beyond India			T	2059	980	1079	994	273	721	91	47	44	4571	2883	16[illegible]8
		D. Other Countries			T	7	5	2	4	1	3	0	0	0	20	12	8
		Total Migration			T	**42948**	**18550**	**24398**	**40627**	**16287**	**24340**	**6766**	**3460**	**3306**	**234475**	**124260**	**110215**
5	Mizoram	**A.** Last residence elsewhere in India			T	101006	46545	54461	20472	2465	18007	4895	2628	2267	65173	36064	29109
					R	75750	35258	40492	15527	1849	13678	2038	1102	936	32864	18602	14262
					U	23088	10244	12844	4575	578	3997	2703	1442	1261	12272	7094	5178
		I. Within the State of enumera-	i. Else-where in the district		T	55223	25972	29251	11277	1413	9864	3116	1686	1430	43636	23826	19810
					R	44578	20982	23596	9300	1148	8152	1426	791	635	20573	11632	8941
					U	9572	4462	5110	1782	243	1539	1583	833	750	6777	3866	2911

1	2	3		4	17	18	19	20	21	22	23	24	25	26	27	28
		tion	ii. In other district	T	33919	15062	18857	7229	768	6461	1487	796	691	15090	8077	7013
				R	23025	10371	12654	5040	507	4533	466	248	218	8495	4576	3919
				U	10135	4326	5809	2069	251	1818	980	528	452	3921	2153	1768
		II. States/Uts in India beyond the State of enumeration		T	11864	5511	6353	1966	284	1682	292	146	146	6447	4161	2286
				R	8147	3905	4242	1187	194	993	146	63	83	3796	2394	1402
				U	3381	1456	1925	724	84	640	140	81	59	1574	1075	499
		B. Last Residence outside India		T	6203	2915	3288	1495	256	1239	65	38	27	4087	2379	1708
		C. Countries in Asia beyond India		T	6192	2909	3283	1494	256	1238	65	38	27	4080	2378	1702
		D. Other Countries		T	11	6	5	1	0	1	0	0	0	7	1	6
		Total Migration		**T**	**107209**	**49460**	**57749**	**21967**	**2721**	**19246**	**4960**	**2666**	**2294**	**69260**	**38443**	**30817**
6	Nagaland	**A.** Last residence elsewhere in India		T	56284	24023	32261	20891	918	19973	3504	1927	1577	215407	116137	99270
				R	35962	15322	20640	13742	701	13041	2125	1153	972	66433	36626	29807
				U	17651	7474	10177	6506	196	6310	1166	652	514	31280	16891	14389
		I. Within the State of enumeration	i. Elsewhere in the district	T	24011	11562	12449	6745	557	6188	1576	863	713	167211	88481	78730
				R	15942	7494	8448	5085	461	4624	1033	558	475	47902	25469	22433
				U	6506	3291	3215	1462	88	1374	451	247	204	18871	9960	8911
			ii. In other district	T	16310	6758	9552	5951	221	5730	741	410	331	25918	13680	12238
				R	9921	4105	5816	3902	157	3745	397	225	172	9424	5175	4249
				U	5874	2428	3446	1908	59	1849	283	155	128	6222	3207	3015
		II. States/Uts in India beyond the State of enumeration		T	15963	5703	10260	8195	140	8055	1187	654	533	22278	13976	8302
				R	10099	3723	6376	4755	83	4672	695	370	325	9107	5982	3125
				U	5271	1755	3516	3136	49	3087	432	250	182	6187	3724	2463

1	2	3	4	17	18	19	20	21	22	23	24	25	26	27	28
		B. Last Residence outside India	T	1140	438	702	550	31	519	59	48	11	2695	1641	1054
		C. Countries in Asia beyond India	T	1100	420	680	522	31	491	57	47	10	1686	1092	594
		D. Other Countries	T	40	18	22	28	0	28	2	1	1	1012	551	461
		Total Migration	**T**	**57424**	**24461**	**32963**	**21441**	**949**	**20492**	**3563**	**1975**	**1588**	**218105**	**117780**	**100325**
7	Tripura	**A.** Last residence elsewhere in India	T	115040	53883	61157	246477	7334	239143	4689	2802	1887	276130	157385	118745
			R	92964	43480	49484	217934	6831	211103	2226	1409	817	93565	53993	39572
			U	17033	7852	9181	22771	372	22399	2268	1277	991	11053	6648	4405
		I. Within the State of enumeration — i. Elsewhere in the district	T	80913	38814	42099	200710	6012	194698	3520	2128	1392	216760	123373	93387
			R	66990	31886	35104	181752	5680	176072	1723	1089	634	59038	34513	24525
			U	9838	4819	5019	14298	229	14069	1647	945	702	7224	4346	2878
		ii. In other district	T	18844	8434	10410	35646	1056	34590	838	498	340	30297	18058	12239
			R	14657	6608	8049	29360	954	28406	382	252	130	10976	6507	4469
			U	3556	1516	2040	5373	81	5292	429	233	196	1854	1146	708
		II. States/Uts in India beyond the State of enumeration	T	15283	6635	8648	10121	266	9855	331	176	155	29073	15954	13119
			R	11317	4986	6331	6822	197	6625	121	68	53	23551	12973	10578
			U	3639	1517	2122	3100	62	3038	192	99	93	1975	1156	819
		B. Last Residence outside India	T	115624	56619	59005	29472	885	28587	623	400	223	103872	66615	37257
		C. Countries in Asia beyond India	T	115610	56612	58998	29463	884	28579	622	399	223	103871	66614	37257
		D. Other Countries	T	14	7	7	9	1	8	1	1	0	1	1	0
		Total Migration	**T**	**230664**	**110502**	**120162**	**275949**	**8219**	**267730**	**5312**	**3202**	**2110**	**380002**	**224000**	**156002**

1	2	3		4	17	18	19	20	21	22	23	24	25	26	27	28
8	Sikkim	**A.** Last residence elsewhere in India		T	32556	15202	17354	43988	846	43142	3500	1996	1504	45604	25887	19717
				R	24077	11478	12599	38072	725	37347	1801	1061	740	21750	12215	9535
				U	6934	2957	3977	4287	93	4194	1565	866	699	5742	3353	2389
		I. Within the State of enumeration	i. Elsewhere in the district	T	17434	8621	8813	25425	496	24929	2088	1203	885	30084	16426	13658
				R	13639	6815	6824	23293	441	22852	1158	690	468	12923	6977	5946
				U	2749	1275	1474	1154	38	1116	839	464	375	3026	1683	1343
			ii. In other district	T	7013	3211	3802	8507	178	8329	635	331	304	6815	3778	3037
				R	5231	2447	2784	7527	156	7371	258	134	124	4142	2293	1849
				U	1519	632	887	621	13	608	355	189	166	870	517	353
		II. States/Uts in India beyond the State of enumeration		T	8109	3370	4739	10056	172	9884	777	462	315	8705	5683	3022
				R	5207	2216	2991	7252	128	7124	385	237	148	4685	2945	1740
				U	2666	1050	1616	2512	42	2470	371	213	158	1846	1153	693
		B. Last Residence outside India		T	3217	1485	1732	4261	118	4143	104	76	28	3701	2332	1369
		C. Countries in Asia beyond India		T	3212	1483	1729	4246	118	4128	102	75	27	3694	2330	1364
		D. Other Countries		T	5	2	3	15	0	15	2	1	1	7	2	5
		Total Migration		**T**	**35773**	**16687**	**19086**	**48249**	**964**	**47285**	**3604**	**2072**	**1532**	**49305**	**28219**	**21086**

Source: website, Registrar General and Census Commissioner, India.

Appendix 9.5

Absolute and Percentage Distribution of Migration according to Reasons as per different Census Years

Sl. No.	Name of the State	Census years	Total Migration from outside/ % of total population	Reasons for Migration (with absolute number and per cent)						
				Employment	Business	Education	Family moved	Marriage	Natural calamities/ after birth	Others
1	2	3	4	5	6	7	8	9	10	11
1	Arunachal Pradesh	1971	69820 (14.93)	-	-	-	-	-	-	-
		1981	83683 (13.24)	29009 (34.67)	-	1415 (1.69)	31058 (37.11)	4870 (5.82)	-	17331 (20.71)
		1991	98966 (11.45)	29937 (30.25)	7235 (7.31)	1752 (1.77)	35231 (35.60)	11530 (11.65)	1630 (1.65)	11651 (11.77)
		2001	153624 (13.99)	52672 (34.29)	8717 (5.67)	1100 (0.72)	42848 (27.89)	14758 (9.61)	2004 (1.30)	31525 (20.52)
2	Assam	1971	1522461 (10.18)	-	-	-	-	-	-	-
		1981	-	-	-	-	-	-	-	-
		1991	710977 (3.17)	81885 (11.52)	86977 (12.23)	11370 (1.60)	216493 (30.45)	153462 (21.58)	5170 (0.73)	155620 (21.89)
		2001	538107 (2.02)	71710 (13.33)	63088 (11.72)	4730 (0.88)	154504 (28.71)	106866 (19.86)	6664 (1.24)	130545 (24.26)

1	2	3	4	5	6	7	8	9	10	11
3	Manipur	1971	37547 (3.50)	-	-	-	-	-	-	-
		1981	27294 (1.92)	5701 (20.89)	-	709 (2.60)	12731 (46.64)	3404 (12.47)	-	4749 (17.40)
		1991	16719 (0.91)	2398 (14.34)	2189 (13.09)	86 (0.51)	6886 (41.19)	2545 (15.22)	170 (1.02)	2445 (14.63)
		2001	16201 (0.75)	2043 (12.61)	1389 (8.57)	182 (1.12)	4186 (25.84)	2460 (15.19)	60 (0.37)	5881 (36.30)
4	Meghalaya	1971	117066 (11.57)	-	-	-	-	-	-	-
		1981	83473 (6.25)	20115 (24.10)	-	4920 (5.89)	27945 (33.48)	11755 (14.08)	-	18738 (22.45)
		1991	83749 (4.72)	15732 (18.78)	6826 (8.15)	3377 (4.03)	25372 (30.30)	16667 (19.90)	2208 (2.64)	13567 (16.20)
		2001	92704 (4.00)	19997 (21.57)	4775 (5.15)	4127 (4.45)	18350 (19.79)	17081 (18.43)	1336 (1.44)	27038 (29.17)
5	Mizoram	1971	-	-	-	-	-	-	-	-
		1981	20125 (4.08)	6304 (31.32)	-	322 (1.60)	9031 (44.88)	545 (2.71)	-	3923 (19.49)
		1991	11309 (1.64)	2826 (24.99)	686 (6.07)	186 (1.64)	4800 (42.45)	811 (7.17)	33 (0.29)	1967 (17.39)
		2001	50780 (5.71)	15715 (30.95)	1654 (3.26)	992 (1.95)	18067 (35.58)	3461 (6.82)	357 (0.70)	10534 (20.74)
6	Nagaland	1971	49515 (9.59)	-	-	-	-	-	-	-

1	2	3	4	5	6	7	8	9	10	11
		1981	63522 (8.20)	19167 (30.17)	-	1707 (2.69)	20516 (32.30)	4123 (6.49)	-	18009 (28.35)
		1991	46438 (3.84)	13014 (28.02)	8819 (18.99)	1043 (2.25)	12464 (26.84)	4723 (10.17)	309 (0.67)	6066 (13.06)
		2001	88370 (4.44)	25360 (28.70)	9912 (11.22)	1031 (1.17)	17103 (19.35)	8745 (9.89)	1246 (1.41)	24973 (28.26)
7	Tripura	1971	555467 (35.69)	-	-	-	-	-	-	-
		1981	86517 (4.21)	10821 (12.51)	-	1167 (1.35)	25650 (29.64)	8088 (9.35)	-	40791 (47.15)
		1991	310752 (11.27)	15732 (5.06)	3002 (0.97)	1569 (0.50)	109893 (35.36)	38081 (12.26)	199 (0.06)	142276 (45.79)
		2001	325409 (10.17)	16222 (4.99)	3281 (1.01)	1507 (0.46)	130907 (40.23)	39593 (12.17)	954 (0.29)	132945 (40.85)
8	Sikkim	1971	21056 (10.03)	-	-	-	-	-	-	-
		1981	32418 (10.25)	10780 (33.25)	-	921 (2.84)	8962 (27.65)	4793 (14.78)	-	6962 (21.48)
		1991	29032 (7.14)	7565 (26.06)	2562 (8.82)	709 (2.44)	7202 (24.81)	6105 (21.03)	68 (0.23)	4821 (16.61)
		2001	64269 (11.88)	21598 (33.61)	2538 (3.95)	1203 (1.87)	11326 (17.62)	14317 (22.28)	881 (1.37)	12406 (19.30)

Source: Calculated from the information of relevant Appendices.

\- means, information not available.

10
Conclusions

Demography is the Scientific study of human population, particularly their size, composition and distribution, which changes over time or space, primarily due to Birth, Death and Migration. The size normally refers to the number of people living in a given place at a given time, composition refers mainly to age, sex, education, religion, social group, marital and residential status, while distribution refers to occupation and activity status of population. The change in the population size due to birth relates to the fertility, i.e. the actual birth performances of the group of women or to the relative frequency with which the births occur in that population. Fertility is again a matter of fecundity, i.e. the physiological capacity of the women to reproduce during their child bearing span. The death has also a vital role in the change of population size. The physiological change in population depends on the absolute increase, i.e. the total number of Births–(minus) the total number of Deaths, over a period of time. But, Migration plays a very vital role in changing the size of population, for which there is no particular reason, time or space.

In the North Eastern Region, there is no separate Demographic Institute or Study Centre or Research Centre, as such. The subject is being taught at the post-graduate level in some of the Universities of this Region, as a paper in Statistics. Perhaps, so far, no comprehensive Study or Research work has been done, nor any Book is available on Demography of the North East India. The Demographic information is available only in the Census Publications. The Census information has its own formats and limitations and that serves the general purposes only, not the specific one. But using the Census information, it is possible to do any kind of Demographic study. The present book, entitled "Demographic Scenario of the North East India" is entirely based on the Census information.

In the North Eastern Region, most of the States are hilly and Tribal dominated. And from the available information, it is seen that the original people of this Region is a mixture of Non-Aryan, Mongolian, Monkhmer, Bodo, Manipuris, Tripuris, Lepchas, Nepalis, Bhutias, Tibetans etc., though there is no record available about their sizes. Not only this, no record was even available about the population of our country till conducting the first population Census in 1872. And in case of North Eastern States, population record is available only from 1901, but for Arunachal Pradesh, it is from 1961. However, it is seen that, the growth of population in the North Eastern States does not follow any particular trend. In the initial years from 1901, the growth was rather slow, but from fifties and sixties, population started increasing very rapidly.

In the present study, an attempt has been made to show the Demographic changes that had been taken place in the North Eastern States over a period of 50 (fifty) years, i.e. the period from 1961 Census to 2011 Census, though there are some lapses due to non-availability of information in some cases for different periods. In the States like Arunachal Pradesh, Nagaland, Mizoram and Meghalaya, where Scheduled Tribe (ST) people are more and Scheduled Caste (SC) people are very less. For the convenience of this study, another group *viz.* 'Others' has been formed with the remaining people, i.e. other than ST and SC. The people in this group are non-ST and non-SC, who have come to these States, mostly from other States of India, primarily for Govt. Service and other Economic activities, as there was a shortage of educated and skilled manpower in the initial periods of Planned Development.

It is seen that, within a period of last 50 (fifty) years, i.e. from 1961 to 2011, the growth of population was much more faster in Urban than Rural, for all the three groups of people, i.e. ST, SC and Others, in almost all the N.E. States. That is also an indication of rapid Urban Development. Further, it is seen that, in Urban areas, the growth rate of ST people was always higher than the growth rate of 'Others', in all the States. It is seen that, within a period of 50 (fifty) years, the growth for ST was ranging from the lowest of 7.62 times of Meghalaya to the highest of 45.69 times of Arunachal Pradesh. And in case of 'Others', it was the lowest of 1.48 times of Meghalaya to the highest of 25.98 times of Mizoram. In Rural areas, the growth rate for ST was not more than 'Others' in all the States. The growth of ST people was the lowest of 1.04 times in Mizoram to the highest of 3.31 times in Manipur.

Whereas, the growth of 'Others' was the lowest of 0.48 times in Sikkim to the highest of 5.21 times in Nagaland, in this period.

In the North Eastern States, mainly, people of 4 (four) major religious groups *viz.* (i) Hindus, (ii) Muslims, (iii) Christians, and (iv) Buddhists, are living. The people of another 2 (two) religious groups, i.e. Sikhs and Jains are also there in all the States, but their numbers are very less. It is seen that, amongst the major religious groups, *viz.* Hindus, Muslims and Christians, the growth of Hindus was comparatively less and over the years, it showed a declining trend in all the North Eastern States. Whereas, the Muslims were growing rapidly in all the NE States and the growth of Christians was also very fast, particularly in Arunachal Pradesh, Manipur, Meghalaya, Mizoram and Nagaland, though the growth rate showed some ups and downs at different points of time.

It has been observed that, within a period of last 40 (forty) years, i.e. from 1971 to 2011, the growth of Hindus was the lowest of 0.42 times in Mizoram to the highest of 2.91 times in Arunachal Pradesh. The growth of Muslims was much faster in all the States. The growth was ranging from the lowest of 2.04 times in Tripura to the highest of 31.12 times in Arunachal Pradesh. The growth rate of Christians was also quite high in many of the Tribal dominated States. The growth was the lowest of 2.06 times in Assam and the highest to the extent of 112.66 times in Arunachal Pradesh during this period. This high growth cannot be attributed to the birth alone. It indicates that, many of the people opted for Christianity, time to time. Buddhist people are mostly in Arunachal Pradesh, Mizoram, Tripura and Sikkim. Their growth rate maintained more or less a declining trend.

It is seen that, in sixties and seventies, the growth rate of Hindus was showing an increasing trend, but later on, it started declining with a faster pace, particularly in the Tribal dominated States. It has been observed that, in the initial period of Planning era, there was a shortage of educated and skilled manpower in these States and as such, many people went there for employment, time to time, from other States of the Country, who were mostly Hindus. But, over the years, the local people became educated and started taking over the jobs and dependency on outside employees started declining. Moreover, many of the local Governments formulated their own recruitment policies and started giving preferences to the local people. Even in C and D categories, almost hundred per cent jobs, kept reserved for the local candidates, in many of these States. Moreover, other than local people, no one has any right to land and properties, therefore, outsiders gradually started leaving the States.

In case of Workers and Non-workers, it is seen that, the proportion of Workers was much less than the proportion of Non-workers in all the North Eastern States except Arunachal Pradesh. In seventies and eighties, in Arunachal Pradesh, the proportion of Main workers was higher than the proportion of Non-workers, and thereafter, the proportion of Non-workers started increasing. Further, it is seen that, in case of Main workers, the proportion of Males was more than the proportion of Females in all the North Eastern States. However, it is also seen that, in some of the tribal dominated States, like Arunachal Pradesh, Meghalaya, Mizoram, Nagaland, Manipur and Sikkim, the proportion of Female Main workers was quite high and in many cases, there was no much difference between the proportional value of Male Main workers and the proportional value of Female Main workers. That indicates that, Tribal Females are more active and they take equal part in Agricultural and other economic activities. It is also seen that, the proportion of Female Main workers was higher in the Rural areas than in the Urban areas. But, Male Main workers did not follow any specific rule. Sometimes, it was more in Rural and sometimes it was more in Urban.

The Marginal workers however, showed a unique trend in all the NE States. It is seen that, the proportion of Female Marginal workers was higher than the proportion of Male Marginal workers in most of the cases, both in Rural and Urban. It is also seen that, the proportion of Female Marginal workers was higher in Rural than Urban with a few exceptions. From this it is evident that, compared to Males, more number of Females, particularly Rural Females, are going for the job of Marginal worker.

The Non-workers play completely a different role. It occupies the major portion of the population of the States or of the country. In some cases, it is seen that, almost three fourth of the population are Non-workers. Further, it is seen that, the Non-workers are more in Urban areas than Rural areas. However, the proportion of Female Non-workers was always much higher than the proportion of Male Non-workers, both in Rural as well as in Urban.

The children are also considered as Non-workers. They occupy a considerable portion of population of the States or of the country. However, their proportion, though vary from state to state and time to time, but not to a large extent. Generally, the proportion of children is higher in Rural areas than in Urban areas. Moreover, the proportion of Girls is higher than the proportion of Boys in many of the North Eastern States. This is also true both in Rural as well as in Urban with a few exceptions. It is also a fact that, the proportion of children is showing a declining trend over the years.

Literacy is one of the most important characteristics of human beings. It defines the ability of a person to read and write. And the literacy rate is also one of the key indicators of human development. That means, higher the literacy rate—higher the number of educated and skilled manpower, which is very much essential for the socio-economic development of a state or of a country.

It is seen that, even in early sixties, the states *viz.* Arunachal Pradesh, Sikkim and Nagaland, were very much lacking in education. In 1961, the literacy rate in Arunachal Pradesh was only 7.13 per cent, in Sikkim, it was 12.33 per cent and in Nagaland, it was 17.91 per cent. However, over the years, the literacy rate started increasing and by 2011, the literacy rate in Arunachal Pradesh reached to 66.95 per cent, in Sikkim, it touched to the height of 82.20 per cent and in Nagaland, it reached to 80.11 per cent. That indicates that, the literacy was increasing with a faster pace in the North Eastern States.

However, it is seen that, the literacy rate for Males is higher than the literacy rate for Females in all the NE States. In the beginning of sixties, the literacy gap between Males and Females was though more, but over the years, this gap narrowed down in all the States except Arunachal Pradesh. In 1961, the literacy gap in Arunachal Pradesh was 10.83 per cent, which increased to 14.12 per cent in 2011. This indicates that, the education of Girl Child is lagging behind or in other words, Girls are not coming forward for education, as the Boys are, in Arunachal Pradesh.

It is a fact that, in urban areas, educational facilities are more. Moreover, Government Offices, Business Establishment, Industry and other economic activities are more in urban and therefore, the number of educated persons are comparatively more in urban areas. That means, the literacy rate is normally more in urban than in rural. But, it is seen that, amongst all the North Eastern States, the Rural-Urban literacy gap is more in Arunachal Pradesh, Nagaland, Meghalaya and Tripura.

Migration is one of the main factors of population change. It affects the size of population mainly in 2 (two) ways, i.e. In-Migration and Out-Migration. But, there is no particular time, place or reason for

Migration. It may be due to natural calamities, wars, fire, drought, political extremism, education, employment, marriage, business and other economic activities etc. The North Eastern States, particularly Assam, Tripura and Meghalaya suffered from the problem of Migration, particularly by the Bengali Hindu Migrants from Bangladesh, the then East Bengal, at different points of times, primarily due to political extremism.

In remaining States of North Eastern Region, Migration was mainly from other States of India. As mentioned earlier, in sixties and seventies, there was a shortage of educated and skilled manpower in these States and as such, many people, who were mostly Hindus, went there for employment and other economic activities, time to time, from other States of our Country. However, from eighties onwards, the situation started changing and there were gradual Out-Migration from these States.

It is seen that, the Hindus, particularly Bengali Hindus are the most sufferer in the North Eastern Region even from the Pre-Independence period. In British days, the Bengali speaking Sylhet District was a part of Assam and many people from that District was in the Government services and was playing a dominant role. This was not liked by the Assamese people and by the Assam Congress and they always tried to get rid of Sylhet District and of Bengali speaking people. In the backdrop of Referendum, held just before Independence, Shri Tathagata Roy mentioned that, "The Assam Congress, led by Gopinath Bardoloi and his group, wanted the district to go to Pakistan so that the hegemony of their group would be assured in the rump province of Assam after independence."[1] Finally, the result of the unfair Referendum went in favour of Assamese people and Sylhet (except a very small portion) went to East Pakistan, the then East Bengal, and they achieved their desired goal.

Regarding separation of Sylhet District and in connection with immigration Shri Sujit Chaudhuri mentioned that, the Assam Pradesh Congress Committee in 1945, in its election manifesto, stated "Unless the province of Assam is organized on the basis of Assamese language and Assamese culture, the survival of the Assamese nationality and culture will become impossible. The inclusion of Bengali speaking Sylhet and Cachar and immigration or importation of lacs of Bengali settlers on wasteland has been threatening to destroy the distinctiveness of Assam and has, in practice, caused many disorders in its administration."[2] Regarding immigration, Shri Chaudhuri further said,

"Immigration has been a matter of concern for the people of Assam since the turn of the 20th century and what is today known as the 'foreigners' problem is simply a projection of this old unresolved issue under a new nomenclature."[3]

Regarding the attitude of the Assam Ministry towards the influx of refugee Shri Chaudhuri mentioned about a government circular issued on 4th May, 1948 which states that, "In view of the emergency created by the influx of refugees into the province from East Pakistan territories and in order to preserve peace, tranquility and social equilibrium in the towns and villages, the government reiterates its policy that, settlement of land should be in no circumstances made with persons who are not indigenous to the province. The non-indigenous inhabitants of the province should include, for the purpose of land settlement during the present emergency, persons who are non-Assamese settlers in Assam though they already have lands and houses of their own and have made Assam their home to all intents and purposes."[4]

Further, to show disregard and to corner the Bengali Hindus, the Assamese leadership did not even hesitate to go for an unholy alliance with the Bengali Muslims. In this connection, Shri Chaudhuri mentioned about Myron Weiner, who stated that, "After 1947 the Bengali Muslims became *de facto* allies of the Assamese in their conflict with the Bengali Hindus. Bengali Muslims have been willing to accept Assamese as the medium of instruction in their schools, and have thrown their votes behind Assamese candidates for the state Assembly and the national Parliament. They have declared Assamese as their mother tongue. In return, the state government has not attempted to eject Bengali Muslims from lands on which they have settled in the Brahmaputra valley, though earlier leaders had claimed that much of the settlement had taken place illegally. There is thus an unspoken coalition between the Assamese and the Bengali Muslims against the Bengali Hindus."[5]

The All Assam Students' Union (AASU) in 1979 started a movement demanding detection and deletion of names of all illegal migrants from the electoral rolls and deportation of all of them under the laws of the land, which lasted for years. In October,1985, a regional political party under the name 'Asom Gana Parishad' (AGP) was again formed. By that time, the central executive committee of AASU was also dissolved and the members joined the AGP.[6] The newly formed AGP then started moving forward the issue of so-called illegal foreigners.

Meanwhile, in April, 1979, a separatist outfit under the name 'United Liberation Front of Assam' (ULFA) was founded. The objective of ULFA was to establish a sovereign Assam via an armed struggle in the Assam conflict. The ULFA established ties with many other outfit organizations and started its operations. The Government of India, however, banned the organization in 1990 citing it as a terrorist organization.[7]

In Tripura, the All Tripura Tribal Force (ATTF) was formed in July, 1990. However, in 1992, it was changed to All Tripura Tiger Force (ATTF). Their main objectives were (i) Expulsion of all Bengali speaking immigrant settlers who entered Tripura after 1956, (ii) Restoration of land to Tribals under Tripura Land Revenue and Land Reform Act, 1960, and (iii) Removal of names of Migrants who entered Tripura after 1956 from the Electoral Roll.[8]

In Meghalaya, the Khasi Students' Union (KSU) was formed in March, 1978. This was basically a student organization and their primary objective was 'Welfare of the State and the Community'. Later on, they extended their objectives and wanted protection from the Government through laws so that the children of the soil may control the Economy, Government and Land. They also wanted to awaken in the Khasi Community a respect for their language, culture, tradition and all that belongs to the Khasi Nation.[9]

The Hynniewtrep National Liberation Council (HNLC) is another Tribal Outfit of Meghalaya. Their main objective is to transform Meghalaya as a province exclusively for the Khasi Tribe, and also to fight against the presence of **'outsiders'**, as they feel that Khasi youths are deprived of the fruits of development in the State.[10]

There are other Organizations, e.g. National Socialist Council of Nagaland (NSCN) formed in January, 1980 which was subsequently divided into 2 (two) groups in April, 1988 *viz.* (i) National Socialist Council of Nagaland-Isak Muivah (NSCN-IM), and (ii) National Socialist Council of Nagaland-Khaplang (NSCN-K). Their sole objective is to establish a 'Greater Nagaland.'[11] Kangleipak Communist Party (KCP) of Manipur, who had been engaged in an arm struggle to achieve 'sovereignty' for Manipur since 1980.[12] Mizo Student Union (MSU), All Arunachal Pradesh Students' Union (AAPSU) etc. who are mainly committed to protect their land and people.

Apart from this, there are many other Ethnic groups, Organizations, Outfits, NGOs etc. in the North Eastern Region. Some of them are very much dedicated to protect their religion and culture, some want independence or separate territory, some are fighting for introduction of Inner Line Permit (ILP) in order to protect their land and people from the hands of Migrants, some are even trying to adopt the policy of 'son of the soil' in the field of education and employment etc. etc.

In sixties, seventies, eighties, nineties, the North Eastern States passed through many unprecedented happenings. The people of this region got divided broadly into 2 (two) groups. In Assam, it was Assamese and Non-Assamese and in other States, it was Tribals (or locals) and Non-Tribals (or others). Non-Assamese and Non-Tribals (or others) were termed as **'outsiders',** who are mostly Hindus, particularly the Bengali Hindus, who came from Bangladesh, the then East Bengal, at different points of times to Assam and to other States. Ultimately, they became the bone of contention in many respects and the local people wanted to get rid of them.

To achieve that objective, different Organizations and Extremist groups started their activities in their own ways. Bandhs, Road blockades, Curfews, arsons, lootings, kidnappings, harassment of people, burning of houses, gutting of shops, extortion, fleeing from houses or hostels, loss of lives etc. became the order of the day. On the other hand, step motherly behaviours were there for **'outsiders'** in case of education and employment. It was quite difficult to get seats in Schools, Colleges and Universities. Due to selection procedure, many meritorious students did not get seats in Engineering Colleges, Medical Colleges, IITs, Management Institutions etc. Similar was the situation for employment and also in case of promotion. Preference was always there for the local candidates. This lowered the standard, at least in the field of education, both in respects of students and teachers, and also in other technical fields. Instances are there that, due to poor performance, students had to leave higher technical courses in the middle of the session. For all these reasons, the so-called **'outsiders',** gradually started feeling, 'as if, they are living the life of a second class citizen'. And that was the beginning of a frustrated life for many of the younger generation. Not only that, there had been a sense of insecurity and indirect mental pressure, that made life miserable for many of the people.

All these factors brought about a change in the minds of Hindus and many of them finally decided to leave North Eastern States and started going back to their own places. The Bengali Hindus, mostly Migrated to West Bengal, Delhi, Mumbai etc. Those who were in service or whose children were in schools and colleges, they had to wait for their retirement or for completion of the education of their children. Many of the professionals and business class people also changed their place of profession and business. Those who could not, many of them, either closed down their business or at least tried to make an alternative arrangement elsewhere. Instances of premature retirement and forceful leaving of jobs and places were there. Abduction and loss of life of many eminent personalities were also there.

The rapid decline in the growth rate of Hindus of different North Eastern States is very much evident from the Appendix-4.8, the details of which have been given in Chapter-4. However, the decline in the growth rate of Hindus is not only in the North Eastern States, but it is also there in the country as a whole, though the rate of decline is with a much slower pace. Amongst other things, one of the reasons of declining the growth rate, might be the attitude of Hindus towards Family Planning and limiting the family size, which is very much needed for bringing up the children in a better way and to give them better education for the establishment in life.

Migration and consequent sufferings of people are rather unfortunate happenings. Sometimes, some people are getting tortured, for no fault of them, at the hands of some other people, having vested interest. People sometimes become very much conscious about protecting their land and people. Religion, culture, language, place of residence, education and employment, hatred etc. become the deciding factors towards fulfilling these objectives. It is a fact that, any kind of violence disturbs the peace and harmony. Not only that, violence is very much detrimental to humanity. It creates a sense of insecurity amongst the people, and that affects industrialization, development and the overall economy. It also affects education very badly in one hand, and generates unemployment, on the other, which is the root cause of many socio-economic evils and problems.

Migration and sufferings of people, now a days, is not confined in a particular place, rather, it is becoming more or less a worldwide phenomenon. This is definitely not a healthy situation. People are not only becoming homeless, rather many of them are losing their lives or their near and dear ones. The survivors are also not always welcomed by others. Politics, economics, social factors etc. stand on their way. Hope, one day, people will feel the pain of Migrants and they will not have to suffer, for no fault of them.

Notes

1. *My People Uprooted*, A Saga of the Hindus of Eastern Bengal, by Tathagata Roy, pp. 128-29.
2. *A 'godsent' opportunity*, by Sujit Chaudhuri, pp. 1-2.
3. *Ibid.*, p. 3.
4. *Ibid.*, pp. 6-7.
5. *Ibid.*, pp. 8-9.
6. website of the AGP, p. 1.
7. website of ULFA, p. 1.
8. website of ATTF, p. 1.
9. website of KSU, pp. 1-2.
10. website of HNLC, p. 1.
11. website of NSCN, pp. 1-2.
12. website of KPC, p. 1.

Bibliography

Arunachal through the Ages by J.N. Chowdhury, published by Smt. Jaya Chowdhury, Shillong, 1982.

An Introduction to the Economy of Meghalaya by D.D. Mali, Ratna's Mascot, G.S. Road, Shillong.

A 'godsent' opportunity, by Sujit Chaudhuri.

Anecdotal History of Partition in Assam by Binayak Dutta, The NEHU Journal, Vol. XII, No. 2, July–December, 2014.

Contribution of India in the War of Liberation of Bangladesh by Salam Azad, Bookwell, New Delhi, 2006.

Digital Library of the Registrar General of India, New Delhi.

Element of Demography by V.C. Sinha and E. Zacharia, Allied Publishers Pvt. Ltd.

Economic Survey, Directorate of Economics and Statistics, Assam, Assam 2005-06.

Economic Survey, Directorate of Economics and Statistics, Government of Manipur, Manipur, 2002-03.

Economic Review of Tripura, 2003-04, Directorate of Economics and Statistics, Planning (Statistics) Department, Govt. of Tripura.

Freedom Struggle, A National by Bipan Chandra, Amales Tripathi, Barun De, 1972, Book Trust Publication, New Delhi.

Glimpses of the Early History of Arunachal Pradesh by L.N. Chakravarty, Published by the Director of Research, Govt. of Arunachal Pradesh, 1973.

History of the Freedom Movement in India, Vol. I, II and III by R.C. Majumdar, FIRMA KLM PVT. LTD., 1997, Calcutta.

Impact of Immigration in Assam (1871–1951) by Nripen Dhar, Published by Biplab Chakraborty of Worldview, Kolkata-700 012.

India Wins Freedom by Maulana Abul Kalam Azad, Orient Longman Ltd. New Delhi, 1988.

India's Fight for Freedom or The Swadeshi Movement (1905-1906) by Prof. Haridas Mukherjee and Prof. Uma Mukherjee, Published by Firma K.L. Mukhopadhyay, 6/1-A, Banchharam Akrur Lane, Calcutta-12, 1958.

India-Bangladesh Relations by Rekha Saha, Published by Minerva Associates (Publications) Pvt. Ltd., March, 2000, 7-B, Lake Palace, Calcutta-700 029.

My People Uprooted, A Saga of the Hindus of Eastern Bengal, by Tathagata Roy.

Mizoram (Historical, Geographical, Social, Economic, Political and Administrative) by S.N. Singh, Mittal Publications.

Manorama Year Book, 1984, Manorama Publishing House, Kottayam.

News Papers viz. *Assam Tribune*, *Telegraph*, *Shillong Times* etc.

Peace and Development in Northeast by P.L. Sanjeev Reddy and P.C. Shekar Reddy, Mittal Publications, New Delhi.

Pak Colonialism in East Bengal by D.R. Mankekar, Somaiya Publications Pvt. Ltd., Bombay–New Delhi, September, 1971.

Partition of India and Other Related Matters by Baren Ray, Published by Badal Ray, IMH Press Pvt. Ltd. New Delhi, 2002.

Partition Diaspora by Anindita Dasgupta and Neets Singh.

Publications of the Registrar General of India, New Delhi.

Social History of Assam by M.L. Bose, Concept Publishing Company, New Delhi.

Sikkim—Land and People by B. Bhattacharya, Omsons Publications, New Delhi-110 027.

Socio-Economic Scenario of the North East India by R.K. Das Choudhury, Concept Publishing Company Pvt. Ltd., New Delhi-110 05.

SRS Bulletins of the Registrar General of India, New Delhi.

The Beautiful India—Nagaland by S.A. Rahman (Chief Editor), Published by Reference Press, New Delhi.

Tripura—Its History and Culture by Omesh Saigal, Published by Concept Publishing Company, Delhi, 1978.

The Other Side of Silence—Voices from the Partition of India by Urvashi Butalia, Penguin Books, 1998.

The Price of Partition by Rafiq Zakaria, 1998, Published by S. Ramakrishnan, Executive Secretary, Bharatiya Vidya Bhavan, Kulapati Munshi Marg, Mumbai-400 007.

The Prolonged Partition and Its Pogroms by A.J. Kamra, Voice of India, New Delhi.

Website of the Registrar General of India, New Delhi.

Websites of different Political, Social and Other Organisations.

Index